Friedrich Hayek

Also by Alan Ebenstein

The Greatest Happiness Principle: An Examination
of Utilitarianism

Great Political Thinkers: Plato to the Present

Introduction to Political Thinkers

Today's Isms: Socialism, Capitalism, Fascism,
Communism, Libertarianism

Edwin Cannan: Liberal Doyen

Hayek's Journey

Friedrich Hayek

A Biography

Alan Ebenstein

The University of Chicago Press
Chicago and London

The University of Chicago Press, Chicago, 60637
The University of Chicago Press, Ltd., London
Copyright © 2001 by Alan Ebenstein
Appendix © 2003 by Alan Ebenstein
Reprinted by arrangement with Palgrave Macmillan, an imprint of St. Martin's
Press, LLC
All rights reserved. First published in 2001 by Palgrave
University of Chicago Press edition 2003
Printed in the United States of America

12 11 10 09 08 07 06 05 04 03   1 2 3 4 5
ISBN: 0-226-18150-2

Library of Congress Cataloging-in-Publication Data

Ebenstein, Alan O.
    Friedrich Hayek : a biography / Alan Ebenstein.
        p.   cm.
    Originally published: New York : Palgrave, 2001.
    Includes bibliographical references and index.
    ISBN 0-226-18150-2 (pbk. : alk. paper)
    1. Hayek, Friedrich A. von (Friedrich August), 1899–. 2. Economists—
Great Britain—Biography. I. Title.

HB103 .H3 E23 2003
330′.092—dc21
[B]
                                                            2002075653

⊗ The paper used in this publication meets the minimum requirements of the
American National Standard for Information Sciences-Permanence of Paper for
Printed Library Materials, ANSI Z39.48-1992.

"That interdependence of all men, which is now in everybody's mouth and which tends to make all mankind One World, not only is the effect of the market order but could not have been brought about by any other means."

—Friedrich Hayek,
Law, Legislation and Liberty

Hayek in his study at the University of Chicago.

Contents

PART ONE

WAR

1899–1931

PART TWO

ENGLAND

1931–1939

Preface and Acknowledgments

The purpose of this work is to trace the intellectual life of Friedrich Hayek. Hayek was the greatest philosopher of liberty during the twentieth century. His contributions to political theory and philosophical economics are immense. The most visible sign of Hayek's importance is the cottage industry of books appearing about him in various languages throughout the world. Intellectual biography may provide greater context for understanding a writer's work. Particularly in the social sciences, the terms in which discussions are held are often, perhaps usually, in contemporary parlance. By knowing a thinker's life and times better, one may obtain greater insight into his thought.

Hayek's life was interesting. His residences in Vienna, London, Cambridge, Chicago, and Freiburg provide snapshots of leading centers of academic debate during the twentieth century. His life is most interesting, though, in helping to elucidate his thought. His universality is demonstrated by the broad and deep interest in him.

It is a delightful opportunity to thank the people who helped in the preparation of this book. Hayek's children and daughter-in-law—Larry Hayek, Christine Hayek, and Esca Hayek—generously answered questions. Larry and Esca put me up for weekend visits to their home on three occasions; their hospitality is among my fondest recollections of this project. Hans Warhanek, the son of Hayek's second wife, answered questions on two occasions. I spoke very briefly over the phone to Helene von Hayek, Hayek's second wife (who died in 1996), and visited their Freiburg apartment.

A number of people agreed to be interviewed. I thank Milton and Rose Friedman, James Buchanan, Ronald Coase, Gary Becker, Edwin Meese, Arthur and Marjorie Seldon, Sir Ernst Gombrich, D. Gale Johnson, Tibor Scitovsky, Ronald Fowler, Lord Desai, Erich Streissler, Peter Rosner, Kurt Faninger, Werner Tschiderer, Reinhold Veit, David Grene, Joseph Cropsey, William Letwin, Charlotte Cubitt, Lord Harris, Manuel Ayau, Christian Gandil, Walter Grinder, Ralph Horwitz, Albert Zlabinger, Harold Dulan, John Kane, W. Allen

Wallis, and Fr. Johannes Schasching. I exchanged correspondence with a number of people, including James Vice, Richard Stern, Stanley Heywood, Paul Post, Sal Soraci, Vera Hewitt, Eric Rose, Henry Toch, Harold Noah, P. M. Toms, Theodore Draimin, Peter Kingsford, the late James Meade, David Jickling, the late Julian Simon, and Edward Lowenstern.

This work has benefited by its review in manuscript form by a number of academics and scholars, some of whom knew Hayek. I thank Bettina Bien Greaves, Jim Powell, Mark Skousen, Peter Klein, Richard Ebeling, Sudha Shenoy, Bruce Caldwell, Bill Herms, David Brooks, Chrysostomos Mantzavinos, Todd Breyfogle, and Stephen Kresge. I particularly thank Tom Schrock and three anonymous reviewers for their comments on preliminary manuscripts. Others who read drafts include Joe Atwill, Robert Bakhaus, Rob Ebenstein, Susan Engel, Jim Gazdecki, Geraldine Hawkins, Gary Rhodes, Michael Rose, Art Rupe, Jim Waddingham, and Laura Wilson. No one who reviewed a manuscript draft should, of course, be held accountable for information and interpretations contained here.

Others who assisted in some way—providing information, encouragement, translation, or other assistance—include Eamonn Butler, Glynn Custred, Gordon Baker, Robert Chitester, Lord Dahrendorf, Barry Smith, Stephan Boehm, Brian Crowley, Greg Ransom, David Gordon, Christian Thiele, Eduard Blanc, Max Gammon, Holly Barber, Isaac Kramnick, Sharon Fuller, Mike Westwood, Tom Campbell, Stephen Weatherford, Scott Pinkner, Andy Ebenstein, Robert Haake, Lee Gientke, Lora Soroka, Rebecca DuBey, Walter Mead, William Breit, and the late Henry Spiegel. I also thank the Mont Pelerin Society, *University of Chicago Magazine, New York Times Book Review, LSE Magazine*, and libraries and special collections at the University of California, Santa Barbara and Los Angeles; the Hoover Institution; the University of Chicago; the London School of Economics and Political Science; Salzburg university; and the University of Vienna. I finally thank Michael Flamini, Alan Bradshaw, Rick Delaney, and Meg Weaver.

I should perhaps mention my background and the process by which this book was written. *Friedrich Hayek: A Biography* was my main endeavor from December 1993 through December 2000. This included extensive and intensive reading of Hayek's work (published and unpublished), much research, and travel. I am, also, son of a political theorist from Vienna, born eleven years after Hayek, who, like him, went to the London School of Economics after graduating from the University of Vienna, and who taught briefly at the University of Chicago. William Ebenstein, my father, was a leading student of two of Hayek's bêtes noires, Hans Kelsen and Harold Laski.

A few stylistic notes: I have sometimes compressed quotations in the main text for readability without the use of ellipses; however, no words have been added to quotes without so indicating. Also, where a quotation's author is not identified, it may be assumed that it is Hayek. Finally, it is useful to think of the six parts of the book as chapters in his life.

I hope that this book is of use to students of Hayek, classical liberalism, libertarianism, and twentieth century political and economic thought and practice, and the relationship between political and economic thought and practice. This work is a history of Hayek's life and thought, and of the libertarian philosophical surroundings in which he worked and lived.

Alan Ebenstein
December 6, 2000
Santa Barbara, California

Introduction

THE BRITISH POLITICAL PHILOSOPHER AND ECONOMIST JOHN STUART MILL, the leading liberal thinker of the nineteenth century, wrote in his immortal *On Liberty* that "ages are no more infallible than individuals—every age having held many opinions which subsequent ages have deemed not only false but absurd; and it is as certain that many opinions, now general, will be rejected by future ages, as it is that many, once general, are rejected by the present."[1] What Mill wrote a century and a half ago remains true today. The twentieth century will be remembered in part as a battle between classical socialism and democratic welfare state capitalism to create future societal order.

The idea that central direction of an economy by government is a more efficient and fair method to create and use productive resources than a free market relying on fluctuating prices, profits, and property is now almost universally discredited. While the extent of classical socialism's hold over the minds of many, as opposed to a relatively few academic writers and teachers, may be questioned in what used to be called the West, there is no question that the economies of the Soviet Union and a score of other nations during the twentieth century were, and in a few places still are, run along classical socialist lines of government ownership and management of all land and capital means of economic production. From the 1930s through the 1980s, Friedrich Hayek challenged the prevailing opinion of many social scientists and others that socialism is a more efficient and just form of economic production than capitalism.

Hayek was often derided within academia for putting forward the position that a competitive market is more economically productive, and conducive to liberty and democracy, than classical socialism. As late as the 1989 edition of his best-selling *Economics* textbook, American Nobel laureate Paul Samuelson wrote that the "Soviet economy is proof that contrary to what many skeptics had earlier believed, a socialist command economy can function and even thrive."[2] Hayek's perspective has become the new conventional wisdom.

Hayek's arguments for the infeasibility of classical socialism had been made by others, notably his teacher Ludwig von Mises. But no one else enunciated the case against socialism with such clarity and force, and extended the argument against socialism so effectively and with such renown from the economic to the more general societal order. Hayek was the great anti-socialist.

Hayek's essential factual as distinct from moral proposition is that knowledge is divided among the minds of all humanity. It is impossible to gather this fragmented knowledge into one brain. It is therefore counterproductive to build societies—as classical socialism attempted—on the belief that central government control of all economic management and business decisions can be more efficient than a decentralized economic order that is created through fluctuating prices, private property, profits, contract, and the ability to exchange goods and services, all of which build on, accommodate, and utilize fragmented and divided information.

Central to Hayek's conception of a classical liberal or libertarian order are fluctuating prices and profits. Prices and profits convey information. They inform producers and consumers of the relative supply of and demand for different goods and services, thereby guiding production. Without fluctuating prices and profits, an economy will not be optimally productive in satisfying human desires. A market society is in largest part defined simply by allowing adult and responsible—autonomous—people to do as they wish as long as they do not harm anyone else.

In his 1944 classic, *The Road to Serfdom,* written in Cambridge where the London School of Economics and Political Science was relocated during World War II, Hayek expanded the argument of the intrinsic economic unproductivity of a classical socialist regime to the realm of political liberty. Now, he argued, it is not just that socialism is unproductive, it is that it is intrinsically unfree. Personal liberty cannot exist where an individual is but a piece in a planner's scheme. The existence of private property is essential for political liberty and economic productivity.

Hayek lived in the United States from 1950 to 1962, after his divorce from his first wife. He was on the Committee on Social Thought at the University of Chicago during this period. He came in contact with Milton Friedman and others at Chicago, but he was relatively little influenced by them except in his focus on certain practical public policy issues. Though Friedman and Hayek agree on many governmental policies, they reach their positions from different philosophical premises. Hayek possesses a Germanic idealist perspective, while Friedman utilizes an Anglo-American empirical approach.

As he developed as a political philosopher, Hayek sought to define societal liberty. He wrote two masterpieces, *The Constitution of Liberty* (1960) and *Law, Legislation and Liberty* (1973-79, mostly written during the 1960s), which will remain landmarks in the field of political philosophy, defining and elucidating the relationship between, and meaning of, law and liberty. His core position in legal and political philosophy, following John Locke, was that there can be no liberty without law.

Hayek put forward the difficult idea of spontaneous order. In a spontaneous order, individuals may exchange and interact with one another as they desire. There is no central management of individual decision making. Individuals may do whatever they wish as long as they harm no one else.

In Hayek's conception of spontaneous order—a concept he saw implicit and explicit in the work of Adam Smith and Carl Menger—the rule of law replaces the rule of men. Order and progressive material development occur in societies typified by law.

Hayek was deeply influenced by the idea of evolution, of which he first became aware in his father's botanical work, and which he developed in his work in both economics and psychology. It is interesting that seminal thinkers as diverse as Darwin, Marx, Freud, and Hayek all had a perspective of evolutionary processes.[3]

Hayek emphasized the importance of material and technological development in the history of mankind. He thought that material development is almost always in unknown directions. There can be no material progress unless individuals are free to move into hitherto unexplored areas. Freedom must include the opportunity to make mistakes.

Hayek was not opposed to government. He emphasized that rules create society, and that without coercive law, no civil society is possible. The essence of his political philosophy may be summarized in the statement that liberty is the supremacy of law, an idea he explored most fully in *Law, Legislation and Liberty.*

Following several fallow decades of public interest in him, Hayek received the Nobel Prize in Economics in 1974. For the rest of his life, he was a leader of the classical liberal and libertarian movements in Great Britain and, to a lesser extent, the United States. His greatest prominence during the last two decades of his life was in Britain, where Margaret Thatcher's public embrace of him during the 1980s established him as her leading philosophical inspirer.

His final work was *The Fatal Conceit* (1988). He took the idea that the market is a threshing process for determining more and less economically productive individuals and practices and tried to expand it to the idea that whole societies are more or less economically productive, and that there exists a competition among different societal systems of rules, laws, customs, and morals. The most economically productive societies—and thus most productive rules and morals—prevail in the end through a process of societal selection.

At the end of the nineteenth century, Karl Marx—much as Hayek now—was considered a significant thinker, but by no means one of the most significant societal thinkers that the nineteenth century produced. In the 1896 edition of Inglis Palgrave's authoritative *Dictionary of Political Economy,* Marx is merely a "distinguished socialistic theorist and agitator."[4] Perhaps the most common conception of Hayek today is as a distinguished libertarian theorist and agitator.

In the formerly communist world, he was an underground inspiration to forces opposed to communism. Tomas Jezek, who became Czech minister of privatization after the collapse of communist rule, said that if the "ideologists of socialism would single out the one book that ought to be locked up at any price and strictly forbidden, its dissemination and lecture carrying the most severe punishment, they would surely point to *The Road to Serfdom.*"[5]

Hayek was a utopian philosopher. He ultimately looked forward to a "universal order of peace." This would be a utopian world that would unite all mankind into one society. His ultimate society would be the one where the highest standard of living would be shared by the most people. He rejected concepts of zero population growth. He sought a world in which as many people as possible would be as wealthy as possible. He thought this could be achieved through a world society bound together not by arbitrary government, but by fixed law. In *Law, Legislation and Liberty,* he wrote that it is "only by extending the rules of just conduct to the relations with all other men, and at the same time depriving of their obligatory character those rules which cannot be universally applied, that we can approach a universal order of peace which might integrate all mankind into a single society."[6] Such a society would secure individual freedom and group order and would have the most advanced technology.

ONE

WAR

1899 – 1931

"The great break of the First World War. I grew up in a war, and that is a great break in my recollected history. The world which ended either in 1914 or, more correctly, two or three years later when the war had a real impact, was a wholly different world from the world which has existed since."

Family

THE VIENNA INTO WHICH FRIEDRICH AUGUST VON HAYEK WAS BORN on May 8, 1899 was cacophonous. The Viennese held divergent views about the future of almost everything. Theodor Herzl, founder of the political Zionist movement, was from Vienna, as was Hitler.

Vienna had long been capital of the Holy Roman Empire and then the Austrian Empire. In 1867, it became capital of the Austro-Hungarian Empire. Vienna was the cultural center of the Germanic world. It was the musical center of the entire world—Beethoven, Mozart, Haydn, and Schubert all lived and worked there.

Hayek's father, August (from whom he received his middle name), was born in Vienna in 1871. August became a medical doctor employed by the municipal ministry of health, but his true passion was botany, in which he wrote a number of monographs. August von Hayek was also a part-time botany lecturer at the University of Vienna.

Hayek's mother, Felicitas (nee) von Juraschek, was born in 1875. Her mother was from a wealthy, conservative, land-owning family. When Felicitas' mother died some years before Friedrich was born, Felicitas received a considerable inheritance that provided as much as half of her and August's income during the early years of their marriage. Hayek was the oldest of three boys. Heinrich and Erich came one-and-a-half and five years after him.

Once, discussing his father and his influence on his career, Hayek said, "I suppose the one thing which might have changed my own development would have been if there didn't exist that esteem for intellectual work. My determination to become a scholar was certainly affected by the unsatisfied ambition of my father to become a university professor. Behind the scenes it wasn't much talked about, but I was very much aware that in my father the great ambition of his life was to be a university professor. So I grew up with the idea that there was nothing higher in life than becoming a university professor, without any clear conception of which subject I wanted to do."[1]

In addition to his father's scholarly pursuits, both of his grandfathers—who lived long enough for Hayek to know them—were scholars. Franz von Juraschek was a leading economist in Austria and close friend of Eugen von Böhm-Bawerk, one of the three key originators of the historical Austrian school of economics (the others were Carl Menger and Friedrich von Wieser, the latter of whom von Juraschek also knew). Von Juraschek was a statistician and later became employed by the Austrian national government. As a result of his own inheritance from his first wife (Felicitas' mother), he became wealthy.

Hayek's paternal grandfather, Gustav Edler von Hayek, taught natural science at the Imperial *Realobergymnasium* (secondary school) in Vienna for thirty years. He wrote systematic works in biology, some of which became relatively well known. One monograph of his at the University of Vienna library is titled (in German), *A Deep Sea Investigation on Board the British Warship "Porcupine" 1869;* other titles include *Compendium of the Geography of Vienna* and *Atlas of Medical and Pharmaceutical Plant Powers.*

The Germanic world at the turn of the twentieth century was different from the present in myriad ways. As an example of the changes in technology that occurred during his lifetime, Hayek described a scene from his youth, before the time of the automobile, when he observed a fireman's horse "standing in its stable ready to be put on the carriage with everything hanging over it; so it required only two or three pressings of buttons and the horse was finished to go out."[2]

Differences between the Germanic world at the turn of the twentieth century and the world just after the turn of the twenty-first go beyond technology. The Germanic world in 1899 was thoroughly prejudiced and anti-Semitism was rampant, particularly in Vienna. Hayek did not share the anti-Semitic views of many, perhaps most, of his Christian contemporaries.

Vienna before World War I has been celebrated and condemned. For some, it was a glittering intellectual paradise in which some of the greatest minds lived. For others, it was a phony city in which superficiality prevailed over substance. Historians of Vienna Allan Janik and Stephen Toulmin, following Viennese author Robert Musil, call Austrian society "Kakania," a name combining two "senses on different levels. On the surface, it is a coinage from the initials K. K. or K. u. K., standing for 'Imperial-Royal' or 'Imperial and Royal.' But to anyone familiar with German nursery language, it carries also the secondary sense of 'Excrementia.'"[3]

Musil himself wrote, "All in all, how many remarkable things might be said about that vanished Kakania! On paper it called itself the Austro-Hungarian Monarchy; in speaking, however, one referred to it as 'Austria'—that is to say, it was known by a name that it had, as a State, solemnly renounced by oath. By its constitution it was liberal, but its system of government was clerical. Before the law all citizens were equal, but not everyone, of course, was a citizen. There was a parliament, which made such vigorous use of its liberty that it was usually kept shut; but there was also an emergency powers act by means of which it was possible to manage without Parliament, and every time when everyone was just beginning to rejoice in absolutism, the Crown decreed that there must now again be a return to parliamentary government."[4]

Viennese author Hilde Spiel called the time between 1898 and World War I the "magical" years in Vienna, when a "seemingly sudden flowering of talent came about—especially in the fields of literature and philosophy."[5] The decades following Austria's defeat by Prussia in the Austro-Prussian War of 1866 were relatively free from war and bloodshed. During these years, Vienna prospered and the middle class expanded.

Vienna was one of the largest cities in the world in 1900. There were two separate eras in its history that are sometimes called golden. The first was the musical golden age of the late eighteenth and early nineteenth centuries. The second was the decades on either side of World War I.

Friedrich—or "Fritz," as his mother and most friends called him throughout life (to his dislike)—displayed an incredibly intellectual and academic bent from a very young age. In unpublished autobiographical notes, he recounts that he read fluently and frequently before going to school.

As a result of his father's serving different neighborhoods as a health officer in the municipal ministry of health, Hayek lived in four apartments while growing up. He recalled in his unpublished autobiographical notes a division within the family between himself and his younger brothers. Although they were only a few years younger than him, he believed that they were somehow of a different generation. Hayek preferred to associate with adults.

After receiving the Nobel Prize in Economics in 1974, he wrote a semi-autobiographical essay, "Two Types of Mind," where he commented that in his "private language" he described "the recognised standard type of scientists as the memory type. It is the kind of mind who can retain the particular things he has read or heard, often the particular words in which an idea has been expressed." This type of mind is the "master of his subject." Hayek was, by way of contrast, a "rather extreme instance of the more unconventional type," the "puzzler," whose "constant difficulties, which in rare instances may be rewarded by a new insight, are due to the fact that they cannot avail themselves of the established verbal formulae or arguments which lead others smoothly and quickly to the result. People whose minds work that way seem to rely in some measure on a process of wordless thought. To 'see' certain connections distinctly does not yet mean for them that they know how to describe them in words."[6]

The issue of "explicit" versus "tacit" knowledge—or the difference between "knowing that" and "knowing how," or between verbal and intuitive knowledge—is one that he explored later in his career, and was vital in his conception of spontaneous order. The "master of his subject" has verbal knowledge; the "puzzler" has intuitive knowledge. Knowledge is not, or may not initially be, verbal. To assume that all knowledge can be verbally expressed at a point in time is false. Knowledge can exist although the words to express it have not been discovered yet. One of the errors of classical socialism was that it relied too much on verbal knowledge.

Hayek characterized his teacher von Wieser at the University of Vienna as in "many respects rather a puzzler," and recalled an intellectual description of Wieser by Joseph Schumpeter, presumably therefore also giving some idea of Hayek's conception of himself. The "fellow economist who enters Wieser's intellectual world at once finds himself in a new atmosphere. It is as if one entered a house which nowhere resembles the houses of our time and the plan and furniture of which is strange and not at once intelligible. There is hardly another author who owes as little to other authors as Wieser, fundamentally to none except Menger and to him only a suggestion—with the result that for a long time many fellow economists did not know what to do with Wieser's work. Of his edifice everything is his intellectual property, even where what he says has already been said before him."[7]

Hayek described characteristics of the Germanic culture in which he was raised. He wrote in *The Road to Serfdom* (though he made a distinction between Germans and Austrians) that "few people will deny that the Germans on the whole are industrious and disciplined, thorough and energetic to the degree of ruthlessness, conscientious and single-minded in any tasks they undertake, that they possess a strong sense of order, duty, and strict obedience to authority, and that they often show great readiness to make personal sacrifices and great courage in physical danger. Deficient they seem in most of those little yet so important qualities which facilitate the intercourse between men in a free society: kindliness and a sense of humour, personal modesty, and respect for the privacy and belief in the good intentions of one's neighbour."[8]

He made these comments about his distant cousin, the philosopher Ludwig Wittgenstein, that shed further light on the society in which he grew to maturity. "What struck me most," Hayek remembered, "was a radical passion for truthfulness in everything (which I came to know as a characteristic vogue among the young Viennese intellectuals of the generation immediately preceding mine). This truthfulness became almost a fashion in that border group between the parts of the intelligentsia in which I came so much to move. It meant much more than truth in speech. One had to 'live' truth and not tolerate any pretence in oneself or others. It sometimes produced outright rudeness and, certainly, unpleasantness. Every convention was dissected and every conventional form exposed as fraud."[9]

Hayek was personally as well as politically a thorough-going individualist. He said in a 1945 lecture that in the "rationalist sense of the term, in their insistence on the development of 'original' personalities which in every respect are the product of the conscious choice of the individual, the German intellectual tradition indeed favors a kind of 'individualism' little known elsewhere. I remember well how surprised and even shocked I was myself when as a young student, on my first contact with English and American contemporaries, I discovered how much they were disposed to conform in all externals to common usage rather than, as seemed natural to me, to be proud to be different and original in most respects."[10]

The focus of the von Hayek household as Hayek grew up was his father's botanical collections. Wherever his family lived, their premises were filled to overflowing with dried plants, prints, and photos of plants. In addition to their own residence, the family, particularly Felicitas and the children, visited the villa of Felicitas' father and his second wife and their children. Hayek's family today remember their father's first family as extended and close-knit. He himself recalled that get-togethers at his maternal grandfather's home were large and extended across ages.

By comparison to his maternal grandparents, his paternal grandparents' circumstances were modest. The von Hayeks had been ennobled over a generation before the von Jurascheks, however, and were "proud of their gentility and ancestry." By way of comparison, the von Jurascheks were "definitely upper-class bourgeoisie and wealthier by far." Hayek remembered that his maternal grandparents' home was "magnificent, even grandiose . . . undoubtedly one of the most beautiful flats in Vienna."[11] They had several servants.

"Von" was the fourth and lowest, as well as most common, of the second of two ranks of nobility in imperial Austria. The higher rank was composed of the royal families who ruled the Germanic world's principalities for centuries, and the lesser rank were those—such as the von Hayeks and von Jurascheks— whose forebears were ennobled during the previous century or so. The English approximation of "von" is "sir."

An "ek" ending on a surname is typically Czech. Hayek traced his ancestry to a "Hagek" from Prague, who was an associate of the famous astronomer Tycho Brahe. Hayek liked to note that on some old maps of the moon there is a crater named "Hagetsius," after his probable ancestor. He observed that families with the name "Hayek" or "Hagek" can be traced in Bohemia (now principally the Czech Republic) from the 1500s, and that—although his family spoke German for as long as he could ascertain—"Hayek" is probably derived from the Czech word "Hajek," meaning "small wood."

He also had ancestors, as did his second wife, from the Salzburg region. In his inaugural lecture at the University of Salzburg, he commenced that in the "course of my life I always introduced myself as a foreigner at the beginning of my lectures. But this time I may permit myself to start with the statement that I am a native. It is now 370 years since a common ancestor of my wife and myself as Duke Archbishop court registry writer received a heraldic letter" to perform a building project.[12] A number of Hayek's ancestors from the Salzburg region were government officials or salt producers. The family later moved to Vienna.

Josef Hayek, the administrator of an aristocrat, was ennobled in 1789 for developing the first Austrian textile factories, through which he became wealthy. His son Heinrich, Friedrich's great-grandfather, became a civil servant in Vienna and, in his great-grandson's words, "spent a long, dignified, and comfortable life as a gentleman." Gustav, Heinrich's son, was originally educated by private tutors and attended an upper-class school reserved for the nobility. Hayek recalled that Gustav became a "naval officer, and indeed seems to have been a bit of a naval dandy."[13] Late in life, by the 1860s, Heinrich lost the family fortune, and Gustav was required to become a schoolmaster. Gustav was August's father.

Hayek told an anecdote about how he recognized Wittgenstein at a railway station in 1918 when both were officers in the Austrian Army that sheds a little light on his childhood. "Very likely Wittgenstein had been one of the handsome and elegant young men whom I remembered around 1910," Hayek recalled, "when my [maternal] grandparents rented for the spring and summer a Swiss cottage on a property adjoining the park of the Wittgensteins in the suburb of Neuwaldegg, having frequently called from their much more grandiose villa for the much younger sisters of my mother to take them to tennis."[14] His relationship with Wittgenstein was not close.

Hayek spent many happy hours on botany with his father, his most sustained childhood hobby. August accumulated a herbarium of between 75,000 and 100,000 sheets and traveled extensively in central Europe, Scandinavia, France, Tunisia, Greece, and Egypt on botanical expeditions. Friedrich had collections of natural specimens of various kinds, including insects and minerals, as well as plants. August edited a "Flora Exotica" supplying and exchanging rare specimens of pressed plants, and Friedrich helped him in practical aspects of this endeavor.[15]

Other hobbies in which Hayek participated as a child and youth included photography, cycling, skiing, sailing, climbing, mountaineering, and theater. He described his attraction to mountain climbing. It was not "so much the technique of rock climbing which fascinated" him, "partly because for that purpose you had to get a guide." He climbed without a guide, and enjoyed "difficult, but not exceedingly difficult, terrain—combinations of ice and rock." He was intrigued by finding his way where there was only one way to get through the face of a mountain. This "needn't be technically difficult. But you knew you would get stuck unless you found the one possible way through."[16] Mountaineering was a family tradition—his maternal grandfather von Juraschek mountain climbed with Eugene von Böhm-Bawerk during the 1880s when they were colleagues in Innsbruck. Friedrich mostly climbed with his brothers and occasionally with his father.

He remarked of his youth that up to his college years his tendencies were "very definitely practical." He wanted to be "efficient."[17] An interviewer wrote and quoted him as saying that the first interest he "pursued systematically was the theatre, and [he] even tried to write tragedies 'on rather violent and more or less erotic themes—Andromache, Rosamunde, and so on.'"[18] Hayek attended plays frequently and read many translations of Spanish and French dramas from the seventeenth and eighteenth centuries and the Greek classics. He read fine German literature, especially the works of Goethe, whom he considered the greatest literary influence on his early thinking. He was a tall, gangly, untidy boy, and a voracious reader.

He was brought up without religious instruction, though both his parents were formally Roman Catholic. His parents never took him to church. There was some religious education in school, but this was minimal. He and his brothers often did not attend the semi-compulsory mass at school whenever a "quite regular"[19] Sunday family excursion occurred during spring and summer, which led to frequent conflicts with scholastic authorities. He and his father sometimes took walks in the woods on Sundays.

However, as a young boy, Hayek remembered the "anguish of feeling that he had sinned between confession and communion."[20] Hayek recalled that when he was thirteen or fourteen, he asked all the priests he knew to explain what they "meant by the word *God*. None of them could. [laughter] That was the end of it for me."[21] "By the age of fifteen, I had convinced myself that nobody could give a reasonable explanation of the word 'God' and that it was therefore as meaningless to assert a belief as to assert a disbelief in God."[22] Few of his family's friends were religious.

His family today remember stories about him as a somewhat rebellious student. This was in contrast to his brothers, who, though excellent students, were not precocious. He showed little interest in any subject except biology. Once, at age fourteen, having failed Latin, Greek, and mathematics, he was required to repeat a grade. He changed *Gymnasium* not just once, but twice, because he had problems with teachers. He would generally "swot up in a few weeks before the end-of-the-year examinations the whole substance of a year's teaching in several subjects" in which he had done "no work whatever."[23]

As a schoolboy, he irritated most of his teachers by his combination of intelligence and disinterest. While he did not do well in school, he was nonetheless considered a very bright boy by his fellows. When he left his first *Gymnasium*—because, he claimed, of deficiency in drawing—he went to another school with poorer boys (schools were separated by gender). Most of the time, he was near the bottom of his class in most required subjects. He was not interested in most of what his fellow students were learning and teachers were teaching, nor did he feel any compunction to be interested.

At home, it was a different matter. Here, he was the little scholar helping his father with botanical work and attending meetings of the Vienna Zoologic and Botanical Society with him. At fourteen or fifteen, growing intellectually dissatisfied with the classificatory aspects of biology, he desired more theoretical knowledge. "When my father discovered this, he put in my hand what was then a major treatise on the theory of evolution. It was just a bit too early. I was not yet ready to follow a sustained theoretical argument. If he had given me this a year later, I probably would have stuck with biology. The things did interest me intensely."[24] He retained interest in evolution throughout his life and career.

The idea of evolution perhaps loomed larger in the first decades after Darwin's work than it has since the end of World War II. The idea of survival of the fit and of unanticipated, undirected evolutionary development were central in Hayek's thought.

His parents were "exceedingly well suited to each other, and their married life seemed (not only to me) one of unclouded happiness."[25] His family life was "probably ideal—three meals together every day, talking about every subject under the sun, always left free by our parents to roam, to think, even to commit minor peccadilloes."[26]

August was, Friedrich recalled, an "extraordinarily educated man" in the field of German literature. Hayek's family today remember him making very positive comments about his father. Hayek recalled the ice-cold bath his father took every morning for discipline of body and mind. As a youth and after World War I, Hayek and the rest of the family spent many evenings listening to August read the great German dramas and German versions of Shakespeare's plays.

August had a great memory and could quote things like "Die Glocke," Friedrich Schiller's poem, from beginning to end. Friedrich would have the academic career his father did not have. August had more influence on his oldest son than anyone else.

CHAPTER TWO

World War I

WORLD WAR I WAS CAUSED BY RIVAL ALLIANCE STRUCTURES, imperial ambitions, international distrust, and German national egoism. The German historical context is different than the Anglo-American one, and it is important to be clear about this in order to understand the culture from which Hayek emerged. Though Rome conquered the west bank of the Rhine separating Germany and France, it never subdued the tribes residing in what is today Germany. Charlemagne, originally king of the Franks (the Germanic tribes who overran Gaul, what is today France), founded and became emperor of the Holy Roman Empire in 800. In that year, he was crowned by Pope Leo III as head of Christian dominions in what had been the west of the ancient Roman Empire and Germany. At its height—during the tenth and eleventh centuries—the Holy Roman Empire included all or most of what are now Germany, Austria, Switzerland, Belgium, the Netherlands, eastern France, northern and central Italy, the Czech Republic, and western Poland.

The empire existed more as a form than a ruling entity as the centuries moved along, and the princes of lesser states in the Germanic world exerted real power within its domains. In 1648, the Catholic emperor in what is now Austria lost sovereignty to the Protestant princes in what is now Germany following the disastrous Thirty Years' War, in which the Germanic population was decimated. The Holy Roman Empire thereafter existed merely on paper. It so endured until Napoleon; Francis II of Austria finally abdicated the imperial title in 1806. The

Holy Roman Empire was in retrospect the First Reich (state) of 1,000 years to which Hitler referred; Bismarck's was the Second Reich (lasting less than fifty years); and Hitler's was the Third *Reich,* also intended to last 1,000 years.

During the French and Napoleonic wars from the 1790s until 1815, the various states of Germany were united under French rule. Through this occupation, ideas of the French Revolution—including liberty, equality, and democracy—were introduced to German-speaking people. This first modern unification of Germany became in time associated with its occupation by what became a despotic foreign regime, and thus the west and its ideas became discredited in the Germanic world.

During the French and Napoleonic wars, Austria's ruling family, the Habsburgs, were France's most consistent adversary. As a result of the settlement at the Congress of Vienna in 1815, Prussia and the Austrian Empire were established as bulwarks between Russia and England to check France. Thereafter an internal struggle followed between Prussia and Austria over which would predominate in the Germanic world, ultimately ratified by a brief war. Prussia prevailed. Under the leadership of Chancellor Otto von Bismarck, and through the Austro-Prussian War of 1866, the Franco-Prussian War of 1870-71, and the intimidation, annexation, and coercion of lesser states in German territory, the Prussian-dominated German Empire was declared in 1871.

Austria as distinct from Germany was the pretended successor to the Holy Roman Empire. The Habsburgs had also reigned over the empire and considered themselves the leading royal family in Europe, associated through marriage or conquest with most countries. Roman Catholic, they considered themselves the defenders of the faith.

Austria-Hungary, as it became, was a cosmopolitan and ramshackle empire located somewhat to the south and east of the traditional Holy Roman Empire, extending deep into the Balkans. The standing description of its political situation during its latter decades was that conditions were "desperate but not serious."

The proximate cause of World War I was the assassination of Archduke Franz Ferdinand, Austro-Hungarian Emperor Franz Josef's heir presumptive, in Sarajevo, Bosnia, on June 28, 1914. Franz Josef decided to suppress Slav nationalism once and for all, and, with Germany's blessing, Austria-Hungary declared war on Serbia on July 28. This brought Russia into the war in defense of its ally Serbia, and Germany entered the war in support of Austria-Hungary. France was an ally of Russia. Germany's plan was to defeat France, its historical enemy, through a Belgian invasion route before taking on Russia, thereby establishing hegemony on the European continent. Germany's invasion of neutral Belgium pulled Great Britain into the conflagration.

The power structure that had basically existed since the Congress of Vienna in 1815, following the French and Napoleonic Wars, was blown to pieces. Notwithstanding that Austria-Hungary started the war, it was secondary as the real fighting started. Germany sought to establish a political position in the world it considered commensurate with its national greatness—a "place in the sun," in contemporary parlance.

Austria marched with high hopes as the Great War commenced. The description by Hayek's later friend Karl Popper of his experiences as a boy in Vienna during World War I undoubtedly sheds light on Hayek's. Popper wrote that "the war years, and their aftermath, were in every respect decisive for my intellectual development. Of course, few people knew at that time what war meant. There was a deafening clamour of patriotism throughout the country in which even some of the members of our previously far from warmongering circle participated. For a few weeks, under the influence of war propaganda in my school, I became a little infected by the general mood. In the autumn of 1914 I wrote a silly poem 'Celebrating the Peace,' in which the assumption was expressed that the Austrians and the Germans had successfully resisted the attack (I then believed that 'we' had been attacked) . . . Meanwhile all of my cousins who were old enough were fighting as officers in the Austrian army, and so were many of our friends."[1]

Hayek's family surely supported the war, in which both Hayek and his father served. Hayek was still a boy, just fifteen, when the war started. Because of his size, he was sometimes harassed for not being in uniform. He later observed that conditions in Vienna did not really change, for the worse, until the last year of the war.

As a boy, like most boys, he had no interest in history and public affairs, though unlike most children he had great interest in biology. With World War I, his intellectual focus moved to the social sciences, following a brief flirtation with psychology. The political excitement connected with the war and later break-down of the Austro-Hungarian Empire shifted his interests from the natural to the social sciences.

His introduction to the social humanities was in a class on the elements of philosophy. The teacher spoke about Aristotle and said that Aristotle "defined ethics as consisting of three parts: morals, politics, and economics." When Hayek heard this, his reaction was, "'Well these are the things I want to study.' It had a comic aftereffect when I went home and told my father, 'I know what I'm going to study. I'm going to study ethics.' He was absolutely shocked. [laughter] Of course, what I had meant by ethics wasn't at all what my father understood when I mentioned the term."[2]

In March 1917, two months shy of his eighteenth birthday, Hayek entered the army. He was sent as an officer to the Italian front after seven months of training. He characterized his self-confident outlook as "the first time I really proved to myself (what I seem never to have seriously doubted) that if I really wanted I could, without much effort, do as well as the best of my fellows was in the officers' school in the army. In spite of a lack of any special natural aptitudes, and even in spite of a certain clumsiness, I emerged among the five or six heading the list of some seventy or eighty cadets."[3] He was far more academically inclined than his fellow soldiers and sexually inexperienced.

He served for over a year in Italy until the war's end in November 1918. Erich Streissler, a colleague during the 1960s, remembers that Hayek was capable of telling "tragic or comic" stories about the war, "e.g., the one of being in charge of a transport of live eels and having to hunt for them in a bedewed meadow where they somehow got loose."[4] A tragic story involved his only close childhood friend, Walter Magg, who also joined the army, and died shortly before Hayek could see him.[5] Hayek could cry decades later when he saw Magg's picture.

Hayek told his last and longtime secretary, Charlotte Cubitt, that during World War I some shrapnel ricocheted and chipped a piece out of his skull without his being aware of it. "His sergeant had been hit at the same time," Cubitt recalls, "the shrapnel unstitching the seams of his tunic and his shirt and leaving a burn on his skin, which made them laugh so much about it that he had taken no notice of his own wound."[6] It was only weeks later when his father felt around his head that the missing bit of bone was noticed.

Hayek remembered his most exciting war experiences as an aborted offensive in June 1918, the Austro-Hungarian army's collapse in October 1918, and two waves of retreat. Retreating from the Piave River, "we were first pursued by the Italians. Since I was telephone officer of my regiment (which meant that I knew all the very few German-speaking men, who were the only reliable men in these conditions), I was asked to take a little detachment for the artillery regiment, first as a rear guard against the Italians following us and then as an advance guard as we were passing the Yugoslav part, where there were irregular Yugoslav cadres who were trying to stop us and get our guns. On that occasion, after having fought for a year without ever having to do a thing like that, I had to attack a firing machine gun. In the night, by the time I had got to the machine gun, they had gone. But it was an unpleasant experience."[7]

He was nearly killed on another occasion when he made the mistake of attempting to parachute out of an observation balloon without disconnecting his earphones. The sound of shells exploding was so loud that he later (probably incorrectly) attributed some of his bad hearing to this source. He said of his war experiences that "in a sense I am fearless, physically, I mean. It's not courage. It is just that I have never really been afraid." Once, during World War I, he was almost killed in an airplane dogfight. An Italian plane fired at his plane from in front, "through the propeller. When they started firing, my pilot, a Czech, spiralled down. I unbelted myself, climbed on the rail. My pilot succeeded in correcting the spin just above the ground. It was exciting."[8]

He more or less decided to pursue economics during the war while in Italy. He recalled in his unpublished autobiographical notes that war consists of long periods of inactivity and boredom, interspersed with intense moments of danger and excitement.[9] He read his first systematic books on economics, given to him by a fellow officer. Although he later remembered these as exceptionally poor volumes—"I'm surprised they didn't put me permanently off"[10]—they introduced him to the discipline.

He perused contemporary socialist and semi-socialist pamphlets, from which he obtained some of his first economic ideas. He was "especially influenced" by the writings of Walter Rathenau, who was "*Rohstoffdiktator* ["raw stuff"—materials—director] in Germany during the war," who had "become an enthusiastic planner. And I think his ideas about how to reorganize the economy were probably the beginning of my interest in economics. And they were very definitely mildly socialist."[11]

He was able to take leaves from the front, and on one of these returned to his *Gymnasium* for a few days to receive his certification to attend university following the war. Had it not been for his active duty status, it was an open question whether he would have received the certificate easily. During these few days, he got into trouble for reading a socialist pamphlet during a divinity lesson.

University of Vienna

IT WAS A CHANGED VIENNA to which the nineteen-year-old Hayek returned in November 1918 following the Austrian rout—after having come close to being taken prisoner during the war's closing days and contracting a case of malaria that he did not shake for a year and a half. The ancien régime was destroyed across central, eastern, and southern Europe. The Romanovs abdicated in Russia in 1917 and were executed in 1918; the Hohenzollerns were out in Germany with the abdication of Kaiser Wilhelm II in 1918; the 700-year-old Habsburg monarchy came to an end in Austria-Hungary in 1918 as well. The whole edifice of societal order was shaken to the core. The internal transformation was exceeded only by the external political reconfiguration. Eight new states and the Soviet Union came into existence, as borders moved all over eastern, central, and southern Europe.

Over one million of Austria-Hungary's population of fifty million perished during the war. Ten million throughout Europe were killed. The Austro-Hungarian Empire was dissolved. The new Republic of Austria was less than one-seventh of the population it had been and was, territorially, a small fraction of the old empire that had gone to war in such high spirits, ironically, to prop up its regime.

Hayek did not really know what he wanted to do as a newly enrolled student at the University of Vienna in late 1918. He was undecided between psychology and economics. He majored in law because economics was a subsection of the law faculty, but he was about equally interested in psychology and economics. He finally had to choose the field in which he was most interested. For primarily financial and career reasons, he decided for economics.

He planned to combine law and economics as part of his career, which he imagined might be in the diplomatic service. He had only a general idea of what he wanted to do. "My development during those three years was in no way governed by thoughts about my future career," he recalled, "except, of course, that tradition in our family made us feel that a university professor was the sum of achievement, the maximum you could hope for, but even that wasn't very likely."[1] A friend predicted he might someday become a senior ministry official.

As most Austro-Germans, he had expected the war would last longer. He decided, while still in the army, to enter the diplomatic academy, "but for a very peculiar reason. We all felt that the war would go on indefinitely, and I wanted to get out of the army, but I didn't want to be a coward. So I decided to volunteer for the air force in order to prove that I wasn't a coward. It gave me the opportunity to study for what I expected to be the entrance examination for the diplomatic academy, and if I had lived through six months as an air fighter, I thought I would be entitled to clear out. All that collapsed because of the end of the war." Hayek got as far as having his orders to join the flying school, which he never did in the end. "Hungary collapsed, the diplomatic academy disappeared, and the motivation lapsed."[2]

Postwar Vienna was desperately poor. The new Austria suffered from famine, lack of fuel, inflation, and an epidemic of influenza. The economy disintegrated. Following the war, the new Republic of Austria abolished noble titles and disallowed individuals from referring to themselves as "von." Hayek discontinued referring to himself as such. Years later, however, "von" was on his birth certificate when he became naturalized in England, and his name in England "became suddenly von Hayek. It was at a moment [1938] when I was very anxious to go on an English passport on a holiday to Europe."[3]

He first experienced in post–World War I Vienna the confluence of ideas and opinions that he later said in *The Road to Serfdom* emerged subsequently in other nations and which he thought laid the foundations for collectivist rule. "The nearness of the communist revolution—Budapest, only a few hours away, had for a few months a communist government in which some of the intellectual leaders of Marxism were active who soon appeared as refugees at Vienna—the sudden academic respectability of Marxism, the rapid expansion of what we have since learned to call the welfare state, the then-new conception of the 'planned economy,' and above all the experience of an inflation of a degree which no living European remembered, determined very largely the topics of discussion."[4] It was a time of intense political, economic, and societal change.

His mild, Fabian socialist phase lasted from about the ages of seventeen to twenty-five. He was "never captured by Marxist socialism. On the contrary, when I encountered socialism in its Marxist, frightfully doctrinaire form—and the Vienna socialists, Marxists, were more doctrinaire than most other places—it only repelled me."[5] He remarked in addition of his early socialism that it made him "interested in economics. I mean, how realistic were these socialist plans which were found so attractive?"[6] World War I heightened the demand for reform—it so thoroughly destroyed the former order, as well as indicated, through war organization, the possibilities of new societal order. He sought to be a part of the coming reform, and his interest in economics was sparked to a considerable degree by his desire to learn whether socialism was feasible, a question that concerned him for the rest of his life, and to which he answered, no.

He characterized the University of Vienna when he enrolled in it as an "extraordinarily lively place." Though economic circumstances were impoverished and the political situation was chaotic, this had "little influence on the intellectual level preserved from pre-war days."[7] In fact, the University of Vienna to some extent benefited from the arrival of scholars from elsewhere around the old empire. He "plunged" into study and a "very active social life."[8] He worked all day and danced in the evening, although coal shortages forced light restrictions. He described his early social life to an interviewer. "'They were mainly university dances,' he says. 'The girls were the relatives of the professors and so on. There was considerable formality. You could ask a girl out—to the opera, say—but there was always a chaperone.' He was allowed to go for walks unchaperoned with the girl who is now his second wife, but that was only because they were distant cousins."[9]

He helped to organize a German Democratic Party as a student in order to have a middle group between conservatives and socialists. The Austrian monetary system collapsed during his studies. Between October 1921 and August 1922, prices rose 7,000 percent.

Hayek was introduced at the University of Vienna to the liberal, free market economic tradition, in the stream of which he traveled for the rest of his life. Primary among those who most influenced him was Carl Menger, founder of the Austrian school of economics. Once, discussing the influence of Austrian economists on him, Hayek said that he was a "direct student of Wieser, and he originally had the greatest influence on me. I only met Mises really after I had taken my degree. But I now realize—I wouldn't have known it at the time—the decisive influence was just reading Menger's *Principles*. I probably derived more from not only the *Principles* but also the *Investigations*." He became hooked on economics when he found Menger's *Principles* "such a fascinating book—so satisfying."[10]

Menger's place in economic and societal thought grows more significant as time goes on, in considerable part, though by no means entirely, because of his prominent intellectual descendants, including Eugen von Böhm-Bawerk, Friedrich von Wieser, Hayek, and Ludwig von Mises. Hayek wrote in 1934 of the Austrian school of economics that its "fundamental ideas belong fully and wholly to Carl Menger."[11] Mises praised Menger in 1929, saying that "every economic thought today is connected with what Menger and his school demonstrated. 1871, the date of the publication of Menger's *Principles of Economics,* is usually considered the opening of a new epoch in the history of our science."[12] Hayek also wrote there can be "no doubt among historians that if the Austrian school has occupied an almost unique position in the development of economic science, this is entirely due to the foundations laid by this one man."[13]

Hayek considered Menger's greatest contribution to have been his individualist or subjective approach, which locates the focus of all economic activity in the actions, decisions, values, and knowledge of individuals. Hayek was also vitally influenced in his technical economic thought by Menger's conception of different "orders" of goods. Menger presented this idea in *Principles of Economics* (1871):

> It appears to be of preeminent importance to our science that we should become clear about the causal connections between goods. The bread we eat, the flour from which we bake the bread, the grain that we mill into flour, and the field on which the grain is grown—all these things are goods. But knowledge of this fact is not sufficient for our purposes. On the contrary, it is necessary in the manner of all other empirical sciences to attempt to classify the various goods according to their inherent characteristics, to learn the place that each good occupies in the causal nexus of goods, and finally, to discover the economic laws to which they are subject. In addition to goods that serve our needs directly (and which will, for sake of brevity, henceforth be called "goods of first order") we find a large number of other things in our economy that cannot be put in any direct causal connection with the satisfaction of our needs, but which possess goods-character no less certainly than goods of first order. In our markets, next to bread and other goods capable of satisfying human needs directly, we also see quantities of flour, fuel, and salt. All these things, or at any rate by far the

greater number of them, are incapable of satisfying human needs in any direct way. That these things are nevertheless treated as goods in human economy, just like goods of first order, is due to the fact that they serve to produce goods of first order, and hence are indirectly, even if not directly, capable of satisfying human needs.[14]

Hayek was also greatly influenced by Menger's *Investigations into the Method of the Social Sciences with Special Reference to Economics* (1883), which grew out of the *Methodenstreit* ("methodological argument") between the dominant German historical school in economics and Menger and his followers. Hayek observed a half-century later that the "main interest" of the *Investigations* to the "economist in our days seems to lie in the extraordinary insight into the nature of social phenomena which is revealed incidentally in the discussion of the origin and character of social institutions."[15] He later said that, in "the form in which Adam Smith put it, the phrase that man in society 'constantly promotes ends which are not part of his intention' describes the central problem of the social sciences. As it was put a hundred years after Smith by Carl Menger, who did more than any other writer to carry beyond Smith the elucidation of the meaning of this phrase, the question 'how it is possible that institutions which serve the common welfare and are most important for its advancement can arise without a common will aiming at their creation' is still 'the significant, perhaps the most significant, problem of the social sciences.'"[16]

The question of spontaneous order was among the most profound that Hayek explored. How is it possible for a peaceful, productive society to emerge in which no one gives orders? Hayek's answer became the rule of law. Right law (*orthonomos*) creates—is—the societal structure or framework in which mankind flourishes.

Menger wrote in the *Investigations* of the "error of those who reduce all institutions to acts of positive common will," and that "institutions are unintended creations." He emphasized that "natural organisms almost without exception exhibit, when closely observed, a really admirable functionality of all parts with respect to the whole, a functionality which is not, however, the result of human *calculation,* but of a *natural* process. Similarly we can observe in numerous social institutions a strikingly apparent functionality with respect to the whole. But with closer consideration they still do not prove to be the result of an *intention aimed at this purpose,* i.e., the result of an agreement of members of society. They, too, present themselves rather as 'natural' products. One needs only to think of language, of the origin of markets, the origin of communities and of states, etc."[17]

Right law creates not the details but the boundaries of interpersonal interaction. Government should not direct an economy but establish and enforce the laws of property and exchange that enable individuals to interact with one another in the most materially productive manner. Liberty, properly conceived, is not the absence of law but its supremacy.

Hayek saw Menger only once, as Menger strode by in an academic procession at the University of Vienna in about 1920 when he was about the age of eighty. He told an interviewer that the "comic part of the story is when later I wrote a biographical essay on him, there's one single sentence which is based on my own experience and that is the only one which is wrong. Because he made a very impressive figure, I described him as a tall man, and afterward everybody told me he was quite medium size."[18] After Menger's death, Hayek was brought in to advise on the sale of his library, so he saw the libraries of all of the original main Austrian economists, though he saw the library of Eugen von Böhm-Bawerk, as he saw Menger's, only after his death.

Besides Menger, the two other key members of the historical Austrian school of economics were Eugen von Böhm-Bawerk (who died in 1914) and Friedrich von Wieser, colleagues and successors of Menger at the University of Vienna, and brothers-in-law and lifelong friends as well. Böhm-Bawerk emphasized capital and interest and stressed the superiority of "roundabout" methods of production, also a source of Hayek's and Mises' business cycle work. Böhm-Bawerk became a leading Austrian statesman and was for a number of decades the most well-known Austrian economist, in part because of his government work. Böhm-Bawerk was also known for his explicit early conflict with Marxian economic thought, which was relatively prominent in German-speaking countries decades before it was in the English-speaking world.

Wieser was more corporatist and intervention-minded than Böhm-Bawerk and Menger. Hayek recalled that when he was a student, he was "very much aware that there were two traditions" in the Austrian school—the "Böhm-Bawerk tradition and the Wieser tradition. Wieser was slightly tainted with Fabian socialist sympathies."[19] Hayek observed of his later relationship with Mises, who "represented the Böhm-Bawerk tradition," that "I perhaps most profited from his teaching because I came to him as a trained economist, trained in a parallel branch of Austrian economics from which he gradually, but never completely, won me over."[20]

Austrian economic historian Joseph Schumpeter, also a student of Böhm-Bawerk, wrote of Menger that it is an "acid test of the power of an argument whether it can be looked upon as decisive in its own right, or whether it stands in need of a long string of supporting subsidiary arguments. The fundamental idea of Menger's theory is that people value goods because they need them. This simple fact and its sources in the laws of human needs are wholly sufficient to explain the basic facts about all the complex phenomena of the modern exchange economy. Human needs are the driving force of the economic mechanism."[21] Economics, in the Austrian view, ultimately concerns the satisfaction of human wants, needs, and desires, and the highest material standard of living, which requires the most scientific knowledge.

Schumpeter also wrote of Menger's work that "all specifically economic events can be comprehended within the framework of price formation. From a purely economic standpoint, the economic system is merely a system of dependent prices. His essential aim is to discover the law of price formation."[22] In closing the preface to *Principles of Economics,* Menger said that he sought to "establish a price theory placing all price phenomena together under one unified point of view . . . the important insights we thereby gain into many other economic processes."[23] Ludwig von Mises explored the role of prices in economic calculation in his attempt to refute classical socialism. Hayek explored the role of prices in spontaneous order more than any of Menger's other intellectual heirs, although Hayek was *sui generis.*

Hayek recalled of the economics faculty at the University of Vienna immediately after the war, that "at first it was dreadful, but only for a year. There was nobody there. Wieser had left to become a minister in the last Austrian government; Böhm-Bawerk had died shortly before; when I arrived there was nobody but a socialist economic historian," Karl Grünberg. Then Wieser returned. Hayek described Wieser as a "most impressive teacher, a very distinguished man whom I came to admire very much. I think it's the only instance where, as very young men do, I fell for a particular teacher. He was the great admired figure, sort of a grandfather figure of the two generations between us. He was a very kindly man who usually, I would say, floated high above his students as a sort of God, but when he took an interest in a student, he became extremely helpful and kind. He was for a long time my ideal in the field, from whom I got my main general introduction to economics."[24] Hayek's maternal grandfather knew Wieser.

Hayek studied mostly psychology during his first year at the University of Vienna. His early interest in psychology was significant. The type of psychology he was interested in was philosophical psychology, which might be described, in his case, as the nature of human mental understanding of the physical world. He was largely influenced in this area by the physicist and philosopher Ernst Mach, who taught at the University of Vienna for a number of years before his death in 1916 and whose philosophical ideas dominated Viennese academic discussion during Hayek's years as a student.

During his second year at the university, he split his time more evenly between psychology and economics, and for a few weeks during a break visited the laboratory of a Zurich brain anatomist, tracing fiber bundles through the brain. During his third year and postgraduate work, he emphasized economics.

His closer contacts with Wieser commenced during his third year at the university as he worked on his second degree. Hayek's first degree, in law, was conferred in November, 1921. He recalled of his university regimen that "I sometimes marvel [at] how much I could do in the three years when you think my official study was law. I did all my exams with distinction in law, and yet I divided my time about equally between economics and psychology. I had been to all these other lectures and to the theater every evening almost."[25] Notwithstanding that he was officially a law student, his legal studies were a "sideline."[26] He was most influenced in this area by a three-semester course on the history of law.

The diverse lectures and courses he attended also included anatomy. "I had easy access. My brother was studying in the anatomy department; so I just gate-crashed into lectures occasionally and even in the dissecting room."[27]

The higher educational program in the Germanic world during the late teens and early 1920s was different than in the United States or elsewhere now. "Instruction was almost entirely confined to formal lectures. There were no tests except three main examinations, mostly at the very end of your study; so beyond the purely formal requirement that the professor testified to your attendance, you were under no control whatever. We were entirely free, really, in what we did, provided that we were ready to be orally examined. We did no written work at all for our whole study, or no obligatory written work. There were some practical exercises in legal subjects where we discussed particular things, but even they were not obligatory. And in the law faculty, especially, the majority of students hardly ever saw the university but went to [a] coach and the coach prepared them for their final exam."[28]

Only a small percentage of students had genuinely intellectual interests. Other students merely wanted to get through exams. The small group of interested students "certainly did not specialize solely in one discipline. I would go to lectures on biology, to lectures on art history, to lectures on philosophy. . . . I sampled around. If you were in that group, you then constantly would meet the same men. It all happened in one building."[29]

There was, in the Germanic universities of this time, a substantial break between the organized discipline of secondary school and the freedom of the university. One had to "learn to find your own way, and most of those who were any good learned to study on their own with just a little advice and stimulus from the lectures."[30] Hayek's university education as he earned his initial degree was intense and short.

The top students, he recalled in an interview,

even in their subject would do more than was essential for examinations. Most of those who would voluntarily attend a seminar beyond the formal lectures would not be interested only in economics but would go outside.

Q: What are your views on the advantages of specialising or of pursuing more than one field seriously, the way you and the best of your contemporaries did?

A: Well, it certainly was very beneficial in our time. I think we were more likely and more ready to ask questions, but we knew factually less than a present-day student does. It didn't matter if you neglected one subject, up to a point. I think on any sort of test of competence in our special subject we were probably less well trained than the present-day student. On the other hand, we preserved an open mind; we were interested in a great many things; we were not well-trained specialists, but we knew how to acquire knowledge on a subject. And I find nowadays that even men of high reputations in their subject won't know what to do for their own purposes if they have to learn a new subject. To us this was no problem. We constantly did it. We had the confidence that if you seriously wanted to pursue a subject, you knew the technique of how to learn about it.[31]

He remarked later in life that Vienna was "one of the great intellectual centers of the world. Nothing could be more exciting than Vienna of the 1920s and the early '30s."[32] Foremost among the influences that made Vienna intellectually great was its Jewish community, one of the largest and perhaps the most talented in the world, a community of two hundred thousand souls, of whom less than eight thousand remained in Vienna following World War II. Early in the twentieth century, Vienna had a population of roughly two million.

Hayek's early interaction with Jews was superficial. Until he went to university, he did not know a single Jew well. Within contemporary Austro-Catholic culture, he was on the liberal or progressive side in his interaction with Jews once he entered the university. He had extensive relationships, both personal and professional, with a number of Jewish students and teachers.

The level of instruction at the University of Vienna was exceptionally high. The *Dozenten* ("private lecturer") system was in operation, in addition to the regular university faculty. *Dozenten* were individuals who were licensed to teach university students and who were not paid by the university, but instead received very modest payment from students. Many *Dozenten* were Jewish, including Mises and Sigmund Freud. "The main people that taught were absolutely first class," Hayek favorably recalled. "Every lecturer, nearly everyone, was intelligent" and perhaps had made a scholarly contribution. "They had to be good or they wouldn't have any students."[33]

Hayek recalled that there were three spheres of interaction within Vienna's particularly intellectual community—the all Christian sphere, a mixed Christian-Jewish sphere, and the all Jewish sphere. Hayek had no contact with the last sphere, and thus no contact with Freud. Hayek interacted with the all Christian and mixed groups.

He said of his study habits that he "soon gave up all attempts to take notes of lectures—as soon as I tried I ceased to understand. My gain from hearing or reading what other people thought was that it changed the colours of my own concepts. What I heard or read did not enable me to reproduce their thought but altered my thought."[34] He said along these lines on another occasion that "it's very curious. I am hardly capable of restating the ideas of another person because I read and embody what I like to my own thought. I cannot read a book and give an account of its arguments. I can perhaps say what I have learnt from it. But that part of the argument which is not sympathetic to me, I pass over."[35]

Hayek was a brilliantly creative writer. He did not always absorb the most light from other minds and this led to inaccuracies in his perspectives. As a result of his overpowering intellect, he was, indeed, able to sustain counterfactual theories for a great distance. Like other great writers, his written word was sometimes better than his thought.

CHAPTER FOUR

New York

HAYEK HAD HOPED THAT AFTER FINISHING HIS LAW DEGREE he would be able to spend a year at a university in Germany, possibly Munich, where sociologist Max Weber taught. Weber died in 1920, though, and the Austrian inflation would have made it infeasible for Hayek's father to afford the cost of a year's study for his son in Germany in any event. Hayek subsequently, from March 1923 to May 1924, lived in the United States, after he received his second degree from the University of Vienna in 1923, in political science, less than a year and a half after his first degree in 1921. He desired to become a professional economist and realized that familiarity with the United States, and greater fluency in English, would be valuable.

Unlike many later postgraduates, he did not go to the United States in the care of the Rockefeller Foundation. "All the later visitors visited America very comfortably and could travel and see everything," he recalled. "My case was unique. I was the only one who came on his own, at his own risk, and with practically no money to spare, and who lived for the whole of a 15-month period on sixty dollars a month. It would have been miserable if I hadn't known that if I was in real difficulty I would just cable my parents, 'Please send me the money for the return.' But apart from this confidence that nothing could really happen to me, I lived as poorly and miserably as you can live."[1]

His opportunity to study in the United States came about through a semi-invitation from New York University professor Jeremiah Jenks, who had just served on an international commission of economists, including John Maynard Keynes, to advise the German government on currency reform. Jenks visited Vienna in 1922, when Hayek met him and explained that he was "anxious to go to America to improve my knowledge of economics. He assured me by saying, 'I am going to write a book about Central Europe; so if you come over, I can employ you for a time as a research assistant.' Now that was immediately after the end of the inflation in Austria; so to collect enough money even to pay my fare was quite a problem. I had saved even the money on the cable announcing that I would arrive. As a result, when I arrived in New York, I found that Professor Jenks was on holiday and left instructions not to be communicated with."[2]

Hayek arrived in New York with "exactly twenty-five dollars in my pocket. Now, twenty-five dollars was a lot of money at that time. So I started first presenting all my letters of introduction . . . which earned me a lunch and nothing else. With the help of another five dollars which somebody had slipped in the box of cigarettes they gave me after the luncheon, I lasted for over two weeks on that money. Finally I was down to—after having reduced my ambitions more and more—accepting a post as a dishwasher in a Sixth Avenue restaurant. I was to start next morning. But then a great relief came to me—but that I never started washing dishes is a source of everlasting regret now. (laughter) But on that morning, a telephone call came. Professor Jenks had returned and was willing to employ me."[3]

Among those who wrote letters on his behalf to American economists was Joseph Schumpeter, who taught at Harvard before World War I, was a bank president in Vienna at the time, and who was influenced in economics by Hayek's maternal grandfather, von Juraschek. Hayek recalled that Wieser asked Schumpeter to "give me letters of introduction to his friends in the States. So I visited Schumpeter in his magnificent office—bank presidents' offices tend to become more and more grandiose as you move East, and Schumpeter's might have been in Bucharest instead of Vienna—and he supplied me with a set of most kind introductory letters, so large in size that I had to have a special folder made to get them uncrumpled to their destination. But they did prove true 'open sesames.' I was received and treated much beyond my deserts."[4]

Hayek's trip to the United States may have prompted the breakup of his relationship with his cousin who later became his second wife. Bill Letwin, a student of Hayek's in London and Chicago, recalls that he once mentioned something like, "I didn't have the wit to say, 'Let's get married,'"[5] when both he and his cousin, Helene, were young in Vienna. He then departed to America for over a year and when he returned, she was in another relationship. According to Stephen Kresge, general editor of Hayek's *Collected Works,* in words reviewed by Hayek's son, through "some misunderstanding of his intentions,"[6] Hayek's cousin married someone else.

He began, though he did not complete, a doctoral program in the United States on problems of monetary stabilization. According to Kresge, it is "not too extreme to say that the encounter with Wesley Clair Mitchell [in New York] shaped the direction of much of Hayek's later work."[7] Mitchell taught at Columbia University and was for twenty-five years director of the National Bureau of Economic Research. Unlike Hayek's Austrian intellectual progenitors, Mitchell emphasized an empirical, statistical, quantitative approach to economics. Among the many prominent economists who studied under Mitchell is Milton Friedman.

In a 1926 letter to Mitchell from Vienna, Hayek wrote that it was "only now that I feel how much I have really learnt during that year [in the United States]. While my theoretical predilections have remained unchanged, I realize now the weak points of abstract theory which seem to most of you to make the pure theory more or less useless. . . . I hope to be on the way to supply some of the missing links between orthodox economic theory and one applicable to the explanation of the processes of modern economic life."[8] There were two basic strands in Hayek's thought—a theoretical strand and an empirical one. To the extent that he was influenced in an empirical direction by Mitchell and his residence in the United States, his time in New York was of great significance to him indeed.

The subject of his intended thesis at New York University was, "Is the function of money consistent with an artificial stabilization of its purchasing power?"— a subject that would concern him in technical economics during the 1930s. Hayek was never a "stabilizer" in contemporary parlance (as Keynes, for example, was). Stabilizers sought stable national prices through internal, domestic, monetary arrangements. Part of Hayek's early goal was fixed international exchange rates through an international gold standard. More to the point, however, from the perspective of his intended New York University thesis, was that he believed stable prices lead to misproduction in economic activity.

The question of a business cycle was far more prevalent in economic theory during the early decades of the twentieth century than it has subsequently become. There were seemingly inevitable and periodic fluctuations in economic activity during the last decades of the nineteenth century and first decades of the twentieth. Hayek developed, following Mises, an explanation of a business cycle that located its source in misstructured economic production that occurs when interest rates do not reflect the real savings of an economy.

What Hayek found of most interest in the United States was work being done on monetary policy and control of industrial fluctuations connected with the Harvard Economic Service and new experiments in central banking policy by the Federal Reserve System. He found discussion of pure economic theory in the United States disappointing. His visit shifted his interest "a little from the pure theory of value and price to the problems of the steering process in the market economy. I was then becoming increasingly aware that the guide function of the process determining the effectiveness of our efforts could operate satisfactorily only if monetary demand corresponded to real demand, not so much in the aggregate as in the relative proportions of the different goods which were demanded and supplied."[9] His conception of economic activity was based on the Mengerian idea of different orders of goods and the Böhm-Bawerkian idea of roundaboutness of production.

He conceived his first major project while in the United States, a book on the development of the Federal Reserve System. While this work never came to pass, his research provided the grist for two of his earliest articles, (in German) "The Monetary Policy of the United States after the Recovery from the 1920 Crisis" and "The American Banking System Since the Reform of 1914." Other benefits of his early trip to the United States included that he gained oral fluency in English, which proved invaluable for his later position at the London School of Economics and Political Science in 1931, and that he became acquainted with newly developed American statistical methods, which assisted in his selection as director of the Austrian Institute for Business Cycle Research that opened in Vienna in 1927.

As well as work affiliated with New York University, he gate-crashed at Columbia University without having any official connection there. At Columbia Hayek attended lectures of Mitchell in economic history, and the seminar of another prominent American economist, John Bates Clark.

He wrote a letter-to-the-editor to the *New York Times* that was published on August 19, 1923, under the title "Germany's Finance." Apparently his first publication in English, the letter remarked on Germany's "impoverishment."[10] The economic circumstances in the Germanic world during his young adulthood were always central in his economic thought. He considered inflation to be the worst misfortune that can befall an economy and looked for a number of years to a gold standard as the best way to maintain a sound and peaceful world economic order.

He hoped to extend his stay in the United States for another year through a Rockefeller Foundation fellowship, for which he was proposed as the first candidate from Austria by Wieser. Before notification of the award reached him, however, he had begun his trip back to Vienna. He intended to return to take advantage of the fellowship in a few years, but before this became possible he married and became director of the Austrian business cycle institute, which made another extended departure from Austria infeasible. He grew a beard while in the United States and liked to joke decades later that "I now use as a very effective opening with American students the phrase, '50 years ago, when I first grew a beard in protest against American civilization—'(laughter)."[11]

His memories of his first sojourn in the United States were not exactly happy. Comparing the varied academic and social world in Vienna to his New York experience, he remembered that his former "sort of life was completely absent. But it was also, of course, that in the United States I was so desperately poor that I couldn't do anything. I didn't see anything of what the cultural life of New York was because I couldn't afford to go anywhere." He had no "real contacts. I wasn't a regular student. I was sitting in the New York Public Library, and there were four or five people at the same desk whom I came to know, but that was the total of my acquaintance with Americans." He met a few Austrian families, but "really had very little contact with American life during that year. I was so poor that my dear old mother used to remind me to the end of her life that when I came back from America I wore two pairs of socks, one over the other, because each had so many holes, it was the only way."[12] Just turning twenty-five in May 1924, Hayek was glad to return to Vienna.

CHAPTER FIVE

Mises

SELECTED IN 2000 AS "LIBERTARIAN OF THE CENTURY" by the editors of *Liberty* magazine, Ludwig von Mises was born in 1881 in Lemberg, then in the Austro-Hungarian Empire. After attending *Gymnasium,* Mises entered the University of Vienna, where he studied history and, after he graduated, participated in Böhm-Bawerk's seminar. His first major work in economics was *The Theory of Money and Credit* (1912). Strongly opposed to inflation, Mises also briefly put forward the theory of a trade cycle that Hayek later developed in more depth: An increased money supply, among its other pernicious consequences, misshapes the structure of economic production.

Following service in World War I, Mises became director of the Austrian chamber of industry, in which capacity he gave Hayek his first position in late 1921 as a legal consultant for a government office carrying out provisions of the treaties ending the war—settling prewar private debts among belligerent nations. Hayek knew French, Italian, and English. Of his appointment to this post, Hayek explained that "the three foreign languages, plus law, plus economics, qualified me for what was comparatively a very well-paid job."[1]

Hayek enjoyed telling the story of how he came to Mises in 1921 with a letter of introduction from Wieser, who "described me as a promising economist. Mises looked at me and said, 'Promising economist? I've never seen you at my lectures.' [laughter]"[2] "This was almost completely true. I had looked in at one of his lectures and found that a man so conspicuously antipathetic to the kind of Fabian views which I then held was not the sort of person to whom I wanted to go. But of course things changed."[3] "We became very great friends afterwards," Hayek remembered, "and while I was working in Austria, he was for the first five years my official head; then he helped me to create the Institute of Economic [Business Cycle] Research and became vice-president while I was director."[4]

As a boss, Mises was "absolutely ideal, considerate and always ready to talk about economics except the work he was doing himself at the moment. . . . After a few months, he used me when a difficult or responsible job was to be done with a very peculiar result, that I had to negotiate on equal terms with bank presidents and ministers of finance who were scandalized at dealing with such a young man. However, when Mises was convinced that I could do it, he completely disregarded routine or rank."[5]

Mises played a crucial role in Hayek's professional development. Mises introduced Hayek to New York University professor Jenks. Without Mises' assistance (which included giving him a salary advance), Hayek would not have gone to the United States nor would he have remained in a professional field close to academic economics. Even more important than this practical assistance, however, was Mises' intellectual stimulation. Hayek's interaction with Mises and participation in his "private seminar" were vital in his intellectual development.

While finishing his law degree, Hayek formed a discussion group—the *Geistkreis* ("intellect" or "spirit circle," perhaps better colloquially translated as "soul brothers")—with fellow student J. Herbert von Fürth, who later became a member of the Federal Reserve Board in the United States. Most of the members of the *Geistkreis* were Jewish. The group met monthly for discussions.

Members of the *Geistkreis*—a number of whom were or became members of Mises' seminar—included Max Mintz, who became a historian in the United States; Erik Vögelin, a political philosopher who taught at the University of Vienna and then in the United States; Alfred Schütz, a sociologist and philosopher; Walter Fröhlich, a historian and lawyer who became a professor at Marquette University; and Felix Kaufmann, a philosopher and legal theorist who later taught at the New School for Social Research in New York. Other participants included Gottfried Haberler, who became an economist and professor at the University of Vienna and Harvard; Oskar Morgenstern, an economist and pioneer of game theory who taught at Princeton; Fritz Machlup, an economist and professor at Princeton; and Friedrich Engel-Janosi, a historian. Both Haberler and Machlup later served as presidents of the American Economic Association. Others who attended at various times included art historians Otto Benesch and Johannes Wilde, musicologist and lawyer Emanuel Winternitz, and psychoanalyst Robert Waelder.

Austrian economic historian Earlene Craver writes of the *Geistkreis* in comparison with Mises' seminar that although there was "considerable overlap between the membership of the Mises seminar and the little circle begun by Hayek and Fürth, the latter filled the needs of those who desired a circle with a broader cultural focus."[6] Fürth kept an agenda that shows the wide variety of topics discussed over a decade. Sessions were devoted to literature, literary figures, art and music history, history generally, and political philosophy. According to economist Stephan Boehm, who has researched interwar Viennese intellectual history, the purpose of the *Geistkreis* was to "establish a discussion group which should, above all, be devoted to the ideals of intellectual freedom, a freedom that they [Fürth and Hayek] saw constantly violated in Othmar Spann's seminar which they attended. In stark contrast to the Mises Seminar a strong emphasis was placed on elaborate, well-prepared presentations of papers, the policy being that the speaker should as a rule not lecture on a topic of his special field."[7]

Historian Engel-Janosi recalled the *Geistkreis* in his autobiography. He wrote that the group emerged from Hayek and Fürth's dissatisfaction with Spann, an economist at the University of Vienna. Hayek and primarily Fürth sought to involve young men in all fields, not just economics.

Hayek described the *Geistkreis* as an "independent discussion group of younger men. Mises had nothing to do with this group."[8] The group's meetings were in private homes. "It went around from house to house—after dinner affairs. I suppose we were always offered a few sandwiches and tea. Sitting around in a circle or sometimes around a table, I suppose a normal attendance would be under a dozen—ten, eleven, something like that." The group was all-male as a result of "then-existing social traditions." Kaufmann was in addition a member of the Vienna circle of logical positivists, so this kept members "informed of what was happening there."[9] The name *Geistkreis* was coined in a somewhat pejorative manner by a fellow young Viennese economist, Martha Steffy Browne, because of the exclusion of women.

Hayek received a second degree from the University of Vienna in early 1923, shortly before he went to the United States in March. This degree was in political science, a new degree for the university. He wrote a thesis for Weiser on imputation, the tracing through of value in economic goods.

Before returning from the United States in May 1924, Hayek was not as intellectually influenced by Mises as he subsequently became when he started to participate in Mises' seminar. Between October 1921, when he began to work for Mises, and March 1923, when he went to America, Hayek was still a student at the university, studying under Wieser.

Hayek remarked of Mises that he became the "chief guide"[10] in the development of his ideas, and that in his interests he was "very much guided by him: Both the interest in money and industrial fluctuations and the interest in socialism come very directly from his [Mises'] influence."[11] Another area in which Mises, following Wieser, influenced Hayek was in his philosophical methodology that emphasizes an internal source of final knowledge. Wieser most clearly expressed the view that Hayek adopted for much of particularly his early career when he wrote that "we can observe natural phenomena only from outside but ourselves from within. The theoretical economist need never deplore a lack of the instruments which are employed in the exact natural sciences. The group of practical sciences, of which economic theory is one, can accomplish more. Economic theory need never strive to establish a law in a long series of inductions. In these cases we, each of us, hear the law pronounced by an unmistakable inner voice."[12] Mises wrote that "what we know about our own actions and about those of other people is conditioned by our familiarity with the category of action that we owe to a process of self-examination and introspection as well as of understanding of other people's conduct. To question their insight is no less impossible than to question the fact that we are alive."[13]

Mises influenced Hayek in a number of other areas, including the following.

APPROACH

My book [*Socialism*] is a scientific inquiry, not a political polemic. I have analysed the basic problems and passed over, as far as possible, all the economic and political struggles of the day.[14]

ATTITUDE AND PROGRAM

It is true that the majority of mankind are not able to follow difficult trains of thought, and no schooling will help those who can hardly grasp the most simple propositions to understand complicated ones. But just because they cannot think for themselves the masses follow the lead of the people we call educated. Once convince these, and the game is won.[15]

The first socialists were the intellectuals; they and not the masses are the backbone of Socialism.[16]

PHILOSOPHY

> Whether civilized humanity will perish forever or whether the catastrophe will
> be averted is a question which concerns the generations destined to act in the
> coming decades, for it is the ideas behind their actions that will decide it.[17]

> Only ideas can overcome ideas and it is only the *ideas* of Capitalism
> and of Liberalism that can overcome Socialism. Only by a battle of ideas
> can a decision be reached. If we could overcome the *idea* of Socialism, if
> humanity could be brought to recognize the necessity of private ownership
> of the means of production, then Socialism would have to leave the stage.[18]

Mises wrote in his magnum opus, *Human Action* (1949), after listing what he
thought were erroneous economic propositions, that there was "only one way in
which a man can respond to them: by never relaxing in the search for truth."[19]

The work of Mises' that most influenced Hayek was *Socialism,* which
appeared in 1922. When asked the books that affected him most, Hayek responded
that there was "no doubt about both Menger's *Principles* and Mises' *Socialism.*"[20]
He wrote in 1978 in the foreword to a new publication of the work that

> when *Socialism* first appeared, its impact was profound. It gradually but
> fundamentally altered the outlook of many of the young idealists returning
> to their university studies after World War I. I know, for I was one of them.

> We felt that the civilization in which we had grown up had collapsed.
> We were determined to build a better world, and it was this desire to
> reconstruct society that led many of us to the study of economics. Socialism
> promised to fulfill our hopes for a more rational, more just world. And then
> came this book. Our hopes were dashed. *Socialism* told us that we had been
> looking for improvement in the wrong direction. . . .

> It was a great surprise to me when this book was first published. For
> all I knew, he [Mises] could hardly have had much free time for academic
> pursuits.[21]

Hayek's outlook did not instantaneously change from a Fabian socialist
perspective to a free market one on meeting Mises. It was a process that took
several years, and even through the later 1920s, Hayek retained more positive
views of government involvement in an economy than he subsequently
developed and maintained.

The question of Mises' influence on Hayek's technical economic thought
is debated. Hayek said that Mises was known primarily as an opponent of

inflation when he first went to work for him. Hayek emphasized, as has been noted, that he came to Mises as a "trained economist, trained in a parallel branch of Austrian economics from which he gradually, but never completely, won me over."[22] During the sixteen or so months that he worked for Mises before going to New York, Hayek was still primarily under the tutelage of Wieser, for whom he was writing a thesis. Moreover, Hayek stated that he developed his views on business cycle theory when he was in New York studying monetary policy and industrial fluctuations. "It was in the studies of my descriptive work on American monetary policy," he later recalled, that he was "led to develop my theories of monetary fluctuations."[23]

Mises did not develop his theory of a business, or trade, cycle as much as Hayek did. Hayek said of the evolution of Austrian business cycle theory that when he "came back from the United States in '24, I wrote an article on American monetary policy suggesting that an expansionist credit policy leads to an overdevelopment of capital goods industries and ultimately to a crisis. I assumed that I was just restating what Mises was teaching, but Haberler said, 'Well, it needs explanation.' So I first put in that article a very long footnote sketching an outline of what ultimately became my explanation of industrial fluctuations."[24] In the introduction to a re-publication of his early economic articles, Hayek added that "one episode in the growth of my expositions may perhaps be worth recording. In the draft of my account I had made use of what I thought was a theory of Ludwig von Mises. But another member of our group persuaded me after reading my first draft that no sufficient exposition of the theory I had used was to be found in Mises' published work."[25] Hayek's referenced footnote begins: "A rate of interest which is inappropriately low offers to the individual sectors of the economy an advantage which is greater the more remote is their product from the consumption stage," and also states that the effect of artificially lowered interest rates is "disproportionate development of goods of higher order"[26]—temporally early capital goods.

Participation in Mises' seminar was by individuals who had already graduated from university. Hayek recalled that, before returning from the United States, "apparently I was regarded as not quite sufficiently mature"[27] for the group. The private seminar was completely distinct from the university. Hayek attended it from 1924, after returning from New York, until 1931, when he left for London. These were discussions among individuals advanced in economic theory and other aspects of the social sciences. They were the most significant discussions of economics and societal theory then occurring in Vienna.

Mises was a short, burly man, given to occasional temperamental episodes. Describing the meetings in retrospect, Mises said that his "main teaching effort" was focused on his "*Privatseminar.* Beginning in 1920, during the months of October to June, a number of young people gathered around me once every two weeks. My office in the Chamber of Commerce was spacious enough to accommodate twenty to twenty-five persons. We usually met at seven in the evening. In these meetings we informally discussed all important problems of economics, social philosophy, sociology, logic, and the epistemology of the sciences of human action. . . . All who belonged to this circle came voluntarily, guided only by their thirst for knowledge. They came as pupils, but over the years became my friends."[28]

Gottfried Haberler was an employee of Mises and a close friend of Hayek's. He recalled that Mises "sat at his desk and the members of the group around him. The meeting would be introduced by a paper by Mises himself or by another member on some problem of economic policy. Sociology, especially of Max Weber and related problems, were favorite topics. The always lively discussion lasted until ten P.M., when the group walked over to the nearby Italian restaurant. There, the discussion continued on finer points of theory and later usually took on lighter tones. At eleven thirty or so, those members who were not yet exhausted went to the Café Künstler, opposite the University, the favorite meeting place of economists in Vienna in those days. Mises was always among the hardy ones who went to the Künstler Café and was the last one to leave for home, never before one A.M. Next morning, fresh as a daisy, he was at his office at nine A.M."[29]

According to Fritz Machlup, "the choice of the topic was left to the members, though the range of subjects for the year was determined in advance. For example, one year was given to discussions of methodology, another year to issues of economic and monetary policy. During the sessions, Mises circulated, to the delight of all the members, a giant box of chocolate candies." Machlup recalled that discussion did not necessarily end following coffee; "emerging after one A.M., there were some who still wanted to enjoy a walk and pursue further the problems that had not been solved during the long evening."[30]

Engel-Janosi emphasized that in addition to the later prominent economists in Mises' seminar—Hayek, Haberler, Machlup, and Morgenstern, as well as Mises himself—there were outstanding philosophers—Kaufmann, Schütz, and Voegelin. Engel-Janosi characterized the theme of the seminar as "the understanding of the understanding" and added that for him the seminar was a "school for precise thinking." Engel-Janosi further recollected that

"Mises was proud of his seminar" and remarked that Mises was not authoritarian, dictated no political line, and "had absolutely nothing to object to contradiction." Engel-Janosi said as well that Mises' liberalism and individualism were "compromiseless,"[31] and that Mises took unpopular political and economic stands in Vienna.

Hayek explained that the seminar sessions were "not instructional meetings, but discussions presided over by an older friend whose views were by no means shared by all members. The discussions frequently dealt with the problems of the methods of the social sciences, but rarely with special problems of economic theory (except those of the subjective theory of value). Questions of economic policy, however, were discussed often, and always from the angle of the influence of different social philosophies upon it."[32] Hayek said that topics at the private seminar included economics, but that the discussion moved into general philosophical, epistemological, and methodological issues, and the relationship between theory and practice.

Mises' private seminar was one of the three great seminars in which Hayek participated, the other two being his joint-seminar with Lionel Robbins at the London School of Economics and his own seminar on the Committee on Social Thought at the University of Chicago. Hayek said of Mises that he was, "contrary to his reputation, an extremely tolerant person. He would have anyone in his seminar who was intellectually interested."[33]

The idea of an Austrian Institute for Business Cycle Research occurred to Hayek while he was in the United States. Paul Silverman, a student of Austrian interwar economic history, writes that Hayek's time in America did "much to expand his knowledge of the problems and techniques of empirical economic research." When Hayek returned to Vienna, he reported his experiences to Mises and urged him to consider the founding of a modern bureau of economic research in Austria. Mises' response was a skeptical one, as such research seemed to carry overtones of both naive anti-theoretical empiricism and the slavish imitation of the techniques of the natural sciences in economic investigations, things which he sharply rejected." In 1926, however, Silverman continues, Mises spent a "number of months in the United States on a lecture tour sponsored by the Rockefeller Foundation, and was able to familiarize himself with the new research techniques which had been developed there. He came to the conclusion that an institute which applied at least some of these techniques could serve a useful purpose in Austrian economic life, and thus on his return he began to promote the establishment of one."[34] The new Institute, of which Hayek was the first director, began operation on January 1, 1927. The Institute collected data and published statistics in a monthly bulletin, also in time publishing a series of books.

Hayek initially had two secretaries to assist him. Gradually, he obtained more personnel; after a couple of years, Morgenstern joined him as the second professional member. Mises "didn't interfere" with Hayek's management, Hayek recalled. Hayek also recollected that he was "completely independent. However, Mises was a great help. He knew how to raise money, finance the thing, etc. But the actual work, he didn't have time for."[35] When Hayek returned from the United States, Mises attempted to create a research position for him in the chamber of industry. When this did not prove feasible, they hatched the institute plan.

Hayek married his first wife, née Helen Berta Maria von Fritsch (also known as "Hella"), on August 4, 1926. She was a secretary in the civil service office in which he was employed. He thought she resembled his first love. Hayek and his first wife have two children—Christine Maria Felicitas, born in 1929, and Laurence Joseph Heinrich, born in 1934. Through the mid-1930s, Hayek anticipated that his permanent home would be Austria.[36]

As Hayek had recently married when the Institute came into existence, its creation was especially beneficial for him. A passage from the recollections of Margit von Mises, the later wife of Ludwig, sheds further light on the Institute and on Hayek and Mises' relationship. She recalled that "when Lu founded the Austrian Institute for Business Research, he did so not only because he thought it to be imperative for Austria, but, according to Lu's secretary, 'because he had to help Hayek find the right start in life.'"[37] Margit von Mises also remembered that "Professor Hayek told me that while he was attending Lu's seminar, Lu sometimes invited him to his house for lunch or dinner. The long table was always set immaculately, Lu sitting at one side and opposite him, Mrs. von Mises [Mises' mother]. 'She never spoke a word,' said Professor Hayek. 'She never participated in the conversation, but one always felt she was there.'"[38]

When Hayek returned from New York in 1924 to Vienna, he began to work research he had done in the United States into a major treatise on monetary theory with which he hoped to qualify for a university position. He was mostly interested in theoretical questions, but what were "mainly appreciated" were his "knowledge of particular facts and the acquaintance with statistical techniques I had acquired in the United States and which were then still largely unfamiliar on the European continent."[39] During the later 1920s, he received an invitation to fill the one remaining volume in Max Weber's series of works on the foundations of social economics—on money. Hayek became "convinced that a satisfactory textbook on monetary theory and policy required a long introduction describing the historical development of these subjects." During his last two or three years in Vienna, he devoted his free time that was not taken by his institute work and later lecturing to an "extensive study of the literature on money. The first four chapters of this, from the seventeenth to the nineteenth centuries, had just been written when an invitation arrived to give some lectures at the University of London."[40]

His father died in 1928 at the age of fifty-seven of a kidney disease resulting from blood poisoning he experienced some years before through a botanical expedition. Hayek recalled that, during his father's last years, his parents had a "fantastic flat" that was "the dancing center of Vienna's upper academia."[41] An obituary said of August that "if we look at the scientific life work of Hayek, we can only admire his work energy as well as versatility and speed with which he published one work after another. If there are some signs of superficiality, when not everything is carried out carefully and exactly, this is probably a natural consequence of the hurry in which he always worked."[42]

Hayek became a *Privatdozent* (lecturer) in economics at the University of Vienna from 1929 to 1931, his final years in Vienna. He sought an academic career, and it would be through serving first as an unpaid lecturer that an eventual full-time position might be attained. What he received from student fees merely covered his taxi expenses. He, Haberler, and Morgenstern led a popular joint-seminar on production theory.

One of the issues Hayek worked on during his last years in Vienna was rent control, which helped him to see the negative outcomes of governmental interference in an economy, and which resulted in a couple of publications. He was active in the Austrian National Economic Association in order to provide a forum in which economists from the University of Vienna and Mises' circle could meet. There were personal animosities among the older Viennese economists fueled in part by anti-Semitism directed against Mises. Hayek served as secretary of the National Economic Association and Mises as vice-president. Lionel Robbins, who became Hayek's great friend at the London School of Economics, told of the subsequent history of the Austrian National Economic Association. Following the *Anschluss* (Austrian unification with Germany), "to his eternal shame, Hans Mayer," Wieser's successor at the University, "instead of closing it down as he could honorably have done, expelled the Jewish members from the famous *Nationalökonomische Gesellschaft*" (National Economic Association).[43]

Hayek lived in the twilight of civilized Austria. His young adulthood was shaped by the unusual interwar era. He remarked in an obituary on Mises, who died at ninety-two in 1973, on his "pessimism which led him often to predictions that did not come true as soon as he had expected but that were usually confirmed in the end."[44] Machlup remembered that as early as 1927 Mises "prophesied the approaching end of freedom in Austria. He was quite sure that all of us would have to emigrate."[45]

The degree to which Vienna attained the greatest intellectual heights during the decades on either side of World War I is debated. Austrian intellectual historian William Johnston wrote that the example of Vienna "teaches that time effaces more than it sustains."[46] Hayek late in life said of the intellectual vitality he knew in Vienna as a young man, "All that is dead now."[47] He remembered a visit to Vienna in September 1932 when "a rather large group of professional colleagues was sitting together, and Mises suddenly asked whether we were aware that we were sitting together for the last time. The remark at first aroused only astonishment and later laughter, when Mises explained that after twelve months Hitler would be in power."[48]

TWO

ENGLAND

*"It is these years in London before the war which in retrospect
seem to me the intellectually most active and satisfying of my life.
Especially the seminar—which was really conducted by Robbins but
for which I nominally shared responsibility—taught me more
economics than anything else."*

CHAPTER SIX

LSE

THE LONDON SCHOOL OF ECONOMICS AND POLITICAL SCIENCE—LSE—was one of the leading institutions of higher learning and research in the social sciences in the world during the twentieth century. John Maynard Keynes biographer Robert Skidelsky identifies five preeminent thinkers in an "anti-collectivist revival"[1] that started during the 1930s: Keynes, Hayek, Karl Popper, Joseph Schumpeter, and William Beveridge. Hayek, Popper, and Beveridge were associated with LSE.

LSE's influence on twentieth-century democratic socialism was similarly extensive. Harold Laski, Richard Tawney, Graham Wallas, Clement Attlee, Hugh Dalton, and Sidney Webb all worked and taught there. LSE was the font from which the revival of classical liberalism, post–World War II democratic socialism, and the welfare state emerged in Great Britain and elsewhere.

During the late 1920s, Hayek wrote a number of articles in which he began to articulate his business cycle theory. One of these, "The 'Paradox' of Saving" (1929), brought him to the attention of Lionel Robbins, recently appointed head of economics at LSE. Simply stated, Hayek did not believe that there is a "paradox" of saving. He referred in this article to William Trufant Foster and Waddill Catchings' "The Dilemma of Thrift" (1926), which put forward an underconsumptionist theory of business fluctuations—that economic activity decreases when consumers purchase fewer goods.

In their *Profits* the year before, Foster and Catchings initiated a competition to seek adverse criticism of their theory, offering a prize of $5,000 for the best criticism. The 1925 competition was a spectacular success. No less than 435 essays were submitted by contestants from at least fifty universities and twenty-five countries, including forty authors of books on economics, fifty professors of political economy, other financial experts, and "several of the most highly-reputed economists in the British Empire."[2]

While Hayek did not participate in the competition, consideration of the underconsumptionist hypothesis of business fluctuations led him to formulate his own theory of a business cycle, building on the work of Ludwig von Mises. Mises' analysis was that artificially lowered interest rates through central bank actions will speed up economic activity through more purchases, particularly of capital goods. In time, this increased consumption will be unsustainable, because the real savings do not exist in the economy to maintain it. The choice then facing central banks would be whether to allow market re-equilibration through increased interest rates, thereby causing economic contraction, or whether to attempt to continue expansion through lowering interest rates yet further, injecting more money into the economy. The result of the latter course is inflation, and in time inflation destroys an economy by eliminating a stable basis for economic transactions.

Hayek built on Mises' foundation by emphasizing Böhm-Bawerk's "periods of production." For Hayek, a business cycle is created through excessive investment in capital, lengthening the period of production. An economy cannot then complete the longer productive processes because the real savings do not exist to complete them. An economy becomes misstructured with excessive temporally early capital when central banks reduce interest rates below the rate indicated by the actual savings and demand for capital in an economy. This temporally early capital must be abandoned later in the cycle.

Hayek first visited England during the late 1920s with the Austrian Institute for Business Cycle Research. He recalled that Mises discovered a "kindred spirit" in Edwin Cannan at the London School of Economics during the early 1920s, and it was from this period that "contacts between the Austrian and London liberal groups date."[3] Hayek corresponded with T. E. Gregory, in economics at LSE, in 1929.

Perhaps because Harold Laski later became so famous and associated with LSE, Edwin Cannan's place is often forgotten. More than anyone else, though, Edwin Cannan founded the classical liberal tradition at the school that, like its socialist influence, has had global impact.

LSE was created in 1895 as the brainchild of British socialist and Fabian leader Sidney Webb, a prominent influence in British politics and society for more than half a century. Among the first instructors who most influenced the fledgling institution were Cannan and Graham Wallas, both at the school from the start. Cannan was in economics, Wallas in political science.

Cannan pierced to the liberal essence—the disinterested but passionate pursuit of knowledge and truth working within a utilitarian moral framework of the greatest good for the greatest number. Writing in 1951, Hayek paid Cannan the very significant compliment that independently of, but together with, Ludwig von Mises in Vienna and Frank Knight in Chicago, he "safeguarded the main body of liberal thought through that eclipse in the intellectual history of liberalism which lasted throughout the fifteen or twenty years following the First World War."[4]

Cannan's colleague and friend A. L. Bowley wrote on his death in 1935 that Cannan was "identified with the School of Economics in the years before the War [World War I], where he always seemed in Common Room and in committee to carry in himself the essential life and character of the institution."[5] Hayek said that Cannan "created the tradition which, more than anything else, determined the intellectual climate in the central department of the school."[6] In response to emerging Cambridgian-Marshallian orthodoxy in economics and mathematical emphasis, Cannan favored heterodoxy and commonsense, verbal communication, in words rather than equations.

Among the elements of Cannan's thought most congruent with Hayek's own was his emphasis on the slow transformation of communities. This is evidenced in Cannan's writings, where he stated that "Political Economy does not tell us beforehand what lines the evolution of society will follow," and that "all important change is gradual, and social institutions are not created by the sudden efforts of inspired geniuses but grow 'of themselves,' usually slower than oak-trees."[7] He was the leading British academic proponent of the gold standard and a great economic historian.

Cannan possessed a similar view to Hayek of government's appropriate role, holding "That there should be an authority possessing jurisdiction over every person and thing existing on a given territory is an absolute necessity for the maintenance of any kind of civilised and settled society. Without such an authority it would be impossible for individualistic effort to be carried on. Individuals would not be able to work for their own benefit in peace, and private property could not be effectively protected in the absence of any organisation for defence against evil doers and well defined rules as to what constitutes evil doing."[8] Thus, rules make society, and are necessary for its function.

Like Hayek through most of his career, Cannan maintained that appropriate functions of the state include such "benefits a[s] more or less complete protection from assault, robbery, and fraud, the freedom of locomotion and transport which results from State-maintenance of roads and streets and State regulation of water traffic, drainage and other sanitary provisions, public parks, elementary education, [and] maintenance of those who cannot or will not maintain themselves and who are not maintained by friends or charitable institutions."[9] He was a classical liberal in the tradition of Adam Smith (of whom he was a great scholar), who favored a considerable range of government activities. Yet Cannan was no dogmatist. It was a boast of his that during the Great War he kept a portrait of Carl Menger hanging from the wall of his office at LSE.

Hayek said of his introduction to the world of British academic economics, "[It] so happened that I had become very friendly with the Cannan tradition. I had reviewed his books, and liked them very much, and Robbins was a Cannan pupil, so I fitted in much better in a group with the Edwin Cannan tradition than I would have fitted in with a Marshall tradition."[10] Alfred Marshall had been at Cambridge, and was Keynes' inspiration—"It's all in Marshall" was the Cambridge line of the day. In a late interview, Hayek remarked that the "Cannan tradition was of greater importance than one is now aware."[11]

One element of a worldview that Cannan saw as essential—which was an integral part of the vision of classical liberals and now libertarians—was, as Lionel Robbins termed it, "internationalism." Robbins wrote of Cannan that he had "no use for the business of frontiers and he regarded civilisation as one. So great indeed was his contempt for the belief that there was any difference between trade within and trade across frontiers that he always steadfastly refused to lecture on international trade and rather ostentatiously chose his examples of inter-regional exchange from counties rather than countries. . . . If there is a difference between a Cannan man and others, it is, I think, that he will perhaps feel a greater instinctive disgust than most at discussions in terms of the desirability of this or that limited advantage for this or that national area—a greater sense of betrayal at the spectacle of economic analysis in the service of economic nationalism."[12] Hayek rejected economic nationalism too, and for the same reason—it hinders the dream of one human race.

Hayek delivered four extremely well-received lectures at LSE in late January and early February 1931 on "Prices and Production." Writing in his monumental *History of Economic Analysis* (1954), Schumpeter said that Hayek's trade cycle theory, elucidated in the lectures, was "presented to the Anglo-American community of economists [and] met with a sweeping success that has never been equaled by any strictly theoretical book that failed to make amends for its rigors by including plans and policy recommendations or to make contact in other ways with its readers' loves or hates. A strong critical reaction followed that, at first, but served to underline the success, and then the profession turned away to other leaders and other interests. The social psychology of this is interesting matter for study. Other successes were more enduring and therefore greater in the end. But they lacked the spectacular quality of Hayek's."[13] Marxist John Strachey contemporaneously wrote that with the 1931 publication of Hayek's *Prices and Production,* a "new comet swam into the ken of the Anglo-Saxon economists."[14] Decades later, economics Nobel laureate John Hicks, who was a young staffer in 1931 at LSE, recalled that much of the reason for the attention Hayek's lectures received was that it was a "time—just when the full dimensions of the World Slump were declaring themselves—at which the need for some new knowledge of the subject of Fluctuations was exceptionally high."[15]

Immediately before giving his early 1931 lectures at LSE, which were his introduction to the school, Hayek gave a one-lecture version to the Keynes-dominated Marshall Society at Cambridge. Richard Kahn, one of Keynes' followers and later his literary executor, described the scene. Hayek had "a large audience of students, and also of leading members of the faculty. (Keynes was in London.) The members of the audience—to a man—were completely bewildered. Usually a Marshall Society talk is followed by a lively and protracted barrage of discussions and questions. On this occasion there was complete silence. I felt that I had to break the ice. So I got up and asked, 'Is it your view that if I went out tomorrow and bought a new overcoat, that would increase unemployment?' 'Yes,' said Hayek. 'But,' pointing to his triangles on the board, 'it would take a very long mathematical argument to explain why.'"[16]

A basic difference between Hayek's and Keynes' approaches can be gathered from an interview in which Hayek said that "I never believed or came to believe that there is a simple function between aggregate [demand] and employment. I insist that if you take the whole production as a stream, the earlier parts of the stream can move to a great extent independently of what happens at the mouth of the stream. And on one occasion I almost got him [Keynes] to understand what I mean when I tried to explain to him that in certain circumstances an increase of the final demand will discourage investment because it became important to produce quickly even at higher cost, while a low demand will force investment to reduce costs. So the relation may be a decrease in demand stimulating investment and an increase in demand discouraging investment. For the moment he was very interested, and then he said, 'But that would be contrary to the axiom that employment depends on final demand. . . .'

Because this was so much an axiom in his life that there was a positive correlation between final demand and total employment, anything which conflicted with it was dismissed as absurd."[17]

Hayek's point was that, in the short run, increase in the demand for consumer goods can redirect production from longer temporal capital processes to the quick production of consumer goods, thereby entailing less capital investment in the longer temporal processes. This would discourage real investment.

Hayek's basic misconception of economic production was concerning the nature of capital. His essential practical thesis in technical economic theory was that artificially lowered interest rates misshape the structure of production by encouraging production of temporally early capital goods. This thesis was based on the Böhm-Bawerkian conception of capital wherein as an economy develops, production increasingly occurs through more and more "roundabout," or long and complex, processes.

Economic downturn was, in Hayek's view, the result of imbalance between an economy's ability to sustain development of longer capital productive processes and its ability to produce immediate consumer goods. In such a circumstance, buying a consumer good prevents the longer capital processes from being completed, thereby resulting in waste. He held in "The 'Paradox' of Saving" that if an "excessive extension of productive equipment has been once begun, and the impossibility of carrying it through has manifested itself in a crisis, the appearance of unemployment and the resulting diminution of the demand for consumption goods may be the only way to set free the means necessary to complete at least a part of the enlarged productive equipment."[18] Keynes, on the other hand, thought that Britain suffered from inadequate consumption and thus that any purchase was a step in the right direction. Robert Skidelsky remarks of Hayek's views as put forward in his 1931 lectures that the "contrast with Keynes' 'Whenever you save five shillings you put a man out of work for a day' could not have been starker."[19]

Hayek "expected nothing less"[20] than that his London lectures would lead to an invitation to teach. Robbins wrote in his autobiography, "I can still see the door of my room opening to admit the tall, powerful, reserved figure which announced itself quietly and firmly as 'Hayek.'"[21] He had arrived. Hayek recalled that he and Robbins became "very close friends, we worked beautifully together."[22]

Robbins featured Hayek prominently in *Economica,* the LSE journal, during the months after Hayek's London lectures. In May, the first edition for which Robbins could get anything in, a translation of Hayek's article in German, "The 'Paradox' of Saving," which first interested Robbins in Hayek, was published as the lead feature in *Economica.* A harshly critical review article by Hayek of Keynes' *A Treatise on Money* was given second place in the next, August number, preceded only by a brief memorial article on Leonard Trelawny Hobhouse. In the November 1931 edition a reply by Keynes to Hayek's August article was given first position, followed by a rejoinder from Hayek. In the next, February 1932 number, the second part of Hayek's review of Keynes' *A Treatise* was given second billing. Hayek's work dominated *Economica* for a full year.

Britain was still arguably the greatest power in the world during the 1920s and early '30s, before Hitler came to power. This was still the empire on which "the sun never set." Its dominions included parts of every inhabited continent and nearly a quarter of mankind. Including the United States, the English-speaking world was perhaps thirty percent of humanity, though most inhabitants in English colonies did not speak English.

Before World War II, the international political world revolved around Europe—almost all of Africa, the Middle East, the Indian subcontinent, and southeast Asia were under colonial control by European nations. Nationalism was among the greatest phenomena of twentieth-century world politics. The number of independent nations expanded almost ten-fold during the century.

Among those who encouraged the new world political order was LSE political scientist, and democratic socialist, Harold Laski. Jewish, Laski was six years older than Hayek. Laski came to LSE in 1920 and became professor of politics in 1926. William Ebenstein, an American political scientist who was a Laski student, wrote that Laski had "perhaps more influence as a teacher than as a scholar or active promoter of political causes."[23]

Many of the nationalist leaders in regions and colonies that after World War II became new independent states studied under Laski. Daniel Patrick Moynihan, who had been a student at LSE, wrote when he was the American ambassador to the United Nations that the school was "the most important institution of higher education in Asia and Africa," and that Laski "molded the minds of so many future leaders of the new majority."[24] Economist John Kenneth Galbraith, a former American ambassador to India and participant in Hayek's seminar at LSE, holds that "the center" of first Indian Prime Minister Jawaharlal Nehru's thinking was Laski, and "India [was] the country most influenced by Laski's ideas."[25] Milton Friedman, who worked in India in 1955, writes that at that time India was "socialist in its orientation, its intellectual atmosphere having been shaped largely by Harold Laski of the London School of Economics, and his fellow Fabians."[26] Hayek wrote in a draft version of his final work, *The Fatal Conceit,* half a century after he arrived at LSE, that when he now traveled through Asia and Africa, he found established men in government who had come to LSE during the 1930s and '40s and been largely motivated by Laski.[27]

One of the great accomplishments of western civilization is its potentially trans-national and trans-ethnic character. Unlike other civilizations, western civilization has not been bound in place and time. To the extent Laski contributed to the great western tradition of the moral equality of all men and women, his contribution was lasting. Western civilization is not a fixed geographical entity, and the idea of the moral equality of all people and peoples throughout the world that developed during the twentieth century was perhaps the century's greatest political advance.

Hayek, who knew Laski well, abhorred him. While he defended Laski against charges that were leveled against him periodically for excessive expressions of opinion, his view of Laski was all but wholly negative. His final opinion was contained in a 1984 letter-to-the-editor in response to a magazine article, in which he said, "John Hunt's description of Harold J. Laski as a representative of leftish views implies that he was mentally sane. An experience with him on a crucial occasion convinced me that this was not the case. It was in August 1939. After dinner Laski had held forth for more than an hour about the marvels of Russian Bolshevism. . . . He then had to stop to let us hear the nine o'clock news of the BBC. We were told about the conclusion of the Hitler-Stalin Pact. The result was an extraordinary explosion by Laski, not only about the treachery of this particular act, but also an unlimited general denunciation of the whole system to which he had given unstinting praise twenty minutes before. . . . After that occasion I could no longer regard him as being mentally sane."[28]

Hayek said elsewhere and more kindly that "curiously enough, Laski and I had a good deal of contact because we are both passionate book collectors. It was only that way." After *The Road to Serfdom* was published in 1944, however, their relationship "ended." Laski was "frightfully offended. He believed it was a book written especially against him."[29] Laski was the main speaker at a December 1945 New York conference attended by Eleanor Roosevelt. He declaimed against the "anarchy of free enterprise." "There is no middle way," he declared, in a very different sense than Hayek. "Free enterprise and market economy mean war; socialism and planned economy mean peace." The American capitalist economy was "the direct road to serfdom."[30]

"For a time Laski was the most important socialist intellectual in the English-speaking world," according to his definitive biographer, Isaac Kramnick.[31] At his death in 1950, one obituary predicted that the "future historian may talk of the period between 1920 and 1950 as the 'Age of Laski.'"[32] Notwithstanding the relative eclipse into which he has gone since his demise, Laski was, with Keynes, the most prominent writer, thinker, and teacher on societal questions in the English-speaking world during his professional lifetime.

Other prominent figures from the left side of the political spectrum at LSE around Hayek's time there included Graham Wallas, Clement Attlee, Hugh Dalton, Richard Tawney, and Sidney Webb. Wallas, like Cannan, was a lecturer at the school from the start. Robbins wrote that as a teacher, Wallas "surpassed anyone I have ever known."[33] In a historical article Hayek wrote on LSE's fiftieth anniversary in 1945, he described Wallas as "one of the early members of the Fabian Society, one of the authors of the famous *Fabian Essays* of 1889, and one of those who had helped to plan the new school from the beginning. He was obviously the person best qualified to develop political science, a subject which both men [Webb and Wallas] had so much at heart that they joined it with economics in the name of the School."[34] Wallas was a humanistic, rather than scientific, socialist. He placed particular hope in the transformation of society through education.

Clement Attlee, prime minister of Great Britain from 1945 to 1951 and first Labour Party prime minister to serve as head of a majority government, was a lecturer and tutor at LSE from 1912 to 1922, excepting World War I. Hugh Dalton, who served as Attlee's chancellor of the exchequer and, like Attlee, in Churchill's wartime coalition government, was a more significant figure at the school. Robbins remembered that during his first year as a student at the LSE, Dalton stood out.

Richard Tawney was a socialist economic historian and, with Professor G. D. H. Cole at Oxford and Laski, one of the three "red professors" during the late 1920s and '30s in Britain. These were the years of the "scientific socialists," the small academic and intellectual minority in Great Britain during the Great Slump (or Depression) years who genuinely believed that a classical socialist regime owning and managing all of the means of a society's economic production—all physical capital—would be the most efficient, as well as fair, form of societal order. Tawney was author of several influential books, including *The Acquisitive Society* (1920) and *Religion and the Rise of Capitalism* (1926). Although Hayek disagreed with Tawney, he had a high regard for him. "There were," Hayek recalled, "many other people whom I greatly respected, like old Tawney. He was a sort of socialist saint, what Americans call a do-gooder, in a slightly ironic sense. But he was a man who really was only concerned with doing good—my Fabian socialist prototype—and a very wise man."[35]

Sidney Webb, together with his wife, Beatrice, was a guiding spirit of British socialism and especially the Fabian Society during the last years of the nineteenth century and first decades of the twentieth. Their goal was the reconstruction of society along socialist and technocratic lines of collective ownership of the means of economic production. Leading historians of Fabianism Norman and Jeanne MacKenzie characterize the Webbs' and other Fabians' aim as "something very like a Positivist state inspired by a Religion of Humanity and governed by a disinterested élite."[36] Sidney played a leading role in drafting the Labour Party's 1918 constitution that called for the nationalization of industry and served in Ramsay MacDonald's two Labour minority government cabinets in 1924 and 1929-1931.

The individual who most influenced LSE as an institution during the 1920s and '30s was Sir William (later Lord) Beveridge, the school's director from 1919 to 1937, with whom Hayek and many other faculty members had a running feud during the '30s. Beveridge was a Liberal and in 1942 primary author of the celebrated *Report on Social Insurance and Allied Services*—the "Beveridge Report"—which proposed an ambitious system of social services in Great Britain that was largely implemented following World War II. Like Keynes, he was not a socialist, though he came to support more government planning and economic macromanagement than Keynes. Beveridge's *Full Employment in a Free Society* (1944) was another popular work.

As even his critics acknowledged, Beveridge was a talented fund-raiser. Staff, facilities, programs, and departments increased substantially during his tenure; the library in particular benefited. The most significant development was growth in the number of full-time faculty. Beveridge recounted in his autobiography that when he came to LSE as director, there were as "full-time teachers two professors, both recently advanced to that position, one reader, and a few of lower rank, seven or eight in all. When I left, there were nineteen professors, fifteen readers, twenty-one lecturers, and twenty-one assistant lecturers and assistants—seventy-six in all—on full time, with another forty-five giving part-time."[37] A standing joke during his directorship was that LSE was the school "on which the concrete never sets." Robbins, despite his ultimate opposition to Beveridge, wrote of his early accomplishments that it was "a very outstanding achievement."[38] Beveridge suggested Hayek for his full-time position at LSE following his highly successful lectures, although, according to Hayek, on Robbins' advice.

CHAPTER SEVEN

Robbins

LIONEL ROBBINS WAS HAYEK'S CONTEMPORARY in age, and became head of economics at LSE in an unusual manner. His predecessor, Allyn Young, a distinguished American economist appointed to replace Cannan, died suddenly of pneumonia in 1929. At the time of Cannan's retirement in 1927, Robbins recalled, it was "felt that the whole organization of teaching of economics" at the school required "substantial overhaul,"[1] which would have been Young's responsibility to accomplish. Thus Robbins, at the age of 30, had a tremendous opportunity to mold economics at LSE. He sought to build a world-leading department, and in considerable part succeeded.

Robbins was intrigued and vitally influenced by Hayek's thought from the first time he was introduced to it, though he gradually worked his way away from much of it in technical economics as his career progressed. What was it in "The 'Paradox' of Saving" that so interested Robbins? Primarily, it was Hayek's attack on the emerging Keynesian thesis (though Keynes was not mentioned in the article) that excessive savings are the cause of a business cycle—Keynes' view was that Britain suffered from too much saving and therefore not enough consumption. Hayek remembered Robbins thinking of "The 'Paradox' of Saving" that "this is the thing that we need at the moment to fight Keynes."[2]

In his autobiography, Robbins defensively remarked on relations between LSE and Cambridge, where Keynes resided, that this is a "matter about which misunderstanding has been rife. A picture is often presented suggesting a state of acute enmity and mutual distrust. This is highly misleading."[3] He conceded, however, that there were "differences of atmosphere"; "differences on matters of practical policy which on occasion provided some justification for the allegation of conflict of outlook"; and "while I should hesitate to involve all my London colleagues in what I now believe to have been a mistaken outlook, I think there was enough manifestation of opposition to policies which were widely supported in Cambridge to provide sufficient substance for the allegation of group conflict."[4] In October 1932, Keynes and several Cambridge economists sent a letter to the London *Times* encouraging public investment to fight the depression. Robbins, Hayek, and other LSE economists fired back a response that supported the government's balanced budget policy.

Among the first generation of LSE scholars, there was no love lost for Cambridge. Cannan had a running feud with Alfred Marshall, and another LSE economist, H. S. Foxwell, left Cambridge angrily when he was not appointed to replace Marshall. LSE faculty were predominantly from Oxford. According to economic historian Gerard Koot, before World War I LSE sought to "mold economic theory and applied economics into an alternative economics to Marshall's vision of the subject then being rooted at Cambridge."[5]

Competition between LSE and Cambridge reached its peak after Robbins became head of economics. He and Keynes served on a five-member "Committee of Economists" appointed in 1930 by Prime Minister Ramsay MacDonald to review economic conditions during the Depression, examine their causes, and recommend solutions. Keynes chaired the committee. Robbins and Keynes clashed on the committee—Robbins refused to sign the final report, after Keynes had originally recommended him for appointment on the committee. Two years after this experience, Keynes refused to debate Robbins on unemployment, saying, "He is so difficult and queer! Also his reasons for differing are so eccentric and so totally different from the ordinary man's, that it may be difficult to bring out the real points which are perplexing the public."[6]

Hayek's lead review of Keynes' *A Treatise on Money*—published by Robbins in the August 1931 *Economica,* a month before Hayek was to take his position at LSE—was vital in creating Hayek's prominence in British academic economics during the next several years, though Keynes' intemperate response in the next issue perhaps played a bigger role in securing Hayek's place than the original review article itself. Hayek criticized Keynes harshly in this review. While he made prefatory comments about Keynes as a "writer who has established an almost unique and well-deserved reputation for courage and practical insight" and praised "passages in which the author displays all his astonishing qualities of learning, erudition and realistic knowledge,"[7] these were preliminary to harsh, pervasive criticism:

The *Treatise* proves to be so obviously the expression of a transitory phase in a process of rapid intellectual development that it would be decidedly unfair to regard it as anything but experimental. . . .

To a Continental economist, this way of approach does not seem so novel as it does to the author. . . .

It was, no doubt, the urgency which he attributes to the practical proposals which he holds to be justified by his theoretical reasoning, which led Mr. Keynes to publish the work in an unfinished state. . . .

The exposition is so difficult, unsystematic, and obscure. . . .

One can never be sure whether one has understood Mr. Keynes aright. . . .

The peculiar method of approach adopted by Mr. Keynes . . .[8]

And so it went. Hayek encouraged Keynes to reply in his final footnote, saying that there had "accumulated so many questions that it is probably wiser to stop for the moment in the hope that further elucidations will provide a firmer basis on which discussion may proceed."[9]

Keynes elucidated, and attacked. After defending his position and critiquing Hayek's for about the first two-thirds of his 11-page response, he observed that "the reader will perceive that I have been drifting into a review of Dr. Hayek's *Prices and Production.* . . . The book seems to me to be one of the most frightful muddles I have ever read, with scarcely a sound proposition in it beginning with page 45. It is an extraordinary example of how, starting with a mistake, a remorseless logician can end up in Bedlam. Yet Dr. Hayek has seen a vision, and though when he woke up he has made nonsense of his story by giving the wrong names to the objects which occur in it, his Khubla Khan is not without inspiration and must set the reader thinking with the germs of an idea in his head."[10]

Despite Hayek's not infrequent complaining of how unfair Keynes was to him in his response to his review of *A Treatise,* Hayek gave as good as he got, not just in his original review, but in his rejoinder to Keynes' reply: "Unfortunately, Mr. Keynes' answer does not seem to me to clear up many of the difficulties I have pointed out. Instead of devoting his answer mainly to clearing up the ambiguities which I have indicated carefully and in detail, and the existence of which he cannot deny, he replies chiefly by a sweeping accusation of confusion . . . in another work. I cannot believe Mr. Keynes wishes to give the impression that he is trying to distract the attention of the reader from the objections which have been raised by abusing his opponent."[11]

Hayek came to be seen in Cambridge as Robbins' and LSE's point man in intellectual combat with Cambridge. Richard Kahn remembered that "possibly wrongly but in Cambridge we had the impression that the intention was to set Hayek up as an idol to serve as an antidote to Keynes." Kahn further recalled that the breach between LSE and Cambridge was the "result of Friedrich von Hayek being brought from Vienna."[12]

In his monumental *The General Theory of Employment, Interest, and Money* (1936), Keynes took a shot at Robbins. Remarking on the tendency of post–Great War economists not to follow their classical economic propositions through in their more pragmatic policy recommendations—beneficially, in Keynes' opinion—he sarcastically observed that it was the "distinction of Prof. Robbins that he, almost alone, continues to maintain a consistent scheme of thought, his practical recommendations belonging to the same system as his theory."[13]

Robbins was considered the intellectual leader among economists at LSE during the 1930s, which, because of the prominence Hayek later attained, is often forgotten. Arthur Shenfield, employed by the LSE-affiliated London and Cambridge Economic Service, recalls that during the '30s he was "aware of the illumination that Hayek spread about him but, bright though he shone, I thought of him only as an associate star to the brightest star among the economists of the time, Lionel Robbins. For on first reading Robbins' *The Nature and Significance of Economic Science* I had felt 'like some watcher of the skies when a new planet swims into his ken.' Hayek, I then thought, was not quite as brilliant a planet as Robbins."[14] Hicks remarked in the 1939 preface to his *Value and Capital* that the ideas there were "not by any means entirely my own; they came into being by a sort of social process which went on among the people who were working there, under the leadership of Professor Robbins";[15] decades later, Hicks titled an introductory essay to early economic articles in his collected works, "LSE and the Robbins Circle."[16] Ronald Coase, another future Nobel laureate in economics who was a student and young staff member at LSE, remembers Robbins as the "most influential figure of all"[17] in economics at the school during this period. Arthur Seldon, long-time editorial director of the London-based Institute of Economic Affairs and an LSE student at the time, says, "Robbins was the intellectual leader in the early-mid 1930s while Hayek was busy on money and the structure of industry"; "Robbins was the leading liberal influence in my early undergraduate years. His lectures and writings were the bugle blast of classical liberalism in counter-attack on socialism"; and Robbins was the "leading light of the economics faculty."[18] Hayek wrote in 1951 that Robbins became the "nucleus of a group of younger economists which emerged at the London School of Economics during the '30s."[19]

Among the other most prominent economists to come forward at LSE during the 1930s, in addition to Hayek and Robbins, were John Hicks, Ronald Coase, Arthur Lewis, Nicholas Kaldor, Abba Lerner, Arnold Plant, and Arthur Seldon. Hicks, co-recipient of the 1972 Nobel Prize in Economics, was among the most influential academic economists of the twentieth century. Hicks taught at LSE from 1926 to 1935. His fame was the result of his theoretical work, including *The Theory of Wages* (1932) and especially *Value and Capital* (1939). While not a follower of Keynes, he played an important role in providing theoretical underpinnings for Keynesianism.

Ronald Coase is most well known for the "Coase Theorem," the proposition that the initial allocation of legal entitlements, or property rights, does not influence their ultimate use as long as transaction costs are nil. That is, a perfectly competitive market would allocate resources over time in the most effective way, for resources would move to higher and better uses. Also important in Coase's thought is that the establishment of property rights and their form are an essential prelude to and shape the content of market transactions. Coase's career, like Hayek's, includes posts at both LSE and the University of Chicago, the former until 1951, the latter until this day.

Arthur Lewis, first black recipient of the Nobel Prize in Economics in 1979, came to LSE as a student in 1933 and stayed as a lecturer until 1948. He described his start in economics by saying, "Fate had decided that I was to be an economist. What kind of economist I was to be was also settled: an applied economist. This did not mean just that I should apply economics to industrial or other structural problems. It meant that I would approach a problem from its institutional background. . . . Professor Sir Arnold Plant was my mentor, and without his word at crucial points I would have received neither the scholarship nor the assistant lectureship. (This was the school's first black appointment, and there was a little resistance.) He and I had intellectual difficulties, since he was a *laissez-faire* economist and I was not; but this did not stand in the way of our relationship."[20]

Nicholas Kaldor was another influential economist during the twentieth century, particularly as a Keynesian in Great Britain, although he was originally much influenced by Robbins and Hayek. His relationship with Hayek was tempestuous. While he was one of the translators of Hayek's early works into English, their personal and professional relationships later soured. Kaldor described their evolving relationship by recalling that Hayek became "frightfully annoyed with me. At first he was terribly for me. But then when I discovered he was so silly I sort of teased him, made him look ridiculous, contradicted him in seminars. I remember one occasion when I had an argument with Hayek. I said 'Professor Hayek, this is intermediate economics.' And Hayek got redder and redder, and afterwards in the tea room Hayek came in [and said,] 'You know what Kaldor said, what Nicky said? He said "Professor Hayek, this is intermediate economics and you ought to know it."' I said, 'I protest. I never said you ought to know it.' Everybody burst out laughing."[21] Kaldor was a student and taught at LSE from 1927 to 1947, before moving to Cambridge, where he became a fellow of King's, Keynes' old college, an environment more to his liking.

Abba Lerner was, like Kaldor, originally a Hayekian who moved in a socialist direction as the 1930s progressed. Unlike Kaldor, he never lost affection and respect for Hayek, which was reciprocated. Lerner enrolled in LSE as a night student at the beginning of the Great Depression. As a student he attempted to foster contact between LSE and Cambridge. According to Tibor Scitovsky, a research student at LSE during the second half of the '30s, Lerner was a "socialist, advocate of market pricing for its allocative efficiency, and believer in private enterprise, whose offer of private employment he considered an essential safeguard of individual freedom."[22] Lerner was, with Oskar Lange, a founder of the notion of market socialism.

Arthur Seldon's influence has been less for his original work than for his editorial efforts through which hundreds of prominent and aspiring classical liberal and libertarian academics and intellectuals have had their work published and improved. As editorial director of the Institute of Economic Affairs from 1957 to 1988, he was an influential source in helping to create the political climate in which Margaret Thatcher could implement market-oriented reforms in Great Britain during the 1980s. In an obituary on Hayek, Seldon wrote that at the LSE, "where he taught me in the mid-1930s (and ever after), he stood out as the austere Austrian whom Lionel Robbins had brought to lecture."[23]

Arnold Plant was the third major figure in economics at LSE during the '30s at LSE, following Hicks' departure to Cambridge in 1935. Plant was a close friend of Robbins and Hayek. Ronald Coase writes of his teacher that "Plant had been a student of Cannan, contemporary with Robbins, but did not share Robbins' delight in high theory. Plant was an applied economist and his main field of interest was what today is called industrial organisation."[24] Coase also recalls that in 1931 he participated in Plant's seminar, and it was a "revelation. He introduced me to Adam Smith's 'invisible hand.'"[25] Seldon remembers that Plant was his tutor for the Commerce degree, "He taught the classical truths of economics, not least the power of markets in trade and industry and the role of private property as seen by Locke and Hume."[26] In many respects, Plant was a more successful teacher than Robbins and Hayek, and he was more influential through his spoken than written word.

Robbins remarked in his autobiography that Arnold Plant's "influence on general development throughout the combined [economic and business] departments was central," and that Plant was a "fine lecturer and a great teacher."[27] Plant recalled of his interaction with Hayek that he had "developed a special interest in the scope of and functions of property and ownership, both public and private. It was a delight to find Hayek as well seized of the economic significance of the ramifications of property law as I was myself. I recall his excitement when I called his attention to the profound discussion of these matters in David Hume's *Enquiry Concerning the Principles of Morals:* section III, Of Justice."[28] In *The Constitution of Liberty,* Hayek remarked that "many years ago"[29] Plant first drew his attention to the importance Hume attached to fixed, invariable rules, particularly regarding property.

In addition to its own talent, LSE attracted many visiting economists from around the world. Robbins remembered these as including Gottfried Haberler and Fritz Machlup from Vienna, Scandinavian economists Bertil Ohlin and Ragnar Frisch (both future Nobel Prize winners), and Frank Knight and Jacob Viner from Chicago. The school was a Mecca for new classical liberal thought. Hayek thought that it "probably became the most important centre of the new liberalism." He also said that "the foundations were laid for a new development"[30] of classical liberalism at LSE during the 1930s, together with developments in Vienna and Chicago.

There were about 3,000 total students at LSE when Hayek began teaching in 1931: 1,250 full-time, including 200 graduate students; 1,250 part-time; and 500 intercollegiate (concurrently enrolled) students. About half of the graduate students and 200 of the undergraduates were from overseas. The school covered the whole range of social sciences: economics, political science, anthropology, sociology, history, philosophy, and for a time social biology, among more applied and other academic fields.

The Robbins-Hayek seminar was a highlight of LSE during this period. Robbins remembered the seminar as the "focus of much of our intellectual activity." The seminar of staff and senior students met weekly to investigate, discuss, and exchange ideas. Robbins continues, "As a matter of form it was usually described as being held by Hayek and myself; and I usually took the chair. But once assembled there was no hierarchy. Staff and students alike were a band of eager seekers after truth and the order of prominence depended upon the excellence of performance. Sometimes the programme would be fixed in advance for a term; more often a number of subjects would be selected and an approximate order; thereafter we would follow the ideas as they disclosed themselves, sometimes changing course completely if new vistas came into sight."[31]

Hayek portrayed the sessions by recalling that there was "always a main topic for the whole year. I think without injustice I can say that Robbins did all the organising work, including the general topic. But once it came to discussion, I more or less dominated discussion. (laughter) It was a large seminar; I suppose thirty or forty people attended. But there was always a front row of people who had been members of the seminar for two or three years already, and they dominated the discussion. This included not only students . . . [but] assistants and junior lecturers."[32]

Plant, too, remembered that "Robbins' economics seminar at LSE became the forum for timeless discussion of Hayek's ideas on monetary influences on the structure of production and industrial fluctuations, and their many-sided implications throughout economic, social and political policy. Hayek's presence added great strength to the magnetic attraction of Robbins' seminar."[33] Works by other seminar participants were also discussed.

Robbins fondly recalled that it was

> all very exciting. The feeling was general that after a period of relative stagnation, economics was on the march again and that we were participating in active operations.
>
> > Bliss was it in that dawn to be alive
> > But to be young was very heaven![34]

Hayek said of his participation in the joint-seminar that he "certainly never again could arouse the same passionate interest in the technicalities of theoretical economics or profit in the same way from discussion with first-class minds with similar interests."[35] He greatly enjoyed and benefited from his years at the London School of Economics during the 1930s.

CHAPTER EIGHT

Keynes

JOHN MAYNARD KEYNES AND MILTON FRIEDMAN are the two most prominent economists of the twentieth century. Born in 1883, Keynes possessed a nineteenth- and even eighteenth-century positivist scientific outlook of the world. Thirty years after his 1946 death, his friend and fellow economist Colin Clark described him, saying, "I think—and I knew him well—that Keynes' ideal world lay in the past, in the world of Edwardian liberalism, of humane conventions, moderate programmes, and hopeful reforms, in which he had grown up."[1] Keynes was temperamentally a moderate.

He appreciated the value of capitalist civilization. Keynes' first great exclamation on the public stage, *The Economic Consequences of the Peace* (1919), was a blistering attack on economic aspects of the Versailles Peace Treaty that followed World War I and the makers of that treaty:

> What an extraordinary episode in the economic progress of man that age was which came to an end in August 1914! The greater part of the population, it is true, worked hard and lived at a low standard of comfort, yet were, to all appearances, reasonably contented with this lot. But escape was possible, for any man of capacity or character at all exceeding the average, into the middle and upper classes, for whom life offered, at a low cost and with the least trouble, conveniences, comforts, and amenities beyond the compass of the richest and most powerful monarchs of other

ages. The inhabitant of London could order by telephone, sipping his morning tea in bed, the various products of the whole earth, in such quantity as he might see fit, and reasonably expect their delivery upon his doorstep; he could at the same moment adventure his wealth in the natural resources and new enterprises of any quarter of the world. . . . He could secure forthwith, if he wished it, cheap and comfortable means of transit to any country without passport or other formality, could despatch his servant to the neighboring office of a bank for such supply of the precious metals as might seem convenient, and could then proceed abroad to foreign quarters . . . and would consider himself greatly aggrieved and much surprised at the least interference. But, most important of all, he regarded this state of affairs as normal, certain, and permanent, except in the direction of further improvement. . . . The projects and politics of militarism and imperialism, of racial and cultural rivalries, of monopolies, restrictions, and exclusion, which were to play the serpent to this paradise, were little more than the amusements of his daily newspaper, and appeared to exercise almost no influence at all on the ordinary course of social and economic life, the internationalization of which was nearly complete in practice.[2]

Keynes expressly rejected socialism (common ownership of the means of economic production) and communism (common ownership of all property). Once, attacking Marxism, he rhetorically asked, "How can I adopt a creed which, preferring the mud to the fish, exalts the boorish proletariat above the bourgeois and intelligentsia who, with whatever faults, are the quality of life and surely carry the seeds of all human advancement?"[3] He wrote to his friend George Bernard Shaw in 1935 that "I've made another shot at old K[arl] M[arx] last week, reading the Marx-Engels correspondence just published, without making much progress. . . . I can see they invented a certain method of carrying on and a vile manner of writing, both of which their successors have maintained with fidelity. But if you tell me that they discovered a clue to the economic riddle, still I am beaten—I can discover nothing but out-of-date controversialising."[4]

Economic circumstances in Great Britain were different than in the United States during the 1920s. While these were the "Roaring '20s" in America, they were depressed times in Great Britain, in which unemployment nudged below 10 percent only once, to 9.7 percent in 1927. Why? Keynes' answer was that Britain had become a rigid and stultified beast. "The forces of the nineteenth century have run their course and are exhausted,"[5] he explained. Britain was, he believed, no longer a growing and vibrant economic organism.

Hayek first met Keynes at a meeting of European business cycle institutes held in London during the late 1920s before Hayek went to LSE to lecture and teach. Keynes was, at this time, one of his "heroes." Was Keynes not, Hayek recalled, "the man who had the courage to protest against the economic clauses of the peace treaties of 1919?" Hayek and his young Viennese contemporaries admired the "brilliantly written books for their outspokenness and independence of thought."[6]

Following *The Economic Consequences of the Peace,* Keynes' next major work was *A Tract on Monetary Reform* (1923), a collection of articles and lectures from the previous three years. Keynes was, in contemporary parlance, a "stabilizer," one who sought stable domestic prices, in contrast to those who believed that the primary goal of monetary policy should be fixed inter-currency exchange rates. He thought a genuine breakthrough was achieved in monetary management through *A Tract on Monetary Reform.* Key essentials of the Keynesian revolution in academic economics were present in embryo form: relative bifurcation of money supply from prices, stress on immediate financial circumstances in setting policy, and a prominent role for government in macromanaging—though not directing the details of—a nation's economy.

Following publication of *A Tract on Monetary Reform,* Keynes waged an unsuccessful battle to prevent Great Britain from returning to the gold standard at prewar parity (the gold standard was suspended during World War I). He considered a policy of a return to gold at prewar parity to be madness. During the period leading up to the restoration, the pound possessed a value somewhere in the vicinity of ten percent less than the dollar at prewar parity. To close this gap would require deflationary policies, further depressing the British economy already suffering from significant unemployment.

After the return to gold at prewar parity, Keynes wrote an attack on it, "The Economic Consequences of Mr. Churchill," who was then chancellor of the exchequer. In 1926, Keynes wrote *The End of Laissez Faire,* where by "laissez faire" he meant the idea that government does not have a large role to play in macromanaging the larger conditions of a society's economic activity.

It was with this background, then, that Keynes wrote what was intended as his *summa* when he released it, *A Treatise on Money* (1930), but by the time it was published, the times had changed. The depressed 1920s in Britain had given way to the even more depressed early 1930s.

Monetary policy became an ineffective policy tool during the early '30s when deflation lowered interest rates to the low single digits. Now, in addition to national monetary policy, Keynes recommended fiscal policy. It became government's responsibility to prime the pump, to get an economy moving again. Government should employ people, perform public works, effect transfer payments, and maintain high spending. Basically, Keynes the monetarist became Keynes the fiscalist as the 1920s evolved into the 1930s, and economic conditions changed from a climate in which monetary policy was more effective to one where fiscal policy could play a greater role.

~

Robert Skidelsky commences the first volume of his three-volume Keynes biography by writing that "John Maynard Keynes was not just a man of establishments; but part of the elite of each establishment of which he was a member. There was scarcely a time when he did not look down at the rest of England, and much of the world, from a great height."[7] It should have been quite heady for the young Hayek to attend a meeting of European business cycle institutes with Keynes in London in 1928 where both were fellow participants.

Some of the source of Keynes' displeasure with Hayek that he manifested in his reply to Hayek's review of *A Treatise on Money* may have been that he thought he had previously been kind to him. In apparently early 1927, Hayek sent Keynes a request for F. Y. Edgeworth's *Mathematical Psychics,* and in 1929 Hayek sent Keynes a copy of his *Habilitation* thesis, (in German) *Monetary Theory and the Trade Cycle.* Keynes' note back to this perhaps unsolicited gift was friendly enough, coming from the leading economist in the world to someone not yet thirty years old, "Many thanks for sending me a copy of your book. I have been particularly interested in the last chapter. But I find your German dreadfully hard to make out!"[8]

In Keynes' *A Treatise on Money,* then, he twice referred to Hayek, most significantly as part of a "school of thought [that] has been developing in Germany and Austria whose theory of bank rate in relation to the equilibrium of savings and investment, and the importance of the latter to the credit cycle, is fairly close to the theory of this treatise"[9]—the referenced members of the school including Mises and Hayek. Keynes generously footnoted that "I should have made more references to the work of these writers if their books, which have only come into my hands as these pages are being passed through the press, had appeared when my own thought was at an earlier stage of development, and if my knowledge of the German language was not so poor (in German I can only clearly understand what I know already!—so that *new* ideas are apt to be veiled from me by the difficulties of language)."[10]

Of Hayek's anti-Keynes introduction to English economics through his review of *A Treatise on Money* in *Economica* a month before he arrived to begin teaching at LSE in September 1931, Keynes editor Donald Moggridge notes that Keynes was "obviously very unhappy, for his copy of that issue of

Economica is among the most heavily annotated of his surviving copies of his journals, with no less than thirty-four pencilled marks or comments on the twenty-six-page review. At the end of his copy of the review, Keynes summed up his reaction by writing, 'Hayek has not read my book with that measure of "good will" which an author is entitled to expect of a reader. Until he can do so, he will not see what I mean or know whether I am right. He evidently has a passion which leads him to pick on me, but I am left wondering what this passion is.'"[11]

Why did Hayek criticize Keynes so harshly? He may in part have realized—possibly encouraged by Robbins—that through challenging Keynes he might most establish his own place in British academic economics. Robbins asked Hayek to write the review of Keynes' *Treatise on Money* for *Economica;* this was in the months following Keynes and Robbins' argumentative interaction on Prime Minister Ramsay MacDonald's Committee of Economists.[12] Hayek also undoubtedly possessed high self-esteem following his tremendously successful January lectures, the unsolicited offer to teach at LSE, and the forthcoming publication of *Prices and Production* and promotion in *Economica.*

Keynes and Hayek engaged in personal correspondence following Keynes' November 1931 reply in *Economica* to Hayek's August review article. Keynes sought greater clarification of Hayek's terminology. They exchanged five letters apiece between December 10, 1931—when Keynes initiated the correspondence—and January 23, 1932—when Hayek gave his final reply to a query from Keynes.

Keynes was dissatisfied with this exchange, which consisted each time of Hayek replying to a letter from him. Keynes wrote Hayek a sixth and final letter on February 11, 1932 that "your [last] letter helps me very much toward getting at what is in your mind. I think you have now told me all that I am entitled to ask by way of correspondence. But I am left with the feeling that I very seldom know, when I read your stuff, exactly what simplified assumptions you introduce or what effect it would have on the argument if these simplified assumptions were to be removed. Going back to the point at which our correspondence started, I am left where I began, namely in doubt as to just what you mean. . . . Many thanks for answering me so fully."[13]

Hayek overestimated Keynes' professional opinion of him. Keynes wrote his Cambridge friends Richard Kahn and Piero Sraffa on February 1, 1932 regarding Hayek. He asked "What is the next move? I feel that the abyss yawns—and so do I."[14] That is, Keynes was bored by his exchange with Hayek. On March 29, 1932, in response to a letter from Hayek, Keynes said "[I have] not studied your *Economica* article [the second part of Hayek's critique of *A Treatise*] as closely as I shall"[15]—this, after presumably having the review in his possession for a number of weeks, and Hayek having made mention of it in correspondence more than two months before.

Keynes wrote on a draft copy of a 1932 article by Hayek, "the wildest farrago of nonsense yet";[16] in a 1933 letter, "Hayek has been here [Cambridge] for the weekend. We get along very well in private life. But what rubbish his theory is—I felt today that even he was beginning to disbelieve it himself";[17] and in a 1935 letter, "God knows what the Austrians mean by the 'period of production.' Nothing in my opinion."[18] According to Robert Skidelsky, March 5, 1933, appears to have been the last time they discussed economic theory in their correspondence, though they thereafter continued to correspond "amiably about their various antiquarian discoveries"[19]—as with Laski, Hayek shared a book-collecting passion with Keynes. In Keynes' well-known, favorable letter to Hayek following *The Road to Serfdom,* he initially admonished, "You will not expect me to accept quite all the economic dicta in it."[20]

Keynes' lack of esteem for Hayek's technical economics—as well as Hayek's inability, in Keynes' opinion, to grasp his position—is well expressed in a footnote Keynes wrote and, "with Prof. Hayek's permission," appended to an article by Hayek in the Keynes-edited Cambridge *Economic Journal.* Hayek was replying to an article by Piero Sraffa attacking him, and concluded his reply, "I venture to believe that Mr. Keynes would fully agree with me in refuting Mr. Sraffa's suggestion . . . the new and rather unexpected fact that he [Sraffa] has understood Mr. Keynes' theory even less than he has my own." Keynes then footnoted, "I should like to say that, to the best of my comprehension, Mr. Sraffa has understood my theory accurately."[21]

The Hayek-Keynes interchange during 1931-32 is sometimes character-ized as a "debate." Actually, as economic historian Bert Tieben writes, "One may conclude that what characterizes the Hayek-Keynes controversy is the absence of debate."[22] Both sides launched their broadsides, and that was about it. There was no sustained, considered, fruitful exchange. Neither side persuaded the other to change its mind, nor even persuaded the other that there was much of value in its own position.

Former Hayek assistant Kurt Leube and economist Albert Zlabinger write that Hayek's work only "shared for a brief moment the academic limelight with the new ideas of Keynes."[23] Hayek's following was strongest at LSE and, by the later 1930s, almost all of those who had been Hayekians a few years before had shifted to Keynes. Ludwig Lachmann, an Austrian-oriented econo-mist who studied with Hayek during this period, recalled that when he arrived at LSE in the early '30s, "everybody was a Hayekian; at the end of the decade there were only two of us: Hayek and myself."[24] Hicks wrote that Hayek's "audience dispersed."[25]

Hayek described Keynes in a 1952 book review that sheds light on both author and subject. Hayek wrote that "whatever one may think of Keynes as an economist, nobody who knew him will deny that he was one of the outstanding Englishmen of his generation. Indeed the magnitude of his influence as an economist is probably at least as much due to the impressiveness of the man, the universality of his interests, and the power and persuasive charm of his personality, as to the originality or theoretical soundness of his contribution to economics. He owed his success largely to a rare combination of brilliance and quickness of mind with a mastery of the English language in which few contemporaries could rival him. . . . As a scholar he was incisive rather than profound and thorough, guided by a strong intuition which would make him try to prove the same point again and again by different routes."[26]

He also described Keynes as someone who was "able to divide his time between teaching economics and conducting a ballet, financial speculation and collecting pictures, running an investment trust and directing the finances of a Cambridge college, acting as the director of an insurance company and practically running the Cambridge Arts Theatre and attending there to such details as the food and wine served in its restaurant."[27] Keynes fascinated Hayek, as he did many others.

Hayek and Keynes' academic and personal relationship was not strong during the 1930s. They became personally close during World War II when the London School of Economics and Political Science moved to Cambridge. However, they were never academically close. According to Ronald Coase, it "must have been very difficult" for Hayek to have lost support at LSE during the '30s, but he "never showed" it.[28]

Much of Hayek's work in technical economics during the 1930s was devoted to a continuation of his initial exchange with Keynes. He became persuaded that to rebut Keynes' views he had to restate the basic theory of capital, which he then intended to apply to monetary issues. In particular, he disagreed with Keynes over whether capital expansion consists primarily of the "widening" or "deepening" of capital, the latter of which Hayek considered to be the most accurate conception and the one most affected by interest rate adjustments.

CHAPTER NINE

Money and Business Fluctuations

STUDENTS OF HAYEK DURING THE 1930s recall what he was like. Ralph Arakie wrote in a 1931 letter, "Read a new book yesterday. It is by old Hayek or *von* Hayek as he is called here. This year he is giving twenty lectures in bad English (God help us) and has recommended us to read [a] book in Dutch!; besides thirty other weighty volumes. But he is a clever chap." Arakie said in a letter the next year that "I have just come home from a very long class in which Hayek got into a bit of a muddle much to mixed feelings of amusement and sorrow on our parts. When such circumstances arise he starts hissing instead of speaking English and he gets rather excited. It was and is all terribly complicated." When Hayek addressed the Socialist Society of University College in 1932, Arakie observed that he gave "a brilliant and very sincere talk. Unfortunately there were a number of hooligans in the audience and they were very insulting."[1]

Theodore Draimin began at LSE in 1932. He remembers that "all of us were excited to hear that Hayek had arrived and was giving a course to graduate students. When we arrived for the first lecture he commenced to talk in English. After a few minutes, it became apparent that none of us could understand a word he said. Some suggested he speak in German. This he did, and those of us unable to understand had to leave the course."[2] Aubrey Jones was another early '30s student. He recalled that Hayek "wore a perpetually benevolent smile, a trait which did not belie his nature. But his accent in English was thick and his thought appeared tangled. One had to sit near the front in order to try and follow."[3]

Ben Higgins was an LSE student from 1933 to 1935. Of the interaction between LSE and Cambridge, Higgins wrote that there was a "joint London-Cambridge seminar which I attended on occasion. We in London regarded the strange things going on in Cambridge as nonsense, and very dangerous nonsense. Moreover, we could see that a man [Keynes] with such grace and wit and charm added to his brilliance might just possibly succeed in persuading some people that he was right. That was a frightening prospect indeed. It wasn't that there was a keen debate between London and Cambridge, because there was hardly any point of contact. We were very much under the influence of Hayek. He was our god." Higgins also recalled the "three-dimensional diagrams with which Hayek presented his ideas and which made them seem like something in the field of engineering—the Structure of Capital."[4]

P. M. Toms attended lectures given by Hayek during 1934-36. She remembers that he "looked to me at least 50, though much later on I discovered he was [in his mid-thirties]. It may have been partly due to his old-fashioned way of dressing, in a thick tweed suit with a waistcoat and high cut jacket. I nicknamed him 'Mr. Fluctooations' as he so often used that word and pronounced it in that way."[5] Vera Hewitt was on the administrative staff and a student beginning in 1936. She remembers Hayek as "so calm and deliberate. A very large quiet man."[6]

Robert Bryce was a Cambridge student who was not just a "convinced" Keynes supporter, but "converted." Sufficiently converted, he "went in the spring of 1935 down to the London School of Economics a day or two a week as a missionary. There I attended von Hayek's seminar on monetary theory and cycle-theory matters. This was the nearest concentration of heathen available from Cambridge and I was encouraged to go and tell them about it. I wrote a paper for the purpose. Hayek very courteously gave me several sessions of his seminar to expose this thing to his students. I must say it was an exciting experience and I found a lot of people quite prepared to give the paper serious attention."[7]

Hicks recalled of himself and his LSE colleagues that "we seemed, at the start, to share a common viewpoint, or even a common faith. The faith in question was a belief in the free market, or 'price-mechanism'—that a competitive system, free of all 'interferences,' by government or monopolistic combinations, of capital or of labour, would easily find an 'equilibrium.' (We were not, at that state, very interested in the welfare characteristics of that equilibrium; 'equilibrium is just equilibrium,' as Robbins said.) Hayek, when he joined us, was to introduce into this doctrine an important qualification—

that money (somehow) must be kept 'neutral,' in order that the mechanism should work smoothly."[8]

Among the most prevalent assumptions by academic economists during the first half of the twentieth century concerning economic activity was the inevitability of a business cycle. During the approximately eighty years from 1860 to 1940, the industrializing world of western Europe and the United States experienced significant periodic contractions and expansions of economic activity. Economies genuinely went into depressions, when unemployment would drastically increase and output would significantly diminish. These periods of contraction were followed by genuine boom times, when employment and production substantially increased. It was a stop-and-go economic world.

Hayek's central factual proposition in economic theory was the existence of different stages of economic production. He believed in essence that production utilizes capital goods that are relatively fixed in their productive capacities. A stock of capital can produce only certain sorts of goods. If the stock becomes misequilibrated with actual demand and savings in an economy, waste will occur.

He perhaps best elucidated what he had in mind with an analogy he used in *Prices and Production*. He posited that the situation following artificial monetary stimulation would be "similar to that of a people of an isolated island, if, after having partially constructed an enormous machine which was to provide them with all necessities, they found out that they had exhausted all their savings and available free capital before the new machine could turn out its product. They would have no choice but to abandon temporarily the work on the new process and to devote all their labour to producing their daily food without any capital."[9] Capital is heterogeneous, not homogeneous. If too much capital is devoted to temporally early stages of production, then, like the islanders' incomplete machine, this capital will remain unutilized unless the capital goods required to finish the productive process are also built.

The problem with modern economies, as Hayek saw them, is that their monetary systems work to misequilibrate economic supply and demand. Because money supply is manipulated through artificially raising and lowering interest rates, production in areas sensitive to interest rate adjustments—capital, he thought—varies not according to actual demand and savings, but on the basis of monetary factors. The structure of production comes in time to reflect not the demand of consumers and supply of savings, but the decisions of central bankers. Eventually, the variance between what is and should be in an economy causes downturns, as unprofitable investments are liquidated. Excessive investment in temporally early capital will not translate into greater final production because the real savings do not exist to complete the productive processes. Temporally early capital will be abandoned.

Importantly, for Hayek, misequilibration occurs in an economy even if the goal of monetary policy is stable prices, for, as an economy grows, its money supply must increase if there is not to be deflation: "In this case, stability of the price-level presupposes changes in the volume of money: but these changes must always lead to a discrepancy between the amount of real savings and the volume of investment . . . and thus, despite the stability of the price-level, it makes possible a development leading away from the equilibrium position."[10] The "point of importance is that the effects of an artificially lowered rate of interest exist whether this same circumstance does or does not eventually react on the general value of money."[11] Even stable prices would lead, in other words, to periodic busts.

Hayek's empirical interpretation of the Great Depression was significantly in error. He wrote in the June 1932 preface to *Monetary Theory and the Trade Cycle* that there could, "of course, be little doubt that, at the present time, a deflationary process is going on and that an indefinite continuation of that deflation would do inestimable harm. But this does not, by any means, necessarily mean that the deflation is the original cause of our difficulties or that we would overcome these difficulties by compensating for the deflationary tendencies by forcing more money into circulation. There is no reason to assume that the crisis was started by a deliberate deflationary action on the part of the monetary authorities, or that the deflation itself is anything but a secondary phenomenon, a process induced by the maladjustments of industry left over from the boom."[12]

This was a highly inaccurate analysis. Far from it being the case that there was a "deliberate policy of credit expansion"[13] during 1929-32, a deflationary policy was followed by the United States Federal Reserve Board. Hayek's language that the deflation was "induced by the maladjustments of industry left over from the boom" and that it was "not a cause but an effect of the unprofitableness of industry" suggests that he did not fully understand the relationship between money and prices. This view, too, is no longer generally accepted.

Furthermore, he inaccurately held in an April 1934 journal article that American monetary "authorities succeeded, by means of an easy-money policy, inaugurated as soon as the symptoms of an impending reaction were noticed, in prolonging the boom for two years beyond what would otherwise have been its natural end. And when the crisis finally occurred [in 1929], for almost two more years, deliberate attempts were made to prevent, by all conceivable means, the normal process of [business] liquidation."[14] It is now almost universally held that the United States Federal Reserve pursued a deflationary policy during 1930 and 1931.

CHAPTER TEN

Capital

·

AFTER KEYNES PUBLISHED *The General Theory of Employment, Interest, and Money* on February 4, 1936,[1] Hayek was virtually forgotten as a technical economist. While there continued to be some interest in him in British economic journals through the late middle 1930s, by the end of the decade, there was little interest in him. The ten monetary and macroeconomists most cited in the *Index of Economic Journals* during the 1930s and early 1940s can be seen on the table on page 80 (number of citations follow names).[2]

Clearly, by the early '40s, Hayek's economic views were no longer a leading topic of academic discussion. This was especially so in the United States, where he was never prominent before *The Road to Serfdom* was published in 1944.

Keynes summarized his position in *The General Theory*:

> I see no reason to suppose that the existing system seriously misemploys the factors of production which are in use. There are, of course, errors of foresight; but these would not be avoided by centralising decisions. When 9,000,000 men are employed out of 10,000,000 willing and able to work, there is no evidence that the labour of these 9,000,000 is misdirected. The complaint against the present system is not that these 9,000,000 men ought to be employed on different tasks, but that tasks should be available for the

Most Cited Economists in the *Index of Economic Journals*					
1931–35		1936–39		1940–44	
Keynes	66	Keynes	125	Keynes	59
Robertson	44	Robertson	48	Hicks	30
Hayek	33	Hicks	33	Haberler	24
Fisher	30	Pigou	31	Robertson	22
Hawtrey	30	Harrod	27	Hawtrey	20
Cassel	22	Hawtrey	25	Kalecki	18
Pigou	20	Haberler	24	Schumpeter	18
Wicksell	17	**Hayek**	24	Hansen	17
Hansen	14	Robinson	20	Kaldor	17
Marshall	13	Clark	18	Kuznets	16
				Lerner	16

remaining 1,000,000 men. It is in determining the volume, not the direction, of actual employment that the existing system has broken down.

I agree that the result of filling in the gaps in the classical theory is not to dispose of the "Manchester System," but to indicate the nature of the environment which the free play of economic forces requires if it is to realise the full potentialities of production. The central controls necessary to ensure full employment will, of course, involve a large extension of the traditional functions of government. Furthermore, the modern classical theory has itself called attention to various conditions in which the free play of economic forces may need to be curbed or guided. But there will still remain a wide field for the exercise of private initiative and responsibility. Within this field the traditional advantages of individualism will still hold good.

Let us stop for a moment to remind ourselves what these advantages are. They are partly advantages of efficiency—the advantages of decentral-isation and of the play of self-interest. But, above all, individualism, if it can be purged of its defects, is the best safeguard of personal liberty in the sense that, compared with any other system, it greatly widens the field for the exercise of personal choice.[3]

Keynes' goal was not state management of business activity—classical socialism—but state management of the economic conditions within which business activity takes place—democratic welfare state capitalism. As he held in *The End of Laissez Faire,* "Capitalism, wisely managed, can probably be made more efficient for attaining economic ends than any alternative system yet in sight."[4] He sought a middle way between contemporary fascism and communism.

Milton Friedman says of Hayek as a technical economist, "let me emphasize, I am an enormous admirer of Hayek, but not for his economics. I think *Prices and Production* was a very flawed book. I think his capital theory book is unreadable. On the other hand, *The Road to Serfdom* is one of the great books of our time. His writings in [political theory] are magnificent, and I have nothing but great admiration for them. I really believe that he found his right vocation—his right specialization—with *The Road to Serfdom.*"[5]

Hayek published four major works in technical economic theory from the late 1920s through the early 1940s. The first was his *Habilitation* thesis at the University of Vienna, *Monetary Theory and the Trade Cycle,* originally published in German in 1929 and republished in 1933 in English; *Prices and Production,* the book form of his 1931 LSE lectures, first published later in 1931 and published in a second edition in 1935; *Profits, Interest and Investment,* a collection of essays on industrial fluctuations published in 1939; and *The Pure Theory of Capital,* the first of an intended two-part *summa* on capital and money, which he abandoned in 1940, publishing the first part in 1941. In addition, a collection of his lectures on an international gold standard, *Monetary Nationalism and International Stability,* was published in 1937.

During much of the 1930s, Hayek was—like Marx, sixty years before—an émigré from the German-speaking world living in London, doing much research in the British Museum, and whose major work in economics was a treatise on capital. Hayek portrayed his conception of himself a number of times in *The Pure Theory of Capital.* He stated in the preface that the "theory of capital is, of course, a field which almost above all others has been the centre of theoretical interest since the beginning of our science,"[6] and held in introducing the work that "it may at first be somewhat disconcerting to be told that the theory of a subject which has been so widely and so vigorously discussed right from the beginning of economic science should need almost complete recasting"[7]— that is, that he was the one able to recast it.

The Hayek family lived in the Hampstead Garden suburb of London. A number of colleagues in economics lived in the immediate vicinity, including the Robbinses, "who became our closest friends,"[8] and the Plants. Hayek's initial salary at LSE was £1,000 per year, which grew to £1,250 after five years. He acquired his first car in 1936. The one luxury he granted himself, which became "very important"[9] to him, was membership in the Reform Club, located on Pall

Mall. The club became a rare geographical constant in his life. He called it decades later the only "home"[10] he had known for close to forty years. The Reform Club is a classic London establishment, a meeting and eating place for academics, civil servants, journalists, and others. Befitting its name, it has historically been "liberal" rather than "conservative"—though, of course, there are no hard-and-fast lines. Jules Vernes' *Around the World in Eighty Days* begins and ends there, and William Gladstone was a nineteenth-century member.

Hayek's home life during the early London years was quiet with "very little social life beyond the occasional entertaining of a visiting colleague. We were of course still running the house with the help of a regular maid. These were usually Austrian girls, one of whom stayed with us for a long time and became quite a member of the family. But this was about all that the then salary of a professor would support."[11]

He happily remembered his relationship with colleagues. "The Economics Department became very rapidly a circle of very close friends," he recalled. "We got on extremely well together. There was very little need for any formality or formal organisation. We had close personal contacts . . . the sort of informal friendship that one just walked into each other's houses at any time of day or evening. For instance, we would not formally entertain each other, but whenever one of us had guests, it was a matter of course that the others would come in after dinner from next door. So it was sort of [an] informal constant relationship which I think was closest between Lionel and myself. . . . I had a big library, but on particular things if I didn't have a book I would walk over to Robbins' and take it out of his library."[12]

Hayek's daily routine consisted of performing most of his "scientific work" at home in the morning and most of his teaching in the afternoon and evening. He usually left home about eleven A.M. and lunched at the school, or "occasionally at the club."[13] Courses he taught during the 1930s included "Theory of Value," "Principles of Currency," "Industrial Fluctuations," and, later in the decade, "The Problems of a Collectivist Economy."[14]

He had an opportunity to know some of the first generation of LSE faculty. During his early years, Edwin Cannan and Graham Wallas occasionally appeared, as did Sidney (and more infrequently) Beatrice Webb. He had enough dealings with the Webbs to form opinions of them. "He [Sidney] was all through the '30s chairman of the library committee, where I was probably the most active member. Sidney and I knew each other fairly well, and for Sidney I had a certain amount of sympathy, a certain respect. But I must say I detested Beatrice. She was a dreadful prig. I disliked her intensely, because she was so conceited. Sidney was a very human person, with whom you could discuss. He was a very skillful politician; I was amused by his mastery of the committee technique. I learned how you managed a committee: If there is a contentious item on the programme, you put it at the very end, and then drag out the rest of the meeting, and then you would say, 'Gentlemen, it's almost time for tea; there's a minor item . . .'!"[15]

Hayek's arguments in capital theory followed from his monetary theory. He believed that the Great Depression was caused by inappropriate capital investment during the 1920s. As a result of interest rates lower than those which would have been justified by the amount of savings in industrialized economies—lower because of the goal of maintaining stable prices—the capital structures in industrialized economies had become misequilibrated with actual savings and demand.

Hayek's essential gist in capital theory was that capital is heterogeneous, not homogeneous—that it cannot be put to many uses. If this empirical assumption of capital's heterogeneity is false, his theoretical system of economic activity falls. In addition, Hayek did not establish his proposition that an increase in economic activity consists, in the short run, of redirection of resources rather than a greater utilization of unused or underused resources, particularly in cases of depression, nor did he establish that changes in interest rates predominantly affect capital investment.[16]

A student of Hayek's during the 1930s, George L. S. Shackle, wrote of the "sustained intensity of thought" that *The Pure Theory of Capital* "cost its author" through several manuscript versions, with "ever-freshly multiplying difficulties." Hayek's work here showed "theory-making as a task not for intellect alone, but for high moral courage and implacable resolve. In this book, Hayek has nailed his colors to the mast and has pursued to the uttermost limits the logic where it led." Shackle also said that it is "inconceivable that any statistical or practical use can be made of the Austrian theory of capital."[17]

Hayek's daughter, Christine, remembers her father as always working in his study when he was home while she was growing up. She adds that, in some ways, she hardly knew him, so preoccupied with work was he, and because of her parents' later divorce.[18] The family spoke German in the home and visited Austria for the summers during the 1930s until the approach of war. They had intended to return to Austria to live. As Great Britain and Germany became increasingly at odds and as the barbarism of the Third Reich manifested itself, they discontinued affiliation with their Germanic heritage, stopped speaking German in the home, and family trips to Austria dwindled. War was soon to break out.

CHAPTER ELEVEN

International Gold Standard

HAYEK LED A SEMINAR OF HIS OWN in addition to his joint seminar with Lionel Robbins. John Kenneth Galbraith was a visitor at LSE during 1937 and 1938. He remembers Hayek's seminar as "possibly the most aggressively vocal gathering in all economic history. It was extensively and imaginatively devoted to telling Hayek why he was wrong. Once, Professor Hayek took his place at the small table from which he presided and said, 'Gentlemen, as I indicated last time, we will today discuss the theory of the rate of interest.' At this point Nicholas Kaldor intervened to challenge the concept of a rate of interest. 'Ridiculous,' he said, 'a contrived capitalist construct.' Others spoke in agreement or disagreement. Hayek listened patiently in compelled silence until the session was over."[1]

Economists at LSE were somewhat apart from the rest of the faculty. "In a sense the economists were a group by themselves," Hayek recalled. "They didn't much let the others interfere with them. In what conflicts might have arisen in the Professorial Council discussion, there Robbins would have been the leading figure on our side, with some support from some of the lawyers, against most of the rest of the School. . . . The Economics Department was not really in the tradition of the School. It was something quite isolated. It existed from the beginning, but as I see it, in the first thirty years of the School, it was just Edwin Cannan as a person, nobody else, who started a new tradition which, in about 1930, saw the appointment of Lionel Robbins and myself, and blossomed into a very important part of the School."[2]

Relations between LSE faculty and school director William Beveridge were a leitmotif during the 1930s. Janet Mair, Beveridge's long-time secretary and future wife, was an unpopular force to be reckoned with during Beveridge's tenure as director. Senior staff revolted when Beveridge requested that her contract should be extended past the normal retirement age. Beatrice Webb recorded in her diary:

> 12 July [1936]. Josiah Stamp and his wife spent the week-end with us. . . . The immediate reason for the meeting was the crisis at the London School of Economics. According to Stamp, who is chairman of the governors, there is a violent upheaval led by the representative committee of the professors on the Committee of governors against the Beveridge-Mair directorship or, as they style it, dictatorship. Mrs. Mair will be sixty this year. Beveridge insists that her term must be extended and threatens to resign if it is not. Robbins and his group—Laski and Eileen Power backed by their friends—in spite of their divergent views on politics and economics, unite to denounce such an extension, and threaten wholesale resignation if Mrs. Mair is retained. But this is not all. Outside authorities—the university inspectors and the U.S.A. donor of funds—object to Mrs. Mair. Sidney and I, in spite of our warm liking for Beveridge and desire not to break with him, agree that the crisis must be ended and *Mrs. Muir must go.*[3]

Mrs. Mair, and Beveridge, went.

There was a brighter side of Beveridge's persona. Robbins recalled once when he and his wife were in Vienna, and had arranged to "spend the evening with von Mises, we ran into Beveridge. It thus came about that, as the three of us were sitting together, von Mises arrived with the evening paper carrying the shocking news of the first academic dismissals by the Nazis. Was it not possible, he asked, to make some provision in Britain for the relief of such victims, of which the names mentioned were only the beginning of what, he assured us, was obviously to be an extensive persecution. This was one of Beveridge's great moments. Thinking aloud, he then and there outlined the basic plan of what became the famous Academic Assistance Council."[4]

As with any academic environment, there were conflicts among different outlooks. Arthur Lewis recalled that during the 1930s, LSE was a "very lively place. Every point of view was represented on the faculty, and as two or three competing courses of lectures were offered on each 'hot' topic, those who understood what was going on had marvellous intellectual feasts. The typical high-achieving LSE student was bright, from the effort to keep up with so many conflicting themes, and skeptical, from learning to distinguish so continually between plausibility and truth."[5] Ronald Fowler, another LSE student and staff member, calls the '30s a "wonderful time" and the "high point"[6] in economics at the school.

When considering the world of British academic economics during the 1930s, it is important to recognize that it was very small both in numerical and geographical extent. Economists were, in Ronald Coase's words, a "tiny group."[7] In the whole of Britain there were perhaps fifty full-time academic economists—a dozen full-time professors, readers, and lecturers at LSE, along with a comparable number or slightly more at each of Oxford and especially Cambridge's colleges together. The University of Manchester was perhaps the next most prominent institution, with four or five economists. Virtually no other schools in the country would have had more than perhaps one professor of economics and one assistant. Moreover, Oxford and Cambridge are both within sixty miles of London.

There were several economic seminars in London during the '30s. Hayek and Robbins' was, somewhat facetiously, the "grand seminar." Hayek often held a seminar of his own (without Robbins) in the evening. Hugh Gaitskell, a social-ist economist and later leader of the Labour Party, and Paul Rosenstein-Rodan, an old Hayek associate from Vienna, sponsored the so-called "pink seminar" at University College, a few blocks from LSE. Discussions were also held at the London Economic Club, and there was a "joint seminar" among primarily junior economists from Cambridge, LSE, and Oxford.

Elizabeth Durbin, daughter of 1930s LSE socialist economics lecturer and later Labour Party member of parliament Evan Durbin, writes of the meetings among younger economists that the main interinstitutional forum for debating theoretical issues was the "joint London-Cambridge-Oxford seminars, which were held regularly during term time in one of the three places. Apparently everybody came, particularly the younger economists—Durbin, Gaitskell, Lerner, Hicks, Kahn, Sraffa, Joan Robinson, Harrod, Meade; occasionally the big guns would also show up—Keynes, Hayek or Robbins. Rosenstein-Rodan vividly remembers one meeting in which he presented a paper on money and its different functions, arguing that both Keynes and Hayek were wrong because they did not take account of the role of time and its effect on anticipations. Hayek responded with a 'lengthy diatribe'; he was followed by Keynes, 'who rose to say he entirely agreed and that in his next book he dealt with it.'"[8]

Hayek was an unreconstructed proponent of a genuinely pure or homogeneous gold standard during the 1930s. "I am a convinced believer in the international gold standard,"[9] he wrote in *Monetary Nationalism and International Stability* (1937), a collection of lectures he gave at the Graduate Institute of International Studies in Geneva where Mises spent the '30s. In these lectures, Hayek set out to demonstrate three propositions: "[1] that there is no rational basis for the separate regulation of the quantity of money in a national area which remains a part of a wider economic system; [2] that the belief that by maintaining an independent national currency we can insulate a country against financial shocks originating abroad is largely illusory; and [3] that a system of fluctuating exchanges would on the contrary introduce new and very serious disturbances of international stability."[10]

Economist Mark Skousen describes the "framework of a pure gold standard":

> Let us first define what we mean by a pure gold standard to distinguish it from a variety of pseudo gold standards that were adopted by Western nations in the 19th and 20th centuries. Even the classical gold standard which existed between 1815–1914 involved a certain degree of fiduciary elements, i.e., paper money combined with a specie base.
>
> A real gold monetary standard, however, would consist of the following attributes:
>
> 1. Gold bullion serves as the official monetary unit of account . . .
> 2. Gold circulates as a general medium of exchange . . .
> 3. Paper banknotes, token coins, checking accounts, and other money substitutes are treated as general warehouse receipts, equivalent to an equal amount of gold coins or bullion stored at the issuing banks. Hence, a true gold standard is a 100 percent banking reserve system and rejects the practice of fractional reserve banking and claims unbacked by specie.
> 4. National currencies are defined as specific weights of gold bullion. Thus, the exchange rate between currencies is fixed by definition.
> 5. The role of government in banking is limited to certifying coins of a fixed weight and the minting of coins. No central bank is necessary.[11]

Hayek's theory of a gold standard on an international basis was that it equilibrates supply and demand among nations. If a nation produces less than it consumes, its money supply will decrease—gold will leave the country. A declining money supply will in turn lead to national deflation. As a consequence, the nation's balance of trade will improve as the prices of foreign goods become higher and the prices of domestic goods become lower.

The practice Hayek saw opposed to a homogeneous gold (or other commodity) standard is monetary nationalism. Under this system, it is not flows of gold among nations that equilibrate international supply and demand; it is changes in the values of currencies. In a system of monetary nationalism, external values of currencies fluctuate, not internal money supplies and prices.

Hayek displayed a thoroughly intellectual conception of the world in *Monetary Nationalism and International Stability:*

> The immediate influence of the theoretical speculation is probably weak, but that it has had a profound influence in shaping these views which to-day dominate monetary policy is not open to serious question. . . .
>
> I am profoundly convinced that it is academic discussion of this sort which in the long run forms public opinion and which in consequence decides what will be practical politics some time hence. . . .
>
> Much must be done in the realm of ideas before we can hope to achieve the basis of a stable international system. . . .
>
> I do believe that in the long run human affairs are guided by intellectual forces. It is this belief which for me gives abstract considerations of this sort their importance, however slight may be their bearing on what is practicable in the immediate future.[12]

He was a convinced intellectual elitist. He could hardly have been more explicit that the ideas that individuals such as himself put forward ultimately guide public opinion and events. Seen from this perspective, he was a great moralist. He sought the common good with intense passion and dedication. While one may question practical outcomes of his early technical economic thought as regards both empirical description and normative prescription, the great interest for the common good that motivated his work should not be doubted, and neither should his stringent intellectual elitism be forgotten.

CHAPTER TWELVE

Socialist Calculation

THE CRITICAL WORKS in Hayek's transition from technical economic theory to broader fields of societal inquiry were the essays he published in 1935 in *Collectivist Economic Planning*. Problems of socialist calculation had long been of interest to economists of the Austrian school. Eugen von Böhm-Bawerk, Mises' teacher, reacted strongly to the work of Karl Marx. According to economic historian Henry Spiegel, Böhm-Bawerk's main argument against socialism was that the "socialist criticism of capitalism was in fact a criticism of the human condition, that is, of the central problem of scarcity, with which socialism would have to cope just as did capitalism"[1]—an argument explored in greater depth by Mises and Hayek.

The socialist calculation debate—inaugurated in 1920 by Mises through his seminal article "Economic Planning in the Socialist Commonwealth"—was long-lasting and significant. Mises' question was brilliant: How would it be possible for an economic system—socialism—to exist in which there are no prices? "There are many socialists who have never come to grips in any way with the problems of economics," Mises wrote, "and who have made no attempt at all to form for themselves any clear conception of the conditions which determine the character of human society. They have criticized freely enough the economic structure of 'free' society, but have consistently neglected to apply to the economics of the disputed socialist state the same caustic acumen. Economics, as such, figures all too sparsely in the glamorous pictures painted by the Utopians. They invariably explain how, in the cloud-cuckoo lands of their fancy, roast pigeons will in some way fly into the mouths of the comrades, but they omit to show how this miracle is to take place."[2] How would a socialist society be organized practically? It is not enough merely to point to deficiencies in capitalism.

Central to Mises' argument was the importance of prices, and the necessity to prices of private property and a competitive market. Economic historian Bettina Bien Greaves emphasizes that, for Mises, the "crucial factor with respect to economic calculation under socialism was not merely that economic agents cannot calculate without prices, but that without private property there can be no prices.... The fundamental necessity for the appearance of prices and profits is private property."[3] The essence of the socialist calculation debate was Mises' attempt to point out that, in the absence of an exchange economy with private property, a competitive market, contract, and profits, there is no such thing as price, and that in this situation, efficient economic decision making is impossible.

Mises made the main point beautifully in the example he used of the importance of prices to direct production: "The [socialist] director wants to build a house. Now, there are many methods that can be resorted to. Each of them offers certain advantages and disadvantages with regard to the utilization of the future building, and results in a different duration of the building's serviceableness; each of them requires [differing] expenditures of building materials and labor. Which method should the director choose? He cannot reduce to a common denominator the items of various materials and various kinds of labor to be expended. Therefore, he cannot compare them."[4] "Socialism," he held in "Economic Calculation in the Socialist Commonwealth," is the "abolition of rational economy."[5]

A number of socialist thinkers acknowledged the force of Mises' argument. Oskar Lange wrote that "socialists have certainly good reason to be grateful to Professor Mises, the great *advocatus diaboli* [devil's advocate] of their cause. It was his powerful challenge that forced the socialists to recognize the importance of an adequate system of economic accounting to guide the allocation of resources in socialist economy. Both as an expression of recognition for the great service rendered by him and as a memento of the prime importance of sound economic accounting, a statue of Professor Mises ought to occupy an honorable place in the great hall of the Ministry of Socialization of the Central Planning Board of the socialist state."[6] The problem of value was to be solved, according to socialist economists, not by freely fluctuating prices in a competitive market with private property, but through very careful accounting by socialist planners.

The classical socialist argument against Mises and Hayek completely missed the point. It is not that there must be careful accounting of resources in production, it is that there must be a method to evaluate the relative values of different resources for optimal production. Capitalism relies on private property, price, the ability to exchange goods and services, and profit.

There were two phases of the socialist calculation debate. In an interview decades later, Hayek remarked that "Mises had conducted this fight with the socialists in the 1920s. When I came to England in the 1930s, I realized that it had gone almost completely unnoticed, so I edited a volume of the literature. The Mises controversy was in the 1920s and mine was in the 1930s."[7]

The Hayek-edited *Collectivist Economic Planning* (1935), subtitled *Critical Studies on the Possibilities of Socialism,* played a major role in the transition of Hayek's work from economic theory to political philosophy. He recalled decades later of his move to what his interviewer called "political-philosophical questions," that this "really began with my doing that volume on collectivist economic planning, which was originally merely caused by the fact that I found that certain new insights which were known on the Continent had not reached the English-speaking world. Being forced to explain this development on the Continent in the introduction and conclusion to this volume I was curiously enough driven not only into political philosophy but into an analysis of the methodological misconceptions of economics [that] seemed to me to lead to these naive conceptions of, 'After all, what the market does we can do better intellectually.'"[8] He left technical economics because he "bec[a]me much too interested in the semi-philosophical policy problems—the interaction between economics and political structure."[9]

His transition from economic theory to other topics was occasioned by his realization that premises he took for granted commanded far less than universal assent. Chief among these was that society is more economically productive when its compound of rules and laws enables each individual to utilize his own knowledge and abilities for his own purposes rather than requiring each individual to conform to a plan established by a central authority. Hayek first enunciated some of the themes that concerned him in the socialist calculation debate and for the rest of his career in his 1933 inaugural address at LSE, "The Trend of Economic Thinking." In this address, he stated that the "majority of men still remain under the erroneous impression that, since all social phenomena are the product of our own actions, all that depends upon them is their deliberate object"; "the coordination of individual efforts in society is not the product of deliberate planning"; and, far too optimistically, "the conviction that, since where there is no directing Will there must be chaos, deliberate planning will necessarily be an improvement on existing conditions, is more and more recognised to be the result of our insufficient understanding of the existing system."[10]

In *Collectivist Economic Planning,* he opposed the idea that it is possible to manage an advanced technological society from a single point. He instead emphasized the idea of spontaneous order (though he did not yet use this term)—that the proper goal of government should be to enable individuals to make as much use as possible of their own knowledge and talents in ways that they themselves see best.

He believed there can be no progress without economic liberty. The attempt to mandate interpersonal agreement by requiring all the members of a society to live in accordance with the dictates of one or some prevents the emergence of the kind of human order in which material and technological advance will occur. Law—rules—should prevail over individual commands. Private property is essential to this order.

His argument against socialism was mostly factual. He observed that the "distribution of available resources between different uses, which is the economic problem, is no less a problem of society [in a command economy] than for the individual."[11] What is missing in a classical socialist economy is any "standard of value."[12]

Another of Hayek's questions in *Collectivist Economic Planning* was, How would uncertain investment decisions be made in a command economy? He elaborated that "risky, and even purely speculative, undertakings will be no less important here [under socialism] than under capitalism. Even if progress is inevitably connected with what is commonly called 'waste,' is it not worth having if on the whole gains exceed losses?"[13] By what criteria should relatively uncertain investment decisions be made in a command economy?

Both Mises and Hayek considered the issue of incentives in their critiques of socialism. For neither was the question of incentive under socialism his primary theme, though for Mises it was a more important concern. Mises wrote that the "motive force disappears with the exclusion of the material interests of private individuals."[14] According to Hayek, "The question [is] whether decisions and responsibility can be successfully left to individuals who are not owners or are not otherwise directly interested in the means of production under their charge."[15]

Hayek emphasized in *Collectivist Economic Planning* that the "constant shift of resources between firms which goes on under capitalism would be equally advantageous in a socialist society. In a capitalist society the transfers of capital from the less to the more efficient entrepreneur is brought about by the former making losses and the latter making profits. The question of who is to be entitled to risk resources and with how much he is to be trusted is here decided by the man who has succeeded in acquiring and maintaining them."[16] The question of who the most effective people are to manage resources is determined in a market economy by who makes the most profits. Those who make profits have the financial ability to manage more resources.

The question of the most effective people to manage resources is no less a factual question under socialism than capitalism, and is intrinsic to Hayek's ideas of undirected societal evolution. It is not necessarily the case that those who can make the most profits are able to express their understanding of the economic process verbally. Rather, their actions determine (under capitalism) that they have more resources to direct. Hayek considered "market socialism"—attempts to merge government ownership with a competitive market—"little more than a sham."[17]

He passionately believed that socialism, as any form of collectivism, literally cannot deliver the goods. Society cannot—not may not—be structured so as to allow government control of the means of economic production if there is to be a decent material living standard. "Central direction of all economic activity presents a task which cannot be rationally solved under the complex conditions of modern life."[18]

Socialism is a factual as well as ethical theory. Hayek's economic argument against classical socialism was not so much that it is normatively undesirable, but that it is factually non-productive.[19]

CHAPTER THIRTEEN

Economics, Knowledge, and Information

THE MOST IMPORTANT SINGLE ESSAY in Hayek's transition to the issues that would concern him for most of the rest of his career was "Economics and Knowledge," which was originally given as his presidential address to the London Economic Club on November 10, 1936. He here put forward the idea of the division of knowledge, which—if true—has appeared to render the possibility of classical socialism unsustainable:

> There is a problem of the *division of knowledge* which is quite analogous to, and at least as important as, the problem of the division of labor. But, while the latter has been one of the main subjects of investigation ever since the beginning of our science, the former has been as completely neglected, although it seems to me to be the really central problem of economics as a social science. . . . Economics has come closer than any other social science to an answer to that central question of all social sciences: How can the combination of fragments of knowledge existing in different minds bring

about results which, if they were to be brought about deliberately, would require a knowledge on the part of the directing mind which no single person can possess? The spontaneous actions of individuals will, under conditions which we can define, bring about a distribution of resources which can be understood as if it were made according to a single plan, although nobody has planned it.[1]

"Economics and Knowledge" marked a break with Hayek's previous methodological thought. Before "Economics and Knowledge," he emphasized an almost exclusively Wieserian and Misesian introspective, theoretical, a priori (before experience) approach.[2] In "Economics and Knowledge," Hayek moved away from a strictly introspective conception of knowledge and achieved greatness.

His discussion in "Economics and Knowledge" grew out of economic equilibrium debates—what constitutes equilibrium, how is equilibrium defined? He remarked in "Economics and Knowledge" of his conception of equilibrium that "separation of the concept of equilibrium from that of a stationary state seems to me to be no more than the necessary outcome of a process which has been going on for a fairly long time,"[3] and in the 1948 republished version of "Economics and Knowledge" referred the reader to chapter II of *The Pure Theory of Capital* for "further developments."[4] There, he held that "most of the shortcomings of the theory of capital in its present form are due to the fact that it has only been studied under the assumptions of a stationary state, where most of the interesting and important capital problems are absent."[5]

John Stuart Mill perhaps best and most famously expressed the concept of a stationary state in *Principles of Political Economy,* in his chapter "Of the Stationary State," "It must always have been seen, more or less distinctly, by political economists, that the increase of wealth is not boundless: that at the end of what they term the progressive state lies the stationary state." This would be a "stationary state of capital and wealth."[6] Hayek's enunciation of equilibrium theory was different than Mill's in two ways. First, equilibrium does not occur in a static economy but in a dynamic one; and second, equilibrium does not occur at a point in time, but over time.

Hayek discussed his concept of equilibrium in "Economics and Knowledge." "A state of equilibrium can hardly mean anything," he held, "but that, under certain conditions, the knowledge and intentions of the different members of society are supposed to come more and more into agreement or, to put the same thing in less general and less exact but more concrete terms, that the expectations of the people and particularly of the entrepreneurs will become more and more correct."[7] He emphasized the idea of foreknowledge, that, in a market, "all knowledge is capacity to predict." He stated that "the concept of equilibrium merely means that the foresight of the different members of the society is correct. Correct foresight is the defining characteristic of a state of equilibrium."[8]

Israel Kirzner, current dean of the Austrian movement in economics, remarks of this last passage of Hayek's that, "in other words, the state of equilibrium is the state in which all actions are perfectly coordinated, each market participant dovetailing his decisions with those which he (with complete accuracy) anticipates other participants will make. The perfection of knowledge which defines the state of equilibrium ensures complete coordination of individual plans." Kirzner continues that the "movement from disequilibrium to equilibrium is at once a movement from imperfect knowledge to perfect knowledge and from uncoordination to coordination. The movement from disequilibrium to equilibrium is a process of communicating information."[9]

The price system was, in Hayek's view, what brings equilibrium about. Prices and profits are information- or knowledge-bestowing tools. Prices and profits overcome the division of knowledge. Hayek explained that the empirical element enters economics through the division of knowledge and communication of information. In his incomplete late article on the Austrian school of economics, he remarked that while it is the case that the "pure logic of choice" by which Austrian economics interprets individual human action is "purely deductive, as soon as the explanation move[s] to the interpersonal activities of the market, the crucial processes [a]re those by which information [i]s transmitted among individuals, and as such [a]re purely empirical."[10]

In a 1978 interview with economist Axel Leijonhufvud, he discussed his methodological views in contradistinction to Mises':

> Q: You have developed your own views on methodology over the years. Did you have a conflict with Mises on methodological matters?
>
> A: No, no conflict, although I failed in my attempt to make him see my point . . . I believe it was in that same article on economics and knowledge where I make the point that while the analysis of individual planning is in a way an a priori system of logic, the empirical element enters in people learning about what the other people do. And you can't claim, as Mises does, that the whole theory of the market is an a priori system, because of the empirical factor which comes in that one person learns about what another person does.[11]

In a 1983 letter to economic theorist and historian Terence Hutchison, Hayek added that his "main intention" in "Economics and Knowledge" was to "explain gently to Mises why I could not accept his a priorism."[12] Economics cannot be a purely deductive, a prioristic discipline because it is not solely about individual actions, but about how individuals communicate information, which is an empirical process about which no a priori statement can be made.

Years after he wrote "Economics and Knowledge," Hayek recalled that it was "somehow in thinking through anew these problems [of socialist calculation] which had much occupied us in Vienna ten or fifteen years earlier that I had suddenly the one enlightening idea which made me see the whole character of economic theory in what to me was an entirely new light."[13] Hayek realized that prices are the essence of a market society, and, with prices, private property, contract, profits, the ability to exchange goods and services, and the laws and societal norms that define and sustain these. Hayek enunciated not merely the negative case against socialism that the division of knowledge renders central control of an economy infeasible, but he stated the positive case for a competitive market society, that fluctuating prices and the concomitants of these are the best, and perhaps only, way to overcome knowledge's fragmentation. The proper role of government is to facilitate effective interpersonal action through creating a market order in which individuals may make maximum use of divided knowledge through fluctuating prices and profits.

Hayek wrote in his autobiographical notes of "Economics and Knowledge" that, together with related articles reprinted in *Individualism and Economic Order* (1948), this sequence of articles "seems to me in retrospect the most original contribution I have made to the theory of economics."[14] Probably his most well-known article after "Economics and Knowledge" is "The Use of Knowledge in Society," originally published in 1945 in the *American Economic Review* and republished in *Individualism and Economic Order.* Milton Friedman writes that prices "transmit information. The crucial importance of this function tended to be neglected until Friedrich Hayek published his great article on 'The Use of Knowledge in Society.'"[15] Hayek held here that the "peculiar character of the problem of a rational economic order is determined precisely by the fact that the knowledge of the circumstances of which we must make use never exists in concentrated or integrated form but solely as the dispersed bits of incomplete knowledge which all the separate individuals possess. The economic problem of society is a problem of the utilization of knowledge which is not given to anyone in its totality."[16] The mistaken assumption that all knowledge can be collected in one mind leads to classical socialism.

In his work from the second half of the 1930s until the end of his career, Hayek emphasized that "to say that planning of the kind we are alluding to is irrational is not equivalent to saying that the only form of capitalism which can be rationally advocated is that of complete laissez-faire in the old sense. There is an essential distinction which must not be overlooked: the distinction between a permanent legal framework and a system . . . [of] central direction. It is this, and not the question of the maintenance of the existing order versus the introduction of new institutions, which is the real issue. In a sense both systems (capitalism and socialism) can be described as being the product of rational planning. But in one case this planning is concerned only with the permanent framework of institutions."[17]

He wrote decades later in *Law, Legislation and Liberty* that "while the rules on which a spontaneous order rests may also be of a spontaneous character, this need not always be the case. . . . The spontaneous character of the resulting order must . . . be distinguished from the spontaneous origin of the rules on which it rests, and it is possible that an order which would still have to be described as spontaneous rests on rules which are entirely the result of deliberate design."[18] He supported the creation of new societal macro-institutions, "the permanent framework of institutions." He opposed government direction of an economy.

Hayek's goal was the highest material standard of living for all people. He thought this would be most likely achieved through a properly designed competitive market order. A competitive market order depends, in turn, on fluctuating prices, private property, profits, contract, and the ability to exchange goods and services. All of these institutional mechanisms are required by the "unavoidable imperfection of man's knowledge"[19]—that is, individual man's knowledge.

He fondly recalled his pre–World War II years at LSE. The senior common room was "an extraordinarily interesting group," and of a size that "made it possible to know most of the members well. It was always a place of lively discussion; in the later 1930s, chiefly about the changing political developments of the world."[20]

He described his transition from technical economics to other areas of the social humanities beginning with "Economics and Knowledge": "I felt in a way, that the thing which I am now prepared to do, I don't know if there's anybody else who can do this particular task. And I rather hoped that what I had done in 'Capital Theory' would be continued by others. This was a new opening. The other would have meant working for a result which I already knew, but had to prove, which was very dull. The other thing was an open problem: How does economics really look when you recognize it as the prototype of a new kind of science of complex phenomena? That was so much more fascinating as an intellectual problem."[21]

He also said of "Economics and Knowledge" that it was "really the beginning of my looking at things in a new light. Up 'til that moment I was developing conventional ideas. With the '36 lecture I started my own way of thinking. It was several ideas converging on [one] subject. It was my essays on socialism, the use in my trade-cycle theory of prices as guides to production, the current discussion of anticipation, . . . to some extent perhaps Knight's *Risk, Uncertainty and Profit*—all that came together. And it was with a feeling of sudden illumination, sudden excitement, that I wrote that lecture. I was aware that I was putting down things which were fairly well known in a new form, and perhaps it was the most exciting moment in my career when I saw it in print."[22]

Prices and profits are essential to communicate information. Much of the rest of his career was devoted to the study and description of the societal order in which mankind can make most use of fragmented knowledge. His focus in time became rules, or law. Rules enable people to live together more or less efficiently, in the most materially productive way with the highest degree of knowledge—the most accurate predictions of the future.

Notwithstanding the prominence that "Economics and Knowledge" gained in his thought, it was read at the time perhaps by only hundreds of academic economists and students worldwide. Most of Hayek's time during the later 1930s, when he was not teaching, was spent on his incomplete work on the dynamics of capital and monetary theory.

The creative sparks from "Economics and Knowledge" were great for Hayek. He said of the essay when he received an honorary doctorate from Rikkyo University, Tokyo, in 1964:

> Its main conclusion was that the task of economic theory was to explain how an overall order of economic activity was achieved which utilized a large amount of knowledge which was not concentrated in any one mind but existed only as the separate knowledge of different individuals. But it was still a long way from this to an adequate insight into the relations between the abstract rules which the individual follows in his actions and the abstract overall order which is [thereby] formed. . . . It was only through

a reexamination of the age-old concept of freedom under the law, the basic conception of traditional liberalism, and of the problems of the philosophy of the law which this raises, that I have reached a tolerably clear picture of the nature of the spontaneous order of which liberal economists have so long been talking."[23]

THREE

CAMBRIDGE

"I do not propose to continue this account into a discussion of the economics of the 1940s as seen from Cambridge. . . . I am not sure that I was still enough of an economist during that period to qualify."

CHAPTER FOURTEEN

The Abuse and Decline of Reason

SO DEEP A CLEFT—emotionally, intellectually, and spiritually—separates the world before and after World War II that it is often difficult for those who were born or came of age after the war to recognize the extent of this divide. Human civilization could have moved in a different way. For those of postwar generations, World War II has always been "the war," notwithstanding other and lesser conflicts and that the generation that lived through and fought it are almost all gone now. For more than five decades, events in the popular mind have been fixed in relationship to before or after the war.

In some ways, the Second World War looms even larger in retrospect than it did at the time. Despite the evilness of the Nazis that was contemporaneously portrayed, the satanic blackness into which they descended was not fully comprehended until the end of the war when widespread discovery (outside of Germany and higher military and political circles) of the concentration-death camps forever focused attention on this part of the Nazi regime. The inauguration of atomic weaponry at the end of the war capped the conflagration. Humanity had, for the first time, the ability to destroy itself.

If World War II ended on shattering notes—discovery of the Holocaust and use of the atom bomb—it began on ones that were also stunning. Hitler came to power following elections in 1932 in which more than sixty percent of Germans supported Nazi and allied parties. After the March 1933 elections in which the Nazis, nationalist parties, and the Roman Catholic Centre Party received over two-thirds of seats in the *Reichstag* (the German parliament), Hitler, who was chancellor, obtained dictatorial powers. All political entities other than the Nazis were outlawed. Other political parties were banned, the Communist Party had already been suppressed, labor unions were abolished, workers were compelled to join the Nazi-led German Labor Front, union leaders were arrested, and all of German industry, state government, and civil service and judiciary functions were brought under the domination of the Nazi Party. The 1935 Nuremberg Laws deprived Jews of citizenship rights and forbade marriage between Jews and non-Jews.

On taking power in 1933, Hitler withdrew from the League of Nations and disarmament talks. He commenced a program of remilitarization and conscription, and in 1936 militarily occupied the Rhineland (adjacent to France), which under the Treaty of Versailles had been intended to remain demilitarized. The Spanish Civil War and the Italian invasion of Ethiopia led, also in 1936, to the Rome-Berlin Axis, followed by a further alliance with Japan. In March 1938, the *Anschluss*—German and Austrian unification, also forbade at Versailles— was accomplished, and in the September 1938 Munich Conference, Great Britain and France forsook Czechoslovakia when Hitler was allowed to occupy the Czech Sudetenland. British-French appeasement came to an end in March 1939 when Hitler occupied the remaining rump Czechoslovakia. World War II finally started in September 1939, following the Nazi-Soviet Pact on August 24 and the German-Russian invasion of Poland on September 1.

Hayek became a naturalized British citizen in 1938, a status he retained the rest of his life. He was unable to serve, as most of his colleagues did, in any governmental capacity during World War II because of his Austrian birth and, perhaps, because of his frequent trips to the Continent during the 1930s. He made a considerable effort to volunteer his services to the Ministry of Information where, as a result of his "exceptional experience," as he wrote in a letter, he thought he might be "of considerable help in connection with the organization of propaganda in Germany,"[1] but his offer was declined.

As a result of his British passport, he was able to travel until the outbreak of war, which he did, visiting his future wife in Austria as "late as July or August of 1939, very much in the awareness that I could risk it, even though it was likely that war might break out at any moment." He knew the mountains well enough that if he were trapped in Austria (by this time Germany) as a result of war, he could "just walk out."[2]

After the German-Soviet invasion of Poland in September 1939, there followed the so-called, and occasionally so-ridiculed, eight-month Sitzkrieg or "phony war" which lasted until Hitler's lightning occupations of Denmark and Norway in April 1940. Then followed the German invasion of Holland, Belgium, and France on May 10. Robbins recalled that after hearing of the German invasions, academic life became "unendurable. Morning after morning brought news of fresh defeats and defections; and here we were, with all our potential unutilized, drooling out routine instruction which had suddenly seemed to lose all relevance."[3] England and the life of western civilization were at stake.

Churchill became prime minister on May 10 following Neville Chamberlain's resignation. Churchill spoke to the House of Commons on May 13, saying he had "nothing to offer but blood, toil, tears and sweat,"[4] which was literally true. For a time, Hayek considered sending his children abroad. When the Battle of Britain started in the summer of 1940, it was not possible for his family to live in London. The London School of Economics and Political Science had moved to Peterhouse College in Cambridge for the 1939-40 academic year and remained there throughout the war. Hayek had a difficult time finding a place to stay in Cambridge, and his family lived for a year with the Robbinses in a cottage outside of London while he stayed in rooms in King's College, Cambridge, which Keynes obtained for him.

Hayek ultimately found a semi-converted barn in Cambridge, in which he and his family lived until the end of the war. The room in which he did his work was about two stories high and was subsequently used as an auditorium for amateur dramatics. Hayek's son remembers the rooms Keynes secured for his father at King's as "very comfortable but cold."[5]

According to wartime LSE student and Fabian historian Norman MacKenzie, "The change was dramatic." In London, there were 3,000 students (half of whom were part-time) and ninety staff. Merely 500 undergraduates (none of whom were part-time) and about half of the faculty, including only nine professors, showed up in Cambridge. "It was also a change in character," MacKenzie recalls. In London, there were about three men students for every woman. In Cambridge, the numbers were at first even, but by the middle of the war there were twice as many women as men. "The decisive change was the conversion of the school from a college of commuters to a residential community."[6]

It is important to emphasize that World War II and its coming greatly changed the worldview of almost everyone in Europe and America. Very few anticipated that a war on this scale or of such a horrific character was in the offing. The future is undetermined.

In the historical article he wrote on the fiftieth anniversary of LSE, Hayek noted that although the outbreak of the war in September 1939 reduced the number of staff and students at LSE in Cambridge, until the war for England really commenced in the spring of 1940, there was not as great a change in the program as happened subsequently. Once France fell and the bombing of London began, though, the "thorough mobilisation of the available brain-power to satisfy the needs of the government departments deprived the school of the greater part of its remaining staff."[7] Robbins, Plant, and many others went into government service.

Hayek became personally closest to Keynes in Cambridge during the war, when Keynes repaired there on weekends from government service in London. It was then, Hayek remembered, that "because he was seeking relief from his arduous duties, or because all that concerned his official work was secret, that all his other interests came out most clearly. I remember particularly one occasion, which seems characteristic of many. Keynes had just returned from an official mission to Washington on a matter of the greatest consequence which one would have assumed had absorbed all his energy. Yet he entertained a group of us for part of the evening with details about the state of the collection of Elizabethan books in the United States as if the study of this had been the sole purpose of his visit."[8] Larry Hayek remembers that his father and Keynes took shifts together watching for fires at night from the top of King's College.

Hayek praised Keynes' proposal for *How to Pay for the War,* the title of a 1940 pamphlet by Keynes that incorporated a suggestion by Hayek for a capital tax following the war. Hayek did not continue work on the second half of *The Pure Theory of Capital,* the preface for the first half of which was written in June 1940, in part because in the second half he would have criticized Keynes. Hayek explained that "a very curious position arose. By then war had broken out. And Keynes was almost the only sensible man who was willing and able to protect us against inflation. So during the war years I was supporting Keynes against his supporters as the one man who actually did succeed in getting through the war without inflation. So during the war, practical politics, I was on Keynes' side, and didn't want to discredit him. An attack on Keynes, during the war years, would have been against what I believed was right. I was grateful for his existence."[9]

Hayek recalled that the "light burden of teaching"[10] and short distances to and from class at Cambridge gave him more time for his own work than ever before. As he wound up his incomplete work in capital and monetary theory, he turned to broader fields of societal inquiry. While he did not intend to leave technical economics, this was the direction his career took.

He became acting editor of the LSE journal *Economica* during World War II as his former colleagues were called into government service. Between 1941 and 1944 he published six articles in *Economica* that were republished in 1952 as *The Counter-Revolution of Science.* He gave as background for this new work that a "very special situation arose in England that people were seriously believing that National Socialism was a capitalist reaction against socialism. So I wrote a memorandum on this subject, then turned it into a journal article, and then used the war to write out what was really a sort of advance popular version *[The Road to Serfdom]* of what I had imagined would be the great book on the abuse and decline of reason."[11] He wrote on a "remote subject matter in a state of intensive concentration with which I reacted to my impotence against the continuous disruptions of falling bombs."[12] His first article of what eventually became *The Road to Serfdom,* "Freedom and the Economic System," was published in April 1938, though Hayek began work in this area several years earlier.

The two parts of the treatise on The Abuse and Decline of Reason, of which *The Road to Serfdom* was an advance popular edition of the second part, were sequentially to be titled "Hubris of Reason" and "The Nemesis of the Planned Society."[13] Decades later, in an initial draft of *The Fatal Conceit,* he wrote that The Abuse and Decline of Reason was intended to be a critique of modern thought. The first part was to be the historical description of modern thought that Hayek did not complete, and the second part—which became *The Road to Serfdom*—was to have been the practical outcomes of the historical ideas that he would have sketched in the first part. The Abuse and Decline of Reason was intended to demonstrate how an excessive conception of what reason can accomplish in society leads to the destruction, through the planned society, of what reason can actually achieve. An erroneous conception of reason leads to its decline.

He distinguished two types of individualism: true—stemming from England and Scotland—emphasizing the insignificance of individual reason; and false—having roots in Cartesian rationalism—stressing the importance of individual reason. Of true individualism, the "first thing that should be said," Hayek stated, "is that it is primarily a *theory* of society, an attempt to understand the forces which determine the social life of man, and only in the second instance a set of political maxims derived from this view of society. Its basic contention is that there is no other way of understanding social phenomena but through our understanding of individual actions. . . . The next step in the individualistic analysis of society is the contention that, by tracing the combined effects of individual actions, we discover that many of the institutions on which human achievements rest have arisen and are functioning without a designing and directing mind. The spontaneous collaboration of free men often creates things which are greater than their individual minds can ever fully comprehend."[14] His position was as much empirical as ethical. He thought that no mind can know in what direction the future will or should head, and that it is therefore counterproductive to attempt to build societies on this premise.

He began the 1941 *Economica* article that eventually became *The Counter-Revolution of Science* with the thought that "never will man penetrate deeper into error than when he is continuing on a road which has led him to great success."[15] He perceived as the source of socialism the mistaken belief that the precision of reason capable in the natural sciences can be obtained in societal planning. He found these ill-advised efforts to have been most pronounced where reason most explicitly engaged culture: Paris. In eighteenth-century France, faith in the future of humanity was unbridled. Human progress was to be founded, moreover, not on evolutionary trial-and-error, but on revolutionary design and intellectual construction.

As an example of the relationship between French rationalism and true individualism, he said, "I cannot better illustrate the contrast in which Cartesian or rationalistic 'individualism' stands to this view than by quoting a famous passage from Part II of the *Discourse on Method*. Descartes argues 'there is seldom so much perfection in works composed of many separate parts as those completed by a single master.'"[16] False individualism exalts what individual minds can particularly accomplish. True individualism is a more humble creed.

Hayek ascribed key roles to Henri de Saint-Simon and Auguste Comte in the rise of socialism. Saint-Simon sought a new societal organization, one founded (as he believed) on science. His schemes were incredible, and the particular forms of organization and his own place in them, fantastic—a Council of Newton, for example, to be presided over by twenty-one scholars and artists to direct the world. Saint-Simon nonetheless bequeathed much socialist legacy. While his manner of organizing humanity was appropriately ridiculed, his concept of organization per se was retained. Hayek cited one particularly influential Saint-Simonian idea, "'All men will work; they will regard themselves as laborers attached to one workshop whose efforts will be directed to guide human intelligence according to my divine foresight. The supreme Council of Newton will direct their works.'"[17] Importantly, "'Anybody who does not obey the orders will be treated by the others as a quadruped.'"[18]

Saint-Simonianism was not a democratic movement. Hayek wrote in *The Road to Serfdom* that socialism "began as a reaction against the liberalism of the French Revolution. . . . Socialism in its beginnings was frankly authoritarian. The French writers who laid the foundations of modern socialism had no doubt that their ideas could be put into practice only by strong dictatorial government. To them socialism meant an attempt to 'terminate the revolution' by a deliberate reorganization of society on hierarchical lines and by the imposition of a coercive 'spiritual power.'"[19] The followers of Saint-Simon did not support individual rights. The movement was an effort to organize all of society along dictatorial lines, for the benefit of all, but nonetheless according to one mind and one will. This direction was seen, furthermore, as inevitable as well as desirable. Hayek did not much consider non-Continental, British idealist socialism, which was a different tradition than Continental socialism.

Hayek considered Comte's addition to socialism to have been primarily in the area of positivist philosophy, which Comte began to explore as a votary of Saint-Simon, whom he later rejected personally. Comte's notion of positivism was a scientific treatment of history. No more would history be regarded as being determined by divine will or happenstance, but in accord with uniform and invariable laws ascertainable by individual human reason. The idea was that a society could be conducted along scientific principles such as were coming to exist in the systematic study of nature.

Comte believed history passes through three phases—religious, meta-physical, and scientific—with the scientific being the last and greatest. Like Saint-Simon, he had little use for individualistic theories of politics, economics, and philosophy. Comte held that "'the vague and metaphysical idea of liberty' 'impedes the action of the masses on the individual' and is 'contrary to the development of civilization and to the organization of a well-ordered system.'"[20]

Hayek's view of Hegel was similar to his perspective of Comte. He observed the paradox of joining Hegel and Comte, for the former is usually considered an idealist, and the latter a (material) positivist. There was, however, little functional difference. For both, history moved in stages above and beyond the individual and removed from his will. What Hayek termed "historicism" is the mistaken belief that there are laws of history as there are laws of nature. Almost by definition, historicism denies moral standards, for it denies free will. Comte's and Hegel's determinism followed from their "peculiarly unhistorical approach to history,"[21] perceiving determinism where it does not exist. The future is subject to man's will.

CHAPTER FIFTEEN

Methodology

HAYEK BECAME COMPLETELY ASSIMILATED TO BRITAIN during the war. He wrote in his autobiographical notes that life in Cambridge during the war years was "particularly congenial" to him and "completed the process" of his "thorough absorption" into English life, which he had found very easy since he moved there in 1931. "Somehow the whole mood and intellectual atmosphere of the country had at once proved extraordinarily attractive to me, and the conditions of a war in which all my sympathies were with the English greatly speeded up the process of becoming thoroughly at home." Of all the available "forms of life," that at one of the colleges of Oxford or Cambridge seemed to him "the most attractive."[1] He said in his LSE fiftieth anniversary article that even with "all its difficulties and inconveniences the years in Cambridge were not without compensation for the students and for those members of the staff who had been fortunate enough to find homes in Cambridge or to be given rooms in Peterhouse or other colleges. The hospitality shown by Peterhouse will long remain for many teachers one of their pleasantest memories of the war years."[2] His time in England—and Cambridge especially—was the high point of his life.

Socialist and Laski biographer Kingsley Martin described LSE's sojourn in Cambridge, also giving some picture of its former conditions: "The character of the London School of Economics was changed by the move to Cambridge. Both teachers and students were affected by being suddenly cut off from the political and economic background of London and finding themselves transformed into a residential university. Now smaller in size, it was able to offer more personal [instruction] and a degree of intimacy which was never possible in the crowded rabbit-warren on Houghton Street. In London, where the tiled passages and the tiers of classrooms and studies were always thronged with students, most of whom were virtual strangers to each other and to all but their most intimate teachers, it had always been difficult to maintain a collegiate life. In Cambridge, faculty and undergraduates alike became friends, mixed socially, and formed a coherent group in Cambridge life."[3]

A wartime LSE student, Joan Abse, recalls that although the "war seemed endless, Cambridge was like a delightful oasis of happiness and fulfillment in a world bent on destruction. LSE in Cambridge was an ideal place in which student life could flourish. The older, enriching virtues of Cambridge were leavened by the easy-going, lively, unconventional atmosphere of the school. We could enjoy the captivating beauty of the place without, as most of us saw it, the disadvantages of segregated [by gender] college life."[4] Ian Gilbert, an LSE student during 1942-43, remembers that his "year at Cambridge was the best year of my life. We worked hard in an extremely stimulating environment. We also played hard, athletically and socially, and even had time to prepare for our war service."[5]

Anne Bohm, an administrative assistant at LSE in Cambridge and longtime school staff member, recalls that Hayek "headed the Economics Department immediately after the British economists disappeared on war service. He was rather stand-offish and I was always a little intimidated by him. He was always, so far as I can remember, in riding boots, striding across a common."[6] A student of Hayek at Cambridge, Eric Rose, remembers that "Hayek's German accent was so thick that it was difficult to understand his English and the material wasn't easy either. He was very anti-Keynes. . . . Hayek particularly objected to the Multiplier which he called the Peter-Outer. Hayek had a hard time because LSE was very left-wing and Marx was compulsory reading."[7]

LSE changed greatly as war progressed, the number of students declined, and the proportion of female students increased. This affected course offerings, women being more likely to major in such fields as sociology. Lectures in most subjects were provided as part of a joint teaching program with remaining Cambridge faculty. Hayek gave lectures in advanced economic theory, while Cambridge economist Arthur Cecil Pigou gave introductory courses. The graduate school shrank to very small numbers as the war wore on, and at the end of the war consisted of little more than a few foreign students stranded in Britain.

Issues of methodology (scientific or philosophical method) are among the most difficult in the social sciences and philosophy. Hayek's interest in these issues was prompted by his participation in the socialist calculation debate of the 1930s. He began to think more deeply on the question of how societal order can form without an orderer. This question followed from the socialist calculation debate, for its answer is really the central contention of capitalism— that without particular government direction, individuals will be more productive than in societies in which government owns and manages all of the means of economic production.

His essential approach in methodology was individualistic. It is by understanding individual human action that collective human action can be understood. He wrote in one of the articles preparatory to The Abuse and Decline of Reason, an article that became part of *The Counter-Revolution of Science,* that it is "probably no exaggeration to say that every important advance in economic theory during the last hundred years was a further step in the consistent application of subjectivism."[8] On the assumption of utility-maximizing behavior, all of an individual's actions may be predicted.

At the same time, he held in "Economics and Knowledge" that questions about collective human action are questions about the transmission of information. Here, the crucial issue is how information is transmitted among individuals. It is not enough to know that individuals are self-motivated. What is as important is how they communicate information and how new information is generated. Individuals can only act on the information they possess. Thus, the transmission of fragmented information through the societal institutions of a competitive market—including private property, prices, profits, contract, and the ability to exchange goods and services—established through law became central in his work.

He emphasized the idea of complexity in his methodological and epistemological thought. Only "pattern prediction" in the world of society is possible because of the complexity of societal life. When he remarked in "Scientism and the Study of Society," one of the essays intended to comprise The Abuse and Decline of Reason, on what he considered to be the mistaken "belief that the commonly used names for historical periods or events, such as 'France during the Revolution' or 'the Commonwealth Period,' stand for definitely given objects, unique individuals which are given to us in the same manner as the natural units in which biological specimens or planets present themselves,"[9] he meant that societal events are more complex than those of, for example, physics.

He thought that facts in the societal world are "compositive."[10] It is not that a fact such as "France during the Revolution" is qualitatively different than biological or other natural specimens, it is that it is quantitatively different and not recognized as such. Because there are so many more elements in the complex societal world, only pattern prediction is possible, as, for the same reason, only general direction or framework rules are—because of the societal world's complexity. He wrote decades later in the "Theories of Social Structures" section of "The Theory of Complex Phenomena" (1961) that "here individual events regularly depend on so many concrete circumstances that we shall never in fact be in a position to ascertain them all; and in consequence the ideal of prediction and control must largely remain beyond our reach."[11] There was in his mind ultimately no difference in kind between the natural and social sciences, merely differences in composition, with the latter being more complex. Because societal life is complex, no attempt should be made to organize it from one point.

CHAPTER SIXTEEN

The Road to Serfdom

THE ROAD TO SERFDOM (1944) revolutionized Hayek's life. Before its publication, he was an unknown professor of economics. A year after it was published, he was famous around the world. *The Road to Serfdom* is, and will likely continue to be, the work by which he is best recognized.

He wrote in the book's introduction that it was the "product of an experience as near as possible to twice living through the same period—or at least twice watching the same evolution of ideas."[1] As a young man in Austria immediately after World War I, he once before experienced a time in which serious consideration was given to nationalizing the means of economic production. Following World War I, nationalization acts were passed by the governments of Germany and Austria. Mises' inauguration of the first socialist calculation debate was prompted by these contemporary actions. Now, Hayek feared, Britain might move in a classical socialist direction.

While books of ideas need not be read by vast numbers in order to be influential, they must be read by some substantial group in order to attain the rank of highest significance. That Hayek considered popular success to be relevant to a work's importance is attested to by his hope, prior to its publication, that *The Constitution of Liberty* would be such a success. He believed fundamentally in the power of ideas. The scope of a book's readers is therefore relevant to its influence. *The Road to Serfdom*—alone among his writings—had some contemporary influence in shaping public opinion—not necessarily immediately, but deeply, and on a broad scale. It sounded as the cry of a voice in the wilderness that classical socialism, if realized, would be political and moral, as well as economic, slavery. This is now conventional wisdom. When Hayek enunciated this idea, it was anything but.

The Road to Serfdom's greatness stems not only from its consequences, however, but from its intrinsic merit. The work may in largest part be considered the political and moral ramifications of the socialist calculation debate, considered not so much from the perspective of economic productivity but from the type of regime and society inevitable in a system of classical socialism. He stated in a 1941 review, "Socialist Calculation: The Competitive 'Solution'"— his final contemporary article in the calculation debate—that "the question how far a socialist system can avoid extensive central direction of economic activity is of great importance quite apart from its relation to economic efficiency: It is crucial for the question of how much personal and political freedom can be preserved in such a system."[2]

The Road to Serfdom was an attempt to reach beyond his fellow economists to a wider audience of social scientists and intellectuals. He did not know when he wrote it how far he would reach, but that he greatly exceeded his expectations is apparent. He did not think it likely that he would become famous around the world as its author. He did not realistically foresee himself as anything other than a professor of economics, though he had much higher hopes. But hoping is not the same as what one reasonably expects. His goal for *The Road to Serfdom* was to reach an audience of educated men and women, and, in influencing them, affect public policy. He saw Britain poised to plunge into full-scale nationalizing socialism after World War II, which he thought would be a grievous error.

"It is necessary now to state the unpalatable truth that it is Germany whose fate we are in some danger of repeating,"[3] he declared in the midst of World War II. To a later generation, as to much of his own, this statement sounds exaggerated. How could early 1940s Britain have been conceived as being in danger of becoming another Nazi Germany? His argument was that government ownership of the means of production—largely supported by academic intellectuals during the 1930s and later—would concentrate power in the state in a manner similar to that in Nazi Germany and the Soviet Union.

Keynes is mentioned only twice in *The Road to Serfdom*—once in a note and once when Keynes himself criticized government management of the German economy during World War I. Hayek's target in *The Road to Serfdom* was not what was then becoming referred to as the welfare state; his target was not Keynes. He clarified in the preface of the book's 1976 edition that "during the interval of time terminology has changed and for this reason what I say in the book may be misunderstood. At the time I wrote socialism meant unambiguously the nationalisation of the means of production and the central economic planning which this made possible and necessary."[4] Nor was his opponent in the book William Beveridge or his 1942 *Report on Social Insurance and Allied Services*. Neither Beveridge nor the Beveridge Report is mentioned in *The Road to Serfdom*.

When *The Road to Serfdom* was published in Britain on March 10, 1944, it was an immediate success and attracted substantial public attention. It appeared at the right moment. Whether one agreed or disagreed with it, the book struck a chord. Should classical socialism—nationalization of the means of economic production— be the direction in which Britain moved following the war?

Sir William Harcourt, a British Liberal leader, said famously in 1884, "We are all socialists now." Hayek now wrote, "If it is no longer fashionable to emphasise that 'we are all socialists now,' this is so merely because the fact is too obvious. Scarcely anybody doubts that we must continue to move towards socialism, and most people are merely trying to deflect this movement in the interest of a particular class or group."[5] Socialism was considered, particularly by academic intellectuals, to be society's next ethical and empirical step.

The book was written between 1940 and 1943, "mostly in '41 and '42."[6] Hayek said of the title that the "idea came from Tocqueville, who speaks about the road to servitude; I would like to have chosen that, but it doesn't sound good. So I changed 'servitude' into 'serfdom,' for merely phonetic reasons."[7] He worked stylistically especially on the introduction and first two or three chapters, "reading it out again and again, getting the swing of the thing." It would have taken him "years to do it for the whole book." He thought that the opening was the "best thing" he ever wrote.[8]

He cited Karl Mannheim's *Man and Society in an Age of Reconstruction* (1940) several times as an example of the philosophy he opposed, and it is worthwhile to turn to this work for a moment to understand the tenor of the times better. Mannheim was a prominent German socialist thinker who was forced to move to England as a result of the Nazis' rise to power. Mannheim believed that at the "present stage of industrial society planning in some form or other [i]s inevitable"; "planning is the reconstruction of an historically developed society into a unity which is regulated more and more perfectly by mankind from certain central positions. The social process is no longer merely the product of conflict and competition. Without recognizing this trend, we cannot understand the age in which we live"; and "it is becoming more and more obvious that the enjoyment of income and interest and the right to dispose of capital are two very different things. It is possible that in the future things will so develop that by appropriate taxation and compulsory charity this unrestricted use could be curtailed, and the disposition of capital could be guided from the center by credit control . . . withdrawing certain functions of capital from the competence of capitalists."[9] Prior to Friedman's reconceptualization of the monetary source of the Great Depression (from which Hayek always dissented), and the great prosperity of the post–World War II period, it was unclear that the Depression was *not* the result of mistakes by capitalists, inherent contradictions in capitalism, and a need for systemic change. Hayek also cited the then-popular work of C. H. Waddington, who looked forward approvingly to an economy that would be "centralised and totalitarian in the sense that all aspects of the economic development of large regions are consciously planned as an integrated whole."[10]

These were genuinely prominent views of the day. If the socialist sentiments of Hayek's intellectual opponents sound dated now, this does not detract from their representativeness of a considerable faction in the contemporary ideological outlook. If, in the same way that some of Hayek's thoughts in *The Road to Serfdom* now sound remote, one remembers how equally far were sentiments of his contemporaries from present discussion—though in exactly the opposite direction—perhaps his remarks will seem less otiose. Hayek misjudged the ranges of the probable and practical in the politics of his day, and was excessively pessimistic as to the likelihood of internal socialist change within western nations and in his evaluation of the capacity for a "middle way" between state socialism and unstructured capitalism to achieve economic productivity and relative personal freedom. He, indeed, endorsed a middle way, though considerably farther to the right than Keynes and Beveridge, and though he did not recognize or call it such.

His achievement was to get the main point right, however, that so many of his intellectual and academic contemporaries got wrong: The practice of private ownership and private direction of many of the means of production in a society is essential to freedom, prosperity, and democracy. Moreover, that classical socialism achieved through democratic means would still be totalitarian.

The British background—intellectual and historical—in which he wrote should be emphasized. Britain was, unlike the United States, a class-riven, inegalitarian, and geographically compact society within which the notion of societal organization was more plausible than in America. Particularly following the experiences of World Wars I and II, when most of the British economy was harnessed to the war efforts in ways far surpassing that in the United States, the idea that such activity could be pursued during peacetime seemed eminently reasonable. From an intellectual perspective, socialism seemed plausible as well. The great British economic and political writers of the seventeenth through nineteenth centuries paved the way for socialism through their emphases on this world, pleasure and pain, and happiness. Socialism was to be the achievement of material happiness through governmental means.

Socialism was, however, explicitly a change from the past—particularly in its Continental variety—though an outgrowth from it. The idea of organizing all of a society's economic aspects could not be conceived until after the industrial revolution. The technology simply did not exist previously to exert such control. Pre-industrial communication was inefficient. A society without even the telegraph and paved roads is difficult to organize comprehensively. While pre-industrial absolutist rulers were tyrants or despots, they generally left their subjects' economic activities to themselves, subject to local, church, and trade guilds and controls, and were for the most part content merely to tax their subjects.

The Great Depression substantially increased support for socialism in both Britain and Continental Europe. When tens of millions were unemployed throughout the western world, it appeared capitalism was a failure, Marx's prophecy of capitalism's demise was accurate, and that collective, state control of the means of production, as in the Soviet Union, was the best way to achieve a stable and productive economy. Herman Finer's vitriolic 1945 response to *The Road to Serfdom, Road to Reaction,* well expressed the conventional view of capitalism's failure from the perspective of the consequences of these deficiencies for preserving democratic government. Finer wrote that the "sense of desperation produced by the downward tug of economic ruin subjected political systems throughout the world to tremendous strain. In Germany, still a democratic form of government, people flew for help to men who were making ready to supplant popular government by dictatorship. In France, the nation was split wide open socially. In the United States and Great Britain, where the democratic system had firmer foundations in history and character of the people, the gravest pressure, almost to the breaking point, was put on the constitutions, which barely survived."[11] For Hayek, on the other hand, "Only capitalism makes democracy possible," and "We have progressively abandoned that freedom in economic affairs without which personal and political freedom have never existed in the past."[12] His argument was the empirical rather than moral one that free market capitalism is the most productive form of economy ever known to mankind and leads to generally freer, more tolerant, and more democratic societies. He believed, moreover, that classical socialism, of necessity, must crimp the soul of man.

∼

While Hayek gave as his ostensible reasons for writing *The Road to Serfdom* that he wanted to clarify that Nazism was not a reaction to socialism but an outgrowth from it, and that there was no one "better qualified"[13] to write on the subject as a result of his colleagues' service in the wartime government, there was more to it than this. The book was his personal war effort, one he found a "duty which I must not evade."[14] Because he was not able to participate in the war effort directly, he did so indirectly. His vital message in the work is the incompatibility of socialism and liberty. This message animates the work, for it broadened the discussion of socialism's failings from economic inefficiency to the elimination of freedom. His argument was not, for the most part, that socialism cannot work economically (he and others had already made that argument), but that socialism is irreconcilable with liberty and freedom.

He began his critique of socialism by observing that it began as a reactionary movement opposed to the French Revolution's liberalism. Under the impetus of the European uprisings of 1848, though, Continental socialists began to ally themselves with democrats. Continental socialists correctly foresaw that democracy was the wave of the future and that no movement seeking wholesale reconfiguration of society could hope to persuade the ruling classes to forfeit their positions voluntarily. By positioning itself alongside the most progressive societal forces, those calling for equal suffrage, socialism began to be seen as the next step forward for humanity.

The tie between socialism and democracy is, however, deeper than political expediency. Moreover, British socialists were always democrats. There was a different socialist tradition in Britain than on the Continent. In Continental Europe, socialism generally was neither democratic nor Christian. Marx, the foremost European socialist, had little, if any, regard for democratic voting, and Continental socialism was generally authoritarian and atheistic.

In Britain, it was a different story. Thomas More's 1516 *Utopia* put forward the idea of a genuinely communist society, and during the Puritan revolution in seventeenth-century England there arose beside the main, more moderate movement a radical group called "Diggers" or "True Levelers," who sought communal ownership of land. While the movement was short-lived, its protest against private property was not entirely forgotten.

Robert Owen, who was born in 1771 and died in 1858, is typically regarded as the founder of British socialism and was first to use the term "socialism." He supported "progressive repeal and modification"[15] of unjust laws and institutions, rejecting revolutionary change. Later in the nineteenth century, John Stuart Mill came to embrace a sort of socialism, favoring cooperation within the working place and competition between working places. Following Jeremy Bentham, Mill became the great proponent and patron saint of governmental reform in Great Britain. The English utilitarians wanted to use government to promote the greatest happiness of the greatest number—really, the goal of British idealist socialism, which ultimately is more this destination than a particular means of achieving it.

Thomas Hill Green, an Oxford don during the 1860s and '70s, exerted considerable influence over British intellectual circles until the early years of the twentieth century. A devout Christian, Green emphasized community, believing that unless men and women are conceived as part of a community—with reciprocal rights and duties—little understanding of either the individual or society is possible. Another influence on the development of British socialism during the last decades of the nineteenth century was the ethical and aesthetic idealism of such poets as John Ruskin and William Morris.

The most significant source of twentieth-century British socialism was the Fabian Society, founded in 1883, whose most significant members included Sidney and Beatrice Webb and George Bernard Shaw. Sidney Webb played the crucial role in founding LSE, and it was at LSE that so many of the great twentieth-century British socialists taught, including Attlee, Wallas, Tawney, Dalton, Gaitskell, Durbin, Kaldor, Lerner, and Laski.

The original vision of British idealist socialism, distinct from Continental socialism, was to create a New Jerusalem in which human brotherhood would replace pecuniary competition. The ultimate goal was not external change of men's lot in life or of their economic order, but internal transformation. The 1920s and '30s greatly influenced, of course, the content and development of political and economic discussion. World War I and the Great Depression blew apart the great nineteenth-century liberal dream of a peaceful and harmonious world united by commerce and free trade. Moreover, the example of the Soviet Union beckoned socialist intellectuals and redirected British socialism from voluntary cooperation toward state initiative and control. Laissez-faire liberalism of the nineteenth-century variety was dead, or at the very least in a state of suspended animation.

To the extent that socialism preaches equality, both of human nature and in sharing the results of human interaction, it is consistent that it would find democracy—the practice of political equality—to be the most appropriate form of government. The program of classical socialism came to be government ownership and management of the means of economic production to be accomplished through democratic means. Though, as Hayek affirmed, socialists' intentions were pure, their goals lofty, that they came to have an essentially egalitarian view of human nature, and that they were democrats, they nevertheless favored coercive direct control by government over a great portion of a society's economy. By way of contrast, Hayek stressed in *The Road to Serfdom* that "it is not the source but the limitation of power which prevents it from being arbitrary."[16] Collectivism is no less so because it is ratified by a majority. The proposition that democracy is the sole condition necessary for good government and a good society is neither logical nor has it stood the test of time.

His position on democracy was essential to his view that socialism is not justified, even though it may be democratically enacted. He thought democracy is intrinsically neutral, emphasizing that he had "no intention of making a fetish of democracy. It may well be true that our generation talks and thinks too much of democracy and too little of the values which it serves. Democracy is essentially a means, a utilitarian device for safeguarding internal peace and individual freedom. As such it is by no means infallible or certain. There is no justification for the belief that so long as power is conferred by democratic procedure, it cannot be arbitrary. Democratic control *may* prevent power from becoming arbitrary, but it does not do so by its mere existence."[17] Democracy is not an end in itself, Hayek believed.

His view of democracy is not in harmony with those that see in the majority right, whatever actions the majority may take, and that praise the majority in and of itself. John Stuart Mill held that if even one man in a million holds an opinion, it would be wrong to suppress him; the opinion he holds might possibly be right. In his presentation of democracy as desirable largely for instrumental reasons, Hayek followed in the Anglo-American tradition, which sees democracy as, in Churchill's words, "the worst form of government, excepting all the other forms." "What is government itself," James Madison asked, "but the greatest of all reflections on human nature? In framing a government which is to be administered by men over men, the great difficulty lies in this: you must first enable the government to control the governed; and in the next place oblige it to control itself."[18] It is not so much that democracy is desirable in itself, Hayek argued; it is that there has been no perceived alternative to it for promoting relative personal freedom, allowing peaceful changes of government, furthering a market order, and educating a citizenry.[19]

If there is no intrinsic relationship between socialism's compatibility with liberty and its democratic enactment, what should next be considered is why socialism is inherently irreconcilable with liberty. Undoubtedly, the primary reason is the degree of power entrusted to government in a classical socialist regime. There can be no personal freedom in a society in which the individual is merely a piece in a planner's scheme. Hayek wrote in "Freedom and the Economic System," the article that became *The Road to Serfdom*, that "economic life is the administration of the means for all our different ends. Whoever takes charge of these means must determine which ends shall be served, which values are to be rated higher and which lower, in short what men should believe and strive for. And man himself becomes little more than a means for the realisation of the ideals which may guide the dictator."[20] He wrote in

"Socialist Calculation: The Competitive 'Solution'" that, with a government-controlled economy, "All economic questions become political questions."[21] He used as an epigraph at the start of the chapter "Economic Control and Totalitarianism" in the book itself, "'The control of the production of wealth is the control of human life itself.'"[22] He said himself, "Whoever controls all economic activity controls the means for all our ends, and must therefore decide which are to be satisfied and which not. This is really the crux of the matter. Economic control is not merely control of a sector of human life which can be separated from the rest; it is the control of the means for all our ends."[23]

The most important feature of his argument against state planning in *The Road to Serfdom* was that it is primarily based on liberty, not economic productivity. His argument was not merely that capitalism is justified because it is more economically productive than classical socialism, but that capitalism is justified because classical socialism is inimical to liberty. This latter argument, if true, has appeared to be more powerful than the economic one, for if the issue of socialism is portrayed as one of liberty, then the debate over it has been lifted away from mere questions of technical efficiency to the sphere of ultimate values and morality. At the time Hayek wrote *The Road to Serfdom,* the collectivist economies of the Soviet Union and Nazi Germany were often considered more productive than those of the bankrupt capitalist system, so the argument against classical socialism from the perspective of liberty was of more relevance than it has since become.

As it appears classical socialism is inimical to both liberty and material productivity, the case against it in its variant of state management of all of the means of economic production seems to be conclusive. The issue of socialism's productive merits was, of course, one that classical socialists emphasized. They genuinely thought that socialism would be more economically productive than capitalism. The current conventional wisdom is that socialists were utterly wrong in this appraisal and that the examples of the former Soviet Union and a host of other formerly Communist nations demonstrate the vapidity of government planning and owner-ship of a society's means of production. If the current conventional wisdom is correct, this would indicate that there is little case for classical socialism. If it is not as materially productive as capitalism, its original main argument from the perspective of many of its proponents has vanished.

∿

Hayek stated in the conclusion of *The Road to Serfdom* that its purpose was not to "sketch a detailed program of a desirable future order of society."[24] A summary conception of the order he favored may nonetheless be gathered from its pages. It was, first of all, an *individualist* society. He remarked on the "individualist tradition which has created Western civilization," and praised "respect for the individual man *qua* man."[25] The essence of both classical liberalism and libertarianism is an appraisal of humanity that places the maximum focus on each individual. Neither supposes that individuals find their greatest good in a collective whole that would somehow be greater than the individuals who compose it. Jeremy Bentham has still stated this aspect of true liberalism best in *An Introduction to the Principles of Morals and Legislation* (1789), when he wrote that the "community is a fictitious body, composed of the individual persons who are considered as constituting as it were its members. The interest of the community then is, what?—the sum of the interests of the several members who compose it."[26] Both classical liberalism and libertarianism teach that individuals are most likely to be happiest and to reach their greatest potential and highest personal productivity when they have the greatest personal liberty possible.

Essential to a classical liberal or libertarian society are private property and a competitive market that incorporates prices, profits, and the freedom to exchange goods and services. Hayek observed that the "gradual transformation of a rigidly organised hierarchic system into one where men could at least attempt to shape their own life is closely associated with the growth of commerce."[27] As a matter of historical record, relative respect for individual rights and democracy has developed first and flourished only in those societies that have practiced a competitive market to some considerable degree. Although he did not believe in the infallible efficacy of democracy, Hayek thought it is most likely to be maintained in a market society. Both democracy and economic liberty emphasize the importance of the individual. Where each individual is considered to have worth and to deserve respect, democracy and economic liberty are able to find an atmosphere in which they can breathe. When the focus is the collective rather than the individual, democracy and economic liberty are threatened.

He saw individualism forming the core of western civilization at its finest. From the Hebrew conception of all men and women as equal children of God, to the Greek emphasis on humanism, to the Christian views of the immortality of each soul, the concomitant worth of every person, and the love of Christ for all, to the Roman perspective of equality before the law— what has made the west different and better than other civilizations at its best is the emphasis it has placed on the importance of each individual. Hayek traced the development of western respect for the individual from its roots in antiquity to the Renaissance, and through the Renaissance to modern times. "From the commercial cities of Northern Italy the new view of life spread with commerce to the west and north, taking firm root wherever there was no despotic political power to stifle it."[28] Individualism became most firmly established in Britain and the Netherlands, where it for the "first time had an opportunity to grow freely and to become the foundation of the social and political life of these countries."[29]

The most important institutional safeguard of individualism is the rule of law. Hayek considered no attribute of a society's political order to be more important than the rule of law. Where not laws, but men rule, no one is free and great coercion is inevitable. He began the chapter "Planning and the Rule of Law" by stating, "Nothing distinguishes more clearly conditions in a free country from those in a country under arbitrary government than the observance in the former of the great principles known as the Rule of Law. Stripped of all technicalities, this means that government in all its actions is bound by rules fixed and announced beforehand—rules which make it possible to foresee with fair certainty how the authority will use its coercive powers in given circumstances and to plan one's individual affairs on the basis of this knowledge."[30] This is the essence of Hayek's desired societal order—not a lawless society but a lawful one. Liberty is the supremacy of law.

His concept of optimal societal order was not based at all on a notion that a society without government and laws is possible. His position was, in fact, exactly the opposite. "Probably nothing has done so much harm to the liberal cause," he stated, "as the wooden insistence on certain rough rules of thumb, above all the principle of *laissez-faire*."[31] He considered government not so much as intrinsically bad as in need of being channeled and kept as minimal as possible.

Classical liberalism is not the absence of the state, as some of its proponents as well as opponents mistakenly maintain. Hayek could not have been more clear on this point. The liberty-maximizing society does not entail "inaction of the state. The question whether the state should or should not 'act' or 'interfere' poses an altogether false alternative, and the term *laissez-faire* is a highly ambiguous and misleading description of the principles on which a liberal polity is based." "Of course, every state must act and every action of the state interferes with something or other. But that is not the point." "In no system that could be rationally defended would the state just do nothing."[32] Some form of organization is necessary in every society, indeed defines every society.

Moreover, he was not opposed to new governmental and societal rules and norms to establish and strengthen a regime of classical liberalism, and his thought has often been misinterpreted on this point. He was clear in "Freedom and the Economic System," the article preceding *The Road to Serfdom*:

We can "plan" a system of general rules, equally applicable to all people and intended to be permanent, which provides an institutional framework within which the decisions as to what to do and how to earn a living are left to the individuals. In other words, we can plan a system in which individual initiative is given the widest possible scope and the best opportunity to bring about effective coordination of individual effort. This task of creating a framework of law has by no means been carried through consistently by the early liberals. After vindicating on utilitarian grounds the general principles of private property and freedom of contract, they have stopped short of applying the same criterion to the specific historic[al] forms of the law of property and of contract. Yet it should have been obvious that the question of the exact content and the specific limitations of property rights, and how and when the state will enforce the fulfillment of contracts, require as much consideration as the general principle.[33]

He similarly held in *The Road to Serfdom* that the "liberal argument is in favour of making the best possible use of the forces of competition as a means of co-ordinating human efforts, not an argument for leaving things just as they are. It is based on the conviction that where effective competition can be created, it is a better way of guiding individual efforts than any other. It does not deny, but even emphasises, that, in order that competition should work beneficially, a carefully thought-out legal framework is required, and that neither the existing nor the past legal rules are free from grave defects."[34]

He emphasized that there is "nothing in the basic principles of liberalism to make it a stationary creed. The fundamental principle that in the ordering of our affairs we should make as much use as possible of the spontaneous forces of society, and resort as little as possible to coercion, is capable of an infinite variety of application. There is, in particular, all the difference between deliberately creating a system within which competition will work as beneficially as possible, and passively accepting institutions as they are."[35]

His argument was not that government should acquiesce in whatever rules exist in a society. His argument was that government should change societal rules to create greater competition and freedom. He well stated his opinions along these lines in a 1945 national radio discussion of *The Road to Serfdom* sponsored by the University of Chicago with two hostile panelists:

There are two alternative methods of ordering social affairs—competition and government direction. I am opposed to government direction, but I want to make competition work. . . . In the way in which you use "planning" in this discussion, it is so vague as to be almost meaningless. You seem to call

all government activity planning and assume that there are people who are against all government activity. There are a good many people who oppose planning who do not mean by that opposition that they think that there ought not to be any government at all. They want to confine government to certain functions. . . . [T]his discussion here, as elsewhere, has been very confused. What I was trying to point out is that there are two basic and alternative methods of ordering our affairs. There is, on the one hand, the method of relying upon competition, which, if it is to be made effective, requires a good deal of government activity directed toward making it effective and toward supplementing it where it cannot be made effective. . . . All I am arguing about is that, where you can create a competitive condition, you ought to rely upon competition. I have always said that I am in favor of a minimum income for every person in the country. I am not an anarchist. I do not suggest that a competitive system can work without an effectively enforced and intelligently drawn up legal system.[36]

Hayek was for human freedom. He thought that people should have the highest material standard of living possible. His fellow-participants on the radio panel were Charles Merriam, a distinguished University of Chicago political scientist, and Maynard Krueger, a former United States Socialist Party vice-presidential candidate. Merriam's biographer recounted of the discussion, "Listeners must have been puzzled at the speed with which hostilities began. . . . What they did not know is that the six-hour warm-up session the evening before had been considerably more heated than was normally the case and that Merriam and Hayek were scarcely on speaking terms as the program started."[37]

When challenged by his interlocutors, Hayek responded, "I am not shaken by what you are saying. You see, you are still talking about an old controversy—about whether the state ought to act or ought not to act at all. The whole effort of my book was to substitute a new distinction for the older silly and vague idea. I had realized that some kind of state action is extremely dangerous. Therefore, my whole effort was to distinguish between legitimate and illegitimate action. I have attempted to do that by saying that, so far as government plans for competition or steps in where competition cannot possibly do the job, there is no objection; but I believe that all other forms of government activity are highly dangerous."[38] A classical liberal order is not necessarily one where government is minimized, but where competition is maximized, neces-sitating, once again, prices, profits, private property, a competitive market, the ability to exchange goods and services, contract, and the rule of law.

Hayek wrote passionately of the modest yet encompassing goal of creating societies that allow the individual "opportunity peacefully and in freedom to build up his own little world." His aim was not a collective whole somehow greater than the individuals who compose it, but the "supreme ideal of the freedom and happiness of the individual."[39]

He wrote in *The Road to Serfdom*'s 1976 preface that, after it, though he "tried hard to get back to economics proper," he could not "free" himself of the "feeling that the problems" on which he had "so undesignedly embarked were more challenging and important" than those he previously considered in technical economic theory. Moreover, much that he said in *The Road to Serfdom* required "clarification and elaboration."[40] He was on a new course.

CHAPTER SEVENTEEN

Celebrity

THE ROAD TO SERFDOM was received positively when it was published in Britain in March 1944. The war was not yet over, but it now was a question of when, not if, Nazi Germany would be defeated. Hayek gave his impression of the book's reception in England when he said later that he could "feel only gratification" at the success *The Road to Serfdom* had in Great Britain. This, while "very different in kind" than in the United States, was "quantitatively no smaller. . . . On the whole, the book was taken in the spirit in which it was written, and its argument was seriously considered by those to whom it was mainly addressed."[1] He became famous in Britain as a result of the work. *The Road to Serfdom* was reviewed in leading papers, journals, and magazines. The initial print run of 2,000 copies sold out within days. According to British intellectual historian Richard Cockett, Hayek's publisher, Routledge, ordered an immediate reprint of 1,000 copies, and in the "following two years they were to be engaged in a losing race to satisfy the huge public demand for the book."[2] Because of wartime paper rationing, Routledge could not print as many copies as it wished. The summer following the work's release, Hayek complainingly referred to it as "that unobtainable book."[3]

There is a small question of his exact intentions for the book—what sort of impact he intended. He wrote to Routledge on May 30, 1943, that he had completed a "semi-popular"[4] work, and perhaps even more significantly wrote on August 9, 1943, "I have made a special effort to get it ready rather earlier than I expected as I believe that there are many signs that the time is becoming rather favourable for the reception of a book of this kind, and I am especially anxious not to miss the opportune moment. I believe you will find it worthwhile making an effort to get it out before the winter."[5] Much of this was, however, merely the promotion that any author engages in with his publisher. In an April 1945 speech, Hayek mentioned that he did not expect more than a few hundred people to read the book.[6]

In November 1943, he wrote Routledge a letter enclosing twelve "Points from the Book": "I don't know whether you will think the enclosed too highly coloured, but after giving the book such a title I might as well be hanged for stealing sheep as for stealing a lamb. After all, I believe what I say is the truth."[7] Among the points were, "Is there a greater tragedy imaginable than that in our endeavour consciously to shape our future in accordance with high ideals we should in fact unwittingly produce the very opposite of what we have been striving for? . . . Totalitarianism is the new word we have adopted to describe the unexpected but nevertheless inseparable manifestations of what in theory we call socialism. . . . We shall never prevent the abuse of power if we are not prepared to limit power in a way which occasionally may prevent its use for desirable purposes. . . . What our generation has forgotten is that the system of private property is the most important guarantee of freedom."[8]

He considered the response of Lady Barbara Wootton, a socialist author, to be typical of the British reception. Hayek recounted that Wootton said, "'You know, I wanted to point out some of these problems you have pointed out, but now that you have so exaggerated it I must turn against you!'"[9] Hayek recalled that the "English socialists, with few exceptions, accepted the book as something written in good faith, raising problems they were willing to consider."[10] The book was received in England as a serious, though overstated, argument against state socialism, not a polemic hit-piece.

Keynes wrote Hayek two letters on *The Road to Serfdom,* one before and the other after reading it. In the first letter, dated April 4, 1944, Keynes thanked Hayek for giving him a copy of *The Road to Serfdom.* The book "looks fascinating. It looks to me in the nature of medicine with which I shall disagree, but which may agree with me in the sense of doing me good. . . . Something to be kept at the back of one's head rather than at the front of it."[11]

Keynes wrote to Hayek again on *The Road to Serfdom* on June 28, 1944:

My dear Hayek, The voyage has given me the chance to read your book properly. In my opinion it is a grand book. We all have the greatest reason to be grateful to you for saying so well what needs so much to be said. You will not expect me to accept quite all the economic dicta in it. But morally and philosophically I find myself in agreement with virtually the whole of it; and not only in agreement with it, but in a deeply moved agreement. . . .

I come to what is really my only serious criticism of the book. You admit here and there that it is a question of knowing where to draw the line. You agree that the line has to be drawn somewhere, and the logical extreme is not possible. But you give us no guidance whatever as to where to draw it. It is true that you and I would probably draw it in different places. I should guess that according to my ideas you greatly underestimate the practicability of the middle course. But as soon as you admit that the extreme is not possible, and that a line has to be drawn, you are, on your own argument, done for, since you are trying to persuade us that so soon as one moves an inch in the planned direction you are necessarily launched on the slippery path which will lead you in due course over the precipice.[12]

Other responses in England by those not inclined to Hayek's perspective included George Orwell, who said that in the "negative part of Professor Hayek's thesis there is a great deal of truth. It cannot be said too often—at any rate it is not being said nearly often enough—that collectivism is not inherently democratic, but, on the contrary, gives to a tyrannical minority such powers as the Spanish Inquisitor never dreamed of."[13] Arthur Cecil Pigou added that "whether we agree with Professor Hayek or not, few who read through this earnest and admirably written plea will fail to be interested and stimulated by his treatment of it, and fewer still to close the book without a feeling of respect for and sympathy with the author."[14] And Richard Tawney commented, "Professor Hayek's book has been composed with genuine emotion and a sincerity which commands respect. His honesty and competence are both beyond question."[15]

"Rather different was the reception the book had in the United States,"[16] Hayek stated. The publishing history of *The Road to Serfdom* in the United States, and of Hayek's impression of this, are interesting. In the 1956 foreword to the work, he said, "I had given little thought to its possible appeal to American readers when writing it. It was then twenty years since I had last been in America as a research student, and during that time I had somewhat lost touch with the development of American ideas. I could not be sure how far my argument had direct relevance to the American scene, and I was not in the least surprised when the book was in fact rejected by the first three publishing houses approached." He then added in a footnote, "I did not know, as has since been admitted by a person advising one of the firms, that this appears to have been due not to any doubts of the success of the book but to political prejudice, which went to the extent of representing the book as 'unfit for publication by a reputable house.'"[17]

Was *The Road to Serfdom* to some extent suppressed as it came to the United States? The support Hayek gave for this proposition were two statements by William Miller, one in an article by William T. Couch and the other in Miller's own work. In his own 1949 *The Book Industry,* Miller wrote of the increasing tendency of university presses to engage in "trade publishing"—that is, offering works not just for scholarly customers but for a wider market. "That university presses have done this is suggested by the publication and promotion by the University of Chicago Press of Friedrich A. von Hayek's *The Road to Serfdom,* a sensational book previously rejected by at least one notable trade house which was quite aware of its sale possibilities."[18]

Couch, then, wrote an article several years later on "undercover censorship by liberals," and wrote Miller inquiring about his enigmatic remark in *The Book Industry.* Miller wrote back, "As to your query whether I intended to suggest that this book was unfit for publication by a reputable house, my answer is that that is what I say, not merely suggest. It just happens that I personally had the opportunity to say as much to the great house for which I read manuscripts, and that I then also took the opportunity to say that in my opinion the book would sell very well. I recommended, nevertheless, that they reject it and remain gratified, as I think they do, that they did."[19] Miller, in other words, was not merely the source for the information that *The Road to Serfdom* was declined for political reasons, he was the person who made the recommendation.

Milton Friedman has remarked on the prevailing intellectual atmosphere of the time. Responding to the question, "There is some indication in the 1956 introduction that *The Road to Serfdom* was to some extent suppressed. Do you think there's much to that?" Friedman said, "I don't have the slightest doubt. You have no idea of the climate of opinion in 1945 to 1960 or '70. I have a hard time knowing how to tell about that, because it really is unbelievable. We had the same experience. I published *Capitalism and Freedom* in 1962. That's seventeen years later. It's a book that's now sold close to a million copies. It was not reviewed by any American publications, other than the *American Economic Review.* It's inconceivable that at the time—I was a full professor at the University of Chicago, I was very well known in the academic world—a book on the other side by someone in that same position would not have been reviewed in every publication, the *New York Times,* the *Chicago Tribune. . . .* No, the evidence is overwhelming about the kind of intellectual atmosphere."[20]

At the same time, Miller was a very tiny figure in the American publishing industry, a reader for a publishing house. Moreover, as Miller himself observed in *The Book Industry,* there are many reasons why publishers do not accept works. Referring specifically to university presses, he commented, "How many of the trade titles were profitable is not known; most of them, like most regular trade books, probably lost money."[21]

Whether *The Road to Serfdom* was rejected initially in the United States by anyone other than William Miller for reasons of political prejudice cannot be said. Two American publishers, Macmillan and Harper, wrote in rejection letters: "Professor Hayek is a little outside the stream of present-day thought, both here and in England," and, "The volume is over-written and he can say all that he has to say in about half the space. Also, it is so completely in the negative vein as to leave the reader without any clue as to what line to take on thought or policy."[22]

Hayek signed a contract with the University of Chicago Press in the beginning of April 1944, about a month after the book appeared in England. Negotiations with other American publishers took place months before, when the book had not yet appeared in Britain, and thus when the question of its potential appeal in the United States—which Hayek did not anticipate—was completely uncertain. In addition, wartime paper rationing constrained publishing decisions in the United States as in Great Britain.

Reviews commissioned by the University of Chicago Press expressed the following views:

1) . . . a masterly performance . . . the whole discussion is pitched at a quite high intellectual and scholarly level. . . . The book is an able piece of work, but limited in scope and somewhat one-sided in treatment. I doubt whether it would have a very wide market in this country, or change the position of many readers. . . .

2) The current discussion between advocates and adversaries of free enterprise has not been conducted so far on a very high level. Hayek's book may start in this country a more scholarly kind of debate. . . . The book is almost exclusively critical, not constructive. Its technique is black-and-white. It is impatient of compromises. It is written with the passion and the

burning clarity of a great doctrinaire. Hayek has the sincerity of one who has had the vision of danger which the others have not seen. He warns his fellowmen with loving impatience.[23]

Historian of liberty Jim Powell provides this summary of *The Road to Serfdom*'s publication in the United States. "Hayek authorized," Powell writes, "Fritz Machlup, then working in Washington, to try finding an American publisher, but he was unsuccessful. He gave a copy of the Routledge page proofs to University of Chicago economics professor Aaron Director [Friedman's brother-in-law] who met Hayek in 1943 when both were teaching at the London School of Economics. Director passed the page proofs to Frank Knight. . . . Knight apparently gave them to William T. Couch, a classical liberal friend at the University of Chicago Press which agreed to publish the book. . . . It was a little wartime edition about 4-7/8 by 6-3/4 inches."[24]

The American edition was published six months after the British edition, on September 18, 1944. As in England, the initial printing was 2,000 copies, proportionately far less in larger and more well-off America. According to a 1945 *Harper's* magazine article, this was "fair indication of the expected demand for what appeared to be a severely intellectual tract for scholars."[25] The book was a largely academic work, directed to a British audience, concerning Britain, and by an Austrian author completely unknown in the United States.

Among the provisos the University of Chicago Press placed on Hayek when accepting *The Road to Serfdom* for publication was, according to Press editor John Scoon, to be "specific about the application to the United States instead of slanting the book directly at an audience limited to England."[26] This was accomplished through an introduction by John Chamberlain, who was a well-known writer and book reviewer affiliated with the *New York Times,* the *Wall Street Journal,* and other publications throughout his career, and whose name appeared prominently on the first edition. Wendell Willkie, the 1940 Republican presidential candidate, was originally contacted to write an introduction to the American edition of *The Road to Serfdom,* but he declined.[27]

Chamberlain praised the work in his introduction. There, he stated that "this book of Hayek's is a warning, a cry in a time of hesitation. It says to the British and by implication to Americans: Stop, look, and listen. *The Road to Serfdom* is sober, logical, severe. It does not make for ingratiating reading. But the logic is incontestable: 'full employment,' 'social security,' and 'freedom from want' cannot be had unless they come as by-products of a system that releases the free energies of individuals. When 'society' and the 'good of the whole' are made the overmastering touchstones of state action, no individual can plan his own existence." Chamberlain concluded that "one can only wish for the widest possible audience for *The Road to Serfdom*."[28]

His wish was fulfilled. On September 24, 1944, *The Road to Serfdom* was the subject of the lead review in the *New York Times Book Review.* Henry Hazlitt, a prominent political and economic writer who had a column in *Newsweek,* was effusive in his praise. He glowingly wrote that in *The Road to Serfdom,* "Friedrich A. Hayek has written one of the most important books of our generation," and the rest of the review was in the same vein. "It restates for our time the issue between liberty and authority with the power and rigor of reasoning that John Stuart Mill stated the issue for his own generation in his great essay, 'On Liberty.' It throws a brilliant light along the direction in which the world has been heading, first slowly, but now at an accelerating rate, for the last half-century. It is an arresting call to all well-intentioned planners and socialists. No one can realize the full force and persuasiveness of this book except by reading it through. Even if the author were not a foreigner by birth, one would say that his English style is remarkably fine. His tone is dignified, temperate and conciliatory." Similarly to Chamberlain, Hazlitt opined that it was a "strange stroke of irony that the great British liberal tradition, the tradition of Locke and Milton, of Adam Smith and Hume, of Macaulay and Mill and Morley, of Acton and Dicey, should find in England its ablest contemporary defender—not in a native Englishman but in an Austrian exile."[29]

Following Hazlitt's review, the University of Chicago Press realized it had a winner on its hands. It placed an immediate order for a second printing of 5,000 copies, and a few days later ordered a third printing of 5,000, increasing this to 10,000 the following day. Press editor Scoon recalls that by the first week of October "many stores were out of stock and we had a tremendous and intricate job of printing, binding, shipping and allotting to customers in both this country and Canada."[30]

There were two sets of responses to *The Road to Serfdom* in both England and the United States, and it is important to be clear about these in order to understand the development of the work's and Hayek's fame. The first response in both countries was during the weeks and months immediately after the book was published. There were reviews in leading periodicals, and *The Road to Serfdom* became known as an academic work of popular interest. Hayek became famous. The second set of responses in each country was the greater public notice that came to the book and to Hayek after a *Reader's Digest* version appeared in the United States during April 1945 under the title "One of the Most Important Books of Our Generation," and when Churchill appeared to make reference to Hayek's ideas the next month during his first speech of the British general election campaign. Hayek became a celebrity, and the work, a symbol.

Hayek personally experienced, and helped to foster, the second success in the United States during a spring 1945 lecture tour. The original plan was for him to repeat a series of lectures at five major universities. On his way across the Atlantic, the *Reader's Digest* version appeared, completely changing the situation. The *Digest*'s circulation at this time was in the vicinity of ten million, and in this pre-television age, it was a significant presence on the American cultural scene. In place of the scholarly tour, the University of Chicago Press turned arrangements for Hayek's visit over to a commercial agency for a popular lecture tour.

He traveled throughout the East and Midwest in the United States during his first visit since his sojourn as a student in 1924. Many articles, interviews, and radio appearances accompanied his journey. He told a humorous story about his first lecturing experience after being informed on arriving in New York that the original plan was off, and he was to

> go on a public-lecture tour around the country. I said, "My God, I have never done this. I can't possibly do it. I have no experience in public speaking."
>
> "Oh, it can't be helped now."
>
> "Well, when do we start?"
>
> "You are late. We've already arranged tomorrow, Sunday morning, a meeting at Town Hall in New York."
>
> Only on the next morning, when I was picked up at my hotel I asked, "What sort of audience do you expect?" "The hall holds 3,000 but there's an overflow meeting." Dear God, I hadn't an idea what I was going to say. "How have you announced it?" "Oh, we have called it 'The Rule of Law in International Affairs.'" My God, I had never thought about that problem in my life. So I knew as I sat down on that platform, with all the unfamiliar paraphernalia—at that time it was still dictating machines—if I didn't get tremendously excited I would break down. So the last thing that I remember is that I asked the chairman if three-quarters of an hour would be enough. "Oh, no, it must be exactly an hour; you are on the radio."
>
> I got up with these words in my ear, without the slightest idea of what I was going to say. But I began with a tone of profound conviction, not knowing how I would end the sentence, and it turned out that the American public is an exceedingly grateful and easy public. I got through this hour

swimmingly. I went through the United States for five weeks doing that stunt everyday.[31]

More than 600,000 additional copies of the *Reader's Digest* version were subsequently distributed through the Book-of-the-Month Club.

Timing undoubtedly contributed to the work's phenomenal success. April and May 1945 was a time of great buoyancy in the United States, although Franklin D. Roosevelt died on April 12. Hitler committed suicide on April 30, 1945, and Germany surrendered eight days later, although the war against Japan remained in full force. The atomic bomb and breach with Russia had not yet developed. Churchill remained prime minister in Great Britain. There was in America, as in Britain, a feeling of, "What's next?"

Lawrence Frank wrote in a May 1945 article on Hayek and *The Road to Serfdom* in the *Saturday Review of Literature* that a "book unobtrusively published last fall by a university press has skyrocketed to national prominence in recent weeks. It is *The Road to Serfdom,* by Friedrich A. Hayek, an Austrian economist who almost overnight has been hailed a major prophet by a section of American business and professional men. He has become the spokesman for the economic beliefs which flourished up to 1929, but since then have not had a wide or sympathetic audience. Various organizations, including the National Association of Manufacturers, are recommending Dr. Hayek's book. Last month the *Reader's Digest* published a somewhat sharpened condensation; and the Book-of-the-Month Club is now publishing reprints. *Fortune Magazine* has praised Dr. Hayek. In the meantime, Dr. Hayek has been making a whirlwind (and some say triumphal) lecture tour of the United States. Seldom have an economist and a non-fiction book reached such popularity in so short a time."[32]

Between April and July 1945, *The Road to Serfdom* became a best-seller in the United States. There was not, at this time, a national best-seller list. Rather, leading sellers were reported on a city-by-city basis. For the week of May 20, the book was the second-leading seller in Chicago and third in Cleveland and Detroit. During the week of June 24, it was number one in Chicago and St. Louis, and number two in Detroit. Other cities in which it reached the top five during this period were Washington and Baltimore.

An editorialist for the *New Republic* opined in April 1945 that *The Road to Serfdom* "found an enthusiastic response in the United States among those who are using the economic theories of the 1880's to justify the business practices of the 1940's. He [Hayek] is being rapidly erected into a leading thinker of reaction. He is being pushed by chambers of commerce, advertising agencies, big business."[33] The writer Stuart Chase, whom Hayek attacked in the book, wrote a critical piece in the May 1945 *Nation,* "Back to Grandfather: Dr. Hayek's Guide to the Pre-War Era."[34]

The most negative response in the United States was Herman Finer's *Road to Reaction.* Finer stated in his preface that he would prove Hayek's "apparatus of learning is deficient, his reading incomplete; that his understanding of the economic process is bigoted, his account of history false; that his political science is almost non-existent, his terminology misleading, his comprehension of British and American political procedure and mentality gravely defective; and that his attitude to average men and women is truculently authoritarian." He also said of Hayek and the work, "worshipper of reaction . . . piece of perverted and pompous logic . . . unscrupulous travesty . . . infamous, malignant outlook . . . betrays most abject ignorance . . . mischievous and unscientific . . . deliberate effrontery . . . thoroughly Hitlerian contempt for democratic man."[35]

Another contemporary response in the United States was by political scientist William Ebenstein. He wrote in *Man and the State: Modern Political Ideas* (1947) that the "most famous anti-planning book is Friedrich A. Hayek's *The Road to Serfdom.* Its excellence was immediately recognized, being digested in the *Reader's Digest,* and distributed widely by all sorts of agencies. . . . Hayek is persuaded that in a planned economy 'the worst get to the top.' . . . The experience in England and other democratic countries which are engaged in socialist planning will tell whether 'intolerance and brutal suppression of dissent, deception and spying, the complete disregard of the life and happiness of the individual are essential and unavoidable' from the 'collectivist standpoint.' . . . As long as Hayek continues to teach his brand of antisocialist economics at the London School of Economics and Political Science, he will still be on the high road to freedom."[36]

While Hayek was on his American lecture tour, the British general election of 1945 was called, in which Churchill was defeated by Labour leader Clement Attlee. Hayek and *The Road to Serfdom* played a part. Churchill began his campaign with a frontal attack on Labour. "My friends," he said, "I must tell you that a socialist policy is abhorrent to the British ideas of freedom. Socialism is inseparably interwoven with totalitarianism and the object worship of the state. It will prescribe for every one where they are to work, what they are to work at, where they may go and what they may say. Socialism is an attack on the right to breathe freely. No socialist system can be established without a political police. They would have to fall back on some form of Gestapo, no doubt very humanely directed in the first instance."[37] According to Harold Macmillan, later Conservative prime minister, Churchill was "fortified in his apprehensions by reading Professor Hayek's *The Road to Serfdom.*"[38]

Churchill's speech backfired, especially his reference to the Gestapo, for he was seen as equating his former partners in the wartime coalition government—Attlee and Labour—with the Nazis right when the worst news about Germany was coming out, the concentration camps and mass murders of Jews. Attlee replied in his nationwide radio speech the following night that Churchill's position was the "second-hand version of the academic views of an Austrian professor, Friedrich August von Hayek."[39]

The "Gestapo" speech undoubtedly hurt Churchill, and it would be an ironic twist if the use by him of ideas from *The Road to Serfdom* contributed in some way to the first majority British Labour government. Hayek responded to an interview question, "The 'Gestapo speech' may well have cost Churchill the election. Do you think there's anything to that?" "I don't regard it as impossible. This phrase of 'a Gestapo' was in that speech used so much against him at the time, it may well be that that whole speech did him more harm than anything else."[40] It would be rash to ascribe Churchill's defeat to the speech, however, and thus somehow indirectly to Hayek. While the British people supported Churchill as a great wartime leader, they sought a different approach for the coming postwar era.

A front-page story headlined "Second-Hand Ideas from an Austrian Professor"[41] appeared in the *Manchester Guardian* the day after Attlee's speech. Hayek was quoted, "I am interested in ideas, not Party politics. I listened to Mr. Attlee's speech and the only thing I could be sure of was that he had not read my book."[42] All the major papers reported the story, and some published excerpts from *The Road to Serfdom.* The *Sunday Graphic* reported two weeks later that the book had become the "nation's number one talking point."[43]

Laski, who was coincidentally at this time chairman of the Labour Party, also played a role in the 1945 British election campaign. During the campaign, Churchill invited Attlee to attend the Potsdam Conference on postwar issues in a few weeks, by which time the election would be over, but votes would not be counted as a result of servicemen and servicewomen's ballots still to be gathered from around the world. Laski then issued this statement, "If Mr. Attlee attends this gathering he shall do so in the role of an observer only. The Labour Party cannot be committed to any decisions arrived at which have not been debated in the Party Executive."[44]

Churchill and the conservative press pounced. Churchill orated in his next radio broadcast, "A new figure has leaped into notoriety. The situation has now been complicated and darkened by the repeated intervention of Professor Laski, chairman of the Socialist Party Executive. He has reminded all of us, including Mr. Attlee, that the final determination on all questions rests, so far as the Socialist Party is concerned, with this dominating Socialist Executive."[45] According to Laski biographer Isaac Kramnick, "Churchill's decision to campaign against socialist planning by equating it with a Gestapo state," combined with Laski's intervention, "created the bizarre phenomenon of a great general election being fought at one level between the rival doctrines of two LSE professors"[46]—Hayek and Laski. In June 1945 the *New York Times* published back-to-back essays, "Is the World Going to the Left?" Laski provided the affirmative argument, and Hayek the negative.

The Conservative Central Office thought highly of *The Road to Serfdom* during the 1945 British general election campaign and offered Hayek's publisher one-and-a-half tons of precious paper to publish an abridged version. This request could not be accommodated before the election, though.

Hayek was initially satisfied with the role his ideas played in the general election campaign. According to Cockett, he "lunched at the Reform Club on the day after Churchill's broadcast, and was pleased that his ideas had been taken up with such gusto."[47] This was over a year after the original British publication of *The Road to Serfdom.*

CHAPTER EIGHTEEN

Mont Pelerin Society

HAYEK WAS VITALLY INTERESTED IN THE PRACTICAL OUTCOMES of economic and political theory. The reason he worked, indeed, ultimately was to influence public policy. When he said in a February 23, 1944, talk to the London School of Economics Students Union in Cambridge, "On Being an Economist," that the societal philosopher should "never directly aim at immediate success and public influence," and that the "desire to gain influence" through positions of power in order to "be able to do good is one of the main sources of intellectual concession," this reflected both his technical view of how influence is most effectively achieved and his deep and abiding commitment to achieve great effect. He believed that in the "search for truth" the economist or political philosopher will most contribute if he focuses on the creation of human knowledge and avoids political offices.[1]

Hayek identified Nazism with socialism as early as the spring of 1933 in a memo.[2] His efforts which were declined to help the British government with war propaganda against Germany flowed from his commitment to use his intellectual powers for good. During the war, he also confidentially proposed, through Robbins, to the British government that a college for social studies should be established after the war to re-educate German leaders.[3] His suggestion was not, however, considered.

Hayek did not intend for *The Road to Serfdom* initially to be so exclusively directed against Nazi Germany, compared to the Soviet Union, as it became. Indeed, in a postscript he contemplated adding to the book four years after it was published, he mentioned that he originally intended *The Road to Serfdom* to depict the struggle between the joint totalitarian powers of the east, Nazi Germany and the Soviet Union (then in tactical alliance), against the liberal democracies of the west. However, following the June 1941 German invasion of Russia and Russia's subsequent alliance with Britain, he deleted most negative references to the Soviet Union. In its suppression of dissenting opinions, he considered the Soviet Union to be worse than Nazi Germany.[4]

Five days after he read "On Being an Economist" to the LSE Students Union—less than two weeks before British publication of *The Road to Serfdom*—Hayek read another paper, "Historians and the Future of Europe," to the King's College Political Society. In this paper, he discussed the role that historians could play in the "re-education of the German people," where by historians he meant "really all students of society."[5] He was concerned, as many others were, that Germany might again move in a totalitarian and aggressive direction following World War II. This latter paper, which he distributed to a number of academics and others, was the genesis of what became the Mont Pelerin Society.

His initial conception was to form a society for the purpose of bringing German scholars back into the mainstream of classical liberal thought, somewhat similar to his idea for a college to re-educate German leaders. The ethical standards of the proposed group would be a dedication to the "sacredness of truth" and a commitment that "ordinary rules of moral decency must apply to political action"— not at all platitudinous goals in light of the German experience. He also put forward that the group should have a "certain minimum agreement on the most general political ideals," including "a common belief in the value of individual freedom, an affirmative attitude towards democracy without any superstitious deference to all its dogmatic applications, and, finally, an equal opposition to all forms of totalitarianism, whether it be from the Right or from the Left."[6] He concluded in this paper that his intention was not to "solicit support for a definite project, but rather to submit a tentative suggestion to your criticism."[7]

Over the next three years the contours of the proposed society changed somewhat, but not its overarching purpose nor Hayek as its driving force. As his fame exploded and over the course of his travels, he came in contact with many who shared his outlook but were alone or almost so among their colleagues. Nearly everywhere he went he "met someone who told me that he fully agreed with me, but that at the same time he felt totally isolated in his views and had nobody with whom he could even talk about them."[8] This gave him the idea to call a conference. As a result of wartime travel and communication restrictions, as well as economic turbulence during the 1930s, contacts among individuals in different nations had been limited for many years; and, indeed, largely for technological reasons, contacts had not been more significant previously.

A conference had been held in Paris in August 1938 to discuss what its participants called "the crisis of liberalism."[9] This gathering, "La Colloque Walter Lippmann," emphasized Lippmann's 1937 book, *The Good Society,* and was attended by Mises, Hayek, twenty-three other academics, and Lippmann. This conference may perhaps be seen as a forerunner of what became the Mont Pelerin Society. At its end, Hayek was charged with forming a British section of the organization that was to issue from the meeting, an International Center of Studies for the Renovation of Liberalism. August 1938 was not, however, a propitious moment to commence a new international organization.

Following the war, there were other academic liberals who sounded the idea of some sort of international gathering, but Hayek's was the idea that bore fruit. His original thought of establishing an international society of liberals to bring German scholars into the mainstream of liberal thought was replaced by one whose focus would be the preservation of classical liberalism itself. He nonetheless considered it an accomplishment of the first conference that the German economist Walter Eucken attended and was "the star," for this "contributed a little to the rehabilitation of German scholars on the international scene."[10]

The other academic who concurrently most actively suggested a gathering of liberal scholars was Eucken's colleague Wilhelm Röpke, like Eucken a member of the Freiburg school of economics, which played an important role in placing West Germany on its postwar free market path. Röpke spent the war years in exile at the Graduate Institute of International Studies in Geneva, where Mises spent the second half of the 1930s and where Hayek gave his *Monetary Nationalism and International Stability* lectures. Like Hayek, Röpke circulated a paper following the war to a number of colleagues and participants in La Colloque Walter Lippmann, calling for an international liberal gathering. In addition to regular meetings of liberal scholars, Röpke suggested an international liberal journal—an issue that would later cause considerable controversy in the Mont Pelerin Society—and raised a certain amount of funds for his project.

A Swiss businessman involved with the Institute of International Studies, Dr. Albert Hunold, invited Hayek to address, in Richard Cockett's words, the "students of the University of Zurich in November 1945 and afterwards dined with Hayek and a group of Swiss industrialists and bankers, at which point Hayek told them of his own plans for a gathering of those intellectuals who shared his views to discuss and redefine liberalism. Hayek proposed that it would be 'an enormous help' if these people 'could come together and meet for about a week somewhere in a Swiss Hotel in order to discuss basic ideas.' Hunold pledged his financial support and that of his fellow businessmen to the project, promising to divert the funds which they had raised for Röpke's periodical to Hayek, as Röpke's idea had proved too costly. During 1946, Hayek took soundings in both Europe and America, and, with Hunold's financial and moral backing, decided to go ahead with the idea of a meeting in Switzerland in the spring of 1947."[11]

The conference was held April 1-10, 1947, on Mont Pelerin, near Vevey, Switzerland. Focusing on his belief in the power of ideas, Hayek wrote in a memo in advance of the conference that if Europe were not to enter a "new kind of serfdom, an intense intellectual effort is needed. We must kindle an interest in—and an understanding of—the great principles of Social organization and of the conditions of individual liberty as we have not known it in our life-time. We must raise and train an army of fighters for freedom. If hands in the face of overwhelming public opinion but work to shape and guide that opinion, our cause is by no means hopeless. But it is late in the day and we have not too much time to spare." He emphasized that the "effort must be essentially a long-run effort, concerned not so much with what would be immediately practicable, but with the beliefs which must regain ascendance if the dangers are to be averted which at the moment threaten individual freedom."[12] If the intellectuals who supported classical liberalism did not join together and promote their vision, humanity might enter a thousand years of night. "Unless we can make the philosophic foundations of a free society once more a living intellectual issue, and its implementation a task which challenges the ingenuity and imagination of our liveliest minds, the prospects of freedom are indeed dark. But if we can regain that belief in the power of ideas which was the mark of liberalism at its best, the battle is not lost."[13]

Thirty-nine individuals from ten countries participated in the Mont Pelerin conference—seventeen from the United States, eight from England, four from Switzerland, four from France, and one each from Belgium, Denmark, Italy, Norway, Sweden, and West Germany. Even this list does not entirely convey the diversity of the group, as several participants, including Mises (who was by this time in New York), Popper (who was in London), and Hayek himself, were transplanted central Europeans. Four at the first meeting—better than ten percent of those in attendance—were later to receive Nobel Prizes in Economics: Hayek, Friedman, George Stigler, and Maurice Allais.[14]

In an article commemorating the fiftieth anniversary of the Mont Pelerin Society, the locale was described: "A visitor is immediately struck by the breathtaking, panoramic view. A broad piazza overlooks Lake Geneva and the alpine Dents du Midi, which are visible in the distance. Across the lake is Evian-les-Bain, France, a spa world-renowned for its bottled water. One nearby resort town is Montreux. From Vevey, a funicular railway travels up the mountainside to Mont Pelerin, a quiet, semi-rural setting conducive not only for reflection, but for hiking as well."[15]

Proceedings of the conference started with a report by Hayek on the aims of the gathering. He was emphatic in his opening address, stating, "I must confess that now, when the moment has arrived to which I have looked forward so long, my feeling of intense gratitude to all of you is much tempered by an acute sense of astonishment at my temerity in setting all this in motion, and of alarm about the responsibility I have assumed in asking you to give up so much of your time and energy to what you might well have regarded as a wild experiment. The basic conviction which has guided me is that, if the ideals which I believe unite us, and for which, in spite of so much abuse of the term, there is still no better name than liberal, are to have any chance of revival, a great intellectual task must be performed."[16] As always, he focused on the intellect.

Session titles during the first conference included "'Free' Enterprise or Competitive Order," "Modern Historiography and Political Education," "The Future of Germany," "The Problems and Chances of European Federation," and "Liberalism and Christianity." According to Max Hartwell, a later president and historian of the Mont Pelerin Society, Hayek "felt it was necessary to bridge the gap between liberals and Christians."[17]

Among those elected to the standing committee for the first conference was Friedman, who traveled to Europe for the first time to attend. Hayek sought a multidisciplinary approach, resulting in attendance by economists, political philosophers, historians, lawyers, and others (though he thought later that the Mont Pelerin Society had become too dominated by economists). He insisted that meetings not be generally open to the public and media, believing such access would hinder the free communication of ideas. This policy resulted in an article in the *Chicago Tribune* on the third day of the first conference, "7 Nations Map Freedom Fight in Secret Talk." The article reported, "The question of publicity was taken up at the opening session. After an hour's debate, it was decided to bar the press and a six man committee appointed to draft a statement to hand to any inquiring reporters who might show up. Dr. Hayek said it would be carefully worded so as to contain no information. Reasons for the secrecy were not altogether clear."[18] This article mistakenly identified Hayek as "Winston Churchill's adviser on economic matters," and had a section heading, "Churchill Adviser Explains"—Attlee's reference to him remained a part of public consciousness.

Aaron Director remembers Lionel Robbins as a "major figure"[19] at the first conference. Robbins drafted the "Statement of Aims," which was adopted at the end of the conference to guide the society. Friedman recalls that there was "nobody else at the meeting who could have reconciled the differences in politics among the participants in that statement as well as Robbins. After we had spent days discussing these issues and tried to draft a statement, Lionel finally took it over and drafted the one we all signed":[20]

STATEMENT OF AIMS

A group of economists, historians, philosophers and other students of public affairs from Europe and the United States met at Mont Pelerin, Switzerland . . . to discuss the crisis of our times. This group . . . has agreed upon the following statement of aims.

The central values of civilisation are in danger. Over large stretches of the earth's surface the essential conditions of human dignity and freedom have already disappeared. In others they are under constant menace from the development of current tendencies of policy. The position of the individual and of the voluntary group are progressively undermined by extensions of arbitrary power. Even that most precious possession of Western Man, freedom of thought and expression, is threatened by the spread of creeds which, claiming the privilege of tolerance when in the position of a minority, seek only to establish a position of power in which they can suppress and obliterate all views but their own.

The group holds that these developments have been fostered by the growth of a view of history which denies all absolute moral standards and by the growth of theories which question the desirability of the rule of law. It holds further that they have been fostered by a decline of belief in private property and the competitive market; for without the diffused power and initiative associated with these institutions it is difficult to imagine a society in which freedom may be effectively preserved. . . .

The group does not aspire to conduct propaganda. It seeks to establish no meticulous and hampering orthodoxy. It aligns itself with no particular party. Its object is solely, by facilitating the exchange of views among minds inspired by certain ideals and broad conceptions held in common, to contribute to the preservation and improvement of the free society.[21]

This first conference proved very successful, and the participants agreed that continuing meetings would be desirable. A permanent association was formed. It should be emphasized that the purpose of the society was not simply to provide intellectual companionship, but, as Hayek said, "we had much to learn from each other since each had pushed his efforts of developing the underlying ideals in a different direction."[22] Recalling how Frank Knight of the University of Chicago blocked his proposal to name the emerging association the "Acton-Tocqueville Society," Hayek later mentioned "one amusing episode about Frank Knight. When I called that first meeting on Mont Pelerin, I had already the idea we might turn this into a permanent society, and I proposed that it would be called the Acton-Tocqueville Society, after the two most representative figures. Frank Knight put up the greatest indignation, 'You can't call a liberal movement after two Catholics!' And he completely defeated it; he made it impossible."[23] Cockett reports that "only a few support[ed] Hayek's original proposal of the 'Acton-Tocqueville Society,' others favoring the names Burke and Smith."[24]

The society officially incorporated on November 6, 1947, simply as the Mont Pelerin Society. Hayek was president, and Walter Eucken (West Germany), John Jewkes (Britain),[25] Frank Knight (United States), W. E. Rappard (Switzerland), and Jacques Rueff (France) were vice presidents. Hunold became secretary and primary administrative mover, fund-raiser, and organizer, a role in which he later came in conflict with Hayek and others in the society, particularly Americans and Britons. The society agreed to meet again in two years, which it did in Seelisberg, Switzerland.

Especially during the society's early years, English participants were disproportionately affiliated with LSE, and those from the United States included a large contingent from the University of Chicago. Within the two countries, the University of Manchester also provided more than its share of members, and the New York-based Foundation for Economic Education (FEE) supplied four first-conference participants. The William Volker Charities Trust in the United States (which subsequently paid for Hayek's and Mises' academic posts in America) and the International Liberal Exchange in England, as well as Hunold's business associates, contributed financially to the fledgling organization.

Hayek considered establishment of the Mont Pelerin Society a genuinely important accomplishment. He observed later, in rare public immodesty, that the "founding and the first conference of the Mont Pelerin Society, I feel entitled to say, was my own idea" and that the first conference and founding "constituted the rebirth of the liberal movement in Europe. Americans have done me the honour of considering the publication of *The Road to Serfdom* as the decisive date, but it is my conviction that the really serious endeavour among intellectuals to bring about the rehabilitation of the idea of personal freedom especially in the economic realm dates from the founding of the Mont Pelerin Society"[26] in 1947.

CHAPTER NINETEEN

Psychology

HAYEK'S WORK IN PSYCHOLOGY IS AMONG THE MOST DIFFICULT of his corpus, as he himself recognized. He never lost his early interest in psychology. He decided to reward himself after *The Road to Serfdom* for doing what seemed a "duty performed"[1] by disregarding what was expected of him and instead doing what interested him the most at the moment, which were his old ideas in theoretical psychology. He had for once "exercised some practical influence"[2] and at the same time earned a considerable amount of money. He wanted to devote his energy for a time to purely abstract inquiry.

He worked on *The Sensory Order* for over five years, both in London and Chicago. His personal life was in transition during this time as a result of his divorce, and he founded the Mont Pelerin Society. His ability to devote concentrated time to academic work was more limited than it had been during the 1930s and early '40s, in part because he acquired more administrative and teaching duties at LSE.

Notwithstanding its difficulty, he considered his work in psychology to be among the most important of his career. He had this exchange in 1978 with Nobel Prize-winning economist James Buchanan:

Q: You wrote a book in psychology.

A: I still believe this is one of my more important contributions to knowledge. It's now twenty-five years old, and the idea is fifty-odd years old.

Q: Could you perhaps summarize that notion?

A: I think the thing which is really important about it, and which I could not do when I first conceived the idea, is to formulate the problem I try to answer rather than the answer I want to get. And that problem is, What determines the difference between the different sensory qualities? The attempt was to reduce it to a system of causal connections, or associations, you might say, in which the quality of a particular sensation—the attribute of blue, or whatever it is—is really its position in a system of potential connections leading up to actions. You could, in theory, reproduce a sort of map of how one stimulus evokes other stimuli and then further stimuli, which can, in principle, reproduce all the mental processes.[3]

He said on another occasion of his psychological work that he wrote a book in which he made an "attempt to provide at least a schema for explaining how physiological processes can generate this enormous variety of qualities which our senses represent. [The book] ends up with the proof that while we can give an explanation of the principle on which it operates, we cannot possibly give an explanation of detail, because our brain is, as it were, an apparatus of classification. And every apparatus of classification must be more complex than what it classifies; so it can never classify itself. It's impossible for a human brain to explain itself in detail."[4]

The milieu of the Vienna circle and logical positivism is useful to review when considering Hayek's work in psychology-related areas. The Vienna circle of logical positivists was founded in 1925 by Moritz Schlick, who had come to hold Ernst Mach's chair of the history and philosophy of the inductive sciences at the University of Vienna. The circle was merely a private seminar arranged by Schlick, whose members were invited by him to participate. Hayek attended lectures by Schlick, although he was never a member of the Vienna circle or a logical positivist.

Logical positivism should not be confused with the French nineteenth-century positivism of Auguste Comte, which Hayek criticized in *The Counter-Revolution of Science.* Comte's positivism sheds light, however, on the twentieth-century variety. Comte coined the term (in French) *positivisme* from *positif,* which in French has more of a connotation of material reality (as opposed to certainty) than its English equivalent "positive." The more physically material aspect of positivism in its French origin helps to explain the later philosophical etymology of the term. Comte attempted to construct a science of society based on strictly material—as opposed to metaphysical or theological—knowledge. He was not concerned predominantly with the nature of truth or knowledge per se, as twentieth-century logical positivists were. His concern was the societal implications of his theory.

Prominent later logical positivist themes included the essentiality of verification to knowledge; the exclusive meaningfulness of mathematics, logic, and science as knowledge; and the rejection (in terms of knowledge) of ethics, metaphysics, and religion. Logical positivists were concerned with the foundations of knowledge: What makes something true, or how is truth applicable to sensory impression/reception? They drew heavily on the work of earlier British empiricists such as David Hume, who believed knowledge must ultimately be reducible to sense impressions, and more recent philosophers of mathematics, logic, and science such as Ludwig Wittgenstein and Bertrand Russell. An essential outlook of the Vienna circle and logical positivists generally may be captured in the statement of Schlick that "the meaning of a proposition is its method of verification."[5] Verification was central in the logical positivist schema. Propositions must be made in a manner that is empirically verifiable in order to be scientific.

Hayek's objection to logical positivism may be gathered in part from the following passage from *The Constitution of Liberty* where he stated that he did not "wish to underestimate the merit of the persistent and relentless fight of the eighteenth and nineteenth centuries against beliefs which are demonstrably false. But extension of the concept of superstition to all beliefs which are not demonstrably true lacks the same justification and may often be harmful. That we ought not believe anything which has been shown to be false does not mean that we ought to believe only what has been demonstrated to be true."[6]

Hayek had a more tentative, yet broader, conception of knowledge than logical positivists. Truth is not restricted, Hayek believed, to what can be empirically proven. Indeed, with Popper and Friedman, he thought that there is no such thing as absolute proof; and that the best fraction of truth that can be obtained is always subject to further revision. This tentative conception of truth is to some extent related to the ideas that not all knowledge can be expressed in words and of the undirected, evolutionary development of society.

∿

Hayek commented in his autobiographical notes that his interest in psychology was stimulated mainly by his interest in the work of physicist and epistemologist

Ernst Mach. It was in reading Mach's philosophical writings that Hayek "conceived the idea which I vainly tried to explain in a brief paper in 1920 and finally published thirty-two years later in *The Sensory Order.*"[7]

Logical positivism and Hayek's psychological ideas were separate offshoots from Mach's work. Hayek said of Mach's *Analysis of Sensations* in a 1977 paper that his

> acute analysis of how what he regarded as the elementary pure sensations corresponding to the individual sensory stimuli came to be further organized by such acquired properties as local signs as a result of experience made me, in a sudden flash of insight, perceive that the presumed core of sensation originally attached to the afferent [initiating] impulse was a superfluous assumption, and that all attributes of sense experience (and soon after that, *all* mental qualities) might be explained in some way by their place in a system of connections. I began to see that there were two orders in which we could conceive of the same set of events—two orders that were in some respects similar but yet differed in exactly that way in which our sensory picture of the world and our scientific conception of it differed from each other.
>
> The conclusion that the world of our mental qualities provided us with an imperfect generic map with its own units existing only in that mental universe, yet serving to guide us more or less successfully in our environment, led me to a philosophical view of the relation between the physical and the sensory world that then had been recently revived by the physicist Max Planck, but that really goes back to Galileo Galilei, who in 1623 had written: "I think that these tastes, odors, colors, etc. are nothing else than mere names, but hold their residence solely in the sensitive body, so that, if the animal were removed, any such quality would be abolished and annihilated."
>
> My conclusion at an early stage was thus that mental events are a particular order of physical events within a subsystem of the physical world that relates the larger subsystem of the world that we call an organism (and of which they are a part) with the whole system so as to enable that organism to survive.[8]

His work here was also in the tradition of Kant, who held that sensory experience occurs in an organism rather than possessing separate ontological status.

Perhaps the most interesting and relevant portion of *The Sensory Order* concerns the "Philosophical Consequences" of Hayek's ideas, which he titled the book's last chapter. He wrote the book in part to show the extreme limits of knowledge of the physical world. Just as there is a limit to what an individual can know of the sensory world of perception, there is even more of a limit to what an individual can know of the actual physical world; indeed, according to Hayek, one can ultimately know nothing at all of the actual, physical world.

In both Hayek's economic and psychological thought, the limits of knowledge are key. The sensory, as societal, world is complex. In both the sensory and societal worlds, the idea of complexity is, in Hayek's thought, paramount. Complexity prevents detailed prediction and control.

He believed that consciousness is determined through an evolutionary process. He held in *The Sensory Order* that the "apparatus [mind] by means of which we learn about the external world is the product of a kind of experience."[9] He wrote in *The Counter-Revolution of Science* that the "classification of the stimuli in our central nervous system is probably highly 'pragmatic' in the sense that it stresses those relations between the external world and our body which in the course of evolution have proved significant for the survival of the species."[10] Evolution runs through his thought in psychology, economics, and societal order. He significantly attributed to *The Sensory Order* the "revival of my interest in the field of biological evolution,"[11] an idea he subsequently applied to societal order.

He always intended to resume work on psychological issues and his student paper of a quarter-century before. He said in introducing *The Sensory Order* that the "few years for which I then thought to put the draft away have become a much longer period." The book was the "outcome of an idea which suggested itself to me as a very young man."[12]

He felt that his work in psychology was not appreciated, and it has not been, other than by a very small number of academic psychologists. For him, however, the "insights I gained both from the first stage in 1920 or later in the 1940s, were probably the most exciting events that ever occurred to me, which shaped my thinking."[13] They taught him a "great deal on the methodology of science, apart from the special subject. What I wrote on the subject, the theory of complex phenomena, is equally the product of my work in economics and my work in psychology."[14]

He remarked in a 1977 conference regarding his economic and psychological thought that in "both cases we have complex phenomena in which there is a need for a method of utilizing widely dispersed knowledge."[15] There is a similarity between the general conception of the physical world that each person is able to form, psychologically, and the desirability of general rules to guide societies. Neither specific individual knowledge nor specific societal control are possible; the best that can be hoped for, Hayek thought, is knowledge of a pattern of the physical world and construction of a legal framework within which individual decision making may occur.

There is another tie between Hayek's psychological, economic, and societal thought. Heinrich Klüver wrote in introducing *The Sensory Order* that from a "broad point of view his theory may be said to substantiate Goethe's maxim 'all that factual is already theory' for the field of sensory and other psychological phenomena. . . . Perception is always an interpretation."[16] In Hayek's other thought, too, he stressed that theory precedes empirical observation.

Knowledge is divided, incomplete, and complex. Each person's fragment of knowledge is infinitesimally miniscule. The idea that the only predictions that are possible as complexity increases are more and more general predictions is congruent with a societal system in which only the broadest parameters for action are established. Laws overcome the complexity of society. In a 1948 letter, he described his work in psychology as "the most important thing I have yet done;"[17] he also expressed years later that "no one understands it yet."[18]

On several occasions late in life, Hayek expressed the view that in "the middle '40s—I suppose I sound very conceited—I think I was known as one of the two main disputing economists: There was Keynes and there was I. Now, Keynes died [in April 1946] and became a saint; and I discredited myself by publishing *The Road to Serfdom*."[19] He said on another occasion that "while Keynes was disputed as long as he was alive—very much so—after his death he was raised to sainthood. I had a period of twenty years in which I bitterly regretted having once mentioned to my wife after Keynes' death [that] I was probably the best-known economist living. But ten days later it was probably no longer true. [laughter] At that very moment Keynes became the great figure, and I was gradually forgotten as an economist."[20]

Hayek's view that on Keynes' death he was considered one of the two leading economists is not shared by others. Coase says that, in Britain, "others would not have thought that."[21] According to Friedman, this "certainly would not have been true in the United States. At no time in the United States that I can remember would Keynes' name have been linked with Hayek as of the same eminence in economics. In fact I would say Robbins would have been more likely to have been linked with Keynes in the American world."[22] Hayek experienced the greatest popular attention in his life to date during the spring of 1945 in both the United States and Great Britain. He undoubtedly saw his ideas in *The Road to Serfdom* emanating from his earlier work in a way not as apparent to adversaries or friends. After Labour won the 1945 general election in a landslide—and after the criticism inflicted on him during his United States tour and the British general election campaign—he "ceased," according to some of his "more leftish acquaintances," to be a "scientist and had become a propagandist."[23] Hayek the thinker became Hayek the symbol in England as well as America following Labour's 1945 British victory.

Hayek's contemporary correspondence indicates that he subsequently thought he made a mistake to remain in Britain following the war. He drifted away from his colleagues at LSE. While he had many articles published in *Economica* during the 1930s and early '40s, following the article on the history of LSE in the February 1946 edition, he had nothing published in the LSE journal during his last four years in London. He wrote to L. B. Miller of the Bureau of Governmental Research in November 1947 saying that he felt useless and unappreciated in Britain, that he taught too much, that his views were considered extreme, and that his advice went unheeded—adding that he should have accepted earlier offers of positions in the United States.[24]

In 1948, Hayek considered a postscript to *The Road to Serfdom,* incorporating developments since its publication. He was distressed by actions of the postwar Labour government, in particular the nationalization and greater regulation of significant aspects of the British economy. Interestingly, Hayek intended to use as an epigraph for this possible postscript the epigraph by Lord Acton that he ultimately chose for the postscript of *The Constitution of Liberty,* that "at all times friends of freedom have been rare, and its triumphs have been due to minorities, that have prevailed by associating themselves with auxiliaries whose objects often differed from their own; and this association, which is always dangerous, has sometimes been disastrous."[25] Perhaps the structure of his later work was distantly taking shape in his mind.

Bruce Caldwell, editor of the ninth and tenth volumes of Hayek's *Collected Works,* writes that "Hayek's stay in England ended sadly. Politically, all that he had fought against was coming to pass."[26] Subsequent history affected how *The Road to Serfdom* became remembered in retrospect. Election of the first majority Labour government led to, as it reflected, a new spirit in which the book was less appealing and more reactionary. Discovery of the Holocaust by the general publics in Britain and the United States made the work appear more extreme. The end of wartime alliance with the Soviet Union and postwar prosperity made it less relevant. Hayek became considered a conservative flash-in-the-pan in the public mind.

The Road to Serfdom was immediately translated into several other European languages and has subsequently appeared in a score worldwide. Hayek noted the "particularly cordial reception by the post-Nazi generation of Germany."[27] He had his "most moving experience" as a lecturer in postwar

Germany. He "discovered that people were circulating hand-typed copies of *The Road to Serfdom,* although it hadn't been published in Germany yet."[28] He lectured elsewhere on the Continent as well.

He visited Austria for the first time during the postwar period in 1946 to see his future wife and other relatives. He usually traveled alone. Once, visiting Stanford, he was put up as the only occupant in a large, common room dorm, which he considered an intentional slight by the administration because of his political views.

CHAPTER TWENTY

Popper

HAYEK'S FINAL YEAR IN ENGLAND was marked by his divorce, which caused a painful rupture in his friendship with Robbins. In a wartime letter to Karl Popper, Hayek described Robbins as his "closest friend whose opinion I value most highly."[1] This happy circumstance did not continue. Hayek left his first wife, Hella, at the end of 1949, divorcing her in 1950 in Arkansas, to which he moved to take advantage of permissive divorce laws. He married his second wife, Helene, in Vienna weeks later.

Robbins considered Hayek's treatment of his first wife to be atrocious. The breach between the two men went deep. Robbins resigned from the Mont Pelerin Society. He wrote in a June 1950 letter that Hayek "behaved in such a way which I find impossible to reconcile with the conception of his character and his standards which I have cherished through twenty years of friendship. As far as I am concerned, the man I knew is dead and I should find it almost intolerably painful to have to meet his successor."[2] The two were not reconciled until after Hella Hayek's death. They re-established their friendship—which again became close—at the wedding of Hayek's son, Larry, in 1961.

Hayek and Robbins' break had important consequences for LSE and academic economic liberalism in Britain. The two leading figures went their separate ways, and Hayek left the country. Robbins was less influential in academic economics during the 1950s and '60s as he moved in the direction of Keynes' middle way than he had been during the 1930s. His practical influence as a pillar of the British establishment substantially increased. He chaired the Committee on Higher Education in Britain from 1961 to 1963, which recommended significant expansion of the higher educational system, and became the leading institutional figure at LSE. Hayek was virtually forgotten in England during the 1950s and '60s. The London-based Institute of Economic Affairs, of which Arthur Seldon served as the editorial director, became almost the only organization that continued to promote him and his work in the country during this period.

The one friendship that Hayek retained at LSE was with Karl Popper, in part because he and his former wife had not known Popper as long and as well as they had known Robbins and the others in economics. Popper only came to the school to teach after World War II and was in the philosophy department.

Popper was deeply appreciative for Hayek's practical assistance to him. At a memorial meeting at LSE in Hayek's honor, he recalled their first meeting:

> My lifelong friendship with Fritz Hayek began in September or October of 1935, when I knocked at the door of his study here. He was only three years older, and I had heard of him in Vienna; but we had never met. He was young and famous, and I was an unknown schoolteacher. I had a letter of recommendation from Professor Hans Kelsen, then teaching political theory in Vienna. Kelsen had told me to visit Hayek, but had warned me that he and Hayek were not seeing eye to eye.
>
> So when I knocked on Hayek's door, having just arrived in London for the first time, I felt anything but confident. Yet Hayek received me with more than friendliness. He assured me that he had been told by his friend Gottfried Haberler that he must read a book I had published a year earlier in Vienna [*The Logic of Scientific Discovery*]. So I gave him a copy; and he assured me that he would read it at once and that, if I came back next week, he would have read it. And when I came back, he really had and with great care. . . . At this second meeting, in which he mainly discussed my book, he asked me to read a paper in his seminar. You can imagine that this was great encouragement.[3]

In a December 1943 letter, Popper wrote that Hayek's "indefatigable kindness to me promises no less than to change the whole course of my life."[4] He wrote a few days later, "Nobody can feel more strongly than I feel about Hayek."[5] In his autobiography, Popper said that his friend Ernst Gombrich, "together with Hayek, who most generously offered his help (I had not dared to trouble him since I had seen him only a few times in my life)," found a publisher for *The Open Society and Its Enemies* (1945), which became Popper's most famous work. Popper continued his praise, "Both wrote most encouragingly about the book. I felt that these two had saved my life, and I still feel so."[6]

Hayek played a crucial role as well in securing Popper's readership at LSE following the war. Popper was the one individual to whom Hayek dedicated one of his books, *Studies in Philosophy, Politics and Economics* (1967).[7] Popper dedicated *Conjectures and Refutations* (1963) to Hayek.

Hayek stated a considerable intellectual debt to Popper. He remarked in an interview that:

> my introduction to what I now almost hesitate to call philosophy—scientific method, I think, is a better description—was to Machian philosophy. It dominated discussion in Vienna. It was the beginning of the Vienna Circle, of whom I was never a member but whose members were in close contact with us. . . .
>
> Well, what converted me is that the social scientists, the science specialists in the tradition of Otto Neurath, just were so extreme and so naive on economics that it was through [Neurath] that I became aware that positivism was just as misleading. . . . I owe it to his extreme position that I soon recognized it wouldn't do.
>
> And it took me a long time, really, to emancipate myself from it. It was only after I had left Vienna, in London, that I began to think systematically on problems of methodology in the social sciences, and I began to recognize that positivism in that field was definitely misleading.
>
> In a discussion I had on a visit to Vienna from London with my friend Haberler, I explained to him that I had come to the conclusion that all this Machian positivism was no good for our purposes. Then he countered, "Oh, there's a very good new book by a man called Karl Popper on the logic of scientific research." To me it was so satisfactory because it confirmed this certain view I had already formed.[8]

British economic historian and theorist Terence W. Hutchison, who knew Hayek and Popper and whose work was well thought of by them, perceptively discusses the development of Hayek's methodological views. Hutchison identifies two phases in Hayek's methodological thought, the first—"Hayek I"—extending to about 1936 and following a Wieserian and Misesian perspective, and the second—"Hayek II"—extending from about 1937 and incorporating a Popperian view.

Hayek followed an almost exclusively Misesian-Wieserian methodology early in his career. This methodology proposes that knowledge is internal and given to men and women. Empirical findings can be used to confirm theories, but not to refute them. Economic theory is based on self-evident axioms. Theory precedes empirical observation. Hutchison quotes Hayek on these themes in *Collectivist Economic Planning*: "'The essential basic facts which we need for the explanation of social phenomena are part of common experience, part of the stuff of our thinking. In the social sciences it is the elements of the complex phenomena *which are known beyond the possibility of dispute* [Hutchison's emphasis]. In the natural sciences they can be at best only surmised. The existence of these elements is so much more certain than any regularities in the complex phenomena to which they give rise that it is they which constitute the truly empirical factor in the social sciences.'"[9]

Hutchison states the "extreme closeness" of Hayek, in his 1935 *Collectivist Economic Planning* introduction, to Wieser and Mises concerning the "two fundamental points of (a) the infallibilist irrefutability of 'the essential basic facts of economics'; and (b) the fundamental contrast between the methods and basic postulates of the social sciences and those of the natural sciences—a contrast drawn with about equally preposterous pretentiousness by Wieser, Mises, and Hayek in favour of economics as a social science."[10] That is, Wieser, Mises, and "Hayek I" thought that, because of self-evident knowledge, economics is potentially capable of more precise statement than the physical sciences.

"Hayek II" adopted a more Popperian view. The question here is not of the provenance of ideas, but of ideas themselves. Hutchison specifically notes that he "renounce[s] any speculations regarding influence."[11] Hayek intended his 1937 "Economics and Knowledge" to explain why he could not accept Mises' a priorism. Hayek adopted a more empirical approach in part of his thought through "Economics and Knowledge," though he simultaneously retained a theoretical emphasis. Hayek said that he never adopted an a priori approach.

The question of Hayek and Popper's intellectual relationship is debated, and some of the gist is that Popper claimed, at least during his last years and after Hayek's demise, more influence on Hayek than was the case and, surely, than Hayek thought to be so. In the same memorial talk in which he described his first meetings with Hayek, Popper continued, "I shall not attempt to say anything about Hayek as an economist. But I may perhaps say a word about Hayek's two great works on the legal framework of a free society . . . *The Constitution of Liberty* [and] *Law, Legislation and Liberty*. I think that I may have had some little influence in turning his interest in this direction—simply because I stressed again and again in some of our conversations that the fight against what was then called, and criticized— especially by Ludwig von Mises—as protectionism, or state-protectionism, could not be conducted in the way of Mises; because in a complex society, anything approaching a free market could only exist if it enjoyed the protection of laws, and therefore of the state. Thus the term 'free market' should always be placed in inverted commas, since it was always bound, or limited, by a legal framework and made possible only by this framework."[12] That is, Popper claimed credit for Hayek's major positive contribution during the last fifty years of his life—the central role of law to establish or create a classical liberal or libertarian order.

Events in Great Britain gradually resumed a normal course following World War II, although the new cold war with the Soviet Union replaced hot war with Germany and Japan. The place of the United States grew phenomenally in the world at the end of World War II with its possession of nuclear weapons and its unrivaled economic production, approximately half of the world's total in the years immediately following World War II.

After the war, Hayek performed a six-week social survey in Gibraltar from which a government report resulted. He was later asked by the British government to do a similar study of Cyprus, but declined. A contemporary political group with which he involved himself was the "Justice for South Tyrol" committee, which sought the return of this area from Italy (which acquired it after World War I) to Austria. He was a frequent contributor to popular media on contemporary issues throughout his life.

Former student Marjorie Grice-Huchinson remembers that in 1947-48, she was

> privileged to follow the series of lectures that Hayek introduced as "a guide to the historiography of economic science." He generally strolled up and down while lecturing, and he talked in a conversational tone, without emphasis or pedantry. His excellent memory and wide humanistic background allowed him to present attractively the ideas of philosophers, jurists, politicians and businessmen of many countries and every period, and he had no difficulty in holding the attention of the large numbers of students who always filled his classroom.
>
> In the first of the twenty lectures that made up the course, Hayek gave us titles of some of the manuals that he thought would be useful for our studies. Among their authors were Alexander Gray, Edwin Cannan, James Bonar, J. A. Schumpeter, August Oncken, Jacob Viner, Charles Gide and Charles Rist. He recommended Erich Roll's *History of Economic Thought*, although Roll was at that time a Marxist. No fewer than nine lectures were devoted to pre-Smithian economic thought, and Hayek always stressed the importance of the earlier writers. I need hardly say that those of us who were thinking of specialising in the history of economics were encouraged to work on original sources.[13]

Grice-Hutchinson also recalls that Hayek "distinguish[ed] in general terms between what he regarded as the two main sources of economic thought, the philosophical and the empirical or practical. The course was chiefly concerned with tracing the origin and development of these two great ideological streams and their mutual relationship, beginning with Greek philosophy and ending with Keynes." She recalls him personally as "courteous but rather aloof," and that he was very helpful to students, including herself, in turning thesis materials into a book. This included practical assistance to secure a publisher.[14]

Former student Henry Toch recollects that he attended Hayek's "Savings and Investment" lectures during the late 1940s, and "the general mood was Socialist, most students in receipt of Labour Government grants and Hugh Dalton becoming a Cabinet Minister. I recall that Prof. Hayek closed his lecture course with words to this effect, 'If you agree with my analysis, put it in your examination answers, but make sure that you argue the case well, since mine is not the accepted view and you may lose marks.' The response was a resounding cheer from the audience, which was quite unusual." Toch also recalls that Hayek participated in Robbins' graduate seminar in 1949, where his comments were "brief, to the point and brilliant."[15] Clearly, the relationship between Hayek and Robbins was changing. This was not the seminar of the early 1930s.

Hayek and Popper corresponded extensively during the latter part of the war, though they did not know each other well. Popper sought Hayek's assistance and ideas in publishing *The Open Society* and then in obtaining his readership at the LSE. He wrote Hayek as often as every two weeks or so between mid 1943 and early 1945. They did not use first names in their wartime correspondence.

Popper completed *The Open Society and Its Enemies* in February 1943. In July, Hayek wrote him that "I have been particularly interested in what you say about your work, as it seems to be extraordinarily close to what I have been doing myself at present."[16] In May 1944, Popper received a copy of *The Road to Serfdom,* which he considered a "most exciting event." He wrote Hayek that "when I came to the passage in the preface in which you described the writing of the book as 'a duty which I must not evade,' I felt that you were driven by fundamentally the same experience which made me write my book."[17]

According to Jeremy Shearmur, who served as Popper's research assistant for eight years, so "astonishingly close" did Popper find some of Hayek's ideas in *The Road to Serfdom* to what he himself was working on that Popper had the "dates on which he had completed the manuscript of his *Open Society* added to the text, to ensure that it did not look as if he had made use of Hayek's ideas without acknowledgement."[18] At the same time, Shearmur writes, "Hayek seemed to him [Popper] to have come from a very different starting-point. . . . Popper privately expressed some unease as to whether Hayek's views were not more conservative than his own; at the way in which—as distinct from the thrust of his own *Open Society*—Hayek did not seem to show as much concern for the protection of the weak, and at the way in which Hayek's work was warmly received by conservatives."[19] Hayek offered to write a preface for *The Open Society,* but in a 1945 letter to his friend Ernst Gombrich, Popper said that he had declined this offer because "I am too proud," and it would "brand the book and myself."[20]

Malachi Haim Hacohen offers perhaps the best views of Popper's intellectual development and Hayek's influence on him. Hacohen emphasizes the Viennese intellectual milieu in Vienna during the decades between World Wars I and II. He sees Popper as having intellectually evolved in a far more radical and logical positivist environment. While Hayek moved in a classical liberal direction as a student, Popper was a communist. Moreover, whereas Hayek was Catholic, Popper was of Jewish ancestry.

Interwar Vienna was a unique place. It was a city of no political power, and as the 1930s progressed, it was only a matter of time before Hitler would subsume control. Austria lost its political independence from Germany during the '30s. As many leftwing and Jewish public intellectuals as possible left Vienna during the middle and later '30s, until 1938.

Popper's ideas came to maturity in the realm including the Vienna circle of logical positivists, although Popper never considered himself to be a logical positivist and, indeed, thought that he had conclusively refuted the premises on which logical positivism is founded. Hacohen writes that Hayek's *Counter-Revolution of Science* essays originally published in *Economica* during World War II "opened his [Popper's] eyes. He discovered a range of discourse on social science unknown to him," and that these essays particularly influenced the last two parts of Popper's "The Poverty of Historicism." At the same time, Hacohen affirms that while "Hayek managed to corrupt [Popper's] socialism," Popper remained considerably to Hayek's political left.[21]

In 1944, Popper wrote to Hayek, "I think that I have learnt more from you than from any other living thinker, except perhaps Alfred Tarski,"[22] and forty years later wrote in a letter to Hayek that Hayek became "a kind of father figure"[23] to him, though they were only three years apart. Nonetheless, Hacohen states that Popper "never accepted Hayek's superiority," and "notwithstanding profuse thanks and adoration, he never accepted Hayek's, or anyone's, authority."[24] Hayek did not develop as close an intellectual relationship with Popper as Hayek would have liked.

Jeremy Shearmur offers thoughts on Popper and Hayek's intellectual relationship. Essentially, he does not see this as having been especially extensive. He remarks in *The Political Thought of Karl Popper* (1996) that "while Popper read some of Hayek's writings when he was in New Zealand and made acknowledgement to them in his work, and while he was later to be influenced by some of Hayek's ideas that he came across after writing *The Open Society,* there does not seem to have been any close intellectual link between them. This made it something of a shock to Popper when, after he had completed *The Open Society and Its Enemies,* he found that Hayek had come to conclusions in some ways similar to his own. . . . Hayek's work was later to make some impact on Popper's social philosophy, notably in respect of his ideas about the importance of institutional procedures as opposed to individual discretion in government. At the same time, it seems to me that while in New Zealand he did not, and did not subsequently, pay much attention to Hayek's argument concerning economic calculation under socialism—an argument which is crucial for the shaping of Hayek's social theory."[25]

Historian of political thought Michael Lessnoff confirms this interpretation. He writes of Hayek and Popper that the "works of each contain laudatory references to the other. Nevertheless, although there are points of similarity in their views, as well as reciprocal influence, the resemblance is less than each, doubtless motivated by their strong personal friendship, seeks to suggest."[26]

Popper perhaps became Hayek's closest friend during the 1950s and '60s, in considerable part because his former friends in economics, most prominently Lionel Robbins, turned their backs so thoroughly on him. This cannot have been easy.

In his 1966 preface to *Studies in Philosophy, Politics and Economics,* Hayek wrote that his earlier readers might notice a "slight change" in his discussion of what he termed "scientism"—the misapplication of positivist, natural sciences approaches to the social sciences. He ascribed this change to Popper, who taught him that "natural scientists did not really do what most of them not only told us that they did but also urged the representatives of other disciplines to imitate. The difference between the two groups of disciplines has thereby been greatly narrowed."[27] Popper's influence here was mostly in Hayek's understanding of the actual scientific method in the natural sciences, which is appropriately tentative in its conceptions of knowledge and truth.

Both Popper and Hayek directed their work in this stage of their careers largely to the left—to rational and secular philosophers and thinkers. In a 1944 letter to the publishing house Routledge, Popper said concerning *The Open Society* that "I feel that nothing is so important at the present time as an attempt to get over the fateful desertion within the camp of the friends of the 'Open Society,' i.e. the camp of humanitarianism, or, if I may say so, within the camp of the 'Left,' if this term is used to include liberals who appreciate the need for social reform."[28] Hayek dedicated *The Road to Serfdom* to "the socialists of all parties," and remarked in his 1945 radio panel on *The Road to Serfdom* that it was not an "attack on socialists; it is rather an attempt to persuade socialists, to whom I have dedicated my book. My main thesis is that they are mistaken in the methods for getting what they want to achieve."[29] He said later that *The Road to Serfdom* had a "very specific purpose: persuading my English Fabian colleagues that they were wrong."[30] The book was an argument to the left from one who largely shared its ethical, though not empirical, views.

Hayek's perspective of the world exalts the spirit—the power of individuals, in freedom and in truth, to build a life fit for themselves and others to live. This is, as he termed it, utopian, though not in the sense of attempting or expecting to attain what is impossible. It is attempting to achieve the best possible. This conception is, moreover, consistent with the Christian one that what is important in life is purity of spirit, that good actions, performed for the wrong reasons, do not justify their doer, and all actions, performed for the right reasons, do. There is only one Christian way forward, and that is in freedom and in truth, for individuals to demonstrate their faithfulness through the voluntary performance of righteous actions. This may not have been Hayek's justification for liberty, but the upshot of his position was similar. Philosophies that attempt to take freedom away from people in order to make them better only destroy what makes people human. Freedom is not just the best, but the only human way.

The conception of human nature on which human freedom is based is, moreover, highly optimistic. Hayek's philosophy is ultimately no more and no less than an injunction to follow the truth wherever it leads. He believed that, left to themselves in the right circumstances, men and women can create decent and even good communities for themselves and others. Such communities would be ones in which all would flourish, because all would be free. There can be no common progress without individual progress, and no individual progress without liberty.

Hayek's views on the power of the individual spirit exalt human individuality and the freedom of the will. He did not believe that men's actions are determined. He rejected both philosophical and scientific determinism. Individuals are, in a deep metaphysical sense, and therefore should be in a practical, political sense, able to design their lives to some considerable degree as they choose. How individuals use their freedom defines them. To deprive others of their freedom steals their humanity.

Near the end of *The Road to Serfdom,* Hayek commented on the "proper field of morals, individual conduct. . . . Issues in this field have become so confused that it is necessary to go back to fundamentals. What our generation is in danger of forgetting is not only that morals are of necessity a phenomenon of individual conduct but also that they can exist only in the sphere in which the individual is free to decide for himself and is called upon voluntarily to sacrifice personal advantage to the observance of a moral rule. The members of a society who in all respects are *made* to do the good thing have no title to praise."[31] He held in *The Constitution of Liberty* that "liberty is an opportunity for doing good. We praise or blame only when a person has the opportunity to choose."[32]

Hayek emphasized the vital significance of the individual in developing ideas, and the concomitant desirability of, in a Hayekian sense, personal freedom, within which alone are personal morality and ethics possible. Classical liberals and libertarians claim a higher moral ground than classical socialists—that humanity may in freedom and in truth create a better life for themselves than under any form of collectivism. Hayek quoted Lord Acton in *The Road to Serfdom* that liberty is "'not a means to a higher political end. It is itself the highest political end.'"[33]

FOUR

AMERICA

1950 – 1962

"To the unknown civilization that is growing in America"
—dedication of The Constitution of Liberty

CHAPTER TWENTY-ONE

University of Chicago

THE UNIVERSITY OF CHICAGO long had been known to Hayek as a bulwark of free market views. While he had some disputes with Frank Knight over capital theory during the 1930s, he thought that Knight was the leader of the American libertarian movement. Together with Mises in Vienna and Edwin Cannan in London Hayek thought that Knight helped to preserve liberal thought during the decades after World War I and helped to prepare the way for new growth of liberal ideas. Henry Simons of the University of Chicago corresponded with Hayek in 1939.

Hayek probably would not have come to the United States on a permanent basis if it had not been for personal, family considerations. He became "completely assimilated"[1] to Great Britain during the 1930s and '40s. Not only did he become a naturalized British citizen, but his sympathies and outlooks took on a distinctly British cast, particularly because of World War II. His children grew up in Britain.

Hayek and his future, second wife, Helene, had been unhappy in their first marriages for a number of years. According to Hayek in 1948 correspondence with Harold Luhnow, president of the Volcker Fund, which paid his salary at the University of Chicago, and in 1950 correspondence with Karl Popper, he and his second wife did not marry when they were young because of simple miscommunication. Helene then married someone else, and Hayek married someone he thought resembled her. Hayek and Helene, who were distant cousins, had been best friends since childhood. They remained in close contact after they were married, and considered divorce as early as the 1930s.

Hayek did not see Helene for over seven years, from 1939 to 1946, as a result of World War II. He sought a relatively high paying position on the Committee on Social Thought at the University of Chicago largely because this would provide the funds to maintain his family in England and himself and Helene.[2]

Following his spring 1945 tour of the United States to promote *The Road to Serfdom*, Hayek returned again to North America in 1946, spending a month at the University of Chicago, a month at Stanford University, and visiting Mexico. He traveled to his family in Vienna in 1946 as well. In 1947, he traveled to Mont Pelerin, and in 1948 he spent the spring at the University of Chicago and the summer at the University of Vienna.

He originally sought an appointment at the Institute for Advanced Studies in Princeton, with which Einstein was affiliated, when he sought to come to the United States after World War II. However, the Institute would not accept someone whose salary would be specifically donated. Jacob Viner (the other major figure with Frank Knight in free market economics at Chicago from the 1920s through mid '40s) now taught at Princeton.

The University of Chicago was one of the several most influential universities in the world during the twentieth century. Of the approximately 400 Nobel Prizes awarded during the twentieth century in Physics, Chemistry, Medicine, and Economics, over sixty were received by individuals associated with the University of Chicago at one time or another as faculty, students, or researchers (though for a number of these recipients, including Hayek, their main academic affiliation was elsewhere). Particularly in Economics—for which the Nobel was instituted in 1969—Chicago has dominated, with a third of total recipients. In Physics, too, the university has had a vastly disproportionate share of Nobel Prize winners associated with it, more than 25.

In a November 1948 letter to John Nef, chairman of the Committee on Social Thought at the University of Chicago, Hayek accepted a position and indicated that he would like to fill it the following fall, in 1949.[3] However, Hayek was unable to obtain a divorce from his first wife in England and was required to go to the United States to obtain a divorce.

Hayek left his first wife and children on December 27, 1949. He flew to New York, where he attended the American Economic Association convention from December 29, 1949, to January 2, 1950. While there, he slipped a note under the door of Harold Dulan, chair of the economics and business department at the University of Arkansas at Fayetteville. (Arkansas had permissive divorce laws.) He wondered whether the department would be interested in him as a visiting professor. Dulan replied affirmatively. Hayek spent the winter quarter in a visiting capacity at the University of Chicago and the spring quarter at the University of Arkansas. He did not teach courses in Fayetteville, but visited classes, met with professors and graduate students, and gave public lectures. John Kane, then an associate professor in economics, remembers Hayek as "very useful, very helpful,"[4] and going to faculty members' houses for meals and discussion.

Hayek's divorce was granted on July 13, 1950, in the chancery court of Washington County, Arkansas. He then married Helene Bitterlich in Vienna, before returning to Chicago for the autumn term.

The divorce was acrimonious. Hella Hayek's opposition to the divorce in response to Hayek's determined perseverance that he must have it led to highly charged personal conditions the last year and a half that he was in England. In February 1950, Hayek submitted his letter of resignation to the London School of Economics. There was no going back.

Hayek was, as his family remains, very reluctant to discuss his divorce and remarriage. He had this exchange in 1978:

> Q: I want to ask you one question which is impertinent. But it's serious, and I hope that maybe you will be willing to answer it. Forgive me for asking it, but I detect a strong respect for moral standards and their importance in society. Now, all of us in our lifetime have faced problems where we have said, "Here is a moral standard, and I want to break it." You must have had some. Would you be willing to maybe indicate what some of them were?
>
> A: . . . I know I've done wrong in enforcing divorce. Well, it's a curious story. I married on the rebound when the girl I loved, a cousin, married somebody else. She is now my present wife. But for twenty-five years I was married to the girl whom I married on the rebound, who was a very good wife to me, but I wasn't happy in that marriage. She refused to give me a divorce, and finally I enforced it. I'm sure that was wrong, and yet I have done it. It was just an inner need to do it.[5]

When asked as a follow-up question whether he would divorce and remarry again, he responded affirmatively, but only after a pause, deliberation, obvious discomfort, and qualifying his answer with "probably."[6]

Hayek saw very little of his children during the 1950s while he was in the United States. They remained in England with their mother. His daughter remembers him taking her on one or two trips during the '50s to Italy and France, and his son also remembers traveling with his father. Hayek's son and daughter were, respectively, fifteen and twenty at the time of the divorce.

CHAPTER TWENTY-TWO

Chicago School of Economics

IT IS IMPORTANT TO BE CLEAR about the distinction between the Chicago school of economics and the economics department at the University of Chicago in order to understand why Hayek did not obtain a position in the economics department at the University of Chicago. Hayek recalled that his early University of Chicago links began during the 1930s with Lionel Robbins' "admiration for Knight's *Risk, Uncertainty and Profit*. And it so happened that later Robbins became very intimately interested in the work of Jacob Viner." Both Viner and Knight were "very well known figures" among Hayek and his fellow economists at LSE; they both lectured there during the '30s, and Hayek came to know them personally, as well as their work. He referred to the "London/Chicago relation in the '30s."[1]

Milton Friedman traces the origins of the Chicago school of economics to James Laughlin, the first chair of economics at the University of Chicago when it opened in 1892. Laughlin was a monetary reformer and leading opponent of the free silver movement. At the turn of the century, he served as a member of the Indianapolis Monetary Commission, and was author of its final report, which was an important step toward the 1913 Federal Reserve Act. Laughlin was closely allied with the Republican Party.

Laughlin's "most important and lasting contribution," Friedman writes, was as chairman of what became the Department of Economics at the University of Chicago. Laughlin "demonstrated an extraordinary degree of tolerance for divergent views in staffing and guiding the Department." Friedman emphasizes that in "more recent years, as in his day, the Department has been widely regarded as a stronghold of proponents of a free market economy. The reputation was justified in the sense that throughout that period the Department had prominent members who held these views and presented them effectively. But they were . . . a minority. The Department has been characterized by heterogeneity of policy views, not homogeneity."[2]

The individual who is sometimes identified as the founder of an explicit Chicago school of economics is Knight, who was born in 1885 and died in 1972. Freidman, George Stigler, Henry Simons, Aaron Director, and others were Knight's students or influenced by him. Knight's personality was well depicted in a story Stigler told about his youth, "Under the suasion of their deeply religious parents, the children signed pledges at church to attend church the rest of their lives. Returning home, Frank (then fourteen or fifteen) gathered the children behind the barn, built a fire, and said, 'Burn these things because pledges and promises made under duress are not binding.'"[3] Knight was an iconoclast. The standing joke at Chicago about him was, "There is no God, but Frank Knight is his prophet." Buchanan says that to Knight, "nothing was sacrosanct, not the dogmas of religion, not the laws and institutions of social order, not the prevailing moral norms, not the accepted interpretations of sacred or profane texts. Anything and everything was a potential subject for critical scrutiny, with an evaluative judgment to be informed by, but ultimately made independently of, external influence. The Knightian stance before gods, men and history embodies a courage and self-confidence that upsets the self-satisfied propounders of all the little orthodoxies, then and now."[4]

Of Viner—the other leading economist at Chicago from the 1920s through middle 1940s—Friedman writes that the "first quarter I was at Chicago, the fall of 1932, one course, with Jacob Viner, who was a great teacher, had a major effect. Viner's course in theory opened up a new world. He made me realize that economic theory was a coherent, logical whole that held together, that it didn't consist simply of a set of disjointed propositions. That course was unquestionably the greatest intellectual experience of my life."[5] Viner made substantial contributions to the theory of cost and, according to economic historian Henry Spiegel, was "without peer in the field of international economics and as a chronicler of intellectual history."[6] Friedman recalls that, as a graduate student, other Chicago faculty members included Lloyd Mints, Paul Douglas, and Henry Schultz; they were an "extraordinarily talented and varied group of eminent economists."[7] Viner left Chicago for Princeton in 1946; Friedman replaced him.

George Stigler had this to say about Henry Simons, who was a follower of Knight. Simons "preached a form of laissez-faire in his famous 1934 pamphlet *A Positive Program for Laissez Faire,* but what a form! He proposed nationalization of basic industries such as telephones and railroads because regulation has worked poorly. Simons urged an extremely egalitarian policy in the taxation of income and detailed regulation of business practices such as advertising. Much of his program was almost as harmonious with socialism as with private-enterprise capitalism. Yet in the area of monetary policy he exerted a strong influence upon the later Chicago School with his trenchant case for monetary policy conducted according to rule rather than to discretionary manipulation. In particular he urged that the rule be the stabilization of a comprehensive index of prices. This rule is clearly the parent of the later proposal that the money supply should grow at a steady rate, say three or four percent a year."[8]

Hayek was initially mooted for a position in the economics department at the University of Chicago, before he received an offer from the university's Committee on Social Thought. Too much credence is sometimes given to an offhand comment in the autobiography of John Nef, chairman of the Committee, regarding Hayek's appointment in 1950. Nef wrote that "my visit to England, where I met T. S. Eliot and Friedrich Hayek in London, enabled me to make those two important appointments to the Committee on Social Thought. Hayek accepted a permanent chair he was destined to hold for almost fifteen years. The economics department welcomed his connection with Social Thought, although the economists had opposed his appointment in Economics four years before largely because they regarded his *Road to Serfdom* as too popular a work for a respectable scholar to perpetrate. It was all right to have him at the University of Chicago so long as he wasn't identified with the economists."[9]

This passage is misleading for several reasons. Firstly, the last sentence, which comes at the end of a paragraph, is, particularly in context, something of a throwaway line. To what extent it was even Nef's considered view that economists did not want Hayek "identified" with them is an open question.

Secondly, regarding the idea that Hayek did not receive a position in economics at the University of Chicago because of *The Road to Serfdom,* Friedman has had this to say:

That had nothing to do with it. They didn't want him—there are two reasons: Number one, they had a very strong feeling that they should choose their own members and not have members appointed from the outside. Independent of the name, they would have reacted negatively to any suggestion from the administration. But number two, they didn't agree with his economics. *Prices and Production,* his capital theory—if they had been looking around the world for an economist to add to their staff, their prescription would not have been the author of *Prices and Production.* So far as *The Road to Serfdom* was concerned, it played no role at all. The fact of the matter is, in terms of ideology, the majority of that department was on Hayek's side. The University of Chicago department of economics was known country-wide in the profession to be distinctive because it was so relatively free market. So, *Road to Serfdom* would have been a plus, not a minus. No, I am sure that the fundamental reason they rejected him was a combination of they would have had to assume responsibility from their funds, he was not a person they would have chosen to add, and they didn't want their membership dictated by the administration.[10]

Some of University of Chicago President Robert Maynard Hutchins' strongest critics were in the economics department, and academic prerogatives were scrupulously guarded.

Friedman also remembers the "story about Luhnow and his offer to finance Hayek a professorship at Chicago for ten years, I think that's what it was, and the administration asked the economics department whether they would be willing to offer a post to Hayek; and they refused. I was there at the time but in a very junior capacity. I was not involved in that decision in any way. But in retrospect, I think they were right. Ted Schultz was chairman then. He was an eminently fair person, and insofar as his principles went, they coincided with Hayek's. He was a very great admirer of Hayek. The fact that Hayek was free market would never have been a disqualification."[11]

During the late 1940s, particularly in academic economics, Hayek was not the great figure in broader societal thought that he has subsequently become in retrospect following his later great works. *The Road to Serfdom* was perceived as a largely popular work. He was off the beaten path, much less the cutting edge, of technical academic economic thought, particularly in the United States. His 1941 *The Pure Theory of Capital* attracted little attention. While he did work in political theory, epistemology, methodology of the social sciences, psychology, and the history of ideas, he was not an active technical academic economist and he did not consider himself to be.

D. Gale Johnson, in the economics department at Chicago since 1944, does not remember the idea of offering Hayek a position in the department ever coming to a formal vote, noting as well that the department acted in such matters by consensus. Johnson also says that Hayek "rendered himself irrelevant" in economics before *The Road to Serfdom*.[12]

Hayek's accounts of not being accepted in the economics department at Chicago were less emphatic than Nef's autobiographical comment. He said in an interview, for example, of going to Chicago that "there was, incidentally, an episode. Somebody proposed me first to the faculty of economics. And they turned me down."[13] Hayek did not expend a great deal of effort attempting to be appointed to the Chicago economics department; indeed, he first sought a position at Princeton when he decided to go to the United States following World War II.

He also recalled of going to Chicago that "I had efforts of my friends in the economics department and they were frustrated I think by the econometricians there. The econometricians didn't want me, and the first attempt to offer me a position at the University of Chicago broke down."[14] He said as well that he "never sympathized with either macroeconomics or econometrics. I was thought to be old-fashioned, with no sympathy for modern ideas, that sort of thing."[15] George Nash writes in his authoritative *The Conservative Intellectual Movement in America* (1976, 1996), covering the postwar era, that it was "one more sign of the times that, like Ludwig von Mises, Hayek was forced to rely on private sources to subsidize his entry into American academic circles"—in the case of both, the Volker Fund. Nash adds that John Nef, Aaron Director, and Henry Simons "persuaded the small, conservative Volker Fund to pay a portion of Hayek's salary."[16]

Friedman was, of course, from the wing of the economics department that was most congruent with Hayek. Hayek remarked in 1978 that he found in Chicago this "very sympathetic group of Milton Friedman and soon George Stigler; so I was on very good terms with part of the department, but numerically it was the econometricians who dominated.... Just Frank Knight and his group were the people whom I got along with."[17]

Hayek looked forward to taking his position on the Committee on Social Thought in part because after teaching economics for two decades, he was "a little tired." He had "become somewhat stale as an economist and felt much out of sympathy with the direction in which economics was developing." He felt it a "release" that he would no longer be required to teach economics.[18] Also, he would not have the administrative responsibilities there that he had acquired during his final years at LSE.

Hayek believed immensely in the power of ideas. That he primarily chose political and societal philosophy over technical academic economic theory during the last fifty years of his life reflected both his mature belief that the former is more important than and incorporates the latter, and personal interest and success. He believed and practiced that ideas rule the world.

He acknowledged that he was not really an economist during his latter decades. He said in introducing *The Constitution of Liberty* that he had "come to feel more and more that the answers to many of the pressing social questions of our time are to be found ultimately in the recognition of principles that lie outside the scope of technical economics."[19] He said on assuming his position at the University of Freiburg in 1962 that while the first half of his career had been "wholly devoted to pure theory, I have since devoted much time to subjects entirely outside of the field of economics."[20] His move from economic theory was also influenced by his view that, with publication of *The Road to Serfdom*, he had discredited himself professionally in the economics field.[21]

Hayek felt great release on his divorce and remarriage. He was unhappy for many years in his first marriage and could not be with the woman he loved. He was happy in Chicago "returning to a general university atmosphere from the narrow atmosphere of a school devoted to the social sciences. The faculty club, the Quadrangle Club, was a great attraction. You could sit with historians one day and with the physicists another day and with the biologists the third. In fact, I still know of no other university where there is so much contact between the different subjects as in the University of Chicago."[22] There were more than 10,000 students at the university when Hayek arrived in 1950.

CHAPTER TWENTY-THREE

Committee
on Social Thought

HAYEK SAID IN RETROSPECT of his position on the Committee on Social Thought that it provided "almost ideal opportunities" to pursue the new interests he was "gradually developing."[1] The committee was a successful outgrowth of the cross-disciplinary approach of university president Robert Maynard Hutchins. Originally called the Committee on Civilization, it was intended to provide graduate education and scholarly opportunities beyond the confines of traditional departmental organization. According to University of Chicago historian William McNeill, "Chaired by John Nef, and funded in large part by his wife's money, the Committee on Social Thought became an elite group. Nef simply gathered persons he liked and admired, picking them from quite diverse professional backgrounds, and asked them to supervise the studies of a select handful of graduate students."[2] Describing conditions on the committee during his tenure as chairman from 1946 to 1964, Nef wrote that "we limited ourselves to training not more than thirty students at once, although the faculty came to number from eight-ten, not counting distinguished visitors."[3] As a result of the low student/faculty ratio, there were close relations between students and faculty. Students in the program came from a wide variety of fields—the humanities, natural sciences, and arts, as well as social sciences. It was a nearly ideal academic environment.

When Hayek arrived in the fall of 1950, the committee was on the upswing. While it took on for a time the character of, in member David Grene's words, a "*salon des refusés*" ("salon of the refused"),[4] its members were brilliant individuals. It was their precocity, indeed, that often led them not to be accepted in traditional departments and also infrequently into conflict with one another.

Hutchins biographer Mary Ann Dzuback says that the committee's work was "unique in the university. Nef initially compiled a list of relevant courses offered by other departments and slowly developed a cross-disciplinary curriculum for master's and doctoral students studying through the committee. Nef invited numerous lecturers in the arts, philosophy, theology, and other disciplines to the campus. After the war, the committee began adding its own faculty members."[5]

Hayek's title was Professor of Social and Moral Science. Shirley Robin Letwin was a student of his and remembered his seminar, observing that Adam Smith, too, had been a "professor of moral philosophy":

> Hayek more than justified his title. Every Wednesday he conducted a seminar of staggering catholicity. On Wednesdays after dinner, a large assortment of the wise and the callow, coming from all disciplines and all nations, assembled around a massive oval oak table in a mock Gothic chamber to talk about topics proposed by Hayek. They ranged, far from idly, across philosophy, history, social science, and knowledge generally. The seminar would have been distinguished if not otherwise by the senior participants: two atomic physicists, one an Italian holding a Nobel Prize, the other a Hungarian, profuse inventor of projects, physical, cinematic, political, and of every other sort; an Irish classicist and farmer, as completely master of Shakespeare, Gibbon, or Tolstoy, as of Sophocles, Plato, and Thucydides; a French Thomist of great piety and philosophical precision who admired Pascal, Proudhon, and T. S. Eliot; an arch grass-roots American and a belligerent atheist with a passion for theological inquiry; the leading monetary theorist, fascinated by the sun-seeking motives of leaves on trees and the optimizing behaviors of economic actors, and game for any argument that came his way; a classical archaeologist, educated in the iconographic traditions of Munich and Berlin, who conducted classes on Nietzsche and tutorials on Proust; the author of *The Gothic Cathedral* and the author of *The Lonely Crowd;* as well as the inventor of the "folk society" and the discoverer of early industrial revolutions. The students, drawn from Japan, the Middle East, Europe, and outlying corners of

America, showed high promise of talents that would as thoroughly defy classification.[6]

Those identified in this passage are respectively Enrico Fermi, Leo Szilard, David Grene, Yves Simon, Frank Knight, Milton Friedman, P. H. von Blanckenhagen, Otto von Simson, David Riesman, Robert Redfield, and Nef. Fermi received the 1938 Nobel Prize in Physics, and Hayek and Friedman later received Nobel Prizes. Einstein's famous 1939 letter to Franklin Roosevelt—which was the genesis of the Manhattan Project, headquartered at the University of Chicago— began, "Some recent work by E. Fermi and L. Szilard leads me to expect that the element uranium may be turned into a new and important source of energy. . . . This new phenomenon would lead to the construction of bombs."[7] The seminar was, to say the least, an august group.

Letwin continued that Hayek "presided over this remarkable company with a gentle rectitude that made his seminar an exercise in the liberal virtues. The general subject was liberalism and no one was in any doubt about Hayek's convictions. But students who hoped to shine by discovering apostasy to an official creed learned to seek other paths to glory. Hunting for the holy grail was definitely out of order. The seminar was a conversation with the living and the dead, ancient and modern; the only obligation was to enter into the thoughts of others with fidelity and to accept questions and dissent gracefully. Hayek's conduct as a colleague and teacher was entirely of a piece with this impeccably liberal colloquium. Standards that have all but disappeared from academic life were meticulously observed by him."[8]

Hayek recalled that the "first seminar I held there [Chicago] was one of the most exciting I have ever held. It was on the relation between the methods of the social and the natural sciences, and I had in my seminar sitting, people like Enrico Fermi, Sewall Wright, the great founder of genetics, and several physicists. It was an all-faculty seminar, in which the best people from the natural and social sciences were sitting together. It was the first time; I never could get so good a crowd together because I never had as good a subject again."[9] About twenty-five could be seated in the seminar room. Students sometimes had to sit on the floor. Another participant was Abba Lerner from Hayek's LSE days, who taught at Roosevelt College in Chicago at this time.

Friedman remembers that they were "wonderful seminars primarily because of the range of people he [Hayek] brought in as speakers. They were very broad ranging in conception. The seminar I remember best is one on methodology in which Enrico Fermi talked. That had a very great influence on my own work. He talked about the concept of measurement, and I will never forget the statement that impressed me most, 'Measurement is the making of distinctions, and the finer the distinctions, the finer the measurement.' It's a marvelously productive idea."[10]

The United States was, at the beginning of the postwar era, at an apex of world power and standard of living. The battle against communism diminished support for collectivism generally. The prosperous 1950s were a reverse image of the depressed 1930s. Unemployment was low rather than high; economic growth was far better than anticipated; the Soviet Union was seen as an opponent of freedom and progress, rather than their beacon; no major world land war occurred or was in the offing. The '50s were a great age of American affluence and dominance.

The changed times may explain part of the reason why Hayek moved away from technical economic theory. A downturn of economic production on the scale that characterized the 1930s did not appear to be in the offing. There was accordingly less interest in business cycle theory, his major area of focus in technical economics. There was little meaningful comparison between Britain's and the United States' economies during the early 1930s and through the 1950s. Moreover, the Soviet system was generally heralded at this time for its economic productivity, so some of the arguments from the socialist calculation debate seemed to have less relevance as well. The economics profession was moving in a mathematical direction that was not his own.

Committee member David Grene remembers that when it was announced Hayek was coming to the committee, some were a "bit shocked." Hayek was perceived as a "stock rightwing man" with a "stock rightwing sponsor." While Grene recalls university president Hutchins as glad that Hayek was coming to Chicago, he also recalls that Hutchins made no special effort to recruit Hayek (as he made an effort to secure other faculty). Grene recollects Hutchins as firm that although Hayek's position was made possible through outside funding, Hayek was not being taken on as a representative of a particular viewpoint, nor would the Volker Fund have any say in the doings of the university or committee. At the same time, Hutchins was clear that no limitations were to be placed on Hayek in any way. Grene remembers Hayek as "pleasant," "tactful," "decent," "punctilious," "gentle," and someone who "never threw his weight around," as well as a very able scholar. He participated well in the details of academia pertaining to oversight of students and the sharing of collegial duties. He struck Grene as an unusual combination—both an "Austrian aristocrat and extremely, extremely English."[11]

Former student Eugene Miller writes that he first met Hayek when he enrolled for graduate study under the committee. His primary responsibility, before his doctoral dissertation, was to study selected great works of western thought, a University of Chicago emphasis. His own list included Thomas

Hobbes' *Leviathan,* Adam Smith's *The Wealth of Nations,* and Edmund Burke's *Reflections on the Revolution in France.* Miller recalls that Hayek "readily agreed to tutor me in these works. In these tutorial sessions, I came to know firsthand the qualities of mind that are so manifest in Hayek's writings—the remarkable breadth of his intellectual interests, his concern for basic issues in moral and political theory, and his unfailing generosity. Hayek knew that intellectual freedom is likely to produce a diversity of ideas. Thus he continued to offer his full help and encouragement when my inquiries led me to question some fundamental principles of his thought. He sought not to cultivate disciples but to challenge his students to face difficult issues with the same integrity and manliness that marks his own thought."[12]

James Vice was another student during Hayek's tenure on the committee, and Hayek served on his dissertation committee. Vice recalls that he was interested in "'Felix Frankfurter's view of judicial reasoning.' Hayek thought this a quite suitable topic and was very sympathetic to Frankfurter. This struck me initially as rather surprising because I identified Frankfurter with economic interventionism. I have come to the conclusion that Hayek and Frankfurter have a common preoccupation with the slow, experimental growth of institutions and a common hostility toward dogmatists." Vice also remembers that Hayek told him his "recommended mode of study was first to skim through a book very rapidly and then to go back over it again in meticulous detail. He was of course a prodigious reader and gave me what seemed a preposterous list of books to study preparatory to doing Frankfurter—Vattel, Grotius, etc." And, "Hayek always seemed to me to be the very model of disinterested and objective search for the best approximation to truth."[13]

Stanley Heywood, an early 1950s student, recollects that he had the "great privilege of taking a seminar in the evening from Hayek on 'The Liberal Tradition.' It was one of the highlights of my Chicago experience. Hayek had that broad and deep kind of European education that made him an ideal seminar leader. He also had the graciousness not to talk too much himself, but to interject, correct gently, and move the discussion into fruitful seas. Each of us was responsible for an author, and for putting forth our author's opinion on the topic of the evening, e.g. 'the Rule of Law.'"[14]

A syllabus from a 1951-52 session of "The Liberal Tradition" lists "Intellectual Freedom" as the first topic to be systematically considered. Here, Hayek placed "*Belief* in power of ideas" as the first item to be discussed, and devoted more space to Intellectual Freedom than anything else on the syllabus. From the belief in the power of ideas, Hayek taught the following: that the "diversity and limitation" of individual intellects follows; that "truth will emerge from the interplay of different intellects in free discussion"; that reason is a social process and that "belief in persuasion" is vital; that "nobody is competent authoritatively to decide [he] knows best"; that "even error has to be respected"; and that "the spreading of opinion is inevitably a gradual process." He listed the following as the "postulates" of Intellectual Freedom: "Tolerance," "Freedom of Thought, . . . Conscience, . . . Speech and Assembly, . . . [and] the Press," "Absence of all Forms of Censorship," and "Academic Freedom" in both teaching and research.[15]

According to Ronald Hamowy, Hayek was an "extremely distinguished-looking man with impeccable manners and a gentle scholarly way about him. I confess to having found him somewhat formal, and although I grew to become quite fond of him and saw him a number of times after having received my doctorate, there always existed a wall, however tenuous, that separated professor from student. Indeed, I never ceased to call him professor even though I last met him when I was in my forties and had been a professor myself for a number of years."[16]

English department member Richard Stern recalls that he

came to Chicago a young instructor, and, in the fashion of those days joined the Quadrangle Club. "Fritz" Hayek sat at the square table in the bay windows, a sort of anyone-can-come table if you missed your usual table and didn't have an engagement. Two or three times a month in those years I'd eat with him. We were separated by decades and many other things, but I found him extremely pleasant and amusing. I have no idea if he knew my name. I can't remember calling him anything or being called anything by him.

Hayek looked unapproachable, haughty, rather as if he were sniffing something disagreeable in his mustache, but I didn't feel patronised by him. He told amusing stories, particularly one I still remember about his LSE colleague Laski. "Laski," he said, "was brilliantly intuitive and an inveterate liar. The combination resulted in amusing but sometimes serious difficulties." It seems that Laski had guessed something that Churchill was planning to do. Churchill got wind that Laski "knew" plans that had been revealed only to the Cabinet. He held a Cabinet meeting and announced that someone had leaked the information to Laski. "It took a while before the truth emerged."

Hayek also talked about the little village in Austria where he'd vacationed for years and where he was still regarded as an outsider unable to buy property.

I remember the story—told me by others—of the early romance interrupted by marriages which was then reignited . . . and the coming together and marriage of the former sweethearts.[17]

Hayek led a number of seminars at Chicago during the 1950s, mostly in political philosophy. They included (by date of first appearance): "Justice and Equality" (twice), "The Liberal Tradition" (thrice), "Scientific Method and the Study of Society" (thrice), "Economic Calculus," "Social and Political Thought" (six times), "The Last Plays of Shakespeare," "Introduction to Social Theory," "British Social Thought Between John Locke and Edmund Burke," and "An Analysis of the Welfare State."[18] In some of the seminars of the later 1950s, he distributed early chapter drafts of *The Constitution of Liberty*.

Hayek's years in Chicago were a time for finding new directions. He recalled Nef's offer to join the Committee on Social Thought was, "You can teach within the field of social science, whatever you like, and if at any time you don't feel like teaching, you needn't teach at all."[19] This opportunity, with a high salary, was outstanding and allowed him to accomplish his highest goals.

CHAPTER TWENTY-FOUR

Mill

THE NINETEENTH-CENTURY BRITISH POLITICAL AND ECONOMIC PHILOSOPHER with whom Hayek is most frequently identified is John Stuart Mill. Some knowledge of Hayek's evolving view of Mill elucidates their intellectual relationship. He said in an interview late in his career that his "many years of work on John Stuart Mill actually shook my admiration for someone I had thought a great figure indeed, with the result that my present opinion of John Stuart Mill is a very critical one indeed."[1] A review of his comments on Mill over the decades reveals the extent to which his point of view changed. In introducing Mill's *The Spirit of the Age* in 1942, he said the value of republishing this essay lay in the "light it throws on one of the most interesting phases in the development of a great figure of the past century."[2]

There are several very favorable references to Mill in Hayek's 1951 *John Stuart Mill and Harriet Taylor: Their Friendship and Subsequent Marriage,* completed before he came to Chicago:

> so eminently sober, balanced and disciplined a mind, and a man who chose his words deliberately and carefully. . . .

> that exceptional capacity of which he justly prides himself in the *Autobiography,* his "willingness and ability to learn from everybody" . . .

> Mill, the most truthful of persons . . .

He will again be recognized as one of the really great figures of his period, a great moral figure perhaps more than a great thinker, and one in whom even his purely intellectual achievements are mainly due to his profound conviction of the supreme moral value of unrelenting intellectual effort. Not by temperament but out of a deeply ingrained sense that this was his duty did Mill grow to be the "Saint of Rationalism," as Gladstone once so justly described him.[3]

He referred to Mill's "great essay *On Liberty*"[4] in *The Road to Serfdom*.

In *The Constitution of Liberty,* Hayek included Mill in lists of great classical liberal thinkers and writers. There are more references to Mill than to any other author, and most references cite him as an authority or are in agreement with him, including:

> One need not be wiser than the great thinkers of the past to be in a better position to comprehend the essential conditions of individual liberty. The experience of the last hundred years has taught us much that a Madison or a Mill, a Tocqueville or a Humboldt, could not perceive.

> The classical argument for tolerance formulated by John Milton and John Locke and restated by John Stuart Mill and Walter Bagehot rests, of course, on the recognition of . . . ignorance.

> [regarding Hayek's distinction between "coercive measures of government and pure service activities"] The distinction is the same as that which J. S. Mill draws between "authoritative" and "unauthoritative" government interference.

> We cannot understand the nature of the opposition of men like Adam Smith or John Stuart Mill to government "intervention" unless we see it against this background [of "the rule of law"].[5]

Hayek also praised Mill in *The Constitution of Liberty* for what he had to say regarding the importance of speculative philosophy,[6] that government control of an economy would be fatal to liberty,[7] of the acceptability of government action to further knowledge,[8] and that government control of education is potentially pernicious.[9] Hayek concluded the text proper on this note, "We cannot think of better words to conclude than those of Wilhelm von Humboldt which a hundred years ago John Stuart Mill put in front of his essay *On Liberty*: 'The grand, the leading principle, towards which every argument unfolded in these pages directly converges, is the absolute and essential importance of human development in its richest diversity.'"[10] A reader might be led to infer that Hayek intended *The Constitution of Liberty* as a prolegomenon to or continuation of Mill's *On Liberty*—its very title, indeed, might be interpreted as pertaining to the earlier work.

John Stuart Mill and Harriet Taylor is an excellent scholarly work tracing their unconventional Victorian romance and marriage (Mill was Taylor's constant companion and travel partner though she was married to another man who eventually died). The book emerged from "the accident" that Hayek obtained the letters contained in it during the war when he had available time and a proficient assistant, Ruth Borchard. This led him to "go much deeper with the project than [he] had intended."[11] In addition to this book and his edition of *The Spirit of the Age,* Hayek wrote several articles on Mill. John Robson, superb general editor of Mill's *Collected Works,* wrote of Hayek on Mill and Taylor that "the tale is well told," and of the "revelatory work of Professor Hayek."[12] Borchard wrote a biography on Mill and acknowledged in its preface her "particular thanks to Professor F. A. Hayek."[13]

Hayek's research considerably influenced Michael St. John Packe, whose *The Life of John Stuart Mill* (1954) Hayek called in the book's preface the "definitive biography of Mill for which we have so long been waiting."[14] Packe thanked Hayek second in his acknowledgements, after only his wife, "To Professor F. A. Hayek, late of the London School of Economics and now at the University of Chicago, I owe far more than he has indicated in the Preface. Indeed, without his many years of fruitful research, neither this nor any other full biography of Mill could have been written: while his constant interest and timely advice have exceeded anything I could have hoped."[15]

Francis Mineka wrote in the preface to *The Earlier Letters of John Stuart Mill, 1812-1848* in Mill's *Collected Works* that "credit for the conception of this edition belongs to Professor F. A. Hayek . . . [whose] decision to assemble as complete a collection [of correspondence] as possible through the year 1848 was wholly sound."[16] Hayek gracefully remarked in introducing Mineka's work that the "tracing of unpublished manuscripts is the kind of detective work which most people will enjoy doing as a recreation in their spare time. But while the pleasure of the hunt was largely mine, the solid hard work to which the reader owes this edition is entirely Professor Mineka's."[17]

In Hayek's four major works in societal philosophy—*The Road to Serfdom, The Constitution of Liberty, Law, Legislation and Liberty,* and *The Fatal Conceit*— the number of references to selected writers is presented in the table on page 187.

Many commentators have noticed similarity between Hayek and Mill. Robert Cunningham begins a collection of papers by various writers on Hayek by

References to Selected Writers					
	RS	CL	LLL	FC	Total
Hume	1	21	43	16	81
Smith	-	17	22	13	52
Mill	3	28	10	10	51
Popper	-	8	25	13	46
Mises	-	20	10	5	35
Burke	-	21	10	4	35
Acton	8	20	5	1	34
Locke	2	10	15	5	32
Aristotle	-	8	11	12	31
Bentham	-	5	20	6	31
Marx	5	6	4	13	28
Kant	1	4	18	2	25
Menger	-	4	8	9	21
Kelsen	-	9	10	-	19
Keynes	2	6	4	7	19
Laski	3	6	3	-	12
Knight	1	8	-	2	11
Friedman	-	7	3	-	10

saying that in "1859 J. S. Mill traced in *On Liberty* the history of what he called civil or social liberty. A hundred years later Friedrich A. Hayek in *The Constitution of Liberty* restated and clarified the traditional doctrine of liberal constitutionalism."[18] Norman Barry writes that there is "little doubt that Hayek's defence of freedom is the most eloquent, persuasive and closely-reasoned since Mill's *On Liberty*."[19] According to John Gray, Hayek intended *The Constitution of Liberty* to "commemorate the centenary of John Stuart Mill's *On Liberty*."[20] A line from Henry Hazlitt's review of *The Constitution of Liberty* has for years been used as the first quotation on the back of the book to entice interest in it: "One of the great political works of our time . . . the twentieth-century successor to John Stuart Mill's essay, *On Liberty*."

Hayek began to display a predominantly negative attitude toward Mill in his later work *Law, Legislation and Liberty*. Mill was no longer the most frequently cited author (Hume, Popper, Smith, Bentham, Kant, and Locke were cited more), and the references now were often in an unfavorable light. Hayek criticized Mill for popularizing the term "social justice."[21] Hayek also criticized Mill in a footnote to the following statement of Hayek's own in the main text calling "nationalism and socialism" the "two greatest threats to a free civilization," "Both of which were characteristically regarded by John Stuart Mill as the only 'elevated' feelings left in modern man."[22]

One of the most prominent examples of Hayek's later negative view toward Mill occurred in the section of *Law, Legislation and Liberty* titled "Unlimited power the fatal defect of the prevailing form of democracy."[23] Hayek began this section by remarking that "The tragic illusion was that the adoption of democratic procedures made it possible to dispense with all other limitations on governmental power. It also promoted the belief that the 'control of government' by the democratically elected legislature would adequately replace the traditional limitations."[24] He then footnoted, "It would seem that James Mill was in this respect the main culprit, though it is difficult to find in his *Essay on Government* a precise statement. But we can trace his influence clearly in his son when, for example, J. S. Mill argues in *On Liberty* that *'the nation did not need to be protected against its own will* [emphasis added].'"[25]

This interpretation of a relatively well-known passage by John Stuart Mill was surprising because it was so inaccurate. (This statement of Mill's, and the lines preceding it, have been given earlier.)[26] The lines following it, as the lines preceding it, make perfectly clear that Mill's point was exactly the same as Hayek's—that democratic voting procedures do *not* vitiate the desirability of restraints on power. Immediately continuing, Mill said of the idea that a nation does not need to be protected against its will that this "mode of thought was common among the last generation of European liberalism. Those who admit any limit to what a government may do, except in the case of such governments as they think ought not to exist, stand out as brilliant exceptions among the political thinkers of the Continent. But, in political and philosophical theories, as well as in persons, success discloses faults and infirmities which failure might have concealed from observation. The notion, that the people have no need to limit their power over themselves, might seem axiomatic, when popular government was a thing only dreamed about, or read as having existed at some distant period of the past. In time, however, a democratic republic came to occupy a large portion of the earth's surface. . . . It was now perceived that such phrases as 'self-government' and 'the power of the people over themselves,' do not express the true state of the case. The limitation, therefore, of the power of government over individuals loses none of its importance when the holders of power are regularly accountable to the community."[27] Hayek got exactly wrong one of Mill's central points in *On Liberty.*

What makes this misinterpretation all the more surprising is that Hayek also referred to this passage from Mill in *The Constitution of Liberty,* but in precisely the opposite context. That is, in *The Constitution of Liberty* Hayek accurately made the interpretation of Mill that he later inaccurately made in *Law, Legislation and Liberty,* raising the questions of the extent to which his later criticism of Mill was based on misinterpretation rather than genuine disagreement, and therefore whether there is not more congruence between the two thinkers than Hayek came to see in his later years. In the main text of *The Constitution of Liberty,* Hayek wrote, "It was at a comparatively late stage in the history of modern democracy that great demagogues began to argue that since the power was in the hands of the people, there was no longer any need for limiting that power."[28] He then added in a footnote, "But see J. S. Mill already arguing against this view in *On Liberty,* ed. R. B. McCallum."[29] In the passage of the McCallum edition to which Hayek referred, the paragraphs from *On Liberty* given here appear.

In *The Fatal Conceit,* Hayek wrote that Mill "early put himself under socialist influence, and through this bias acquired a great appeal to 'progressive' intellectuals. He probably led more intellectuals into socialism than any other single person."[30] Hayek's emphasis on Mill's socialism was excessive. While it is the case that in his posthumously published autobiography Mill said that their "ideal of ultimate improvement would class us [Mill and Harriet Taylor] decidedly under the general designation of Socialists," and that after the 1848 first edition of *Principles of Political Economy* he made (under the influence of Taylor and of the European uprisings that year) concessions to socialism in subsequent editions, the socialism he foresaw was workers' cooperatives within a competitive economy, not all-encompassing state control—Hayek's definition of socialism.

Indeed, again in *The Constitution of Liberty,* Hayek agreeingly quoted Mill on this very point, "'If the roads, the railways, the banks, the insurance offices, the great joint stock companies, the universities, and the public charities, were all of them branches of the government; if, in addition, the municipal corporations and local boards, with all that now devolves on them, became departments of the central administration; if the employees of all these different enterprises were appointed and paid by the government, and looked to the government for every rise in life; not all the freedom of the press and popular constitution of the legislature would make this or any other country free otherwise than in name.'"[31] In the last book of *Principles of Political Economy,* Mill wrote, in almost Hayekian, *Constitution of Liberty* terms, that there "is a circle around every individual human being, which no government ought to be permitted to overstep; there is a part of the life of every person who has come to years of discretion within which the individuality of that person ought to reign uncontrolled either by any other individual or by the public collectively."[32]

While Mill's thought evolved through various phases of diverse emphases, his ultimate and decisive commitment was to liberalism, not at all state socialism. He concluded *On Liberty,* which he correctly predicted would last longer than any of his other works, "The worth of a State, in the long run, is the worth of the individuals composing it; a State which dwarfs its men, in order that they may be more docile instruments in its hands even for beneficial purposes—will find that with small men no great thing can really be accomplished; and that the perfection of the machinery to which it has sacrificed everything will in the end avail it nothing, for want of the vital power which, in order that the machine might work more smoothly, it has preferred to banish."[33]

Hayek traveled to international and national intellectual and academic conferences during the 1950s. He participated in a 1955 world congress in Milan of intellectuals from western democracies on the theme "The Future of Freedom." After a week of relative agreement among the intellectuals representing left, right, and center, he went on the offensive. According to participant Seymour Martin Lipset,

> Professor Hayek, in a closing speech, attacked the delegates for preparing
> to bury freedom instead of saving it. He alone was disturbed by the general
> temper. What bothered him was the general agreement among the delegates,
> regardless of political belief, that the traditional issues separating the left
> and right had declined to comparative insignificance. In effect all agreed
> that the increase in state control which had taken place in various countries
> would not result in a decline in democratic freedom. The socialists no longer
> advocated socialism; they were as concerned as the conservatives with the
> danger of an all-powerful state. The ideological issues dividing left and right
> had been reduced to a little more or a little less government ownership and
> economic planning. No one seemed to believe that it really made much
> difference which political party controlled the domestic policies of
> individual nations. Hayek, honestly believing that state intervention is bad
> and inherently totalitarian, found himself in a small minority of those who
> still took the cleavages within the democratic camp seriously.[34]

Hayek delivered the opening address on the occasion of the Mont Pelerin Society's tenth anniversary conference in 1957, and, in reference to the society's purpose in its Statement of Aims "to contribute to the preservation and improvement of the free society," remarked that things looked considerably less dark than they did in 1947, although he was still not optimistic. The 1957 meeting in St. Moritz, Switzerland, revitalized the society. The 1954 Venice gathering attracted only forty-one members, down from fifty-seven in 1953. In 1956, only twenty-five members attended in Berlin. There were, in 1951, 167 members in the society. The 1957, tenth anniversary conference was the largest meeting to date, with seventy-three members in attendance and forty-nine guests. Hayek gave his "Why I Am Not a Conservative" talk at this meeting, which became the postscript of *The Constitution of Liberty.* Hayek was against modern liberalism in 1955 in Milan; he spoke against old-fashioned conservatism in 1957.

Topic sessions from Mont Pelerin conferences during the 1950s give an idea of transitory as well as more permanent issues. Titles included "The European Iron and Steel Authority," "Soviet Expansion in Underdeveloped Countries," and "Liberalism and Colonialism."[35] John Davenport, a *Fortune* book reviewer, was a Mont Pelerin member. He remembered that Hayek had a "famous confrontation" with American conservative thinker Russell Kirk at the St. Moritz conference, and noted Kirk was never elected to the society "despite many friends."[36] Kirk subsequently criticized the society in the American conservative magazine *National Review,* writing that during its early years members of the society promulgated "liberal dogmas"[37] and hostility toward Christianity. Aaron Director, Milton Friedman, and George Stigler replied in a letter that "the participants of the initial conference were not characterized by any simple position, let alone 'rigid adherence to nineteenth century liberal dogmas and a rationalistic hostility toward Christianity.'"[38] Several early society members, including Walter Eucken and Wilhelm Röpke, were Christians.

James Buchanan recalls that he was "invited to become a member of the Mt. Pelerin Society in 1957. I do not know who nominated me for membership, but I do know that everyone acknowledged that the society was really Hayek's and that any new member must have been approved by Hayek himself. By 1957, the membership had grown somewhat from its small beginnings, but there was still a club-like aspect to the meeting with an underlying tension between the central European and American members (the latter mostly with Chicago connections). To those of us who had libertarian-populist blood in our veins, there was too much deference accorded to Hayek, and especially to Ludwig von Mises, who seemed to demand sycophancy. Hayek dominated the group, and he was, quite properly, treated with respect that approached awe. His direct contributions to the discussions were invariably profound as well as relevant."[39]

Longtime Dutch Mont Pelerin member Christian Gandil remembers that early society meetings were dominated more by Europeans than by Americans, while the latter have dominated subsequent meetings. He also recalls early society conferences as much more intimate than they have become.[40]

Hayek experienced personal fulfillment during the 1950s. While he also experienced moral angst at his decision to leave his first wife and children, Helene (also known as "Lena") was the love of his life, his best friend since childhood, and their marriage was the realization of a long and deeply held dream.

Friedman remembers Hayek's second wife as a "very intelligent woman."[41] She sometimes attended Hayek's seminar in Chicago, translated *The Counter-Revolution of Science* into German, and, Hayek said, "practically redid"[42] *The Constitution of Liberty* translation into German. In the preface of *The Sensory Order,* perhaps his most difficult work, he thanked her, acknowledging that "without the acute criticism of the manuscript by my wife the book would contain even more obscurities and so slovenly expressions than it undoubtedly still does."[43] As well, Helene Hayek was a beautiful woman, though possessed of a difficult personality. In a 1948 letter, Hayek wrote that Helene had been his partner in his intellectual work prior to their separation in 1939.[44]

A project which Hayek initiated during the second half of the 1950s and spent a considerable amount of time on through the first years of the 1960s was an unsuccessful attempt to revive the intellectual tradition at the University of Vienna. He was always fundamentally a continental European—he said in *The Road to Serfdom* that he was "one who, whatever the law may say, must forever remain a foreigner."[45] He wrote a number of memoranda and sought funding from the Ford and Rockefeller Foundations for the project. He intended to persuade prominent intellectuals to return to the University of Vienna to rekindle its past academic greatness. His "idea was to create something like an institute of advanced studies, and to bring all the refugees who were still active back— people like Schrödinger and Popper . . .—Oh, I had a marvelous list!"[46] His own frequent changes of residence led him to think that other academics could be persuaded to relocate to Vienna.

CHAPTER TWENTY-FIVE

The Constitution of Liberty

THE CONSTITUTION OF LIBERTY owed its origins to a trip that was surely among the most enjoyable duties a scholar ever had to perform. In editing John Stuart Mill's correspondence with Harriet Taylor, Hayek omitted most of the long letters that Mill wrote her from a trip in Italy and Greece during the winter and spring of 1854-55. Hayek conceived the idea of repeating Mill's journey by exactly one hundred years to the day after it took place and producing an annotated volume of Mill's letters. He secured foundation funding for this sojourn, and he and Helene spent a "delightful"[1] seven months traveling by car through France, Italy, and Greece. From Greece they made a side trip to Egypt, where he delivered lectures on "The Political Ideal of the Rule of Law," which comprise five chapters in *The Constitution of Liberty*.

The work evolved over a number of years. When Hayek came to the University of Chicago in 1950, he had two completed manuscripts–*John Stuart Mill and Harriet Taylor*, which was already at a publisher, and *The Sensory Order*, for which negotiations were pending. He attempted to interest Karl Popper in the latter. However, while Popper wrote Hayek a few letters in response to Hayek's letters regarding it and further thoughts along these lines, Hayek was not able to interest Popper in his ideas in psychology. Hayek sometimes expressed the hope that Popper could join him in Chicago, as he later hoped Popper might participate in the endeavor to re-create the University of Vienna's intellectual tradition, and when he was in Salzburg, that Popper might join him in Salzburg.

Hayek's thought moved in a new direction with the *Collectivist Economic Planning* essays. While he before had been a practicing technical academic economist, he now became a societal theorist and philosopher. In writing these essays, he became increasingly aware of the function of prices and profits to guide production. Prices and profits are production signals.

In "Economics and Knowledge," he followed up his idea that prices guide physical production to suggest that the fundamental issue of a societal order is whether prices and profits exist to guide production, which is much of material activity. He postulated that the most important question facing a society is how effectively it utilizes divided and fragmented knowledge. He further postulated that the institutional concomitants of a liberal order–private property, freedom of labor and exchange–in sum, the rule of law–are absolute prerequisites for a materially productive and intellectually free society.

Hayek's thoughts on constitutional order stemmed from his work in economics, methodology, and psychology. In his recent work in psychology, he became even more impressed with human ignorance, how little people really know about the actual scientific world, particularly individually. How is it possible for a human system to exist in which knowledge is so fragmented? As well, Hayek's work in psychology suggested to him the importance of evolution.

His work in economics led him to believe that business fluctuations are caused by changes in relative prices between capital and other goods in a structure of production. His conception of economic activity was, or at least so the view is here, inaccurate. Nonetheless, the idea of the guiding function of prices that emerged from it was of great value apart from its incorporation by Hayek in Austrian trade cycle theory.

When he came to Chicago in 1950, Hayek's work program was about as follows. For a number of years, he had been working on The Abuse and Decline of Reason essays, some of the preliminary results of which had appeared in the collection of articles *Individualism and Economic Order* (1948) and which would appear, with additional material, in *The Counter-Revolution of Science* (1952). *The Road to Serfdom* was published in 1944. He was interested in the relationship between societal change and the presentational format of scientific work. He had interdisciplinary interests. He was much better off on the Committee on Social Thought than if he had been a member of the economics department.

He wished to explore the idea of the utilization of divided, fragmented, incomplete, and inaccurate knowledge further. He sought further clarification of the idea that societal order can emerge although no one is directing it, and of the use of knowledge by a group of individuals that no one individual possess in its entirety. He found significant wisdom and knowledge in (culturally) transmitted institutions and practices. He thought that these had evolved over time to lead to the most materially productive societies.

On March 7, 1954, he wrote the Guggenheim Foundation to ask for funding for his travels in Italy and Greece, not just for his intended work on John Stuart Mill, but because he thought that traveling to these non-industrialized areas would help him to gain greater understanding of the development of tradition and culture in agrarian societies. He was interested in how nonverbally explicit rules and customs—not irrational, but nonrational—develop. The title of a book he intended along these lines, which he said he had been working on for years, would be close to the title he gave to the second chapter of *The Constitution of Liberty*, "The Creative Powers of a Free Civilization."[2]

Hayek never really wrote this book. The "Philosophy" articles in his *Studies* (1967) and *New Studies* (1978) come closest to expressing his ideas of his published work in this area. "The Creative Powers of a Free Civilization," as originally conceived, was intended more to be a work that incorporated his ideas in psychology than his economic ones. The individual philosophy that Hayek saw undergirding his ideas of societal order was one that emphasizes individual ignorance, evolution, group intelligence, communication, and originality–liberalism. He was interested in the relationship among morals, ignorance, and societal order.

He came to recognize that the attempt to strive for the same degree of prediction, and thus control, that is possible in the physical sciences is impossible in the social ones. Therefore, societies should not strive for the same degree of predetermined outcomes as is possible in the physical sciences. The limits of knowledge dictate limits of government. Individual ignorance is inerradicable. He was interested in the idea of the use of knowledge that no one has in its totality.

As a result of his Cairo lectures and "constant preoccupation with Mill's thinking," the plan for *The Constitution of Liberty* suddenly "stood clearly" before Hayek's mind on returning to the United States.[3] He originally intended to write two works on liberal order when he returned to the United States. The first was to be *The Constitution of Liberty*, and the second, "The Creative Powers of a Free Civilization." He worked on *The Constitution of Liberty* for the next four years. He concluded the 1959 preface to the German edition of *The Counter-Revolution of Science* (which was originally intended to be the first part of The Abuse and Decline of Reason) by stating that "the work of which this is a part will not be continued in the form originally conceived. I now hope to present the body of thought in another volume that is less historical but more systematic"[4]—*The Constitution of Liberty*. He completed *The Constitution of Liberty* by writing its preface on his sixtieth birthday, May 8, 1959.

He stated his conception of liberty in the book's first chapter as "the state in which a man is not subject to coercion by the arbitrary will of another."[5] His point was not that complete absence of coercion is possible or characterizes liberty. His point was that law may create liberty through the establishment of a societal framework that allows individuals to live their lives rationally. What he thought essential is that coercion not be *arbitrary,* that individuals should know in advance what is permissible and what is not permissible in a society.

The larger times in which he wrote influenced the book. The late 1950s were a period of intense rivalry between the United States and the Soviet Union. There was a real political and philosophical struggle as to which system would prevail—that of the Soviet Union or that of the United States. Many thought it would be the former. In this context, *The Constitution of Liberty* may be considered a restatement of and justification for liberal capitalism.

Hayek's hopes for *The Constitution of Liberty* were higher than for any of his other works. The volume was intended as his magnum opus. A number of the chapters were published in some form before they appeared in the final book, and they were circulated to friends, associates, and students for comments. He listed twenty-six individuals in the acknowledgements and notes who reviewed the manuscript in some form before publication, unprecedented for any of his other works (he mentioned in the acknowledgements, "I have never learned even to avail myself of the aid of a research assistant").[6] He hoped *The Constitution of Liberty* would be *The Wealth of Nations* of the twentieth century.

The five chapters of *The Constitution of Liberty* that comprised his Cairo lectures primarily concern the rule of law. He emphasized the importance of law to liberty. Without law, there can be no liberty. Right law constitutes, defines, creates liberty—right law is liberty. He used as the epigraph of the chapter "The Origins of the Rule of Law" the following passage from John Locke: "The end of law is, not to abolish or restrain, but to preserve and enlarge freedom. For in all the states of created beings capable of laws, where there is no law there is no freedom. For liberty is to be free from restraint and violence from others; which cannot be where there is no law: and is not . . . a liberty for every man to do what he lists [desires]. (For who could be free when every other man's humour might domineer over him?) But a liberty to dispose, and order as he lists, his person, actions, possessions, and his whole property, within the allowance of those laws under which he is, and therein not to be the subject of the arbitrary will of another, but freely follow his own."[7] Hayek approvingly quoted Locke in *The Road to Serfdom* as well, that "There can be no liberty without law."[8]

The idea that right law creates liberty may seem unusual to those who conceive of liberty in society either as a certain material standard of living or the ability to participate in political governance. While Hayek held that both of the latter typically are good things, he argued that they are distinct from liberty properly conceived, which pertains solely to the society in which one man's coercive will over another is reduced to the absolute minimum through known general laws applicable to all.

In the first part of *The Constitution of Liberty*, "The Value of Freedom," Hayek sought to paint a picture of the great productive possibilities of a political order characterized by the rule of law. This was essentially a continuation of economic arguments he made earlier in his career against classical socialism, but from a more positive perspective. He here stressed not the infeasibility of classical socialism, but the material productivity of a political-economic order in which the rule of law, private property, contract, and freedom of exchange lead to the highest standard of living possible.

The essentiality of the rule of law to productivity is based on the psychological necessity of a rational context for individuals to be maximally productive. Hayek stated that "the importance which the certainty of law has for the smooth and efficient running of a free society can hardly be exaggerated. There is probably no single factor which has contributed more to the prosperity of the West than the relative certainty of the law which has prevailed here."[9] The societal rationality that law creates was, in Hayek's view, law's justification. If the rules of a society are uncertain as to what one may do and what one's property is, individuals will not be as productive as in a society where these rules are more certain. Without laws and societal morés, individuals cannot know the consequences of their actions.

Laws and rules are a metaphysical or abstract order. They in large part depend on others following the same laws and rules. They create societal order and thereby the possibility of productive activity.

The content of law, as well as its existence, is, of course, essential. Hayek thought that the appropriate content of law is to create private domains for individuals wherein, as Locke and Mill held, they may act as they desire. Liberty, Hayek held in "The Value of Freedom," "presupposes that the individual has some assured private sphere, that there is some set of circumstances in his environment with which others cannot interfere."[10] Furthermore and importantly, because material objects play such a large role in individuals' lives, individuals cannot be considered free if they have no liberty to dispose of at least some material objects as they desire. For this reason, private property is essential to liberty, as is some opportunity to choose employment.

Hayek emphasized the importance of material progress by observing that "the aspirations of the great mass of the world's population can today be satisfied only by rapid material progress. At this moment, when the greater part of mankind has only just awakened to the possibility of abolishing starvation, filth, and disease; when it has just been touched by the expanding wave of modern technology after centuries or millennia of relative stability; even a small decline in our rate of advance might be fatal."[11]

Hayek challenged hundreds of years of egalitarian thinking. Perhaps the most readily apparent examples of this in *The Constitution of Liberty* are his discussions of underdeveloped nations and of the importance—indeed necessity—of inequality within societies. Concerning world inequality, he wrote that there "can be little doubt that the prospect of the poorer, 'undeveloped' countries reaching the present level of the West is very much better than it would have been, had the West not pulled so far ahead. If today some nations can in a few decades acquire a level of material comfort that took the West hundreds or thousands of years to achieve, is it not evident that their path has been made easier by the fact that the West was not forced to share its material achievements with the rest— that it was not held back but was able to move far in advance of the others?"[12]

Concerning inequality within a community, Hayek believed that "it is one of the most characteristic facts of a progressive society that in it most things can be obtained only through further progress. This follows from the necessary character of the process: new knowledge and its benefits can spread only gradually, and the ambitions of the many will always be determined by what is as yet accessible only to the few. The rapid economic advance that we have come to expect seems in a large measure to be the result of inequality and to be impossible without it."[13]

In his inegalitarianism, he was outside the mainstream of liberal political thought. While passages from the following authors could be found that express contrasting views, the prevailing sentiment of preceding liberal political thought was nonetheless different than the one Hayek enunciated:

HOBBES: "Nature has made men so equal in the faculties of the body and mind, as that though there be found one man sometimes manifestly stronger in body or of a quicker mind than another, yet when all is reckoned together the difference between man and man is not so considerable as that one man can thereupon claim to himself any benefit, to which another may not pretend, as well as he."[14]

LOCKE: "Let us suppose that the mind to be, as we say, white paper, void of all characters, without any ideas; how comes it to be furnished? To this I answer in one word, from experience: in that all our knowledge is founded, and from that it ultimately derives itself." Locke also approvingly quoted Richard Hooker that "equality of men by nature" "'hath brought men to know that it is no less their duty to love others than themselves; for seeing those things which are equal must needs all have one measure, how should I look to have any part of my desire herein satisfied, unless myself be careful to satisfy the like desire, which is undoubtedly in other men, being of one and the same nature? My desire, therefore, to be loved of my equals in nature . . . '"[15]

SMITH: "The difference of natural talents in different men is, in reality, much less than we are aware of. The difference between the most dissimilar characters, between a philosopher and a street porter, for example, seems to arise not so much from nature, as from habit, custom, and education."[16]

JEFFERSON: "All men are created equal."

Though Hayek was inegalitarian in his view of individuals' potentialities, he was not conservative in the sense of seeking to preserve the status quo or protect existing relationships of power and privilege in a society. Indeed, he sought radically to upset the status quo in societies to the extent that the status quo does not create genuinely meritocratic, inegalitarian, competitive market orders. "The freedom that will be used by only one man in a million," he wrote, "may be more important to society and more beneficial to the majority than any freedom that we all use."[17] Most importantly, "It has been the fashion in modern times to minimize the importance of congenital differences between men and to ascribe all the important differences to the influence of the environment. However important the latter may be, we must not overlook the fact that individuals are very different from the outset. As a statement of fact, it just is not true that 'all men are born equal.'"[18]

The significance of Hayek's inegalitarian outlook of humanity's intrinsic propensities is that it undercuts societal orders based on an idea of the desirability of equality or uniformity within societies. If humanity is not diverse physiologically, communities in which significant diversity of outcomes exists may, to this extent, be less than optimal. If individuals naturally are very diverse, on the other hand, optimal—or natural—societies will be ones in which human diversity manifests itself.

He held in *The Constitution of Liberty* that from "the fact that people are very different it follows that, if we treat them equally, the result must be inequality in their actual position. . . . [F]reedom leads to material inequality."[19] This is perhaps the heart of the Hayekian message with respect to desirable human communities—there can be no material progress without inequality and diversity of outcomes. He said decades later in an interview that "we will have to recognize that only a system where we tolerate grossly unjust differences of reward is capable of keeping the present population of the world in existence"[20]

He put this proposition forward, moreover—similarly to his arguments against socialism—not as an ethical precept but as an empirical fact. Individuals may not like this fact, but there cannot be materially productive human communities in any other way. There is a choice between equality and productivity. One may have one or the other, or neither, but one may not have both, or at least such was Hayek's argument. He chose inequality and productivity in the material outcomes of a societal order over equality and poverty.

Material inequality in a society should be based, moreover, on innate human diversity. This is paradoxically achieved through the equality of all before the law. It is precisely when people are treated the same that innate human diversity manifests itself. Hayek thought the optimal society would be one where place and material possessions would be established by ability impartially determined through a competitive market typified by freedom of exchange and private property, not by government management of all of the details of economic activity.

He was criticized in a respectful manner by a student of his at Chicago, Ronald Hamowy, who wrote in the *New Individualist Review* on "Professor Hayek's use of the term 'coercion' within the context of state activity. He states that 'the conception of freedom under the law that is the concern of this book rests on the contention that when we obey laws, in the sense of general abstract rules laid down irrespective of their application to us, we are not subject to another man's will and are therefore free.' The inference is, of course, that these abstract rules are non-coercive, despite any qualification as to their content."[21] Hamowy's criticism—that Hayek's macro-conception of liberty and law was non-contentual—has been made by others as well.

Hayek responded that the "issue on which Mr. Hamowy dissents is the practical one of the manner in which the power of coercive action by government can be so limited as to be least harmful. Since government needs this power to prevent coercion, it might at first seem as if the test should be whether it is in the particular instance necessary for that purpose. But to make necessity for the prevention of worse coercion the criterion would inevitably make the decision dependent on somebody's discretion. . . . While we want to allow coercion by government only in situations where it is necessary to prevent coercion, we do not want to allow it in all instances where it could be pretended that it was necessary for that purpose. We need therefore another test to make the use of coercion independent of individual will. It is the distinguishing mark of the Western political tradition that for this purpose coercion has been confined to instances where it is required by general abstract rules, known beforehand and equally applicable to all. Combined with the requirement that such general rules authorizing coercion could be justified only by the general purpose of preventing worse coercion, this principle seems to be as effective a method of minimizing coercion as mankind has yet discovered."[22] His position, in other words, was not only that law should have a certain, general form, but a coercion-minimizing content.

Hamowy also said that Hayek's "main thesis is that freedom may be defined as the absence of coercion."[23] To this, Hayek responded, "It was not the main thesis of my book that 'freedom may be defined as the absence of coercion.' Rather, as the first sentence of the first chapter explains, its primary concern is 'the condition of men in which coercion of some by others is reduced as much as is possible in society.' I sympathize with disappointment about my admission that I know of no way of preventing coercion altogether and that all we can hope to achieve is to minimize it. Coercion can only be reduced or made less harmful but not entirely eliminated."[24] The essential rub is that to "prevent people from coercing others is to coerce them."[25] The state, Hayek believed, in some form or other, is here to stay.

As well as emphasizing the essentiality of law to liberty, he stressed that progress is for the most part into the unknown. There should not be coercive direction of a society because no one knows what the future may bring and how technological changes may affect future societal life. He strongly believed in everyone's "unavoidable ignorance."[26] "Mind can never foresee its own advance," he wrote, and he quoted Oliver Cromwell that "'Man never mounts higher than when he knows not where he is going.'"[27] Hayek emphasized that it would be an "error to believe that, to achieve a higher civilization, we have merely to put into effect the ideas now guiding us. It we are to advance, we must leave room for a continuous revision of our present conceptions and ideals which will be necessitated by further experience."[28] Mind is unable to foresee its own advance.

He believed in reason. He wrote in *The Constitution of Liberty* that "reason undoubtedly is man's most precious possession. Our argument is intended to show merely that it is not all-powerful and that the belief that it can become its own master and control its own development may yet destroy it."[29] His argument was not against reason, but was itself the reasonable argument that there is a limit to what individual reason may know and accomplish, and optimal societies should be based on this premise, rather than on one that sees an all-powerful individual reason.

The third part of *The Constitution of Liberty* is "Freedom in the Welfare State." Mises reviewed the work, providing this appraisal:

> It was the great merit of Professor Friedrich von Hayek to have directed attention to the authoritarian character of socialist schemes. Now Professor Hayek has enlarged and substantiated his ideas in a comprehensive treatise, *The Constitution of Liberty*. In the first two parts of this book the author provides a brilliant exposition of the meaning of liberty and the creative powers of a free civilization.
>
> Unfortunately, the third part of Professor Hayek's book is rather disappointing. Here the author tries to distinguish between socialism and the Welfare State. Socialism, he alleges, is on the decline; the Welfare State is supplanting it. And he thinks that the Welfare State is under certain conditions compatible with liberty. Professor Hayek has misjudged the character of the Welfare State.[30]

Hayek was not doctrinaire. Based on his own conception that emphasizes the insignificance of an individual's reason, it was consistent that he favored merely piecemeal tinkering with the welfare state rather than its wholesale replacement. Thinkers of a future time may be able to imagine a world without government, but this was not the next practical step when Hayek wrote *The Constitution of Liberty*. The welfare state was at this time the most productive form of human society ever to emerge and required reconfiguration as opposed to replacement in its global confrontation with world communism.

Hayek's hopes for *The Constitution of Liberty* were higher than for any of his other work. He had this exchange with James Buchanan in 1978:

> Q: I've heard you say that you were so surprised by the reaction to *The Road to Serfdom*. On the other hand, I've heard people say that you were greatly disappointed by the reaction to *The Constitution of Liberty*—that you expected much more of a reaction than you got. Is that right?

A: Yes, that is true.[31]

Hayek hoped that, like *The Road to Serfdom, The Constitution of Liberty* would be a tremendous popular success. The work was officially published on February 9, 1960, but review and advance copies were available during late 1959. Hayek personally sent, or had sent by others, scores of copies to leading academics, corporate leaders, and government officials, as well as to journals and magazines, in the United States particularly but throughout the world. While some of this large prepublication promotion was paid for by the University of Chicago Press and foundations, he also dipped into his own pocket.

He sought a wide readership. In a personal letter to an editor at *Time* unsuccessfully encouraging a review, he observed that, while it appeared to be a scholarly work, *The Constitution of Liberty* was intended for the general reader. In a more or less form letter he sent to many with a copy of the book, he expressed that it was intended mostly for businessmen and leaders of public affairs and opinion. He personally sent copies to former President Hoover, Vice President Nixon, *Time* publisher Henry Luce, Walter Lippmann, members of the President's Council of Economic Advisors, and others. Nixon apparently at least glanced at *The Constitution of Liberty* and was basically in sympathy with it.[32]

Hayek sent a copy of *The Constitution of Liberty* to *Reader's Digest,* in the hope that it would condense it, as it had *The Road to Serfdom.* In a letter with *The Constitution of Liberty* to DeWitt Wallace of *Reader's Digest,* he described it as the great positive statement of a free society's principles on which he had been at work since *The Road to Serfdom. Reader's Digest* replied, to Hayek's disappointment, that it would not be possible to condense the work.

Some of the letters and copies of the book he sent were intended to solicit remarks that could be used for further promotion. Roscoe Pound wrote back to Hayek, for example, that "if you feel it is worthwhile to quote me I should not hesitate to say that the book is timely, sound, and well written."[33] In much of Hayek's prepublication correspondence with advance copies, he noted publication would be February 9, hoping to engender the widest possible publicity for the book when it was released.

He was disappointed by the response. No review was published in either *Life* or *Time,* and the book was reviewed unfavorably by Sydney Hook in an interior article in the *New York Times Book Review,* which gave *The Road to Serfdom* a banner, front-page reception sixteen years before. Hook said that as a "cautionary voice Mr. Hayek is always worth listening to. He is an intellectual tonic. But in our present time of troubles, his economic philosophy points the road to disaster."[34]

Hayek's great disappointment in the response to *The Constitution of Liberty* was not entirely warranted and reveals both his extremely high conception of himself and unrealistic expectation of what he thought was likely to be a popular work. Actually, for a work of its sort, it received considerable, as well as positive, attention. John Davenport wrote in *Fortune* that it was a "timely and timeless book";[35] the *Chicago Sunday Tribune Magazine of Books* opined that it "should be the book of the year in the field of ideas";[36] Arthur Kemp said in the *Journal of the American Medical Association* that *The Constitution of Liberty* "provides the most significant contribution in the twentieth century to a restatement of the principles of a free society on which the growth and even the survival of western civilization depends";[37] and Henry Hazlitt, who wrote the 1944 *New York Times Book Review* article on *The Road to Serfdom* that so contributed to its success, praised *The Constitution of Liberty* in his *Newsweek* column.

A reviewer for the *Wall Street Journal* noted in June 1960, four months after its publication, that "the book was well received; the reviews, even in quarters that are normally hostile to the anti-statist position, were respectful. Yet *The Constitution of Liberty* had none of the shattering effect of *The Road to Serfdom*. In one sense this is encouraging. For what it would seem to prove is that Hayek's position has been rehabilitated as a respectable mode of thought. No longer is a libertarian, the 'Old Whig,' the believer in thorough-going individualism, regarded as a freak."[38]

Lionel Robbins wrote in *Economica,* in a review signaling rapprochement with Hayek, that "I have written as I should talk if we were having a friendly discussion in the staff seminar here, as we have done so often in the past. The recognition of an order in society which has not been planned as a totality is clearly fundamental; and never has the pathbreaking significance of the great eighteenth century discoveries in this respect been better set forth than in Professor Hayek's luminous exposition, itself the source of many new insights. Propositions that have been repeated more or less parrot-wise for a hundred and fifty years acquire a meaning and depth seldom before realized," concluding that it is a "work which surely no one with even a bare minimum of magnanimity and sense of what is fine can read without gratitude and admiration—gratitude for a splendid contribution to the great debate, admiration for the moral ardour and intellectual power which inspired it and made it possible."[39] The rift between the two men healed, following the death of the first Mrs. Hayek.

Hayek chose to direct his final thoughts in *The Constitution of Liberty* against conservatism, in its postscript, "Why I Am Not a Conservative." He noted that in the contemporary battle against increasing state power, supporters of classical liberalism had at times to make alliances with conservative forces, but he did not consider these tactical associations to reflect the intrinsic liberal or libertarian positions, which are as opposed to conservatism as to socialism. He saw, indeed, more similarities between socialism and conservatism than between either and classical liberalism or libertarianism, "Conservatism, though a necessary element in any stable society," he wrote, "is not a social program; in its paternalistic, nationalist, and power-adoring tendencies it is often closer to socialism than true liberalism; and with its traditionalistic, anti-intellectual, and often mystical propensities it will never, except in short periods of disillusionment, appeal to the young and all those others who believe that some changes are desirable if this world is to become a better place."[40] Conservatism's opposition, before socialism's rise, was liberalism.

He especially opposed conservatism because of its approach to knowledge. Classical liberalism and libertarianism celebrate the acquisition of new knowledge. They recognize that human advance is into the unknown, and that humanity can never move forward unless one pursues truth wherever it leads. Such has not always been the case with conservatism, which has a "propensity to reject well-substantiated new knowledge because it dislikes some of the consequences which seem to follow from it. By refusing to face the facts, the conservative only weakens his own position."[41] Classical liberalism and libertarianism are committed to reason and truth.

If he had to choose between left and right, he chose left at the time he wrote *The Constitution of Liberty,* in the same way that he dedicated *The Road to Serfdom* to "the socialists of all parties." He wrote in *The Constitution of Liberty* that the "belief in integral freedom is based on an essentially forward-looking attitude and not on any nostalgic longing for the past or a romantic admiration for what has been. In a world where the chief need is once more to free the process of spontaneous growth from the obstacles and encumbrances that human folly has erected . . . [the political philosopher's] hopes must rest on persuading and gaining the support of those who by disposition are 'progressives,' those who, though they may now be seeking change in the wrong direction, are at least willing to examine critically the existing and to change it wherever necessary."[42]

Classical liberalism and libertarianism are forward-looking, rational philosophies. They see potential worlds that yet may be, not that never were. Hayek concluded *The Constitution of Liberty* by writing that "I doubt whether there can be such a thing as a conservative philosophy. Conservatism does not give us any guiding principles which can influence long-range developments."[43] He was a true liberal.

CHAPTER TWENTY-SIX

Influence

INFLUENCE IS SO DIFFICULT TO MEASURE. Hayek quoted Mill approvingly in *The Constitution of Liberty* on the "'lesson given to mankind by every age, and always disregarded—that speculative philosophy, which to the superficial appears a thing so remote from the business of life and the outward interest of men, is in reality the thing on earth which most influences them.'"[1] He himself wrote in *Monetary Nationalism and International Stability* that "I regard it not only as the privilege but as the duty of the academic economist to take all alternatives into consideration, however remote their realisation may appear at the moment."[2] He concluded *The Counter-Revolution of Science,* "I doubt whether it is possible to overestimate the influence which ideas have in the long run."[3] He stated in "Why I Am Not a Conservative" that the "task of the political philosopher can only be to influence public opinion. He will do so effectively only if he is not concerned with what is now politically possible."[4] He approvingly quoted G. Mazzini in *Law, Legislation and Liberty* that "Ideas rule the world and its events. A revolution is the passage of an idea from theory to practice."[5] He himself wrote in *Denationalisation of Money* that the "chief task of the economic theorist or political philosopher should be to operate on public opinion to make politically possible what today may be politically impossible."[6]

Among his favorite lines were those of Keynes' closing to *The General Theory,* where Keynes asked of his work there, "Is the fulfillment of these ideas a visionary hope? It would need a volume of a different character from this one to indicate even in outline the practical measures in which they might be gradually clothed. But if the ideas are correct—an hypothesis on which the author himself must necessarily base what he writes—it would be a mistake, I predict, to dispute their potency over a period of time. The ideas of economists and political philosophers, both when they are right and when they are wrong, are more powerful than is commonly understood. Indeed the world is run by little else. Practical men, who believe themselves to be quite exempt from any intellectual influences, are usually the slaves of some defunct economist. Madmen in authority, who hear voices in the air, are distilling their frenzy from some academic scribbler of a few years back. I am sure that the power of vested interests is vastly exaggerated compared with the gradual encroachment of ideas. . . . Soon or late, it is ideas, not vested interests, which are dangerous for good or evil."[7]

Hayek said in *The Constitution of Liberty* that "the belief that in the long run it is ideas and therefore the men who give currency to new ideas that govern evolution . . . have long formed a fundamental part of the liberal creed."[8] He also held there that "so far as direct influence on current affairs is concerned, the influence of the political philosopher may be negligible. But when his ideas have become common property, through the work of historians and publicists, teachers and writers, and intellectuals generally, they effectively guide developments."[9] Applying this standard to Hayek himself, he intended and sought to guide societal evolution.

Regardless of the immediate success—or lack thereof, in Hayek's opinion—of *The Constitution of Liberty,* the United States was ready for a number of the ideas contained in it. Barry Goldwater, the 1964 Republican presidential nominee against Lyndon Johnson, was significantly influenced by Hayek. According to Goldwater's biographer Lee Edwards, "Echoing Hayek, whom he had read as a young businessman in Phoenix almost twenty years before, Goldwater endorsed a government that 'attends to its inherent responsibilities of maintaining a stable monetary and fiscal climate, encouraging a free and competitive economy, and enforcing law and order'. . . . Goldwater's favorite president was Thomas Jefferson; his political philosopher, F. A. Hayek."[10] Goldwater occasionally quoted Hayek in speeches, and wrote in his 1988 autobiography that during his early years in the Senate he was "much influenced by the work of Professor F. A. Hayek."[11]

Goldwater's *The Conscience of a Conservative*—ghostwritten by Brent Bozell (brother-in-law of William F. Buckley)—was published in April 1960, two months after *The Constitution of Liberty*. It became a huge popular success, illustrating a point Hayek made that the greatest merit of *The Road to Serfdom* is its brevity. *The Conscience of a Conservative* is barely one-eighth the length of *The Constitution of Liberty.* Eventually more than four million copies sold, catapulting Goldwater to the leadership of American conservatism.

While Hayek and Goldwater's terminology differed, their general philosophical views were similar. Goldwater wrote that "the Conservative" (Hayek would have said "Liberal") "looks upon politics as the art of achieving the maximum amount of freedom for individuals that is consistent with the maintenance of social order. The Conservative is the first to understand that the practice of freedom requires the establishment of order: it is impossible for one man to be free if another is able to deny him the exercise of his freedom."[12] It is essential to recognize that order is the first requirement of any society. Without order, nothing else can be accomplished. It is for this reason that liberty is the supremacy of law.

Ronald Reagan received his introduction to American national politics through the Goldwater campaign. In a nationally broadcast speech on Goldwater's behalf a week before the 1964 election, Reagan said that there was "only an up or down: up to man's age-old dream—the ultimate in individual freedom consistent with law and order—or down to the ant heap of totalitarianism."[13] To the interview question "What philosophical thinkers most influenced your conduct as a leader?" Reagan later responded that "I've always been a voracious reader—I've read the economic views of von Mises and Hayek."[14] Those close to Reagan studied Hayek. Of seventy-four economists employed in six task forces during the Reagan administration, twenty were members of the Mont Pelerin Society.[15] Former Attorney General Edwin Meese recalls that individuals high within the Reagan administration influenced by Hayek include Richard Allen, Glenn Campbell, Martin Anderson, and himself. He also remembers Reagan quoting and being familiar with Hayek's work. Meese adds that Friedman was the more important influence on the Reagan administration.[16]

Jack Kemp—primary House of Representatives sponsor of the Kemp-Roth tax bill cutting taxes across-the-board, which Reagan embraced in 1980, as well as Robert Dole's 1996 vice presidential running-mate—wrote Hayek after he received the Nobel Prize that "Your books, especially *The Constitution of Liberty,* gave me the desire to run for Congress."[17] David Stockman, Reagan's first director of the Office of Management and Budget, described his intellectual development, "I plunged into economics with unusual vigor. Before long I emerged a disciple of F. A. Hayek."[18] Just a few of the others in the United States influenced by Hayek include writers William F. Buckley, Frank Meyer, Thomas Sowell, R. Emmett Tyrell, and George Will, Republican Congressmen Tom Campbell, Ron Paul, Marc Sanford, Dana Rohrabacher, John Kasich, and Richard Armey, Senator Phil Gramm, and former Massachusetts governor William Weld.

In the United States, Hayek's appeal generally has been to the right/ libertarian side of the political spectrum. In Great Britain, there has been considerable intellectual interest in Hayek from the left, through such academic writers as Lord Desai, John Gray, David Miller, and Raymond Plant, building on such historical interest there from the academic left. In England, however, the primary interest in Hayek is from the right, most prominently Margaret Thatcher and the Institute of Economic Affairs.[19] Keynes biographer, Robert Skidelsky, is also very interested in Hayek.

When Reagan said in his first presidential press conference of the government officials of the Soviet Union that they have "openly and publicly declared that the only morality they recognize is what will further their cause, meaning they reserve unto themselves the right to commit any crime, to lie, to cheat,"[20] he could have been paraphrasing Hayek. When Reagan stated that the Soviet Union was an "evil empire," he expressed Hayek's thought exactly. For Hayek's thesis that the political philosopher and economist guides events, it is surely relevant that the four leading conservative political leaders in the Anglo-American world during the twentieth century—Reagan, Thatcher, Goldwater, and Churchill—have all been influenced by him, though in somewhat different ways.

Hayek left Chicago for financial reasons. He was "much concerned about the inadequate provision for my and my wife's old age which that position offered me: a lump sum at a comparatively early retirement age (sixty-five),"[21] which would have occurred in 1964. D. Gale Johnson, who has served in the administration as well as in the economics department at the University of Chicago, remembers Hayek talking with him about retirement. Hayek had not accumulated many assets because of his divorce and also because he lived a relatively expensive lifestyle for a university professor, with annual summer trips to the Austrian Alps. He never received any royalties for the condensed version of *The Road to Serfdom,* nor did he write any textbooks, which usually are the most remunerative form of academic writing. From the late 1940s through receiving the Nobel Prize in Economics in 1974, royalties from Hayek's books never exceeded £5,000 in a single year, and, a journalist wrote in 1975, that would have been a "high figure for any of those years."[22] *The Road to Serfdom* sold 100,000 copies in English during its first two or three years, which earned Hayek $30,000. By the early 1960s, there was only a small amount of royalties each year from the book.

Ralph Horowitz, a Mont Pelerin Society member, recalls Hayek telling him that he had lost his savings in a financial swindle (though perhaps after the Chicago period).[23] Hayek did not make his living through writing; his primary source of income during his academic years was his professorial positions. His last and longtime secretary, Charlotte Cubitt, reports that he once told her that every move he made was for financial reasons. Hayek also said, of leaving the United States, that as much as he "enjoyed the intellectual environment that the University of Chicago offered," he "never came to feel as much at home in the United States" as he had in England.[24]

Hayek was not exclusively at Chicago during his years in the United States. In addition to his semester at the University of Arkansas during 1950, he was a lecturer on political economy at Harvard during the 1952-53 academic year, and lectured at the University of Virginia in 1961. Later, during 1968-69, he was visiting Flint Professor at the University of California at Los Angeles. While he never broke through to popular consciousness while in the United States, he increased his exposure within American academia substantially, thereby gaining the opportunity for greater mediated influence in the United States, and thereby internationally.

He said of his time in Chicago that "I was very happy and spent twelve years at the Committee on Social Thought, with very friendly personal relations with the Economics Department. Viner had moved and gone to Princeton, but Knight was still there, and [I] very soon established a very close relationship with Friedman and Stigler. I enjoyed these twelve years in Chicago very much."[25]

Friedman says that, in contrast to the economics department, "Hayek's influence on Chicago was much more through the students he brought, through the group that established the *New Individualist Review*—his influence there was very strong and very great."[26] The *New Individualist Review* was published between 1961 and 1968. Friedman also writes that when the *New Individualist Review* was founded, "belief in 'free, private enterprise, and in the imposition of the strictest limits to the power of government' and in 'a commitment to human liberty'—to quote from the editorial introducing volume 1, number 1— was at a low ebb even in the countries of the so-called free world. Yet, at the same time, there were many signs of an intellectual reaction against collectivist views, of a resurgence of interest in the philosophy of classical liberalism. Two organizations in particular served to channel and direct this resurgence: the Mont Pelerin Society and the Intercollegiate Society of Individualists. . . . The Intercollegiate Society of Individualists (ISI) operated at the other end of the age scale. It promoted the establishment of chapters among undergraduate and graduate students on college campuses. The members of these chapters too were a minority, but also one that had more than its share of independence, integrity, selflessness, and breadth of vision."[27] Others organizations in which Hayek participated in the United States included the Foundation for Economic Education (FEE), Philadelphia Society, American Enterprise Institute, and later, the Heritage Foundation and Cato Institute.[28]

Latin American interest in Hayek perhaps follows interest in him in the English- and German-speaking worlds. As early as the 1950s, there were government officials in Latin American countries interested in his work. Alvaro Alsogaray, minister of economy in Argentina from 1959 to 1962, later ambassador to the United States, and founder of the Institute of Social Market Economy, wrote Hayek in 1968 that "we are reaching the culmination of our struggles and the present economic platform of the Government is based on the ideas you have developed."[29] A number of think-tanks and university academicians in Latin America during recent decades have been influenced by Hayek. Guatemalan and past president of the Mont Pelerin Society Manuel Ayau calls Hayek "the intellectual torchlight for the libertarians in Latin America."[30]

Hayek's son, Larry, himself a Mont Pelerin member, remarks that the society was "very much" his father's "baby."[31] The society genuinely was a fledgling organization during the 1950s, with the question of its future completely open. Society historian and former president Max Hartwell writes that as early as 1948 there were "tensions about the character and size of the society and about the appropriate strategy for reviving and sustaining liberalism."[32] Not all agreed with Hayek's conception of a strictly intellectual association with no advocacy, not even a journal or publication of conference proceedings. Albert Hunold, the fund-raising secretary, sought a society publication and was continually rebuffed by Hayek. The 1958 and 1959 meetings were held in Princeton and Oxford. "At these meetings," Hartwell writes, "the society began to fall apart."[33]

By common consensus among the Hayek/anti-Hunold faction, Hunold prevented the sort of cooperation among members that is required for a private association like the Mont Pelerin Society to be effective, harmonious, and enjoyable. At the 1958 and 1959 meetings, Hunold interfered with previously made arrangements regarding speakers and sessions, and basically attempted to run the show completely. Tempers flared. Personal relations became strained. There were allegations of petty financial improprieties by Hunold, which he reciprocated. Friedman, who strongly supported Hayek, wrote in a 1959 letter on problems the society faced that the "immediate provocation is the increasingly impossible and insubordinate behavior of Hunold, involving proceeding against actions of the Council and without the consent of the President, and indeed against his request, insulting and libeling members and those who assist in organizing meetings."[34] Hayek and Hunold had been a president and secretary team since the society's founding.

A showdown ensued at the 1960 conference. According to Hartwell, the "conflict shows that if a small group of people who know each other well begin to quarrel, there is a tendency toward increasing hostility because each side feels that it is being betrayed by former friends. If, in addition, the combatants are very intelligent, they argue the *casus belli* with great skill and with a meticulous dissecting of each other's communications. Letters become a combination of learned article and lawyer's brief. If, finally, there are some real issues involved, whether those of power or strategy, then further passion is added to the conflict, and the whole affair passes beyond the boundaries of reasonableness and good sense. Finally attitudes harden and compromise becomes impossible, so that one side must win and the other side must lose and be banished."[35] Hartwell notes of the communiqués sent by both sides in the run-up to the 1960 conference that the "increasing length of the letters and the increasing rapidity of their circulation are quite revealing, as are the passion and intensity of feeling they display. The combatants argued as though great issues were involved and great stakes were at risk."[36]

The September 1960 meeting was very unsatisfying for Hayek. He had sent a letter to all members a month before the conference announcing his intention to step down as president, adding "I should not wish to remain connected with a Society of which Dr. Hunold is Secretary."[37] Both Hayek's and Hunold's allies attempted to collect proxy votes for the meeting—George Stigler was Hayek's key ally in collecting proxies from American members. Hayek did not arrive until the third day of the conference. A compromise over the society's governance was reached in which Wilhelm Röpke (a Hunold ally) became president and Hunold stepped down as secretary but became a vice president. Hunold noted that when, at the final meeting, members were invited to applaud his and Hayek's service to the society, he received more spontaneous applause than Hayek did.[38]

Hayek was completely absent from the 1961 conference. This confabulation featured three board meetings in a single day, and was a defeat for Hunold and Röpke, the latter of whom had intended that Hunold would succeed him as president. The American contingent came to the conclusion that either Hunold must go or they would resign from the society. Hunold and Röpke resigned in December 1961, and their resignations were followed by about a dozen more in their support in 1962. In a 10,000-word valedictory that Hayek contemplated sending to all Mont Pelerin members in late 1961—before Hunold and Röpke's resignations—but that he then never did, he intended to announce his resignation from the society because it had been destroyed by these two men in whom he had placed his trust. In 1964, after the dust settled, Hayek was made honorary president of the Mont Pelerin Society and remained its guiding spirit for the rest of his life.

As Hayek completed *The Constitution of Liberty,* he did not really know what his next major project would be. James Buchanan recalls that Hayek "came to Charlottesville in January 1961, for a semester-long visit. He had just published *The Constitution of Liberty,* and he expressed an interest in using the Virginia lectures as the format for returning to economic theory and particularly to his early major contribution on the use of knowledge in society. . . . He announced a series under the overall title 'A New Look at Economic Theory,' and he presented four lectures on (1) 'The Object of Economic Theory,' (2) 'The Economic Calculus,' (3) 'Economics and Technology' and (4) 'The Communication Function of the Market.' . . . The lectures were failures, at least by Professor Hayek's own standards. Those who listened to them were, of course, rewarded by a careful review of the earlier analysis of knowledge in relation to economic interaction. But Hayek was unable to go beyond that which he had developed two decades before; no new insights emerged as he reviewed the earlier thought processes."[39]

Hayek's thought changed over his career more in the areas he emphasized than in his essential views. Indeed, after his youthful flirtation with socialism, he rarely changed his opinions, although they developed. He wrote in a late essay on Keynes of "the great scientist whose growing insight moves along a single path"[40]—presumably Hayek's experience of his own intellectual development.

Hayek began to suffer from truly significant depression from about the time of his 1961 visit to Charlottesville, which was later diagnosed as in part the reaction to a mild heart attack that was not discovered at the time. His depression became intermittent during the coming years and was most pronounced from about 1969, when he had another, somewhat more significant, heart attack (also not discovered at the time), until 1974, shortly before he received notification that he won the Nobel Prize in Economic Science.

He accepted a position at the University of Freiburg, West Germany, for the fall of 1962. A surprise testimonial dinner was given for him and Helene at the Quadrangle Club on May 24 by the Intercollegiate Society of Individualists. He was tricked into attending by some students who led him to believe that he would merely be having dinner with them. His old friend Fritz Machlup came from Princeton to serve as master of ceremonies.

Friedman paid tribute to Hayek. He observed that Hayek had "succeeded in straddling two kinds of worlds"—the world of scientific knowledge and the world of public opinion. "This attempt to influence opinion is something that is very seldom combined with thorough, deep, and profound scholarly work that can influence the course of science. There are few men who have exercised the kind of influence which Fritz Hayek has on the ideas in the whole western world and not only in the United States."[41]

George Stigler also honored Hayek. He said that Hayek was "one of the few three or four professional economists who have had a noticeable influence on the course of his time in the twentieth century," but lamented that Hayek had not devoted more attention to the history of economic thought. "Mrs. Hayek," Stigler concluded his comments, "I want you each day in the future to address your husband and inquire what his progress has been in what I consider to be one of the most interesting and intriguing fields, the evolution of the work of scholars."[42]

Ludwig von Mises, who was at New York University at this time, sent the following statement that was read at the banquet. "We are not losing Hayek entirely," Mises wrote. "He will henceforth teach at a German University, but we are certain that from time to time he will come back for lectures and conferences to this country. And we are certain that, on these visits, he will have much more to say. In this expectation, we may take it as a good omen that the name of the city of his future sphere of activity is Freiburg. 'Frei'—that means free."[43]

In impromptu remarks, Hayek said that the twelve years—or actually seventeen since he had been visiting Chicago almost every year—had been of great importance to him. The opportunity to do what he chose, and follow the interests he picked, was very valuable. He was able to move beyond technical economics to larger societal issues within which economics is subsumed. He was both apprehensive and hopeful regarding the future trends of political and economic thought and practice. He said later of his dedication of *The Constitution of Liberty* to "the unknown civilization that is growing in America" that the "moral views of the next one hundred years are going to be determined by the United States more than anywhere else."[44]

FIVE

FREIBURG

*"A new statement of the liberal principles of justice
and political economy"*

—*subtitle of* Law, Legislation and Liberty

CHAPTER TWENTY-SEVEN

Law, Legislation and Liberty

HAYEK LIKELY EXPERIENCED A MAJOR CHANGE IN WORLDVIEW after *The Constitution of Liberty* was published. He may have thought that his picture might appear on *Time* magazine, not that he would be unable to secure a review in it. While he was periodically identified during the 1950s in the United States as a leading conservative thinker, he never broke through to the popular consciousness while he was in Chicago, as he had with *The Road to Serfdom*.

He began teaching at the University of Freiburg, West Germany, in the fall of 1962. His work during the 1960s in Freiburg was highly productive. *Law, Legislation and Liberty,* one of his two greatest works, along with *The Constitution of Liberty,* was mainly written in Freiburg.

Erich Streissler, a colleague at the time, recalls a number of Hayek anecdotes, including that a real effort was made to obtain his services for the university. The dean at Freiburg in particular appreciated his thought, though Hayek was largely forgotten in continental Europe. Streissler also remembers that it was nonetheless quite an event in the German academic world when Hayek came to Freiburg.

Hayek was popular among students. His seminar during the 1960s was well attended, including by socialist professors. When Hayek arrived, he was second in seniority on the faculty based on first employment as a professor—faculty sat by seniority. Hayek emphasized economic policy, rather than contemporary theory, in his teaching. He almost became rector of Freiburg, but spoiled his chances when he supported government efforts to discontinue winter break and by his suggestion of Otto von Habsburg (of the former royal family) for the political science department.

Economic historian Henry Spiegel and his wife Cecile visited Hayek during the mid 1960s in Freiburg. They recall him as being cross when he could not attend a presentation of *The Magic Flute* with them because only three tickets, rather than four, had been purchased (on the basis that Hayek's poor hearing would prevent him from attending). Hayek also complained to them about the high rate of West German taxation.

On returning to Europe, he resumed more frequent contact with his children. His daughter-in-law remembers her husband saying, "Now, I have a father again,"[1] after Hayek returned to Europe. Hayek saw his family in Austria more as well, including his mother and brothers, and Helene's family. His mother lived until she was ninety-two in 1967.

He characterized his years at Freiburg during the 1960s as "very fruitful,"[2] and observed that in addition to academic work he and his wife traveled more than ever before. This included four trips to Japan with side trips to Taiwan, Indonesia, Tahiti, Fiji, New Caledonia, Sydney, and Ceylon, as well as an academic term at the University of California, Los Angeles. He said of his time in Freiburg from 1962 to 1969 that he retained until almost the end of that period his "full energy," "health," and "working capacity."[3]

Law, Legislation and Liberty—particularly its first volume, *Rules and Order*—is the unduly neglected great work of Hayek's career. The relationship between *The Constitution of Liberty* and *Law, Legislation and Liberty* is not always understood, as the latter is not always understood. It is often forgotten when considering the two works that, although the latter was not published until the 1970s, it was for the most part written during the 1960s, just a few years after *The Constitution of Liberty*.

Law, Legislation and Liberty should be seen more as a continuation of ideas in the earlier treatise than as a completely different work. It was written after the ideas and new information stirred up by writing *The Constitution of Liberty* settled in Hayek's mind, and was finished during his highly productive and creative later seventies.

Describing the relation between his two greatest works in the introduction of *Law, Legislation and Liberty*, Hayek wrote that in "another book I have attempted to restate, and hope to have in some measure succeeded in clarifying, the traditional doctrine of liberal constitutionalism. But it was only after I had completed that work that I came to see clearly why those ideals had failed to retain the support of the idealists to whom all the great political movements are due."[4] *Law, Legislation and Liberty* was the more original of his two *chefs-d'oeuvre*. He remarked in the preface to its third volume that though *Law, Legislation and Liberty* was "supplementary to and not a substitute for" *The Constitution of Liberty*, it was "more original." He said here as well that to the "non-specialist reader" he would therefore recommend *The Constitution of Liberty* before proceeding to the "more detailed discussion or particular examination of problems to which I have attempted solutions in these volumes."[5]

Law, Legislation and Liberty is written at a higher level than *The Constitution of Liberty*, as the earlier work was intended for a more general audience. Hayek realized that his work would not penetrate to a more popular readership, and therefore in *Law, Legislation and Liberty* did not even attempt to pitch it to anyone other than specialists. It is appreciated most by reading it several times, as well as by possessing significant background in political and economic theory and history generally, and in Hayek's other work.

This second treatise was originally conceived as a "little pamphlet,"[6] apparently in 1962. Hayek intended at first to follow *The Constitution of Liberty* with additional work in the field of the division of knowledge. He wrote to Popper in 1960 that "Though I do not mean to concentrate mainly on methodology, The New Look at Economic Theory which I am taking and which may result in a book of that title inevitably began with an attempt to restate my views of the nature of economic theory, and the conception of higher level regularities which I then formed continues to occupy me and seems fruitful far beyond the field of economics."[7]

Hayek referred to A. P. d'Entreves' *Natural Law* (1951) in *Law, Legislation and Liberty*, and said earlier that the "best brief survey"[8] of the various natural law theories he knew was d'Entreves' work. It is worthwhile to turn to this work for a moment to attain a fuller understanding of Hayek's conception of law. D'Entreves wrote that the "essential function of law is to make life in society possible. Law presupposes society. Legal experience is tied to the notion of a community. Human laws cover only those aspects of human behaviour which imply a co-ordination with other men. Thus, properly speaking, the laws of men do not primarily aim at promoting virtue, but only at securing a peaceful living together: they do not forbid all that is evil, but only that which imperils society; they do not command all that is good, but only that which pertains to the general welfare."[9]

Hayek agreed and disagreed with this statement of law. While he, too, believed that law pertains to the common, as opposed to individual, good, he also thought that customs and morals play a vital role. They are a fundamental part of the glue that binds people together in a society, but, unlike law, are not coercively enforced by government. Laws, customs, and morals together create a society. Law is what may be demanded of people coercively through government. Customs and morals are a non-coercive standard.

He was vitally interested in the concept of system, that, in physical terms, there can be no action without an equal and positive reaction somewhere and sometime else in the system. This is in part the idea of equilibrium, and economic theory is in certain respects an attempt to apply to society truths of the physical world.

Law, Legislation and Liberty stemmed from his work in economic theory. He came to see that the laws, customs, and morals of a society define and create that society. Laws, customs, and morals are a way of looking at the world, a *Weltanschauung,* a worldview, a paradigm. They do not exist so much in bricks and mortar as in the minds of a society's members. They are shared values. They provide consistency, rationality, and stability for the members of a society, thereby allowing more, or less, fruitful interaction.

Freiburg is a beautiful city of 200,000 people. Its Albert-Ludwigs University has about 25,000 students and was founded in 1457. It is the third oldest university in Germany. The city is located in the southern- and westernmost niche of Germany, within twenty-five miles of France and Switzerland. Thousand-meter hills rise adjacent to the city center on one side, and it is surely the case that the old mountain climber Hayek walked through these. Vineyards are adjacent to the city on a plain in the opposite direction. The city itself is dominated by the Münster, "Cathedral of Our Lady." The name "Freiburg" means "free castle." During the Middle Ages, a market was located here. The city experienced significant destruction during World War II, but was restored following the war.

The unanticipated offer to teach at Freiburg allowed Hayek to work three years longer than he would have in Chicago and included a pension for life, which was financially important to him. Financial concerns weighed heavily on him. A reporter described him when he was in London shortly after he assumed duties in Freiburg, "The voice is quiet and measured, heavily accented. On Wednesday evening he loomed genially above the other guests at the Institute of Economic Affairs, a big shambling man with a small grey moustache, in elephantine grey suit and a wayward collar, as defiantly unmodish in dress as in opinion, looking more like a country auctioneer than the Prussian *savant* (he is in fact an Austrian anyway), drinking not schnapps but homely sherry."[10]

He said in his inaugural lecture on assuming the professorship in political economy at Freiburg that he did not know to what "good star" he owed it that for the "third time in the course of one life that faculty has honoured me with the offer of a chair which I would have chosen if an absolutely free choice in such things were possible." As Freiburg is halfway between Vienna and London, "the two places which . . . shaped me intellectually" and is located in an area that was for centuries part of the Austrian Empire, moving to it was "something like coming home."[11]

Academic circumstances at the University of Freiburg were more similar to those he experienced at the University of Vienna more than three decades before than to those at either the London School of Economics or the University of Chicago. Economics was located in the faculty of law. He "valued particularly the opportunity to teach again in a faculty of law, in the atmosphere to which I owe my own schooling. After one has endeavoured for thirty years to teach economics to students possessing no knowledge of law or the history of legal institutions, one is sometimes tempted to ask whether the separation of legal and economic studies was not perhaps, after all, a mistake."[12] The fact that German and Austrian scholars place greater emphasis on the relationship between law and the economic system than many Anglo-American economists do, reflects, perhaps, this institutional arrangement.

As Hayek resettled in the German-speaking world, his focus shifted to some extent. He began to speak German again to colleagues and students, and wrote more in German as well. He and his second wife almost always spoke German. He had, moreover, "once again, to become an economist." As he was able to concentrate on problems of economic policy as opposed to pure theory, though, he thought he "still had something of importance to say."[13] He resumed more active teaching responsibilities, offering classes, leading seminars, and advising students. He said in his inaugural address that he hoped during the remainder of his active career to pass along the fruits of his experience after "long years of study in various parts of the world which were devoted more to research than to teaching."[14] In a preliminary version of *The Fatal Conceit* he remarked that the first half of his life was devoted to learning and the second half to teaching.

Hayek's argument, following d'Entreves', that rules pertain to the common good, deserves emphasis. What may be demanded of one by others is not what is in one's own interest, but that one not harm others. The common good is the domain of rules—that is, laws, customs, and morals. Personal good may not be demanded of one by others, either through coercive laws or non-coercive morals.

Hayek had been familiar with the University of Freiburg for many years as a result of his close friendship with the classical liberal economist Walter

Eucken, who died a dozen years before Hayek accepted his position. Hayek had also known several other professional colleagues at Freiburg, but they too had passed away before he arrived. The Walter Eucken Institute, which has played a considerable role in publishing Hayek in the German-speaking world, is now located at the University of Freiburg.

The 1960s are recalled in retrospect as a time of tumult and change, but they were not so for Hayek during most of his Freiburg years. The cultural explosions of the decade did not really occur until its last years, and through 1967 or so the prosperous and relatively calm societal circumstances that characterized the 1950s continued through much of the developed western world.

CHAPTER TWENTY-EIGHT

Liberty and Law

THE ISSUES WITH WHICH HAYEK GRAPPLED in *Law, Legislation and Liberty* are among the deepest and most fundamental in political philosophy. John Locke, the great English liberal political philosopher, grounded government in men's partiality toward themselves and their associates: "It is unreasonable for men to be judges in their own cases, self-love will make men partial to themselves and their friends: and on the other side, ill-nature, passion and revenge will carry them too far in punishing others; therefore God hath certainly appointed government to restrain the partiality and violence of men. Civil government is the proper remedy for the state of nature."[1]

Hayek completely followed Locke. True liberty, far from being inconsistent with law, is in fact dependent on it. Genuine law is the embodiment of liberty. Law is the essential ingredient of liberty. Without law, there can be no liberty. Right law (*orthonomos*) is liberty.

The idea that liberty is properly defined as law may be unusual to those who consider freedom to be either the complete absence of government or a certain material standard of living. With respect to the former, there is a great difference between libertarianism and anarchism. Hayek observed that the distinction between his view and "some of my friends who lean into the anarchist camp is that within the territory where I live I can assume that any person that I encounter is held to obey certain minimal rules. I cannot form voluntary groups of people who obey the same rules and still have an open society. I must know that within the territory in which I live, any unknown person I encounter is held to obey certain rules which are known to me. Libertarianism quite easily slides into anarchism, and it's important to draw this line. An open society in which I can deal with any person I encounter presupposes certain basic rules on everybody." [2]

Anarchists believe in no government and no laws. They desire to live in what Locke called "the state of nature." Libertarians, on the other hand, believe law creates liberty because laws enable individuals to interact most productively in a material sense. Without effective and optimal law, people's opportunities for interaction are circumscribed. In a society in which there were no law, human life would be, as Thomas Hobbes put it, "solitary, poor, nasty, brutish, and short." [3] Law is required not so much for individual as collective life, and, in the libertarian view, for collective life that is the most productive materially.

Hayek rejected the conflation of liberty, or freedom, with a certain material standard of living. Though liberty and a high standard of living may both be desirable, this does not imply that liberty is the same thing as a high material standard. Liberty, in society, refers to one thing and one thing only, Hayek thought. Liberty is the society in which coercion is reduced to the minimum possible through known general laws applicable to all with a coercion-minimizing intent. Liberty is the supremacy of law.

Hayek favored explicit government creation of laws and societal imposition of new non-coercive rules. He was clear on this point. He was a radical who sought to change existing laws and institutions to the extent to which they do not lead to the greatest competition possible. While he also affirmed that there may be great wisdom contained in the inherited laws and other rules of past generations, his decisive commitment was to change, not stasis. His philosophy was a dynamic, progressive creed that emphasizes the desirability of great societal change. He was explicitly not a conservative.

During the 1960s and 1970s, he proposed significant alterations in legislative and monetary arrangements, which he described as "radical" and "far-reaching change[s] in our political institutions." [4] In replying to those who suggested that his later monetary proposals were inconsistent with his emphasis on evolutionary development in a society, he responded that it "has been said that my suggestion to 'construct' wholly new monetary institutions is in conflict with my general philosophical attitude. But nothing is further from my thoughts than any wish to design new institutions. What I propose is simply to remove the existing obstacles which for ages have prevented the evolution of desirable institutions in money."[5] He sought to remove impediments to new, competition-maximizing institutions, not to create the details of such institutions himself.

Although he decried "constructivist rationalism," Hayek sought great change in societal macro-institutions. He stated in the penultimate paragraph of *Law, Legislation and Liberty* (which, when he wrote it, was intended to be his final work) that "government is of necessity the product of intellectual design. If we can give it a shape in which it provides a beneficial framework for the free growth of society . . . we may well hope to see the growth of civilization continue."[6] He thought that the ideas that guide, and practical implementation of, government are vital. Unlike classical socialists, however, who seek to direct all of the details of a society's economic activity, Hayek's goal was to create a philosophical framework to guide future societal order. He sought new, competition-maximizing institutions, which he thought would require great change from existing institutions. He said of his later radical monetary proposals that if he were "responsible for the fate of a country dear" to him, he would "gladly take the risk in the field I have been considering here."[7]

He advocated government activity in what are usually considered environmental and local "quality of life" issues. Hayek posited that it is "often impossible to confine the effects of what one does to one's own land to this particular piece; and hence arises those 'neighbourhood effects' which will not be taken into account so long as the owner has to consider only the effects on his property. Hence also the problems which arise with respect to the pollution of air or water and the like."[8] After he received the Nobel Prize, he offered use of his name for endorsement purposes to the World Wildlife Fund. Other environmental organizations of which he approved included the Audobon Society in the United States and Natural Trust in Great Britain.

He listed "arms" among the "dangerous goods" he defined in *Law, Legislation and Liberty* as amenable to "restrictions on sale,"[9] and said that it is "probably undeniable that where the sale of firearms is involved, it is both desirable and unobjectionable that only persons satisfying certain intellectual and moral qualities should be allowed to practice such trades."[10] He was not what in the United States would be considered a strong supporter of the second amendment to the U.S. constitution. He approved of military conscription.

Of homosexuality, he said that "private practice among adults, however abhorrent it may be to the majority, is not a proper subject for coercive action for a state whose object is to minimize coercion."[11] He referred to the British *Report of the Committee on Homosexual Offences and Prostitution,* and declared his agreement with the logic that led the committee to recommend the legalization of these activities. The question was that of "whether the existence of strongly and widely held moral convictions in any matter is by itself a justification for their enforcement. The answer seems to be that within a spontaneous order the use of coercion can be justified only where this is necessary to secure the private domain of the individual against interference by others, but that coercion should not be used to interfere in that private sphere where this is not necessary to protect others."[12] Liberty is freedom of individual action and association created through law.

CHAPTER TWENTY-NINE

Marx, Evolution, and Utopia

IDENTIFICATION OF ASPECTS OF HAYEK'S OR AUSTRIAN ECONOMIC THOUGHT with Marx is a common academic view. Hayek's technical economic thought—while not his practical economic advice—in part resembles that of Marx. Robert Skidelsky comments of Hayek's early economic work that Hayek's "conclusion was that a credit-money capitalist system is violently unstable . . . [and] nothing could be done about it. One can understand why Hayek's doctrines attracted a certain kind of socialist: they seemed to reach Marx's conclusions."[1]

Lord Desai observes that there are "many parallels" between Hayek and Marx; "their life's work was concerned with *modelling* capitalism, its cyclical character, the importance of money and credit, its long-term prospects. . . . There is much that is common to Marxian and some variants of Hayekian thought. Their analysis of the dynamics of capitalism is similar . . . There is also much in common in capital theory between Hayek and Marx. Compare if you will the middle third of the second volume of *Capital* and Hayek's *Pure Theory of Capital,* and you will discover a similar enterprise."[2]

In an early LSE lecture, "The Marxian Theory of Crises," Hayek praised book II of Marx's *Capital* in his lecture notes, emphasized it in his lecture bibliography, and placed Marx at almost the level of Adam Smith in general economics.[3] Hayek's praise of book II of *Capital* followed Böhm-Bawerk's, who, while strongly faulting other parts of Marx's system, held of the second part of *Capital* that these "parts of the system . . . by their extraordinary logical consistency permanently establish the author as an intellectual force of the first rank. This long middle part of his work is really essentially faultless."[4]

Marxian writer Karl Kühne wrote that "Marxian ideas have had certain repercussions in conservative circles. The great conservative von Hayek has had the courage to admit that he has been influenced by Marx *via* Tugan-Baranovsky and Spiethoff." Kühne continued that "Marxist theory and over-capitalisation theories overlap. The true heir to this theory is an arch-conservative, von Hayek, who paradoxically and honestly recognized Marx's paternity. . . . The essential point is not to be found in von Hayek's conservative conclusions, but in his analysis of the causes of the boom and depression, which strongly resembles the Marxian one."[5]

In the 1933 English edition of his *Monetary Theory and the Trade Cycle*, Hayek said that there was less divergence between his own theory of the trade cycle and non-monetary theories than between his own theory and other monetary explanations. Commenting on this line in the original text—"There can, at the present time, be no more important task in this field [of explaining a trade cycle] than the bridging of the gulf which divides monetary from non-monetary theories"[6]—he later footnoted, "Since the publication of the German edition of this book, I have become less convinced that the difference between monetary and non-monetary explanations is *the most important* point of disagreement between the various Trade Cycle theories. It seems to me that within the monetary group of explanations the difference between those theorists who regard the superficial phenomena of changes in the value of money as decisive factors in determining cyclical fluctuations, and those [such as Hayek himself] who lay emphasis on the real changes in the structure of production brought about by monetary causes, is much greater than the difference between the latter group and such so-called non-monetary theorists as Prof. Spiethoff and Prof. Cassel."[7] That is, his own position was closer to non-monetarists such as Spiethoff and Cassel, and, by implication, Marx, than to monetarists who ascribed an inflationary or deflationary source to a trade cycle.[8]

The stream of thought explaining Hayek's conception of the monetary influence on economic activity was closer to that of Marx than to monetarists. Hayek wrote of the former, Marxian stream in *The Pure Theory of Capital* that "in all these different versions of [business cycle] theory the crucial point is that, towards the end of a boom, a scarcity of circulating capital and a consequent rise in the rates of interest make it impossible either to complete the large projects for investment in fixed capital or profitably to use the additional plant so created. It would lead us too far afield to discuss here the relations which are supposed by the different writers to exist between these phenomena and credit expansion. Nor is it possible here to trace the important influence which these views have had on the theory of crises of Karl Marx, through him on M. v. Tougan-Baranowski, and through the latter on such contemporary authors as G. Cassel, A. Spiethoff . . ."[9]

In his lecture file for his early 1930s lecture "The Marxian Theory of Crises," Hayek had twenty pages of notes and a bibliography including works by Marx, Hilferding, Tougan-Baranovsky, and Spiethoff. Regarding Tougan-Baranovsky (who based his work on Marx), Hayek wrote in his lecture notes that Tougan-Baranovsky's work was the most influential source of modern trade cycle theory.[10]

Hayek said of his own theory of the trade cycle in *Prices and Production* that "the central idea of the theory of the trade cycle which has been expounded in the preceding lecture is by no means new. That industrial fluctuations consist essentially in alternating expansions and contractions of the structure of capital equipment has often been emphasised. . . . In the German literature similar ideas were introduced mainly by the writings of Karl Marx. It is on Marx that M. v. Tougan-Baranovsky's work is based which in turn provided the starting point for the later work of Professor Spiethoff and Professor Cassel. The extent to which the theory developed in these lectures corresponds with that of the two last-named authors, particularly with that of Professor Spiethoff, need hardly be emphasised."[11]

Analyst of Marxian economics Michael Perelman maintains that Marx realized that "credit was a central factor in the upheavals that occurred. . . . Marx integrate[d] his analysis of credit into his economic theories. The lynchpin that connects this analysis is the notion of fictitious capital"[12]—capital financed through the monetary system without real savings. Perelman also writes of his conception of Marx's theory that "the more fictitious capital distorts the price signals, the more important information about the economy disappears. Decisions about production become increasingly unrelated to the underlying structure. Pressures build up in the economy, but they are not visible."[13]

Such was essentially Hayek's view. He remarked in *Prices and Production,* referring to the stream of thought including Marx and Spiethoff that "at one time, at the beginning of the second half of the last century, such theories enjoyed considerable vogue and the financial journalists of those days frequently used a terminology which seems to imply essentially the same argument as that used here. The creation of 'fictitious capital' makes it impossible to continue or to complete the new undertakings and so causes collapse."[14]

Hayek and Marx were of one mind regarding the initial outcomes of capitalism. Marx and Engels wrote in *The Communist Manifesto* that "The bourgeoisie has played a most revolutionary role in history. The bourgeoisie has been the first to show what man's activity can bring about. It has accomplished wonders far surpassing Egyptian pyramids, Roman aqueducts, and Gothic cathedrals; it has conducted expeditions that put in the shade all former migrations of nations and crusades . . . The bourgeoisie has given a cosmopolitan character to production and consumption in every country. The bourgeoisie, by the rapid improvement of all instruments of production, by the immensely facilitated means of communication, draws all nations, even the most barbarian, into civilisation."[15] Hayek scarcely saw it differently.

Where Marx and Hayek differed—and where Marx was in error—was on the subsequent development of capitalism. Far from capital concentrating, it has dispersed; far from the living standards of workers diminishing, they have fantastically increased; far from material conditions becoming worse around the world, they have incredibly improved; far from capitalism ending in a crash, it flourishes more abundantly than ever for more people than ever before.

Continental socialism always had a strong atavistic element, as stated by Marx in *The Communist Manifesto*. In addition to his rueful comment there that capitalism has put an end to "idyllic relations," there is the ninth of the measures in *The Communist Manifesto* that "will be pretty generally applicable" as to the "means of entirely revolutionising the mode of production" from capitalism to socialism to consider "9. Combination of agriculture with manufacturing industries; gradual abolition of the distinction between town and country, by a more equable distribution of the population over the country."[16]

The idea of a more even distribution of people over the land conjoined with the idea of agriculture and industry existing side-by-side has been possible thus far only in relatively primitive societies (three million people died in Cambodia between 1975 and 1979 in an attempt in part to implement this measure). Furthermore, Marx's vehement denunciation of "Free Trade"— "that single, unconscionable freedom"[17]—and of the changes that capitalism has wrought was in part an attempt to turn back the clock of human progress. Marxism looks to the past, as well, perhaps, to the future, in conceiving ideal societal institutions.

Marxism should in many respects be considered a conservative, even reactionary, movement that was an outgrowth of European Romanticism, not the European Enlightenment. Hayek's ultimate complaint against Marx was, indeed, not that he was too radical, but that he was too reactionary. He emphasized the reactionary character of the classical socialist idea particularly in a draft version of *The Fatal Conceit*. He remarked in a 1976 essay on Adam Smith that the "demand for 'social justice,' for an assignment of the shares in the material wealth to the different people and groups according to their needs or merits, on which the whole of socialism is based, is an atavism"[18]—reversion to an earlier type. Hayek argued that the idea that all knowledge can be accumulated in one mind, as was the case for the primordial chief or head-man, is fallacious.

He also said in the piece on Smith that "if we persevere in the atavism and, following the inherited instincts of the tribe, insist on imposing upon the great society principles which presuppose the knowledge of all the particular circumstances which in that society the chief could know, back to the tribal society we shall go."[19] He emphasized in *The Fatal Conceit* that "Karl Marx was thus right to claim that *'capitalism' created the proletariat: it gave and gives them life."*[20] Hayek believed that Marx misunderstood the actual forces of economic production, and that to follow his prescriptions would bring death to billions.

Hayek worked on *Law, Legislation and Liberty* for longer than any of his other works, over a period of sixteen years between commencing it in 1962 and completing it in 1978, with most of the work done between 1962 and 1969. Though he was not completely satisfied with the final form of the work, and lamented in its preface and elsewhere the passing of years that for a time diminished his capacity to work, it was a deeper contribution than *The Constitution of Liberty*.

He emphasized in *Law, Legislation and Liberty* that it has been the "desire to make central governments strong in their dealings with other countries that has led to their being entrusted also with other tasks which could probably be more efficiently performed by regional or local authorities. The main cause of the progressive centralization of government powers has always been the danger of war."[21] He also clarified here the difference between his own view and that of Social Darwinists, "'Social Darwinism' concentrated on the selection of individuals rather than on that of institutions and practices, and on the selection of innate rather than on culturally transmitted capacities."[22]

There are three main sources of biological evolution: individual differences, environmental selection pressures, and random genetic drift. Of these, the first two are generally emphasized in the popular mind. Without individual variation, evolution cannot occur. Only if and as there is variation can genetic or societal evolution occur. If the individuals within a biological group or societies were stationary and uniform, a species or society could not develop further.

In addition to the necessity of diversity for biological and societal evolution, there are environmental factors. Different environments call forth different attributes over time as long as diversity among members of a species or within and between communities exists. Both the environment and individual variation condition attributes that emerge from biological and societal selection.

Preparation for national war was undoubtedly one of the greatest societal environmental factors influencing the development of government during the twentieth century. World Wars I and II caused great increases in government activity and power, as did the Cold War. During war, more nationalist mind-sets come to characterize societies, and these paradigms or worldviews, as well as practical government activities, spill over into facets of societal order other than purely military ones.

Hayek remarked along these lines in *Law, Legislation and Liberty* that "now, when at least in Western Europe and North America we believe we have excluded the possibility of war between the associated nations and are relying for defence on a supranational organization, we ought gradually to discover that we can reduce the centralization and cease to entrust so many tasks to the national government, merely to make that government strong against external enemies."[23]

He believed that the idea of evolution occurred first in the societal realm and was then applied to biology. He said in *The Fatal Conceit* that "Darwin was reading Adam Smith just when he was formulating his own theory."[24] In *Law, Legislation and Liberty,* he quoted C. S. Pierce that in *The Origin of Species* "Darwin merely extends politico-economic views of progress to the entire realm of animal and vegetable life," and expressed there himself that a nineteenth-century "social theorist who needed Darwin to teach him the idea of evolution was not worth his salt."[25]

Societal evolution was a core Hayekian topic. The idea of societal evolution is vitally related to spontaneous order. In the same way that biological evolution occurs without a tangible orderer, so does evolution within and among societies. In societal evolution, however, Hayek thought, selection occurs mostly through culturally transmitted characteristics, institutions, and practices rather than by the physiological selection of individuals. The behavior of successful individuals and groups becomes generally adopted, and these practices dominate over time. He said in *Denationalisation of Money* that it is "always the new ideas of comparatively few which shape evolution. . . . People who have the better ideas will determine developments because they will be imitated."[26]

The market is an evolutionary mechanism. The economically more successful prosper, and those who are not as economically successful do not. When the sifting function of the market is disrupted, just as when the winnowing process of physical natural selection is, economic development stops.

For societies as wholes, an evolutionary process also occurs. In his later theories of societal evolution, Hayek took the evolutionary function and process of a competitive market and applied this to whole communities over time and their webs of rules, laws, customs, and morals. The more successful laws and customs—and thereby more successful societies—prevail over time. The most successful societies are those that are materially and technologically the most developed and advanced.

Hayek's argument for liberty was in largest part that it allows successful development to occur within and among societies. The "unfortunate necessity of making central governments strong for the task of defence against external enemies"[27] has prevented much desirable evolution through the centralization of government it has fostered.

Hayek was a utopian philosopher. He wrote in 1949 that "We must make the building of a free society once more an intellectual adventure, a deed of courage. What we lack is a liberal Utopia, a program which seems neither a mere defence of things as they are nor a diluted kind of socialism, but a truly liberal radicalism. The main lesson which the true liberal must learn from the success of the socialist is that it was their courage to be Utopian which gained them the support of the intellectuals and thereby an influence on public opinion which is daily making possible what only recently seemed utterly remote."[28]

The possible utopia Hayek saw before much of his late 1970s and early '80s work in *Law, Legislation and Liberty* and *The Fatal Conceit* was a classical liberal, as distinct from libertarian, society in which government would play a substantially smaller role than it now does. As much as possible, competition would be the general principle by which society would be organized both in its economic activity and government services. Laws, customs, and morals would provide a societal framework emphasizing private property, contract, and exchange. As a proportion of gross domestic product, total government spending would be reduced from the 30-60 percent range that currently typifies most economically developed nations to the 10-20 percent or so of gross domestic product that was the norm during the latter half of the nineteenth century and pre–World War I twentieth century. Welfare would be provided at the local and (in the United States) state levels—as well as voluntarily, charitably—rather than by national governments.

While there might continue to be, particularly during a transitionary period, mandatory retirement, unemployment, and disability insurance programs, these would become more market-oriented with more choice by consumers of the specific programs in which they would wish to participate. Competition among non-governmental entities to provide these services would become the standard—it might be required, for example, that individuals have unemployment insurance, but this insurance could be provided through a competitive market of private insurers rather than by one, universal government program. Pollution control would be on a more market basis. Vouchers would be implemented in education. All of this is a long way from classical socialism, but also from pure theoretical libertarianism.

He put forward his conception of optimal realizable utopia for humanity as he saw it in *Law, Legislation and Liberty*—"the transformation of local and even regional governments into quasi-commercial corporations competing for citizens. They would have to offer a combination of advantages and costs which made life within their territory at least as attractive as elsewhere.... To re-entrust the management of most service activities of government to smaller units would probably lead to the revival of a communal spirit."[29] He remarked in *The Constitution of Liberty* on "competition between municipalities,"[30] and said in an interview, "I'm inclined to give the local authorities power which I would deny to the central government, because people can vote with their feet against what the local governments can do."[31]

Classical liberalism possesses a strong communitarian element. Hayek rejected the conception that central national government provision of welfare services is either the most cost-effective or morally best way to provide these services. Rather, there is a great advantage—in creating a sense of community— to providing welfare services at the local instead of national level, and voluntarily instead of mandatorily.

Hayek saw utopia—as he considered the appropriate issue in much of his other work—not so much as an ethical but empirical question. It is not just, What would be desirable? But, What would be possible? Hayek thought that an "ideal picture of a society, or a guiding conception of the overall order to be aimed at, is not only the indispensable precondition of any rational policy, but also the chief contribution that science can make to the solution of the problems of practical policy."[32] Utopia was valuable to Hayek not mainly for reasons of inspiration but for reasons of conceptualization. His primary purpose was to enlighten the mind, not to enflame the heart. Utopia is a factual theory, not merely an ethical ideal.

He best presented his conception of utopia in *Law, Legislation and Liberty* where he wrote that "it is not to be denied that to some extent the guiding model of the overall order will always be an utopia, something to which the existing situation will be only a distant approximation and which many people will regard as wholly impractical. Yet it is only by constantly holding up the guiding conception of an internally consistent model which could be realized by the consistent application of the same principles, that anything like an effective framework for a functioning spontaneous order will be achieved."[33] What Hayek felt was urgently required in contemporary political and economic discourse was the "courage to consider utopia."[34] Utopias are to guide governmental and other societal order by providing a blueprint, a pattern, for how things might be.

CHAPTER THIRTY

Government and Morals

ALTHOUGH HAYEK DERIDED LEGAL THEORIST HANS KELSEN, Kelsen stated the essential point that law is fundamentally moral, that it is about the way a community should act in an ethical manner. Kelsen stated in *The Pure Theory of Law* (1934) that "by [legal] 'norm' we mean that something *ought* to be or *ought* to happen, especially that a human being ought to behave in a specific way."[1] Law pertains to the future. It thus is, of necessity, moral, prescribing a certain way of life.

Law is the coercive societal structure within which common life, particularly economic activity, takes place. Hayek's view of law was that it is largely an abstract order—a metaphysical framework, as it were—that defines a society. It is, moreover, only by creating the conditions within which human activity takes place and not by determining specific outcomes of human activity or directing particular actions that societal evolution and progressive material development can occur.

Hayek observed in *Law, Legislation and Liberty* that "what is required if the separate actions of individuals are to result in an overall order is that in those respects in which the success of the action of the individuals depends on some matching action by others, there will be at least a good chance that this correspondence will occur. . . . [What] rules can achieve in this respect is to make it easier for people to come together and to form that match."[2]

Much of the purpose of rules is merely practical. They enable more effective human interaction. They provide a rational societal framework. Different rules have different results. "Our problem is what kind of rules of conduct will produce an order of society and what kind of order particular rules will produce."[3]

"Law" did not include much governmental activity for Hayek. There was in his mind a difference between the framework laws that define a society and more day-to-day measures to handle public welfare functions. His essential concern regarding the latter was that government should be small rather than large, implemented at a local or state (rather than national) level, that government services should be administered competitively, and that as many public welfare services as possible should be provided privately.

The concept of spontaneous order was among Hayek's greatest contributions. Though neither the phrase nor idea were original to him, he perhaps more than anyone else gave currency to the idea that material progress can occur and societal organization can develop, though the details of a specific societal order are not determined by an orderer. Giving perhaps his best analogy of the idea of "spontaneous order" in *The Constitution of Liberty* through his description of crystals in the section "Order without Commands," he wrote that though "people more familiar with the manner in which men order physical objects often find the formation of spontaneous orders difficult to comprehend, there are, of course, many instances in which we must rely on the spontaneous adjustments of individual elements to produce [even] a physical order. We could never produce a crystal if we had to place each individual molecule or atom in the appropriate place in relation to the others. We must rely on the fact that in certain conditions they will arrange themselves in a structure possessing certain characteristics. Similarly, we can produce the conditions for the formation of an order in society. The task of the lawgiver is to create conditions in which an arrangement can establish and ever renew itself."[4]

He further developed the idea of spontaneous formation of human order in *Law, Legislation and Liberty*. He held here in its crucial first volume that when "Montesquieu and the framers of the American Constitution articulated the conception of a limiting constitution that had grown up in England, they set a pattern which liberal constitutionalism has followed ever since."[5] It is essential that government should be defined as well as limited if liberty is to characterize a society—that individuals should know what they may and may not do. This particularly includes rules regarding property. It is vital that government should not direct most economic decision making, though government plays the greatest role in creating the larger societal order within which economic activity takes place. For reasons both of liberty and economic productivity, government's role should be delimited and circumscribed.[6]

Hayek was never a conservative, including in old age. He always favored change, ultimately of and between societies. He was against the left, but this does not mean that he was necessarily for the right. It is significant that in *The Constitution of Liberty*—which, when he wrote it, he intended as his magnum opus—he chose to direct his final fire at the right, at conservatives. That he mentioned it was the challenge of "rationalist philosophy"[7] that led him to his views indicates his constructivist roots. He was a radical anti-socialist. He said throughout his career that he always retained many values of socialists, and that if socialist conceptions of the way the world is were true, one should adopt many socialist practices. Where he primarily differed from socialists was not in values, but in his perspective of facts. If socialists could have persuaded him that their version of facts were correct, a socialist he again would have become.

He termed the different societal patterns and outcomes that emerge from design-oriented and evolutionary development to be, respectively, "organizations" and "orders." The former are planned; the latter spontaneously grow. He thought that as society becomes more technologically advanced, it becomes more, not less, difficult to engage in central planning. The division of labor and, more importantly, division of knowledge is greater, thereby reducing the capability of one mind to direct the totality of a society. He wrote in a 1940 socialist calculation article, referring to his seminal 1937 "Economics and Knowledge," that it is the "main merit of real competition that through it use is made of knowledge divided among many persons which, if it were to be used in a centrally directed economy, would have all to enter the single plan. To assume that all this knowledge would be automatically in the possession of the planning authority seems to me to miss the main point."[8] He held later in his career that the "whole economic problem is a problem of utilizing widely dispersed knowledge which nobody possesses as a whole"; that the "economic mechanism is a process of adaptation to widely dispersed knowledge"; and that "our society is built on the fact that we serve people whom we do not know."[9] Much of the advantage of a competitive market typified by freedom of exchange, private property, prices, profits, and contract is that it accommodates incomplete and imperfect individual knowledge. Competition is a process of discovery.

He emphasized the "Great" or "Open Society." By these appellations he intended the society in which the spontaneous and non-coercively coordinated actions of individuals bring about—through appropriate laws, customs, and morals—continuous development toward greater material production. He observed that the division of labor is one historical development of the Great or Open Society. He stated in *Law, Legislation and Liberty,* though—and it is in this that his primary contribution lay—that much less emphasis has been placed on the "fragmentation of *knowledge,* on the fact that each member of society can have only a small fraction of the knowledge possessed by all, and that each is therefore ignorant of most of the facts on which the working of society rests."[10] An order dependent on omniscient human orderers for its existence has not, thus far, been practicable. Order is a descriptive term as well as an ethical ideal.

The essentiality of his premise that societies cannot, as well as should not, assume omniscient intelligence on the part of any one or some is that this destroys much of the design-oriented approach to society that attempts to direct all of the details of economic life, and thus paves the way for reconceptualizing optimal society along Hayekian lines. Socialism is not so much morally unattainable as intellectually infeasible. According to Hayek, "In none but the most simple kind of organization is it conceivable that all the details of all activities are governed by a single mind"; "the struggle between the advocates of a free society and the advocates of the socialist system is not a moral but an *intellectual* conflict."[11]

He advocated a prominent role for custom and tradition, in opposition to Mill, who held in *On Liberty* that a society's "means of tyrannising are not restricted to the acts which it may do by the hands of its political functionaries. Society can and does execute its own mandates: and if it issues wrong mandates instead of right, or any mandates at all in things with which it ought not to meddle, it practises a social tyranny more formidable than many kinds of political oppression, since, though not usually upheld by such extreme penalties, it leaves fewer means of escape. Protection, therefore, against the tyranny of the magistrate is not enough: there needs protection also against the tyranny of the prevailing opinion and feeling."[12] Hayek believed, on the other hand, that the "fact that conduct within the private sphere is not a proper object for coercive action by the state does not necessarily mean that in a free society such conduct should also be exempt from the pressure of opinion or disapproval. Mill directed his heaviest attack against such 'moral coercion.' In this he probably overstated the case for liberty."[13]

Stephen Kresge calls attention to Hayek's emphasis on the importance of custom and morals in his discussion of Hayek's divorce. Kresge quotes a passage from *The Constitution of Liberty* that it is "indeed a truth that freedom has never worked without deeply ingrained moral beliefs and that coercion can be reduced to a minimum only where individuals can be expected as a rule to conform voluntarily to certain principles. There is an advantage in obedience to such rules not being coerced because it is often desirable that rules should be observed only in most instances and that the individual should be able to transgress them when it seems to him worthwhile to incur the odium which this will cause. It is this flexibility of voluntary rules which in the field of morals makes gradual evolution and spontaneous growth possible, which allows further experience to lead to modifications and improvements."[14]

Hayek also held that "moral rules and conventions that possess less binding power than the law have an important and even indispensable role . . . and probably do as much to facilitate society as do the strict rules of law." Among other roles, customs and morals "secure a certain minimum of uniformity of conduct."[15]

Customs and morals, together with law, are building blocks of a society. The difference between morals and government law is that the latter is coercively enforced, and the former are merely commonly held beliefs that an individual may transgress, though potentially at a loss of intercourse with others. Libertarianism is neither legal nor moral anarchy.

Richard Cockett observes that the "founding fathers of the Mont Pelerin Society included most of the world's foremost liberal economists, many of whom were to have considerable influence in their own countries, especially in Germany, America, France, and Britain."[16] Prominent Mont Pelerin members who influenced postwar German economic policies included those of the Freiburg school of economics, who provided theoretical underpinnings for West Germany's highly successful move to a market economy. Early Mont Pelerinians associated with the Freiburg school included Walter Eucken and Wilhelm Röpke. Another most significant Mont Pelerin member from West Germany was Ludwig Erhard, West German minister of economic affairs from 1949 to 1963 and then federal chancellor until 1966. His advisers included Röpke and Eucken, and he was the key government official in postwar West Germany responsible for its transition to a market economy.

Hayek *Collected Works* editor Peter Klein remarks on Erhard's accomplishment in light of the prevailing ethos that the "intellectual climate of this period is captured by the economists' reaction to Minister Ludwig Erhard's decision to free prices and wages in newly created West Germany. . . . Hayek recalls Erhard's own contemporary account, 'He has gleefully told me how the very Sunday on which the famous decree about the freeing of all prices accompanying the introduction of the new German mark was to be published, the top American military commander called him and told him on the telephone, "Professor Erhard, my advisers tell me you are making a great mistake," whereupon Erhard replied, "So my advisers also tell me."'"[17]

Lord Dahrendorf writes that Erhard was a "man who had his moment in history and grasped it. As head of the Economic Department of the administration which preceded the creation of the Federal Republic of Germany, he was the author of the decision to combine the currency reform of 1948 with the abolition of rationing, and of restrictive regulations concerning production, distribution and capital movements. Many have argued that Germany's 'economic miracle' owes much to these decisions."[18] Replying to an interview question regarding "examples" of nations that, having "flirted with socialism or the welfare state," were able to "reinstate the rule of law," Hayek responded "Oh, very clearly Germany after World War II, although in that case it was really the achievement of a single man almost . . . Ludwig Erhard."[19] He also said that Erhard "could never have accomplished what he did under bureaucratic or democratic constraints. It was a lucky moment when the right person in the right spot was free to do what he thought right, although he could never have convinced anybody else that it was the right thing."[20]

Walter Eucken was theoretical leader of the Freiburg school. Within the German-speaking world, he is often considered the leading German economist of the twentieth century. Perhaps because economics in the Germanic world has been taught as part of university faculties of law, there has been greater focus on ties between economics and law, which was reflected in Hayek's work. Similarly to Hayek, Eucken stressed the distinction between the economic order—which is the framework within which economic decisions are made—and the economic process, which are economic activities themselves. Hayek remarked in 1983 that Eucken was "probably the most serious thinker in the realm of social philosophy produced by Germany in the last one hundred years." He noted Eucken's "role at the very beginning of an international movement in the service of understanding the preconditions of freedom. For it is a real problem that many people hold the illusion that freedom can be imposed from above, instead of by creating the preconditions with which people are given the possibility to shape their own fate."[21]

Hayek said in his 1962 Freiburg inaugural lecture that his listeners knew "better than I what Eucken has achieved in Germany. I need therefore not explain further what it means if I say here today that I shall regard it as one of my chief tasks to resume and continue the tradition which Eucken and his friends have created at Freiburg and in Germany. It is a tradition of the greatest scientific integrity and at the same time of outspoken conviction on the great issues of public life." He also remarked there that he had the "closest agreement on scientific as well as on political questions with the unforgettable Walter Eucken."[22] He said elsewhere that Eucken was a "valuable friend for me. In the later 1930s, before the outbreak of the war, when I first acquired a car and made the trip from London to Austria by automobile, I regularly made a stopover in Freiburg just to visit Eucken and to keep in touch with him."[23]

Of Wilhelm Röpke, Hayek said during happier times than their bitter disputes in the Mont Pelerin Society that if the "existence of a neo-liberal movement [in Germany] is known far beyond the narrow circles of experts, the credit belongs mainly to Röpke."[24] Röpke's focus was applied economics as opposed to pure theory, and his A Humane Economy: The Social Framework of the Free Market (1958) was an especially popular work. Henry Hazlitt grouped Röpke relatively early in the postwar period with Mises and Hayek as "one of the three most influential leaders of the neoliberal movement away from state controls and toward a restoration of individual freedom."[25] Erhard said, "My own services toward the attainment of a free society are scarcely enough to express my gratitude to him [Röpke] who, to such a high degree, influenced my position and conduct."[26] While Hayek and Röpke ultimately had their falling-out in the Mont Pelerin Society, Hayek said of the society's early development that he "received a great deal of support in its organisation especially from Röpke."[27]

Hayek's discussion of the West German "social market economy" sheds light on his conception of optimal, or at least adequate, societal order. Relating a story about Erhard, Hayek recalled that "we were alone for a moment, and he turned to me and said, 'I hope you don't misunderstand me when I speak of a social market economy (Sozialen Marktwirtschaft). I mean by that that the market economy as such is social not that it needs to be made social."[28] In Law, Legislation and Liberty, Hayek commented on the term "social market economy" that "I regret this usage though by means of it some of my friends in Germany (and more recently in England) have apparently succeeded in making palatable to wider circles the sort of social order for which I am pleading."[29]

He responded in 1976 to a London Times letter praising policies in West Germany by his old LSE adversary Nicholas Kaldor, "For Lord Kaldor to describe a country that for twenty-seven years has known no nationalization, no price controls, no exchange controls, no investment controls and whose now governing 'social democratic' party has publicly committed itself to a market economy as 'much ahead in "socialist policies" of either France, Britain or Italy' suggests an ignorance of the policies he himself has been advising which is somewhat astounding."[30] This same year, he wrote in a new preface to The Road to Serfdom that "Sweden is today very much less socialistically organised than Great Britain"[31] because, though Sweden had a larger welfare state than Great Britain, it possessed fewer nationalized industries.

During the years that Hayek praised West Germany, its government share of gross domestic product was in the vicinity of forty to fifty percent. Hayek's belief was that it is more important what government does and how it does it than the percentage of gross domestic product it taxes and spends.[32]

In France, Mont Pelerin member Jacques Rueff was a prominent government advisor to General Charles de Gaulle on free market policies. Mont Pelerinian Reinhard Kamitz played a similar role in postwar Austria. Luigi Einaudi, a future president of Italy, was a charter Mont Pelerin member.

CHAPTER THIRTY-ONE

History of Ideas

HAYEK'S MAJOR PUBLICATION during the 1960s in Freiburg was *Studies in Philosophy, Politics and Economics* (1967). He was always successful in getting his major articles republished in book form, from *Prices, Interest and Investment* (1939) to *Individualism and Economic Order* (1948) to *The Counter-Revolution of Science* (1952) to the 1967 *Studies* to *New Studies in Philosophy, Politics, Economics and the History of Ideas* (1978).

In a 1955 memorandum to himself, in which he outlined potential future writing projects, Hayek indicated that he might write two works on liberal order, *The Constitution of Liberty* and a work on the creative powers of a free civilization, noting that this second potential work would concern how societal institutions emerge and grow with no one designing them. He saw a substantial tie between his work in psychology, *The Sensory Order,* and his philosophical work.[1]

He inscribed in a copy of *The Sensory Order* that the volume was a "contribution to the problem of how a part of the ordered universe can adapt its actions to the fact that the whole is ordered," recommending in particular its penultimate section, "The Limits of Explanation," in the final chapter, "Philosophical Consequences," of the book. He held here that there is an "absolute limit to what the human brain can ever accomplish by way of explanation" because "any apparatus of classification must possess a structure of a higher degree of complexity than is possessed by the objects which it classifies."[2] That is, mind would have to be higher than mind, as it were, to explain itself.

He displayed a thoroughly Kantian conception of the nature of existence (ontology) in his psychological thought; he traced his ontological views, however, to Galileo. Essentially, Hayek believed that all meaning resides in the mind. There is no such thing as an external world apart from what the mind perceives. He rejected the view of the "physical," which ascribes absolute existence to a world external to the mind; to maintain such a conception "implies a metaphysical belief in the ultimate 'reality' and constancy of the phenomenal world for which there is little justification." He was a philosophical skeptic in the tradition of David Hume, who, too, saw nothing in reality other than what the individual himself senses. According to Hayek, one will "never be able to bridge the gap between the realm of the mental and the realm of the physical."[3]

In a piece on his cousin Ludwig Wittgenstein—on whom he once intended to write a biography—Hayek mentioned that when Wittgenstein's *Tractatus Logico-Philosophicus* appeared in late 1921, he was one of its "first readers," and the work "made a great impression on me."[4] According to British political philosopher John Gray, Wittgenstein's influence on Hayek ran "deep, and is seen not only in the style and presentation of *The Sensory Order,* . . . but in many areas of Hayek's system of ideas."[5] In addition to the notational format that *The Sensory Order* shares with the *Tractatus,* there are echoes of Wittgenstein's substantive thought in Hayek's presentation.

In the *Tractatus,* Wittgenstein discussed the nature of language. He held in the work's preface that the "whole sense of the book might be summed up in the following words: what can be said at all can be said clearly, and what we cannot talk about we must pass over in silence. Thus the aim of the book is to draw a limit to thought, or rather . . . to the expression of thoughts . . . It will . . . only be in language that a limit can be drawn, and what lies on the other side of the limit will simply be nonsense."[6] When Hayek wrote in *The Sensory Order* that the "whole idea of the mind explaining itself is a logical contradiction— nonsense in the literal meaning of the word,"[7] he expressed something of the Wittgensteinian ideas of the limitation of language and that not everything can be expressed.

In a paper he wrote in 1977, Hayek said (as previously noted) that the conclusion of his psychological thought was that "mental events are a particular order of physical events within a subsystem of the physical world that relates the larger subsystem of the world that we call an organism (and of which they are a part) with the whole system so as to enable that organism to survive."[8] In *The Sensory Order,* he referred to The Abuse and Decline of Reason essays that became *The Counter-Revolution of Science,* where he emphasized that "the independent actions of individuals will produce an order which is not part of their intentions."[9]

In both Hayek's psychological and economic thought, the idea of the unanticipated and undeliberate evolution of an order of action—individual and collective—toward what benefits the individual and group through the utilization of knowledge which no one individual possesses in its entirety is central. In response to an audience question on his 1977 paper on the connection between his psychological and economic thought, he said that in "both cases we have complex phenomenon in which there is a need for a method of utilizing widely dispersed knowledge. The essential point is that each member (neuron, or buyer, or seller) is induced to do what in the total circumstances benefits the system. Each member can be used to serve the needs of which it doesn't know anything at all."[10] His psychological and economic thought were largely parallel.

In the 1955 memorandum to himself in which he outlined potential future writing projects, Hayek noted that his work in psychology was really precedent to his philosophical work on the nature and requirements of a free and materially progressive society because his philosophical thought was based on a view of human psychology that emphasizes the limitations of individual knowledge and the evolutionary survival of modes of perception (and, in the case of society, institutions) that further life. Both human institutions and sensory perceptions are "based upon our developmental history."[11] He became interested in the societal evolution of institutions in large part through his work in psychology.

After Hayek completed *The Sensory Order,* he intended to write a work on "systems within systems," both of what can be said about a system and what can be said within a system—to some extent following from his idea that an agent of classification cannot classify something of a higher degree of complexity than itself—but he found this work "excruciatingly difficult." In addition, "nobody I tried it upon could understand" it.[12] This included Popper. He instead wrote a paper "Degrees of Explanation," which was intended to be the first in a series of articles in which he further presented his ideas in this line. In "Degrees of Explanation," he held that while it is "evidently possible to predict precisely without being able to control, we shall clearly not be able to control developments further than we can predict the results of our action. A limitation of prediction thus implies a limitation of control."[13] Kresge points out that "arguments both for and against the efficacy of the central planning that socialism inevitably requires either stand or fall on the . . . ability to predict the consequences of actions."[14] The limitations of knowledge preclude classical socialism.

Later works aligned with "Degrees of Explanation" were collected by Hayek in the first part of the 1967 *Studies in Philosophy, Politics and Economics.*

To some extent, these essays were a continuation of Hayek's project to outline the philosophical foundations of a theory of freedom that relies on the evolutionary development of undesigned institutions and societal norms. The winnowing process of the market became, in Hayek's mind, the prototype for societies as wholes and their complexes of rules, laws, customs, morals, and institutions. Just as there is competition in the market among producers of different goods and services, there is competition among societies as to which are the most materially productive. In the end, the most materially productive societies, and thereby most materially productive rules and institutions, prevail. In the fourth chapter of *Studies in Philosophy, Politics and Economics,* "Notes on the Evolution of Systems of Rules of Conduct," he observed that the "natural selection of rules will operate on the basis of the greater or less efficiency of the resulting order of the group," and cited a statement by Alexander Carr-Saunders (William Beveridge's successor as director of LSE) in support of this position, that the "groups practicing the most advantageous customs will have an advantage in the constant struggle with adjacent groups."[15]

A number of writers have praised Hayek's work as a historian of ideas. In addition to George Stigler, economic historian Henry Spiegel said of Schumpeter's monumental *History of Economic Analysis* that it "was informed by an almost unparalleled erudition matched in modern times only by Hayek's contributions to the history of ideas and by Jacob Viner."[16] Schumpeter himself wrote of Hayek's edition of Henry Thornton's *Paper Credit* that it is "prefaced by an essay by Professor von Hayek, the scholarship of which is surpassed only by its charm. The reader who misses it deprives himself not only of much valuable information but of an exquisite pleasure."[17] According to economic historian Ben Seligman, Hayek was, as a historian of economic thought, "top rank."[18]

Hayek's work in the history of ideas extended across his career. During the early years of his academic career in Vienna, he studied monetary history as well as theory. His first major foray in the history of ideas was four chapters on the development of monetary policy and theory between 1663 and 1848, "Genesis of the Gold Standard in Response to English Coinage Policy in the 17th and 18th Centuries," "First Paper Money in 18th-Century France," "The Period of Restrictions, 1797-1821, and the Bullion Debate in England," and "The Dispute Between the Currency School and the Banking School, 1821-1848."[19]

While he never completed his early anticipated treatise on the history and theory of money, he gave his remaining historical notes for the project to a doctoral student at LSE, Vera Smith (later Lutz). She then used them in writing her dissertation, published in 1936 as *The Rationale of Central Banking*. Undoubtedly something further of his intellectual flow can be gathered from her chapter titles—"The Development of Central Banking in England," "The Scottish System," "The Development of Central Banking in France," "The Organisation of Banking in America: Decentralisation Without Freedom," "The Development of Central Banking in Germany," "Discussions on the Theory of the Subject in England and America Prior to 1848," "The Discussions in France and Belgium," "The Discussions in Germany," "The Post-1848 Discussions in England," "Discussions in America Prior to the Foundation of the Federal Reserve System," and "The Arguments in Favour of Central Banking Reconsidered." Smith stated in her concluding chapter that the origin of central banking was to be found in the "establishment of monopolies, either partial or complete, in the note issue." She noted as well that "monopolies in this sphere outlasted the abolition of protectionism in other branches of economic activity."[20] Hayek came late in his career to support what might be considered a variant of free banking—the denationalization of money—and believed that ending the government monopoly of the money supply is vital to the preservation of a free society.

His early historical essays on economists included an obituary article on his teacher Friedrich von Wieser in 1926 and introductions to Hermann Heinrich Gossen's *Development of the Laws of Human Relationships* (1929), Richard Cantillon's *Essay on the Nature of Commerce in General* (1931), collected works of Carl Menger (1934), and Henry Thornton's *An Enquiry into the Nature and Effects of the Paper Credit of Great Britain* (1939). He also wrote on the history of the Austrian school of economics generally and, later in his career, penned several essays on Mises. He considered his work in the history of ideas in *The Counter-Revolution of Science*—on the Saint Simonians and Comte—to be his "most ambitious attempt in a field which has long interested me."[21] His extensive work on John Stuart Mill followed from this last endeavor. He at one time considered writing a book on great British economists and on the Whig tradition.

Political philosophers and economists on whom he wrote later in his career included David Hume, Bernard Mandeville, and Adam Smith. Of Hume, Hayek said that he "gives us probably the only comprehensive statement of the legal and political philosophy which later became known as liberalism. It is in Hume that we find the fullest statement of that doctrine."[22] In *The Constitution of Liberty,* he remarked that Hume "will be our constant companion and sage guide."[23] In a 1963 Freiburg lecture, Hayek called Hume "the outstanding philosopher of liberal political and legal theory."[24] In the preliminary draft of a 1980 talk, Hayek described Hume as his chief inspirer, and in a 1982 lecture he referred to "my great idol David Hume."[25]

His attraction to Hume, whom he quoted more than anyone else in his major works, stemmed from several sources. Hayek explained that it "is in his analysis of the circumstances which determined the evolution of the chief legal institutions, in which he shows why a complex civilization could grow up only where certain types of legal institutions developed, that he makes some of his most important contributions to jurisprudence. In the discussion of these problems his economic and his legal and political theory are intimately connected. Hume is one of the few social theorists who are clearly aware of the connection between the rules men obey and the order which is formed as a result."[26]

Hayek was a rule utilitarian in ethical approach.[27] While he strongly opposed act utilitarianism (whereby actions are evaluated by the immediate application of a moral standard), he supported the ethical goal of the greatest good for the greatest number, which he thought is obtained through known general rules applicable to all.[28] He approvingly quoted Christian Bay that "'Hume may be called a precursor to Darwin in the field of ethics. In effect, he proclaimed a doctrine of the survival of the fittest among human conventions— fittest in terms of maximum social utility.'"[29]

Hayek observed of Hume that he "concisely describes the advantages of the 'partition of employments' (what Adam Smith was to make popular under the Mandevillian term 'division of labour')."[30] He concluded his 1963 lecture on Hume by stating that Hume was "very far from denying that government had positive tasks. Like Adam Smith later, he knew that it is only thanks to the discretionary powers granted to government that 'bridges are built, harbours opened; everywhere, by the care of government, which, though composed of men subject to all human infirmities, becomes, by one of the finest and most subtle inventions imaginable, a composition, which is, in some measure, exempted from all these infirmities.'"[31]

Hayek's interest in Bernard Mandeville was significant, and as much as any other historian of thought he placed Mandeville in an important position. Hayek's praise for Mandeville included the following: "That we do not know why we do what we do, and that the consequences of our decisions are often very different from what we imagine them to be, are the two foundations of that satire on the conceits of a rationalist age which was his initial aim. I do mean to claim for Mandeville that the speculations to which that *jeu d'esprit* led him mark the definite breakthrough in modern thought of the twin ideas of evolution and of the spontaneous formation of an order." He said of the relationship between Mandeville and Hume that "I do not intend to pitch my claim on behalf of Mandeville higher than to say he made Hume possible. It is indeed my estimate of Hume as perhaps the greatest of all modern students of mind and society which makes Mandeville appear to me so important."[32]

Hayek wrote of Adam Smith on the 200th anniversary of *The Wealth of Nations* in 1976 and a decade earlier in "The Results of Human Action but not of Human Design." In the earlier essay, he observed that Smith's conception of an "invisible hand," whereby "man is led to promote an end which was no part of his intention," is the central contention of the concept of spontaneous order.[33] On the occasion of the 200th anniversary of *The Wealth of Nations,* he wrote that the "recognition that a man's efforts will benefit more people, and on the whole satisfy greater needs, when he lets himself be guided by the abstract signals of prices rather than by perceived needs, and that by this method we can best overcome our constitutional ignorance of most of the particular facts, and can make the fullest use of the knowledge of concrete circumstances widely dispersed among millions of individuals, is the great achievement of Adam Smith."[34] Hayek's historical interests tended to move over the course of his career as his primary interests shifted.[35] His appreciation for Smith rose over his lifetime.

Perhaps the specifically historical work of Hayek's that attracted the most attention at the time it was published was the collection of essays by Mont Pelerin Society members he edited, *Capitalism and the Historians* (1954). Here, he argued, contrary to much of the prevailing academic wisdom of the time, that the Industrial Revolution—far from having been an era of increasing misery of the masses—was the time of the greatest improvements in the living conditions of more people than ever before in history.

"Who has not heard of the 'horrors of early capitalism,'" he rhetorically asked, "and gained the impression that the advent of this system brought untold new suffering?" He expressed his views on the importance of historical presentation in *Capitalism and the Historians*. "Public opinion and views about historical events ever have been and always must be closely connected," he wrote. "In the end even those who never read a book and probably have never heard the names of the historians whose views have influenced them come to see the past through their spectacles."[36]

Interpretations of the past help to shape the future. Hayek's writings on the history of ideas were intended to help to shape the future he wished to see.

CHAPTER THIRTY-TWO

Salzburg

HAYEK SUFFERED FROM ILL HEALTH AND ACUTE DEPRESSION from 1969 through about 1974, and he retained intermittent depression for the remainder of the 1970s. After 1985 significant depression, as well as old age and ill health, struck him. He previously, in 1960 and 1961, was hindered from working by depression.

There are a number of reasons why *Law, Legislation and Liberty* has not received the attention it deserves. The first is that its three parts were published separately, in three volumes, in 1973, 1976, and 1979. As a result of ill health, Hayek decided to issue the parts independently. This had the effect of destroying the unity of the work as it appeared, for it was impossible to discern what came later. Secondly, *Law, Legislation and Liberty* is very difficult and written on a high level. Extensive knowledge of Hayek's other works and of political, economic, and legal philosophy and history generally are required to obtain the most from it, as is reading it more than once. Thirdly, the practical policy proposal he put forward in it—separate legislative and governmental assemblies, with restricted suffrage—has not appeared fruitful.

Hayek did not feel that voting should be as extensive as it now is in democratic polities. Specifically, he opposed granting the franchise to those who receive benefits from government. Also, he thought that there should be two representative assemblies—a *legislative assembly* for framework laws and a *governmental assembly* for more day-to-day public welfare functions. Election to the legislative assembly would be at the age of forty-five for a single fifteen-year term, and election would be only by those who were themselves forty-five. Individuals would, thus, be able to vote for, and seek election to, the legislative assembly only once in their lifetime, at forty-five; one-fifteenth of the legislative assembly would be elected each year. The governmental assembly would be elected and function much like current representative bodies.

As earlier noted, most of *Law, Legislation and Liberty* was much closer in date of composition to *The Constitution of Liberty* than the respective dates of the two works' publications—1960 and 1973-79—would indicate. Hayek said in the preface to *Law, Legislation and Liberty*'s second and third volumes that most of the manuscript was in "fairly finished form as long ago as the end of 1969 when indifferent health forced me to suspend the efforts to complete it."[1] He had not completed *Law, Legislation and Liberty*'s final chapter when he left Freiburg for Salzburg, Austria, in 1969, and about this time he began to suffer from significant health problems.

He attributed some of these problems to misdiagnosis. He said in a 1985 interview that "there was a period when I was in a very bad state of health. For two or three years I was suffering from what the doctors called depression. I always said that is nonsense; I am depressed because I can't work, not the other way round. Now there is a modern technique of electrocardiography that discovered that apparently I have had two heart attacks, and the second one knocked me out for three years, and it has only been discovered in retrospect. From about '69 'til '73 I couldn't do any work at all. That was when my work on *Law, Legislation and Liberty* got stuck. My impression was 'I am finished; I have finally aged.' Then suddenly I recovered."[2] He remarked on another occasion that "not being able to work made me frightfully depressed and pessimistic."[3]

His first period of depression and ill health, during 1960 and '61, coincided with his belatedly discovered first heart attack. He ascribed some of his health problems during the early 1970s to misdiagnosis—his Salzburg doctor treated him erroneously for diabetes, which gave him too low a blood sugar level. Hayek went so far as to say that he was "intellectually disabled"[4] during this latter period.

Time began to take its toll. His hearing deteriorated. Even when he was in Cambridge, he had difficulty following conversations—he was deaf in his left ear and the hearing in his right began to diminish. His hearing loss "increasingly deprived" him of the "enjoyment of society and almost completely of the theater," which once was one of his "regular pastimes."[5] Also, from a personal perspective, he had developed no hobbies, which in old age he regretted. He was almost apologetic in some of his later books about his reduced capacity to work. He remarked in the second volume of *Law, Legislation and Liberty* that "I shall do my best to bring the volume concluding this series out as soon as the advance of old age permits,"[6] and in the 1977 preface to *New Studies in Philosophy, Politics, Economics and the History of Ideas* he said that for years he had doubted his ability to finish *Law, Legislation and Liberty*.

He took antidepressant medication for a number of years. University of Chicago historian of political thought Joseph Cropsey remembers Hayek being very open about his health circumstances on one occasion when, returning to Chicago for a visit, Hayek mentioned that he took medication for depression. Cropsey also recalls that once, when Hayek was on the Committee on Social Thought, he dropped over to introduce himself and just to engage Cropsey in philosophical discussion. Cropsey, co-editor with Leo Strauss of *History of Political Philosophy,* remembers no contact at all between Hayek and Strauss in Chicago, though both were there during the same period.

Arthur Seldon visited Hayek in 1972 in Salzburg, and found Hayek so unwell that he could not get up from his bed. Seldon remembers Hayek as in low spirits, feeling his life's work had been wasted—that no one was interested in what he had said or written. It may have been on this occasion that he mentioned to Seldon that part of the reason he did not marry his cousin, who eventually became his second wife, when they were young was because of potential hereditary implications.

Larry Hayek recalls of his father during this period that "we used to talk on the telephone, and I could tell that he was depressed. He couldn't summon up any energy to do anything."[7] Hayek remarked of his lesser, 1960-61 episode that he suffered a "severe depression."[8] He lost weight during his later years, going from almost 200 pounds to about 160.

Hayek's 1969 move to Salzburg was occasioned largely by financial consider-ations, as his earlier relocations to Chicago and Freiburg had been. Salzburg is also closer to Vienna than is Freiburg, and Helene's son's family live in Vienna. The University of Salzburg was willing to buy Hayek's library, and by moving there, Hayek would still be able to use it. He was not financially independent before he received the Nobel Prize. He titled a section in *The Constitution of Liberty,* "The importance of the man of independent means,"[9] and expressed there, "I wish I could command the eloquence which I once heard the late Lord Keynes expatiate on the indispensable role that the man of independent means plays in any decent society."[10] Hayek himself would undoubtedly have enjoyed greater economic resources to pursue his goals during most of his career, though

his last secretary, Charlotte Cubitt, remembers him as not having been a good
financial manager.

Salzburg is even more beautiful than Freiburg; it is certainly more quaint.
Located on the river Salzach, the city has been inhabited since Roman times as
a result of nearby salt mines (*Salz* is German for "salt"). Mozart was from
Salzburg, and Emperor Franz Josef had his hunting villa here. Like Freiburg,
Salzburg was heavily damaged during World War II but was restored.

Salzburg University is not as distinguished as the University of
Freiburg. Its campus is split among several locations and its enrollment is less
than 6,000. Kurt Leube, Hayek's research aide, calls Hayek's years in Salzburg
from 1969 to 1977 "somewhat disappointing."[11] It was in part ill health and
the times, but it was also that the economics division of the university was
small—a couple of professors and perhaps four lecturers. "The faculty's and
the students' level did not meet his academic expectations,"[12] Leube writes.
In a summer 1974 interview just before receiving notification of his receipt of
the Nobel Prize, Hayek responded to a question regarding whether his work
was known and whether students sought him out, "It wasn't when I arrived.
And even now there is not a great deal of interest outside of the few who have
come to my classes."[13]

He had few friends in Salzburg and was intellectually isolated. He
commented in the preface to the 1976 second volume of *Law, Legislation and
Liberty* that in revising the work in Salzburg he no longer had "easy access to
adequate library facilities,"[14] which he had had when he prepared the original
draft. In a February 1977 letter to the editor explaining why he was leaving
Salzburg, he commented, "People frequently ask why I am leaving Austria. I
must confess that I began to have doubts after only a few months. My doubts
were reinforced by a circular reminding me of an old ministerial decree,
'University professors must notify the Federal Minister of any foreign travel
they undertake.' Over and above this, however, I must mention that the
University of Salzburg is not authorized to bestow doctorates [in the social
sciences]. Thus, there are no serious students of economics here. I made a
mistake in moving to Salzburg."[15]

A reporter from London wrote a story on Hayek during his Salzburg
interlude. He depicted him as living in a "slightly rundown suburb, between
a retired fireman and a retired blacksmith, in a house somewhat inconvenient
of access either to the centre of the city or to the university. The choice of a
retirement home was dictated partly by the preference of his (second) wife
and partly by the fact that the purchase by Salzburg university of his library
financed the acquisition of his home."[16] When Hayek left Salzburg to return

to Freiburg after receiving the Nobel Prize, the university, would not sell his library back to him.

The early 1970s were the worst of times from Hayek's perspective, apart from his physical condition. Inflation ignited throughout the western world. The United States imposed wage and price controls. Britain appeared to some, including Hayek, to hover on the brink of social and economic collapse. The counterculture movement was in full swing. The Soviet Union's position in the world seemed to grow inexorably. Developing nations were in revolt against the morés and institutions of their former colonial overlords.

His return to the German-speaking world on a day-in, day-out basis during the last third of his life affected his English writing style. He remarked jokingly in a 1978 interview that he had retained one consequence of his German-speaking background—his sentences were "much too long."[17] This perhaps shows particularly in *Law, Legislation and Liberty*. His departure from the English-speaking world deprived him of working colleagues with whom he regularly discussed his work in English (though virtually all German academics know English), and he also wrote more in German. In 1969, a collection in German of articles which have mostly appeared in English, *Freiburger Studien* (*Freiburg Studies*), appeared. He and his wife continued to speak German in the home. Marjorie Seldon, Arthur Seldon's wife, recalls Helene saying that she could not speak English well enough to talk with them when the Seldons visited the Hayeks in Salzburg in 1972, though in fact she could.

Hayek once joked as a young man that he would someday like to be president of the Austrian *Nationalbank,* and while he was in Freiburg during the 1960s, he apparently had the chance. "I was asked by the then right-hand side chancellor of Austria, after he had vainly asked Machlup, whether I would be willing to take over the presidency of the national bank, [to] which I assented on one condition, 'If I can engage one of the great international accounting firms to check out the nationalized industries.' That was the end of the conversation!"[18] He was later publicly criticized by an Austrian chancellor on the left of the political spectrum, Bruno Kreisky, after he returned to Austria to live.

In 1971, Hayek participated in a Viennese symposium celebrating the 100th anniversary of Carl Menger's *Principles of Economics*. He stated in his paper that "though there is no longer a distinct Austrian School, I believe there is still a distinct Austrian tradition."[19] Looking back, he recalled of other historical work during this time that before 1974, he was "almost for five years out of action intellectually, or at least unable to do any original work. I did such things as, for instance, that survey of the history of liberalism for an Italian encyclopedia which not only just reproduces my old knowledge but even makes some awful blunders of pure memory. If you know my writing at all you will see how absurd it is to write an intellectual history of liberalism and to forget to even mention Lord Acton, who was one of my great figures. But that kind of thing could happen to me at that time."[20]

James Buchanan recalls the 1972 Mont Pelerin meeting in Montreux, Switzerland, which was the closest location to Mount Pelerin large enough to accommodate the expanded membership. During the conference, the group made a pilgrimage to Mount Pelerin, where Hayek "addressed the group from the portico of the original hotel on a very hot afternoon. He was enthusiastic as well as nostalgic on the 25th anniversary, and he more or less forgot the time limits dictated for those of us who stood in the heat of day."[21]

When Hayek and his wife lived in Freiburg during the 1960s, they had an attractive apartment not far from the city center, yet on the outskirts of the city. They "particularly enjoyed the beautiful environment"[22] of Germany's Black Forest. During the summers, they vacationed in Obergurgl, Austria, a small village in the Tyrolian Alps, where Hayek visited all his life.

Hayek reemerged on the popular intellectual scene through his 1972 paperback, *A Tiger by the Tail: The Keynesian Legacy of Inflation*, compiled by Sudha Shenoy[23] and published by the Institute of Economic Affairs in London. He commented at the 1969 Mont Pelerin Society conference in Caracas that twenty years before he "lost interest in monetary matters because of my disillusionment with Bretton Woods. I was wrong in my prediction that the arrangement would soon disappear. Its main innovation has been to impose the responsibility for restoring balance in international payments on the creditor nations. This was reasonable in the deflationary 1930s, but not in an inflationary period. Now we have an inflation-borne prosperity which depends for its continuation on continued inflation. If prices rise less than expected, then a depressing effect is exerted on the economy. I expected that ten years would suffice to produce increasing difficulty; however, it has taken twenty-five years to reach the stage where to slow down inflation produces a recession. We now have a tiger by the tail: how long can this inflation continue? If the tiger (of inflation) is freed he will eat us up; yet if he runs faster and faster while we desperately hold on, we are *still* finished! I'm glad I won't be here to see the final outcome."[24]

In *A Tiger by the Tail,* Shenoy quotes a reply by Keynes to Hayek's 1943 *Economic Journal* article "A Commodity Reserve Currency," in which Hayek proposed that a basket of commodities, not merely gold, should function as an international commodity standard—acting as an ideal gold standard would. Keynes argued against Hayek that the primary policy argument against a gold standard is not practical (that it is potentially difficult for the amount of gold to increase with the demand for money) but, rather, is policy-driven. Keynes argued that the "fundamental reason for limiting the objectives of an international currency scheme is the impossibility, or at any rate the undesirability, of imposing stable price-levels from without. The error of the gold-standard lay in submitting national wage-policies to outside dictation. It is wiser to regard stability (or otherwise) of internal prices as a matter of internal policy and politics. Commodity standards which try to impose this from without will break down just as surely as the rigid gold-standard."[25]

Since this response comprised Keynes' last public reply to an economic proposal of Hayek's, as well as being a rare economic response from Keynes to Hayek following his 1931 reply to Hayek's critical review of *A Treatise on Money,* Keynes' response merits further discussion. Keynes argued against Hayek's 1943 proposal for a commodity reserve standard to maintain stable prices, saying that it is important for nations to be able to control their internal money supplies in order that they not experience deflation, because under contemporary conditions economies cannot deflate without experiencing economic contraction. Hayek argued that only a commodity standard among nations would impose the discipline to achieve stable prices. Hayek appears to have been empirically wrong on this point. Stable prices, or largely stable prices, have been achieved under a system of flexible exchange rates. Moreover, international trade has skyrocketed, also contrary to what he predicted would happen with flexible international exchange rates.

In the 1978 second edition of *A Tiger by the Tail,* Shenoy included the 1945 review by Hayek of William Beveridge's *Full Employment in a Free Society,* in which Hayek stated, "Lord Keynes assured us that we had all been mistaken and that the cure could be painless and even pleasant: all that was needed to maintain employment permanently at a maximum was to secure an adequate volume of spending of some kind."[26] Here, Hayek saw Keynes as having recommended easy monetary and easy fiscal policies, and in these factual appraisals, Hayek was more accurate. It is important to observe, though, the circumstances within which Keynes advocated these policies—the depressed 1920s and '30s in Britain, when these were optimal policies and Hayek's recommendations of tight monetary and tight fiscal policies would have been counterproductive.

A Tiger by the Tail played the significant role in England and Europe of reintroducing Hayek to the public eye. The work was reviewed in many popular and academic publications. To what extent the publicity engendered by *A Tiger by the Tail* contributed to making it possible for Hayek to receive the Nobel Prize in Economics in 1974 is an open question. Fritz Machlup was apparently among the nominators, and nominated Hayek, when Hayek received the Nobel Prize.

Hayek wrote in his autobiographical notes in 1972 on the "sort of life on the borderline of purely academic and public work which probably, in the later part of my life, I should have found most satisfactory."[27] During the last stage of his life, as he lived to an extremely active and productive old age as the grand old man of classical liberalism—and as his ideas of limited government and more emphasis on a competitive market came into vogue—he far exceeded his hopes for combining scholarly and practical activity.

But this lay in the future during the early 1970s. He was asked in 1974, shortly before he received notification that he had won the Nobel prize, "I am curious as to how you see the prospects of liberty in our times or in the future?" "What I expect is that inflation will drive all the Western countries into a planned economy via price controls. Nobody will dare to stop inflation because to discontinue inflation will inevitably cause extensive unemployment. So assuming inflation stops it will quickly be resumed. People will find they can't live with constantly rising prices and will try to control it by price controls and that of course is the end of the market system and the end of the free political order. So I think it will be via the attempt to regress the effects of a continued inflation that the free market and free institutions will disappear. It may still take ten years, but it doesn't matter much for me because in ten years I hope I shall be dead."[28] A decade later, looking back on his inactive, unhappy period from 1969 to 1974, he commented, "Sometimes I feel these five years have been a period of rest."[29]

SIX

NOBEL PRIZE

1974 – 1992

"Now that the Nobel Prize for Economic Science has been created, one can only be profoundly grateful for having been selected as one of its joint recipients. Yet I must confess that if I had been consulted whether to establish a Nobel Prize in economics, I should have decidedly advised against it. I feared that such a prize would tend to accentuate the swings of scientific fashion."

Laureate

IF HAYEK HAD NOT RECEIVED THE NOBEL PRIZE in Economic Sciences, it is an open question what his reputation would now be. In retrospect, the decision by the Swedish National Bank in 1968 to endow a Nobel Prize in Economic Sciences, and the decision by the Nobel Foundation to accept this gift, potentially constitutes a watershed in modern economic development. It was not so much, as Hayek was inclined to think, that the creation of this award recognized economics as a science, but that through bestowing the award to heterodox thinkers such as himself and Milton Friedman, the prize has played a role in channeling academic economics in new directions. It is no longer as possible as it once was to dismiss the views of free market economists out of hand. Indeed, Swedish socialist economist and political figure Gunnar Myrdal, with whom Hayek shared the Nobel Prize in economics in 1974, later proposed that the economics prize should be removed because it had been given to such reactionaries as Friedman and Hayek. (A standing joke at the time the Nobel was awarded in 1974 was that Hayek was surprised that he received it at all, and Myrdal was surprised that he had to share it.)

The award of the 1974 Nobel Memorial Prize in Economic Sciences to Hayek, which was announced on October 9, 1974, was the great rejuvenating event in his life. He became not merely the author of a best-selling book three decades before, but the first free market economist to win the Nobel Prize. It is ironic that Sweden—which was praised for its exemplary welfare state programs from the 1930s through the 1960s and was seen by some as an evolving "middle way"—first between fascism and communism and then between capitalism and communism—stemmed an institution, the Nobel Prize in Economic Sciences, which has played a considerable role in influencing academic economics in the direction of capitalism.

Hayek was genuinely surprised that he received the award in 1974. He assumed that the Nobel committee would treat him as "too old, as already out of the running." He "didn't think the Nobel Prize ought to be given to people that had done something in the distant past." He thought it should be awarded for "some specific achievement in the fairly recent past."[1] He acknowledged as well that he moved from technical economics as his career progressed.

That the Nobel Committee gave the prize simultaneously to Myrdal and Hayek indicated, in Hayek's mind, the controversial esteem in which he was held and the out-of-favor character of his ideas. Reflecting the differences between them, Myrdal (who was listed first on the official announcement of the award) held a press conference and called for wage and price controls and the immediate rationing of gasoline in the United States.[2] Hayek, by way of contrast, was quoted as saying that "all major crises have been caused by previous inflation, which sooner or later leads to a collapse."[3]

Award of the Nobel Prize to Hayek was completely unanticipated by most on both the left and right. He had been almost completely forgotten in the American popular mind. His most recent major and complete work was *The Constitution of Liberty*, which appeared in 1960. So much had happened since that time—the assassinations of President John F. Kennedy, Martin Luther King, and Robert Kennedy; the civil rights movement; the Vietnam War; the American and world cultural revolution. Hayek had lived outside of the English-speaking world for the previous dozen years. He had written outside of the field of economics proper for most of the previous thirty.

John Chamberlain—who wrote the foreword to the initial American edition of *The Road to Serfdom*—observed in an opinion piece in the *Wall Street Journal* that, in contrast to the satisfaction that could be taken from the award itself, it was "less heartening to note the incomprehension, even stupefaction, expressed in some mass media quarters that such a relatively 'unknown' person as Hayek could have been so honored."[4]

Friedman perhaps best summarized the view of Hayek's friends in a congratulatory note that read, "Dear Fritz: I cannot tell you how delighted I am that the Swedes finally overcame their political biases sufficiently to recognize your contributions. It took them much too long, & even then they went only half the way, but that is more than I had expected them to do."[5] Friedman said later that the "rules of the Nobel, when the Nobel Prize was set up in economics, were that it could not be given for five years to a Swede. This was the sixth year. They wanted very badly to give the prize to Myrdal. But Myrdal was way over on the left of the spectrum, and—this is my reconstruction; I cannot give documentary evidence—they thought they would be subject to great criticism, so they decided to link Myrdal with Hayek, left with right, and off-set the criticism."[6] In an interview, saying much the same thing, Hayek admitted that "I never expected to receive the Nobel Prize. That came as an entire surprise because I did not think Keynesianism had already lost its reputation in intellectual and professional circles. I am not certain that this was the real cause. The Swedish Nobel Committee seems to have been very anxious to keep a certain balance between different views and therefore selected a rather peculiar pair, of which I was one!"[7]

Richard Ebeling observed in a contemporary *Reason* editorial that the "common denominator" among previous Nobel economics recipients was their "general acceptance of the Keynesian framework, a belief in the validity of State intervention in economic affairs and the use of mathematical, static models. Thus, it came as no surprise when it was announced that the 1974 award had been given to the Swedish economist Gunnar Myrdal. What came as a surprise was the economist chosen to share this year's award with Myrdal . . . Friedrich von Hayek! Professor Hayek thus became the first thorough-going free-market economist to receive the prize."[8]

The Nobel Prize in Economic Science was first given in 1969, unlike the other Nobel Prizes in Peace, Literature, Physics, Medicine, and Chemistry, which were begun in 1901. Myrdal and Hayek were the eighth and ninth recipients of the economics Nobel. A number of other market-oriented economists, starting with Milton Friedman in 1976 and mostly from the University of Chicago, have since received Nobel Prizes in Economics.

The Nobel ceremony in December 1974 was most significant because of Aleksandr Solzhenitsyn's attendance to receive the prize in Literature that had been conferred on him in 1970, but that he had been unable to receive at that time for fear of not being allowed to return to the Soviet Union. He was able to attend in 1974 only because the Soviet Union had by this time expelled him. Hayek remarked in both *The Constitution of Liberty* and the 1956 foreword to *The Road to Serfdom* that "powerful literary form" played a great role in creating a "sobered mood"[9] toward socialism. He said later of Solzhenitsyn that he is a "very complex figure. I made his acquaintance because he received his Nobel Prize the same time as I did. I have recently taken the opportunity of a Russian translation of *The Road to Serfdom* appearing to send him a copy. Evidently he saw the book for the first time and he wrote me a letter that he could hardly believe that somebody who had not lived in Russia could see the effects of socialism as clearly as I had seen them."[10]

Hayek's health significantly improved shortly before he received the Nobel Prize. While some have suggested a connection between his receiving the award and his improved health, he indignantly rejected any correlation. He had "not been cured, as some of my friends maliciously suggest, by the Nobel Prize. I had already started publishing again early in the summer of '74 before I had any idea."[11]

His mood improved considerably following the early 1970s. He observed in 1984 that he was "more optimistic"[12] than he used to be. Some of his positive attitude may have been a consequence of changes in medication, as well as improved health. It was also a result, however, of the changed public perception of him, of the new opportunities he had, and of better times. While there may have been no physical link between his receiving the Nobel Prize and his greater activity following it, the new prominence the award brought him was personally enjoyable and presented him with many pleasing opportunities. Walter Grinder, who was with the Institute of Humane Studies at this time, remembers Hayek as "almost two different people"[13] before and after he received the Nobel Prize.

The times changed considerably during the 1970s. During the late 1960s and early 1970s, it appeared to some that not just cultural revolution but political revolution led by young people was possible in western nations, and that most of Europe and the third world might follow the lead of the Soviet Union or become "Finlandized." By the middle 1970s, notwithstanding American withdrawal from Vietnam, these eventualities appeared less likely or imminent.

Economic circumstances of high inflation and high unemployment brought economists such as Hayek and Friedman to a wider public vogue than ever. Hayek gave his perspective of the role that public acknowledgement plays in one's life or work in response to an interview question along these lines:

Q: Is it important, in the sense of joy that one receives, that there is external recognition of excellence?

A: Yes, although I don't think I was ever guided in the choice of subjects I worked on by the aim at recognition. But when it comes it's very pleasant. But I would not have very much regretted having spent my life on something which I still thought was important but had not found recognition. I might have found it an inconvenience if it didn't bring an adequate income; but it would not have been a major obstacle to me if I was convinced something would ultimately be recognized as important.[14]

Perhaps the most significant consequence of Hayek's receiving the Nobel Prize was that it brought him greater public prominence. If he had not gained the renown the award gave him, it is an open question whether Prime Minister Margaret Thatcher's later public embrace of him would have been as newsworthy, and it was from Thatcher's recognition of him that he gained his greatest later celebrity.

CHAPTER THIRTY-FOUR

Friedman

THE MOST PROMINENT TWENTIETH-CENTURY ECONOMIST with whom Hayek is now most frequently identified is Milton Friedman. Hayek mentioned, and to some extent discussed, Friedman in interviews, articles, and books. It cannot be said, however, that Hayek engaged Friedman—that he fruitfully considered Friedman's thought and modified his own in response to it. This is not so for Friedman. While he is forthright that Hayek is not the major inspiration of his thought, and certainly not of his economic thought, he regularly cites Hayek for having exercised a beneficial influence on him. There are relatively few references by Hayek, on the other hand, that he was positively influenced by Friedman, or that he thought Friedman was a particularly important societal thinker (other than as a popularizer), except in the area of school vouchers.

Friedman has on a number of occasions stated his intellectual debt to Hayek. In his first major foray attempting to influence public opinion, *Capitalism and Freedom* (1962), Friedman wrote that he "owe[d] the philosophy expressed in this book and much of its detail to many teachers, colleagues, and friends . . . at the University of Chicago: Frank H. Knight, Henry C. Simons, Lloyd W. Mints, Aaron Director, Friedrich A. Hayek, George J. Stigler"; and he wrote in the introduction that "the great threat to freedom is the concentration of power. Government is necessary to preserve our freedom . . . ; yet by concentrating power in political hands, it is also a threat to freedom."[1] Hayek held in *The Road to Serfdom* that it is "not the source but the limitation of power which prevents it from being arbitrary."[2] Friedman also wrote in the introduction to *Capitalism and Freedom* of unlimited democratic power that "even though the men who wield this power initially be of good will . . . , the power will both attract and form men of a different stamp."[3] Hayek emphasized, too, that in a collectivist system, "the worst get on top."[4]

In introducing a 1976 collection of essays on Hayek by Mont Pelerin members, Friedman wrote that "over the years, I have again and again asked fellow believers in a free society how they managed to escape the contagion of their collectivist intellectual environment. No name has been mentioned more often as the source of enlightenment and understanding than Friedrich Hayek's. I cannot say that for myself, since I was influenced in this direction by my teachers at the University of Chicago before I had come to know Hayek or his work. But I, like the others, owe him a great debt. From the time I first read some of his works, and even more from the time in the mid-1940s that I first met Friedrich Hayek, his powerful mind, his moral courage, his lucid and always principled exposition have helped to broaden and deepen my understanding of the meaning and the requisites of a free society."[5] The person most influenced by Hayek who has himself most significantly influenced public opinion and policy is Friedman, although Friedman's contributions are independent of Hayek's.

Hayek and Friedman were not as personally close during the dozen years both were at the University of Chicago as is sometimes thought. They did not interact departmentally, which is how academics get to know one another best. They were more friendly associates than close personal friends or colleagues. The two couples "saw one another on and off,"[6] Friedman recalls, and Helene and Rose Friedman occasionally took walks together. Hayek was perhaps personally closer to Keynes than to Friedman, giving an indication of his relationship with each man.[7]

Friedman is described by his former student and colleague, and fellow Nobel laureate, Gary Becker:

> Milton Friedman came to Chicago's department of economics in 1946 and
> remained until 1977. He was clearly the dominant influence in a department
> that may well have been the most innovative and lively one in the profession.
> He solidified and expanded the reputation of the Chicago school. . . . The
> economics department increasingly reflected his approach and interests.
> These included deep commitment to the truth, appreciation of markets and
> free enterprise, frank and blunt discussion, and enormous zeal to convince
> the heathen. But most important was the commitment to economic analysis
> as a powerful instrument for interpreting economic and social life.

During most of his Chicago career, he gave one section of a two-quarter sequence on price theory taken by all graduate students in economics. Friedman was at his best in this course. He developed theory in clear, systematic, logically consistent fashion. He also gave numerous illustrations and applications. These applications helped students absorb Friedman's vision.

Friedman encouraged give-and-take with students. He welcomed questions, restated them much more clearly than struggling students were able to, and then usually showed why they revealed confused thinking. Some students found the intensity of the course, the high standards demanded, and the bluntness of Friedman's comments on questions and written work too difficult to absorb. Most, however, found Friedman's approach an eye-opener, and were willing to be exposed to his brilliant insights.[8]

When Becker was a graduate student at Chicago, he once asked Hayek to read a draft paper on economic analysis and political choice, but Hayek declined as he did not read handwritten manuscripts.[9]

Hayek did not participate in the Money and Banking Workshop through which, according to Becker, Friedman mainly influenced research at Chicago. D. Gale Johnson remembers that few economics students during the 1950s were interested in Hayek. Friedman recalls that "as far as Hayek's influence on Chicago is concerned, it was not through the economics department, except as he influenced individuals like myself who went to his seminar and interacted with him."[10]

Largely because they were not in the same department, Hayek and Friedman did not develop a close working relationship except through mostly extracurricular activities. During the dozen years Hayek spent at Chicago, he was gone for extended periods to, among other places, Harvard, the University of Virginia, and Europe; and Friedman spent a year traveling the world and another year at the Center for Advanced Study in the Behavioral Sciences in Palo Alto, California, and did not attend a Mont Pelerin Society conference after the first one until 1957.

The Friedmans' memoirs reinforce the view that Hayek and Friedman were not especially close in academia or socially. There have been dozens of colleagues over the course of his career to whom Friedman has been closer than Hayek. They personally drew closer during the late 1950s as Friedman began to participate in the Mont Pelerin Society more and with the founding of the Intercollegiate Society of Individualists, of which both served on the editorial advisory board of its journal, the *New Individualist Review*. Friedman strongly supported Hayek during and after the crucial 1960 and 1961 meetings of the

Mont Pelerin Society that set the society's future course. Friedman was secretary of the society in 1963 and president in 1970-72.

Friedman has responded to the question, "How would you describe him personally?"

> A: Hayek was a very complicated personality. He was by no means a simple person. He was very outgoing in one sense but at the same time I would say very private. He did not like criticism, but he never showed that he didn't like criticism. His attitude under criticism, as I found, was to say, "Well, that's a very interesting thing. At the moment I'm busy, but I'll write to you about it more later." And then he never would. [laughter]
>
> Q: Would you say that he was a proud man?
>
> A: Oh yes, no question that he was a proud man. . . . He was very sure of his own ideas.[11]

Though Friedman is little influenced by Hayek in technical economics, he remarks in his autobiography that his "interest in public policy and political philosophy was rather casual before I joined the faculty of the University of Chicago. Informal discussions with colleagues and friends stimulated a greater interest, which was reinforced by Friedrich Hayek's powerful book *The Road to Serfdom,* by my attendance at the first meeting of the Mont Pelerin Society in 1947, and by discussions with Hayek after he joined the university faculty in 1950."[12] In his 1976 Nobel address, "Inflation and Unemployment," Friedman said that an "effect of increased volatility of inflation is to render market prices a less efficient system for coordinating economic activity. A fundamental function of a price system, as Hayek emphasized so brilliantly, is to transmit compactly, efficiently, and at a low cost the information that economic agents need."[13]

Hayek's later prominence in part reflected Friedman's brighter presence. From the 1960s forward, other than in Britain, Friedman is the more publicly prominent intellectual libertarian. Making this point in a negative vein, economic historian Brian McCormick writes that "in the 1960s and 1970s . . . [Hayek] was never able to dominate the stage and he tended to be overshadowed by Friedman."[14] Hayek's longtime and final secretary, Charlotte Cubitt, recalls Hayek noting in 1985 that, "Friedman seemed to have taken his place."[15] An obituarist for the Institute of Economic Affairs wrote on Hayek's demise that "in the early 1970s, when Hayek appeared to be at his lowest point . . . the emergence of Milton Friedman began to bring him back to prominence."[16] In the milieu of nascent and emerging libertarianism from the 1940s through 1990s, Hayek and Friedman played the key roles.

Hayek's greatest contribution was in societal philosophy. He, more than anyone else, put forward the ideas of spontaneous order, of the division of knowledge, and of the crucial role of prices to overcome this division. Friedman says of Hayek as a monetary theorist that "the truth of the matter is, he really got out of that side of the business."[17] Hayek said much the same thing that, following Keynes' death, "I did only incidental work in economics."[18]

~

Hayek and Friedman differ in their methodological approaches. Hayek had this exchange in 1985 with an interviewer:

Q: The Chicago school—were they influenced by you being at Chicago?

A: Simons had great hope, and his death was a catastrophe. The others, in a methodological line, they are in effect macroeconomists and not microeconomists. Stigler least of all, Friedman very much. And this is a continuous problem for me. Milton and I agree on almost everything except monetary policy. But it creates an awful problem in the Mont Pelerin Society with the constant danger of the society splitting up into Friedmanite and Hayekite groups. And to avoid this, I try to avoid discussions of monetary theory.

Now, in this sense, the whole group, whose sources derive from Wesley Clair Mitchell's creation of the Institute of National Economic Research, are, in effect, logical positivists, methodologically. They believe economic phenomena can be explained as macro-phenomena, that you can ascertain causal effects from aggregates and averages. But, in a sense, an observation is true, though there is never a necessary [empirical] connection. It is quite likely, in fact I should prefer to demonstrate historically, that every period of inflation ends with a crash. But the historical demonstration is no proof that this must be so. The reasons why it happens can now be accounted for by microeconomic analysis and not by macroeconomic analysis. That, Milton Friedman just pooh-poohs. Stigler, yes, you can discuss it with him. He will see the problems.

The other, probably the most gifted, man in that Chicago school is Becker. And he's also theoretically the more sophisticated thinker. But Friedman has this magnificent expository power. He's on most things, general market problems, sound. I want him on my side. I want nothing less than the whole Friedman group would leave the Mont Pelerin Society. But you know, I ought to add, I have often publicly said that one of the things that I most regret is not having returned to a criticism of Keynes' [*The General Theory*]. But it's as much true of not having criticized Milton's *Positive Economics,* which in a way is quite as dangerous.[19]

Wesley Clair Mitchell taught at Columbia University in New York and for twenty-five years was director of the National Bureau of Economic Research. He emphasized a quantitative and empirical approach to economics. Hayek wrote in a 1948 obituary that Mitchell "probably contributed more than any other economist of his generation to shape the general approach to the subject which during the last thirty years has been distinctive of much of the work done in the United States."[20]

When Hayek criticized Friedman and others for being macroeconomists, he meant that Friedman did not share his Austrian conception of a trade cycle wherein there are different orders of particularly capital goods which, during economic contraction, become misstructured compared to the actual supply of savings and demand for capital in an economy. Hayek wrote that the "Chicago school thinks essentially in 'macroeconomic' terms. They try to analyze in terms of aggregates and averages, total quantity of money, total price level, total employment";[21] "You cannot build a theory on the basis of statistical information, because it's not aggregates and averages which operate upon each other, but individual actions."[22] Hayek's criticism of Friedman's macroeconomic approach was vitally tied to his own particular, Austrian conception of economic activity and a trade cycle.

When Hayek criticized Friedman and other Chicago economists for being "logical positivists," he was mistaken. Verification was essential in the logical positivist schema, but there is a difference between holding (as logical positivists were inclined to do) that unless a statement can be empirically proven, it should not be considered scientific, and maintaining, as Friedman does, that a theory that cannot in any way be empirically evaluated is usually without much worth. As Rudolph Carnap, one of the central figures in logical positivism put it, the aim of logical positivism was "conclusive justification for every statement."[23]

Friedman's methodological position is close to some aspects of Hayek's own. In his seminal "The Methodology of Positive Economics," Friedman wrote, in passages for which similar outlooks can be found in Hayek's works:

The fact that economics deals with the interrelations of human beings, and that the investigator is himself part of the subject matter being investigated . . . , raises special difficulties in achieving objectivity. . . .

The ultimate goal of a positive science is the development of a "theory" or "hypothesis" that yields valid and meaningful (i.e., not truistic) predictions about phenomena not yet observed. . . .

Factual evidence can never "prove" a hypothesis; it can only fail to disprove it, which is what we generally mean when we say, somewhat inexactly, that the hypothesis has been "confirmed" by experience. . . .

Empirical evidence is vital at two different, though closely related stages: constructing hypotheses and in testing their validity. . . .

The necessity of relying on uncontrolled experience rather than on controlled experiment makes it difficult to produce dramatic and clear-cut evidence to justify the acceptance of tentative hypotheses. . . .

Descriptive material on the characteristics of our economic system and its operations have been amassed on an unprecedented scale. This is all to the good. But, if we are to use effectively . . . abstract models and this descriptive material, we must have a comparable exploration of the criteria for determining what abstract model it is best to use for particular kinds of problems.[24]

Friedman's methodological position is close to parts of Hayek's own. One should question whether Hayek was misled by Friedman's use of the word "positive" into confusing Friedman's conception—which in significant part is simply the importance of some empirical corroboration of theories in order provisionally to accept them—with logical, strict verificationist, positivism. Friedman had the following exchange in 2000:

Q: As I understand your methodology, it is, empirical corroboration is important in trying to validate theory.

A: It's strictly Popperian.

Q: Okay. Well, here's the question. . . . Hayek, too, said that he was influenced by Popper.

A: Yes, but he didn't come all the way. Hayek retains—he's not as bad as von Mises. But he retains a large element of the praxeological approach of Mises, that knowledge comes from us inside, that we have sources of data we can rely on and we can reach truth by. . . .

Q: I just think it's a nonsensical view.

A: I think it's an utterly nonsensical view. I've never been able to understand how anybody could accept it.[25]

In 1995, Friedman made the following comments about Hayek's and particularly Mises' methodological positions:

> I never could understand why they were so impressed [at LSE] with the lectures that ended up as *Prices and Production,* and I still can't. As of that point, he [Hayek] had not freed himself from the methodological views of von Mises. And those methodological views have at their center that facts are not really relevant in determining, in testing, theories. They are relevant to illustrate theories, but not to test them, because we base economics on propositions that are self-evident. And they are self-evident because they are about human beings, and we're human beings. So we have an internal source of final knowledge, and no tests can overrule that. Praxeology.
>
> That methodological approach, I think, has very negative influences. It makes it very hard to build up a cumulative discipline of any kind. If you're always going back to your internal, self-evident truths, how do people stand on one another's shoulders? And the fact is that fifty, sixty years after von Mises issued his capital theory—which is what's involved in Hayek's capital theory—so-called Austrian economists still stick by it. There hasn't been an iota of progress.
>
> It also tends to make people intolerant. If you and I are both praxeologists, and we disagree about whether some proposition or statement is correct, how do we resolve that disagreement? We can yell, we can argue, we can try to find a logical flaw in one another's thing, but in the end we have no way to resolve it except by fighting, by saying you're wrong and I'm right.
>
> On the other hand, if you take more like a Karl Popperian approach, an approach which says what we do in science is to offer hypotheses about the consequences of certain events and, if we disagree, we test those by trying to seek empirical evidence that contradicts our predictions—if you and I disagree, we have another way to solve our problems, resolve our differences. I say to you, what facts can I find that will convince you I was right and you were wrong. You say to me, what facts can I find that will do the opposite. Then we go out and observe the facts. That's how science progresses.

Now, as I said, I believe that Hayek started out as a strict Misesian, but he changed. The more tolerant atmosphere of Britain, then subsequently of the U.S., and his exposure to a wider range of scholars, led him to alter that position.[26]

Hayek's methodological thought was an amalgam of theoretical and empirical Misesian and Popperian perspectives. Friedman's conception of prediction is not so distinct from Hayek's of "foresight"—"all knowledge is capacity to predict,"[27] as Hayek put it in "Economics and Knowledge"–although Hayek certainly did not state this to be the case.

Hayek disputed the value of statistical information. He remarked during a 1977 interview that his "argument is that we know so much detail about economics, our task is to put our knowledge in order. We hardly need any new information. Our great difficulty is digesting what we already know."[28] He wrote early, in words he never reconsidered, that "the use of statistics can never consist in a deepening of our theoretical insight."[29] He quoted A. Lowe favorably that "'our insight into the *theoretical* interconnections of economic cycles has not been enriched at all by descriptive work or calculations of correlations,'" and "we entirely agree with him [Lowe] when he . . . say[s] that 'to expect an immediate furtherance of *theory* from an increase in *empirical* insight is to misunderstand the logical relationship between theory and empirical research.'"[30]

Hayek misinterpreted Friedman's methodological views in at least one other important sense. Not only is Friedman not a logical positivist in the sense of a strict verificationist, his use of "positive" is intended largely to differentiate facts from values. He also wrote in "The Methodology of Positive Economics" that "positive economics is in principle independent of any particular ethical position or normative judgments. As Keynes [John Neville, father of John Maynard, and a significant economist in his own right] says, it deals with 'what is,' not with 'what ought to be.'"[31] Friedman's concern with positive economics here, so defined, is because many differences about optimal economic policy derive from different opinions about the consequences of actions. This use by Friedman of "positive" has nothing to do with logical positivism, and raises the question of the extent to which Hayek's differences with Friedman in this case, as in his later differences with Mill, were based on misinterpretation.

Hayek appears to have made no reference in his written work to Ayn Rand, who, together with Mises, Friedman, Popper, and Hayek, is among the writers with the most appeal to twentieth-century libertarian-inclined readers. Hayek's secretary Charlotte Cubitt remembers him orally remarking during the early 1980s that Rand was one of three outstanding woman economists (the other two, Hayek thought, were Joan Robinson and Vera Lutz).[32]

Rand achieved prominence predominantly through her extremely popular and influential 1957 *Atlas Shrugged.* She offered views of Hayek on several occasions. In 1946, she wrote to Leonard Read, founder of the Foundation for Economic Education, that "I fully sympathize with your anger at the conservatives who claim that they oppose compulsion except for their particular pet cause. That is their usual attitude. . . . All so-called respectable publications, owned by conservatives, have been staffed with pinks who maintain a blockade against all real advocates of our side. Only the Hayeks and such other compromisers are allowed to get through, the kind who do more good to the communist cause than to ours."[33]

Rand wrote similarly in a 1946 letter to Rose Wilder Lane, author of *The Discovery of Freedom* (1943), "Now to your question: 'Do those almost with us do more harm than 100% enemies?' I don't think this can be answered with a flat 'yes' or 'no,' because the 'almost' is such a wide term. There is one general rule to observe: those who are with us, but merely do not go far enough are the ones who may do us some good. Those who agree with us in some respects, yet preach contradictory ideas at the same time, are definitely more harmful than 100% enemies. As an example of the kind of 'almost' I would tolerate, I'd name Ludwig von Mises. As an example of our most pernicious enemy, I would name Hayek. That one is real poison."[34]

Milton and Rose Friedman praise Rand. On several occasions, the Friedmans have used a "tide" metaphor to describe the evolution of societal thought and action, stating that the "hypothesis is that a major change in social and economic policy is preceded by a shift in the climate of intellectual *opinion,* itself generated, at least in part, by contemporaneous social, political, and economic circumstances." They write of three tides—"the rise of *laissez-faire* (the Adam Smith tide)," "the rise of the welfare state (the Fabian tide)," and "the resurgence of free markets (the Hayek tide)." The Friedmans see a fundamental change in opinion during recent decades, and ask, "Why this great shift in public attitudes? The persuasive power of such books as Hayek's *Road to Serfdom,* Ayn Rand's *Fountainhead* and *Atlas Shrugged,* our own *Capitalism and Freedom,* and numerous others," observing that *The Road to Serfdom* was "probably the first real inroad in the dominant intellectual view."[35]

In a 1977 *Individual Liberty* survey of its readership, seventy percent named Rand as "most influential" in initially causing them to adopt libertarianism.[36] In 1988 and 1998, *Liberty* magazine surveyed its readers and Libertarian

Table 34.1		
	1998	1988
Rand	3.51	4.02
Jefferson	3.51	3.10
Friedman	3.08	2.95
Mises	2.76	3.65
Hayek	2.74	3.02
Rothbard	2.72	3.93
Goldwater	2.39	2.49[37]

Party activists, asking them to rate by whom they had been most influenced intellectually on a scale of one to five, with five being most influential (see table above).

Friedman's greatest praise for Hayek was contained in a 1992 obituary of his old friend. He here called Hayek "unquestionably . . . the most important intellectual leader of the movement that has produced a major change in the climate of opinion."[38]

CHAPTER THIRTY-FIVE

Later
Monetary Thinking

DURING THE MIDDLE 1970s, Hayek's two main projects were to complete the long-delayed *Law, Legislation and Liberty* and to develop ideas in the area of monetary reform. In his Nobel Prize address, he said of himself and fellow economists that, as a result of inflation then occurring, as a "profession we have made a mess of things."[1] Hayek resumed participation in more technical monetary discussion, after a hiatus of almost thirty years, as a result of the accelerating inflation that occurred in western nations during the late 1960s and early 1970s. Just as inflation in post–World War I Austria initially focused his attention on monetary issues, the inflation of the early 1970s refocused his attention.

Hayek remained firmly convinced that the primary problem inflation causes is that it misshapes an economy's productive structure. He wrote in an October 1974 opinion piece in the London *Daily Telegraph* that "the chief harm which inflation causes . . . [is] that it gives the whole structure of the economy a distorted, lopsided character which sooner or later makes a more extensive unemployment inevitable."[2] There would be, in Hayek's conception, excessive production of temporally early capital.

He opposed the monetarism of Milton Friedman. In a 1980 letter to the editor of the London *Times*, he said that the "newfangled word monetarism means no more than the good old name 'quantity theory of money.'" He went on in this letter to say that "the problem" with the quantity theory of money in its "crude," Friedmanian form is that it "provides no adequate measure of what is the supply of money and that not only the supply of all kinds of money but also the demand for them determines its [money's] value."[3]

He made the following criticism of Friedmanian monetarism in the 1978, second edition of his great, incomplete late contribution to monetary theory and policy, *Denationalisation of Money*. The problem with the quantity theory of money is that by its "stress on the effects of changes in the quantity of money on the general level of prices it directs all-too exclusive attention to the harmful effects of inflation and deflation on the creditor-debtor relationship, but disregards the even more important and harmful effects of the injections and withdrawals of amounts of money from circulation on the structure of relative prices and the consequent misallocation of resources and particularly the misdirection of investments which it causes."[4]

To follow the course that Friedman recommends of a fixed rate of increase in money supply would, Hayek thought, "probably produce the greatest financial panic of history." Such a course could result in insufficient monetary liquidity. "As regards Professor Friedman's proposal of a legal limit on the rate at which a monopolistic issuer of money was to be allowed to increase the quantity in circulation, I would not like to see what would happen if it ever became known that the amount of cash in circulation was approaching the upper limit and that therefore a need for increased liquidity could not be met," to which he footnoted, "to such a situation the classic account of Walter Bagehot would apply: 'In a sensitive state of the English money market the near approach to the legal limit of reserve would be a sure incentive to panic.'"[5]

In addition, Hayek believed that it is impossible to bring inflation down gradually. He also remarked in 1980 on what he regarded as the too "wet" or moderate course that new Prime Minister Margaret Thatcher was following that his "hopes of Britain saving herself have shrunk a little. . . . I'm afraid Mrs. Thatcher is following the advice of Milton Friedman. He is a dear friend of mine and we agree on almost everything except monetary policy. He thinks in terms of statistics, aggregates and the average price level and does not really see that inflation leads to unemployment because of the distortion of the structure of relative prices. If you have a long period of inflation in which much misdirection of effort has taken place as a result of the distortion of the price structure, extensive unemployment becomes inevitable."[6]

Hayek thought it is politically infeasible to slow inflation down gradually. Rather, he thought, inflation must be stopped dead in its tracks, once and for all, because once the process of disinflation starts, there must be a crisis as a result of business liquidations to accommodate a misshaped structure of production. His Austrian conception of a trade cycle greatly influenced his views of the practicability of the successful course to reduce inflation that Great Britain, the United States, and many other nations adopted during the late 1970s and early '80s in significant part through Friedman's influence.

Hayek was pessimistic of Britain's chances to summon the will to cure inflation as he thought it must be done, at one fell swoop. He predicted that "if this is not done by a determined Government it will not be done before, after a vain attempt of concealing inflation by price controls, the pound finally collapsed entirely."[7] He thought that wage and price controls would be implemented by governments unwilling to control inflation through monetary means, and that wage and price controls would, in turn, destroy the free market economy through hyperinflation and eventual state management of the means of economic production. His experience of hyperinflation as a young man in Austria impressed him greatly.

Hayek's ideas in technical economic theory were not understood by the general public during the early 1970s. On a number of occasions, he expressed sentiments to the effect that the only thing worse than the general public not understanding the quantity theory of money would be that they would place too extensive reliance on it. He always thought that the most significant negative symptom of an increase in monetary supply is that it would misshape a structure of production.

He had very little practical influence—at least as he intended—on monetary discussions during the late 1960s and early 1970s. Particularly after he received the Nobel Prize, he was again a prominent symbol, who was perceived as opposed to Keynes, inflation, and excessive government. The exact details of his arguments were perhaps less important in the public mind than this broad conception of him. His monetary ideas had little influence in academia.

He expressed pessimistic thoughts throughout his career on various issues. In *The Constitution of Liberty,* he feared that "concentration camps" for the elderly might result from social security programs that grew as projected in inflationary circumstances; he also expressed here the fear that "the day may not be far off when authority, by adding appropriate drugs to our water supply . . . will be able to elate or depress, stimulate or paralyze . . . the minds of whole populations." For a "none too pessimistic" presentation of the future that might occur, he referred the reader to Aldous Huxley's *Brave New World* and B. F. Skinner's *Walden Two.*[8]

In 1978, Hayek expressed the view that western economies had not performed as well during the decades following World War II as at any time in history:

> Q: . . . I suppose that you would have to say that the world's economies, by
> some objective measure, have functioned as well during those [the "last"]
> thirty years as in any previous time.
>
> A: Well, I doubt that . . . [9]

He always anticipated that what he considered the excessively inflationary period
of the 1950s through 1970s would be followed by economic collapse on a scale
comparable to, if not exceeding that of, the Great Depression. He remarked in a
1975 lecture that the "inevitable end is now near if it has not already arrived."[10]
He said in 1983 that the "stupidity of the politicians may very easily lead to a
similar outcome to that of 1930-31."[11] He made many similar predictions
throughout the entire period following World War II.

He considered the events of intervening decades since he did his work in the
later 1920s and during the 1930s in monetary theory to have confirmed his work.
He responded in 1978 to the question, "Have the economic events since you wrote
on trade-cycle theory tended to strengthen or weaken your ideas on the Austrian
theory of the trade cycle?" "On the whole, strengthen."[12] He did not shift his early
1930s views in economics one significant iota. In 1981, giving his essential view of
the British economic condition at this time, he stated that "unemployment is the
necessary effect of stopping inflation dead. I would take any amount of unemployment which is necessary for this purpose, because that is the only way of bringing
Britain back on a self-maintaining order and standard where it can in [the] future
begin a new growth. . . . The conditions which make unemployment inevitable were
laid during the previous inflation. . . . I have often regretted that there haven't been
more bankruptcies in the past; the British economy would be in a better position
now if more firms had been eliminated and not kept artificially alive."[13] The
misshaped structure of British production required unemployment and bankruptcies
after disinflation. He also said in 1981 that food shortages might confront Great
Britain if Prime Minister Thatcher failed: "The problem is essentially one of paying
for imports. Britain imports large quantities of raw materials and though it produces
more of its food than it did before the last war it is still nothing like self-sufficient.
First, the problem will take the form of scarcity and rationing. It could arise within
the next ten years."[14]

A special conference of the Mont Pelerin Society was held in Hayek's honor in
1975. For reasons of modesty, he did not attend. The assemblage broke into

applause when a communication from him was read that he had completed the second volume of *Law, Legislation and Liberty*. He appeared on the American news interview program "Meet the Press" in 1975 as well.

A reporter portrayed Hayek and his wife at this time, shortly after he received the Nobel Prize:

> These days his mornings are devoted to writing, and to serious reading. He is preparing his essays on law, legislation, and liberty. Then he takes a constitutional, often to an idyllic lake overlooked by the Austrian Alps. For leisurely reading, mainly in bed, Trollope is much favoured. Then there is music on records, though his wife is more of a music-lover than he. His favourites: Beethoven and Mozart. Wagner? "Not very often. Too dissonant. A little of him goes a long way."
>
> When he was being photographed in his house, Frau Hayek arrived home from a walk. Hayek left us and the two talked outside in German. He returned to explain that Frau Hayek would come with us to take some pictures of him on condition that she did not appear in the pictures. Agreed. She then emerged—a handsome lady two years younger than Hayek.
>
> She shared her husband's preference for exact statement. "I like the great line of classics, from Mozart to Brahms," she said, when asked about her love of music. Mahler? "No, he wasn't in that line. He came after Brahms." Schubert, then? "Of course. He came between Mozart and Brahms. Therefore I like him, as I've explained."[15]

When Hayek left Salzburg to return to Freiburg in 1977, he and Helene moved to the same apartment in which they had lived in Freiburg during the 1960s. This was very important to her, and almost a condition to the university authorities for his return.

Hayek's exceptional late contribution to monetary theory and policy was his proposal for competing, an idea he first explored in-depth in a 1975 address, "Choice in Currency: A Way to Stop Inflation." With the exception of the two centuries that the gold standard was practiced, Hayek felt that "practically all governments have used their exclusive power to issue money in order to defraud and plunder the people. . . . What is so dangerous and ought to be done away with is not governments' right to issue money but the *exclusive* right to do so and their power to force people to use it and to accept it at a particular price."[16]

His idea for competing national currencies was brilliant. "The concrete proposal for the near future," he wrote, "is that the countries of the Common Market, preferably with the neutral countries of Europe (and possibly later the countries of North America), mutually bind themselves by formal treaty not to place any obstacles in the way of the free dealing throughout their territories in one another's currencies or of a similar free exercise of the banking business by any institution legally established in any of their territories."[17] This would require abolition of exchange controls and any sort of regulation on the movement of money among countries, and create the freedom to use any currency anywhere.

The "generalisation of the underlying principle" on which his near-term proposal was based was that if "we are to contemplate abolishing the exclusive use within each national territory of a single national currency issued by the government, and to admit on equal footing the currencies issued by other governments, the question at once arises whether it would not be equally desirable to do away altogether with the monopoly of government supplying money and to allow private enterprise to supply the public with other media of exchange it may prefer. There is no necessity or even advantage in the now unquestioned and universally accepted government prerogative of producing money."[18]

He said on a number of occasions during his later years that he made one "discovery" and two "inventions"—the discovery was of the division of knowledge, and the inventions were his thoughts on reforming representative government and his proposals for monetary reform. His thoughts in the area of currency reform were ahead of his time. Arthur Seldon quotes an "august personage in the British banking system" as calling them possibly for "the day after tomorrow."[19]

Hayek's initial proposal for monetary reform—simply to allow a competitive market among national currencies (as a preliminary step toward the allowance of private currencies)—was embraced by the Thatcher government in European monetary discussions. Nigel Lawson, Thatcher's chancellor of the exchequer, recalls that in 1989 he and Thatcher decided that in forthcoming European monetary talks the "alternative form of monetary union we should propose should be based on the Hayekian idea of competing currencies. . . . Currency creation would remain in the hands of the national Central Banks. . . . With complete interchangeability and no legal impediments, good currencies would threaten gradually to drive out the bad, in a happy reversal of Gresham's law, until eventually Europe might theoretically find itself with a single currency, freely chosen."[20]

Thatcher writes in her memoirs that "we had to agree [on] the line which Nigel would take at the forthcoming meeting of European Community Finance ministers on EMU [European Monetary Union]. Nigel had devised an ingenious approach, based on Friedrich Hayek's idea of competing currencies, in which the market rather than governments would provide the momentum for monetary union. (Unfortunately, this proposal did not in fact get very far, not least because it was not at all in the statist, centralised model which our European community partners preferred.)"[21]

Hayek was not able to develop his late thoughts in monetary theory and practice that call for competing and private currencies in other than preliminary form. He soon became involved in a work that he thought would be the summation of his life and thought—*The Fatal Conceit.*

CHAPTER THIRTY-SIX

IEA

IN THE FALL OF 1978, Hayek participated in a series of interviews conducted through the Oral History Program of the University of California, Los Angeles. The idea was beginning to emerge that he was not simply a thinker for the contemporary period, but potentially for centuries. The interviews were organized by Armen Alchian, professor of economics at UCLA and member of the Mont Pelerin Society, who described Hayek's personality and traits as "calm, imperturbable, systematic, questioning, uncompromising, explicit, and relaxed."[1]

Hayek was described by others during this period, including Eamonn Butler, director of the Adam Smith Institute in London, on whose academic advisory board Hayek served as the nominal chairman. "Hayek's manners both in print and in person are impeccable," Butler wrote in 1983; Hayek believed that it is "the little qualities of personality which are so important in fostering good relations between men and therefore crucial in making the liberal society possible; values such as kindliness and a sense of humour, personal modesty and respect for other people's good intentions. One might add punctuality and reliability, and then Hayek could be the model himself: for those who know him are agreed that in his writings and in person he approaches as near to the ideal of the liberal scholar as perhaps human frailty will admit."[2]

His former LSE student George Shackle described him in 1981 as "aristocratic in temper and origins; physically, morally and intellectually fearless; clear and incisive in thought; the embodied principle itself of following the logic where it leads; the soul of scholarly generosity; Friedrich August Hayek is one of the outstanding sculptors of this age's thought."[3] His old friend Fritz Machlup remarked that "memorable traits noticeable in almost all of his writings are Hayek's chivalry and tolerance in criticism and polemics, and his modesty and humility not only in acknowledging the contributions of his intellectual forebears but also in arguing against the views of his intellectual opponents."[4]

In 1976, Hayek participated in a conference sponsored by the Institute for Humane Studies at Windsor Castle that was one of three conferences held between 1974 and 1976 that helped to provide an initial institutional framework and fillip for the Austrian movement in economics during recent decades. Hayek remarked in a 1978 interview that Mises was "the real founder of the American school of Austrian economics. I mean the American school of Austrian economics [i]s very largely a Mises school."[5] He also had the following exchange:

Q: So in the revival of interest in the Austrian school that has taken place in recent years in the United States—

A: It means the Mises school. . . . I am now being associated with Mises, but initially I think it meant the pupils whom Mises had taught in the United States. Some rather reluctantly now admit me as a second head, but I don't think people like [Murray] Rothbard or some of the immediate Mises pupils are really very happy that they are not.[6]

Seldon made the interesting remark in the 1976 preface to Hayek's *Denationalisation of Money* that during the 1930s Robbins and Hayek "helped to make the works of Menger, Wieser, Böhm-Bawerk and Mises known to British students and teachers, but little further has been heard of the Austrian School until the last year or two."[7] Hayek's 1974 Nobel Prize played a significant role in publicizing Austrian economics to new generations.

The most important institution to emerge from Hayek's influence is the London-based Institute of Economic Affairs, IEA, which helped to generate ideas that were implemented during Margaret Thatcher's eleven years as prime minister from 1979 to 1990. According to Friedman, "Without the IEA, I doubt very much whether there would have been a Thatcherite revolution."[8]

Hayek described the IEA's genesis, "Almost at the same time as the founding of the Mont Pelerin Society," he recalled, "a second development along the same lines took place. A young English pilot who had made a great deal of money came to me and asked what he could do to thwart the ominous growth of socialism. I had considerable trouble persuading him that mass propaganda was futile and that the task consisted rather of convincing intellectuals. I convinced this man by the name of Antony Fisher of the need to establish such an institution, which led to the founding of the Institute of Economic Affairs. Its progress was very slow at first, but today [1983] it is not only enormously influential but also serves as the model for a whole set of comparable institutions scattered around the entire western half of the globe, from which sound ideas emanate."[9]

The IEA's intellectual roots may be traced to the LSE economics department during the 1930s. Arthur Seldon, IEA's prodigious editorial director from 1957 to 1988, was a student and research assistant at LSE from 1934 to 1941. Friendly, soft-spoken, and helpful, as a secondary school student he read Cannan. He was originally a student of Plant's; "as my interest turned from economic theory to applications in policy the strongest influence became Hayek through his writings on capitalism and the market"[10] in *Collectivist Economic Planning*. In an essay commemorating the fortieth anniversary of *The Road to Serfdom*, Seldon continues that "Hayek's intellectual assault on the economics of collectivism fortified five post-graduates in 1938-39 to form a small group to discuss ways of refuting collectivist economic heresies. The war prevented it from evolving into an embryo IEA-type organisation of liberals."[11]

British political historian Dennis Kavanagh well describes the philosophy and development of the IEA, which was founded as a "'research and educational trust' to study the role of markets and pricing in allocating resources and registering preferences. It was run by Arthur Seldon and Ralph Harris. The starting point of much of the IEA's work is that the climate of opinion colours the thinking of politicians. Rather than capture a political party or politician, it believed that the case for the free market would be enhanced more effectively by shaping opinion in the educational and academic world." Through 1997, the IEA had published more than 500 papers, had a monthly journal, and regularly hosted lunches and seminars for political, business, and opinion leaders. According the Kavanagh, "by 1979 the IEA was firmly established as the intellectual home of free markets, economic liberalism, and monetarism in Britain. It published a number of Hayek's essays. By publishing Hayek, the IEA played an important part in reviving interest in his work."[12]

Hayek noted that his own greatest later intellectual prominence occurred somewhat after the initial flush of interest following the Nobel Prize. In response to a question in 1985, "To what do you attribute the late reaction?" he said, "The Nobel Prize had very little effect. From '74 'til about '80, oh yes, external effects and so on. But I could not yet feel that it had stirred the interest of the younger generation. And for the past five years there's been such a flood that I can no longer follow it. I don't think I'm exaggerating—I get every month a new book dealing with my problems. And I'm concerned with my own tasks. I can't even read them"; "there is now such a flood of books by Hayekians that I can no longer master it."[13]

Hayek began to experience virtual adulation in some quarters during the early 1980s. He was perceived to have been right about Keynes, inflation, and the welfare state, and later he was perceived to have been right about socialism and communism all along as well—that collective, government control of all land and economic means of production in a society is wasteful and dictatorial. While there had always been a (small) segment of the intellectual community who considered him to be a genuinely profound and significant thinker, this view became more pronounced during the early '80s. He began to be considered a virtual prophet who saw and defined the consequences of socialism for a longer period of time than anyone else.

Eamonn Butler observes that after receiving the Nobel Prize, Hayek began "writing and lecturing even more widely than before."[14] Hayek always traveled. His *Studies* and *New Studies* contain lectures given in twelve different locations around the world—Rikkyo University, Tokyo; the University of Freiburg; Chicago; Mont Pelerin; Cambridge, England; Sydney; New York City; Salzburg; London; Stockholm; the University of Kiel, (then, West) Germany; and Canberra, Australia.

The pace quickened after he received the Nobel Prize, notwithstanding that he was entering his late seventies. Butler quotes Hayek as saying that "looking back on his period of ill health, he often remarked, 'Some years ago I tried old age, but discovered I didn't like it.'"[15] Butler notes as well that in 1973 Hayek was unsuccessfully proposed for the honorary position of Chancellor of the University of St. Andrew's in Scotland, which John Stuart Mill had once held, but the electorate had decided that he was too old and frail for the job. Hayek laughed uproariously nine years later when told that he was the only candidate still alive."[16]

Recognitions began to stream in from around the world. Hayek had been elected a Fellow of the British Academy in 1944, on the recommendation of Keynes. He was awarded honorary doctorates by Rikkyo University in 1964 and the University of Salzburg on his seventy-fifth birthday in 1974. In 1971, the University of Vienna had made him an honorary senator. Following the award of the Nobel Prize, he received honorary doctorates from universities in Guatemala, Argentina, and Chile, all in 1977. In 1978, he received another honorary doctorate, from the University of Dallas, where long-time associate William Hutt (who wrote one of the essays in *Capitalism and the Historians*) now taught. A university was named after Hayek in Guatemala. He remarked to an interviewer in 1978, though, "I have—this is always apparently inevitable—since my Nobel Prize been collecting quite a number of honorary degrees. But not one from what you call a prestigious university. The prestigious universities still regard me as a reactionary; I am regarded as intellectually not quite reputable."[17]

The progress of new ideas is almost inevitably slow and, at first, often invites ridicule. As Hayek emphasized so well, society is in large part based on shared conceptions of the way the world works. Although change is inevitable— and though "yesterday's heresy is tomorrow's dogma"—few recognize during their lifetime that much, if not most, of what they believe to be objectively true about the world will later be shown to have been false or, more certainly, incomplete and inaccurate. Human conceptions of the truth are tentative, hypothetical, and changing, subject to constant checking, validation, modification, or rejection. The discovery of truth is an endless process of evaluating old and new hypotheses by new experience. The truth is not a mountain peak to be conquered, but an endless journey on an endless road. Each discovery of knowledge opens up new areas of ignorance; the more one discovers of nature and reality, the more one is aware of what one does not know.[18]

Though one may readily assent to these principles in theory, to implement them in fact is a different question. New ideas of the way the world works and is, if they are to become accepted, should eventually become clothed in words. It is the understanding (in German, *Verstehen*) that is at first important and which may only be conceived by one or a few; only later may new understandings be placed into words to which all (or most) give assent and comprehend.

When Hayek and Mises put forward the idea of the impracticality of classical socialism, they expressed a notion that to many sounded strange and false because it was so contrary to accepted opinion. Of course socialism would work better and be more productive than capitalism. Would not the planned development of an economy be more productive than the chance outcomes of capricious competition? How could it plausibly be maintained that capitalism would be more productive than socialism?

Hayek responded that no matter how persuasive these words might appear, they reflect a false concept of reality, a false understanding. He put forward an idea that he thought more accurately reflects actual reality—that there is a division of knowledge among the minds of all humanity, and that the fundamental societal question is not how to gather this knowledge in one place, but how to enable societal orders that make the most use of fragmented and divided knowledge and information.

These words had little influence for many years. The accuracy of their (provisional) truthfulness was not evident to many politicians, citizens, or intellectual leaders—they were seen as a false concept of reality. But, in time, the manifest unproductivity of Communist systems, combined with their political tyranny, led to a circumstance in which Hayek's words became perceived as a more accurate description of the way the world works and is than socialist conceptions. Hayek the eccentric became Hayek the major societal philosopher, and attention that was long denied him has come in abundant quantities.

Arthur Seldon's roles in the IEA and in sustaining interest in Hayek's thought were and are vital. Seldon remarks of his early IEA involvement with Hayek's work that *The Constitution of Liberty* "led us to invite ten authors to assess Hayek's biggest book so far. They produced an assortment of praise and criticism in the IEA book, *Agenda for a Free Society* (1961). Hayek had left Britain for the USA. My impression was that in Britain knowledge of his work had fallen away. I found the wide sweep of *The Constitution of Liberty* magisterial and profound, its scholarship massive and its insights brilliant."[19]

Richard Cockett writes that under the "direction of Arthur Seldon, the IEA tried to apply the principles of economic liberalism to as wide a range of areas of economic activity as possible, and to bear topical relevance in mind. It was a testimony to Arthur Seldon's skills as an editor that the IEA achieved its aim of reaching a wide audience. Seldon was careful with his choice of authors for IEA publications, and the IEA's almost exclusive reliance on academic economists ensured that it acquired the reputation for excellence. Undoubtedly one of the IEA's most important achievements was to create a public platform in Britain for Hayek and Friedman." Cockett also observes that Hayek and Friedman's Nobel Prizes "helped to cement the academic and intellectual credibility of the IEA's work, which, all along, had been its greatest asset."[20]

Seldon recalls that he first heard of Hayek in his "Sixth Form in 1932 as a new foreign economist at the LSE with a funny name (Hake? Hike? Hayeck?). In the end I knew him from 1934, when I arrived at LSE, until 1987 at a seminar in Freiburg. . . . We students—and some junior staff—saw Hayek as a tall, lean, austere Austrian 'Herr Professor' teaching technical economics with a Germanic accent. . . . I remember him as the model of academic courtesy. The IEA was his spiritual home. Scholars have enlightened their times, and some beyond. Hayek was a scholar for all seasons."[21]

Seldon edited Hayek's works published by the IEA. When Hayek doubted, for a time, that he would be able to see *Law, Legislation and Liberty* through to publication, Hayek left instructions that, if he did not, Seldon should finish it. Seldon comments that Hayek's 1972 IEA-published *A Tiger by the Tail* began his "way back to fame."[22] Had it not been for Arthur Seldon and the IEA, it is an open question whether Hayek would have received the Nobel Prize.

Thatcher

THE COUNTRY IN WHICH HAYEK IS BEST KNOWN IS GREAT BRITAIN, primarily as a result of Prime Minister Margaret Thatcher's public embrace of him as her leading philosophical inspirer during the 1980s. Hayek's prominence rose in England after Thatcher became leader of the Conservative Party in 1975 and skyrocketed after she became prime minister in 1979.

Thatcher remarks in her memoirs that as a young woman the "most powerful critique of socialist planning and the socialist state" she read, and to which she has "returned so often since," was *The Road to Serfdom.*[1] She has also been greatly influenced by Hayek's other work, including what she describes as his "masterpieces,"[2] *The Constitution of Liberty* and *Law, Legislation and Liberty.*

Richard Cockett, describing Hayek's first encounter with Thatcher, writes that "soon after she had become Leader of the Opposition in 1975, the IEA arranged for Mrs. Thatcher to meet Hayek for the first time at Lord North Street [IEA headquarters]. Mrs. Thatcher arrived and was ushered into the boardroom for a private audience with Hayek, which lasted for about thirty minutes. At the end, Mrs. Thatcher left and the staff of the IEA gathered around an unusually pensive Hayek, seeking his reaction to the meeting. After a long pause, all he said, with obvious feeling, was 'She's so beautiful.'"[3]

A Conservative Research Department officer remembers one occasion when a colleague "prepared a paper arguing that the 'middle way' was the pragmatic path for the Conservative Party to take, avoiding the extremes of Left and Right. Before he finished speaking to his paper, the new Party leader reached into her briefcase and took out a book. It was Friedrich von Hayek's *The Constitution of Liberty*. Interrupting our pragmatist, she held the book up for all of us to see. 'This,' she said sternly, 'is what we believe,' and banged Hayek down on the table."[4]

The depth of Hayek and Thatcher's personal and political, as distinct from philosophical, relationship can be overemphasized. Hayek commented in 1978, a year before she became prime minister, that "I'm very interested in politics; in fact, in a way I take part. I now am very much engaged in strengthening Mrs. Thatcher's back in her fight against the unions. I write articles; I've even achieved recently the dignity of an article on the lead page of the London *Times* on that particular subject. I'm represented in England as the inspirer of Mrs. Thatcher, whom I've only met twice in my life. I enjoy this, but on the principle that I will not ask, under any circumstances, what is politically possible now. I concentrate on what I think is right and should be done if you can convince the public. If you can't, well it's so much the worse, but that's not my affair."[5]

After Thatcher was elected prime minister, Hayek occasionally tried to advise her on practical, political issues, particularly early in her prime ministership, perhaps by sending her a letter with a polished interview transcript or a lecture text. In August 1979, he wrote to her to suggest a national referendum on trade union reform, but she politely declined his advice.[6] He sent her a copy of the third volume of *Law, Legislation and Liberty* when it was published in 1979, and the first copy of the fortieth anniversary leather bound edition of *The Road to Serfdom* in 1984. Thatcher was not much influenced by Hayek in topical political issues. During her entire time in office, they were in any sort of significant contact perhaps only once or twice a year or so.

Hayek was nonetheless identified in popular British media as her behind-the-scenes guru. A 1976 *Daily Mirror* headline asked, "Who the heck is Hayek?"—to which the answer was provided in the article, "An Austrian-born professor is the shadowy figure behind a flaming row inside the Tory Party. He is still virtually unknown among the British people."[7] The *Mirror* headlined another article four years later, "Mrs. Thatcher's Godfather!"[8] and titled another story, "The Priest and the Premier," in which the writer said, "Professor Friedrich August von Hayek is the inspiration behind the Government's policies which, if pursued, will push the unemployment figures beyond two million and lead to multiple bankruptcies and a revival of the class war."[9]

Patrick Cosgrave in his *Margaret Thatcher: A Tory and Her Party* (1978) noted the "extent to which Hayek's reputation has risen again in the 1970s (he spent some years in virtual seclusion and silence), and how he has commanded a far greater audience than he ever enjoyed immediately after the war."[10] As a result of stagflation, excessive union power, and the award of the Nobel Prize—and especially Thatcher's rising position—Hayek gained greater prominence in Britain than he ever had before, and far more than he ever acquired in the United States or anywhere else. In 1978, Michael Foot, then Labour Party leader in the House of Commons, attacked Hayek as a "mad professor,"[11] and accused Thatcher, somewhat similarly to Attlee's criticism of Churchill over thirty years before, of being in his clutches.

Hayek met Ronald Reagan through Thatcher. She introduced him to Reagan in 1982 in London. Reagan mentioned that he had read one of Hayek's books and "learned a great deal from it."[12] As prime minister, Thatcher said in the House of Commons, "I am a great admirer of Professor Hayek. Some of his books would well be read by some honourable members."[13]

Other politicians in the United Kingdom who have been influenced by Hayek include Enoch Powell and Thatcher Cabinet members Keith Joseph, Geoffrey Howe, John Biffen, and Nigel Lawson. Edward Heath, British prime minister from 1970 to 1974, attended a 1953 Mont Pelerin Society regional meeting.

Hayek regularly took part in the public policy debate in Great Britain. Particularly after he received the Nobel Prize, he frequently wrote letters-to-the-editor to the London *Times* especially and had longer opinion pieces published in a variety of outlets. One particular 1978 letter that generated controversy was when, in the course of praising Thatcher's call for an end to immigration, he wrote, "Nobody who has lived through the rise of the violent anti-Semitism which led to Hitler can refuse Mrs. Thatcher admiration for her courageous and outspoken warning. When I grew up in Vienna the established Jewish families were a generally respected group and all decent people would frown upon the occasional anti-Jewish outbursts of a few popular politicians. It was the sudden influx of large numbers of Galician and Polish Jews [during World War I] . . . which in a short period changed the attitude. They were too visibly different to be readily absorbed."[14]

This letter elicited no less than five negative responses during the next week, and two further letters from Hayek. *Times* columnist Bernard Levin wrote that Hayek's argument was that "racialism is really all the fault of the victims, who only have to remain sufficiently inconspicuous and sufficiently unsuccessful for it to go away."[15] Professor Willi Frischauer wrote that "when Professor Hayek traces the rise of Austrian anti-Semitism to the immigration of 'visibly different' Jews from Poland, he is either deceived by his memory or ignorant of Austria's political and social history."[16] Dr. George Fink said that "Professor Hayek's assertion that it was the influx of Polish Jews which 'changed the attitude' of Viennese society is as offensive as it is facile. Anti-Semitism in Austria was endemic."[17] Nicholas (now Lord) Kaldor weighed in to challenge Hayek's economics,[18] and Ruth Glass declared that Hayek's letter "started with a monstrous distortion—that it was 'the rise of the violent anti-Semitism which led to Hitler,' not the other way round."[19]

Defending himself in his final response, Hayek said that he was "puzzled why the indignant protests about my letter should insist to treat as a problem of race what I had been at pains to show was a problem of acculturation. I had in my first letter deliberately dragged in the example of Czech immigration into Vienna before 1914 which led to street riots. Nothing like these riots demanding discriminatory government action had in recent history there been directed against the Jews until the flood of (differently dressed!) refugees from Galicia arrived."[20]

Hayek could be culturally insensitive and stereotypical of particular nationalities.[21] He did not, however, perceive meaningful physiological diversity among humanity's races. In *The Road to Serfdom,* he considered it criticism of central planning on a global basis that, "Can there be much doubt that this would mean a more or less conscious endeavour to secure the dominance of the white man, and would rightly be so regarded by all other races?"[22] He wrote in a *Fatal Conceit* draft that the west had no obligation to provide less developed nations with the capital that would raise the productivity of their workers, implicitly implying that it is lack of capital and education that causes underdevelopment, not different natural propensities among peoples.

In a 1961 South African interview, commenting on recent racial discrimination legislation there, Hayek said that this "appears to be a clear and even extreme instance of that discrimination between different individuals which seems to me to be incompatible with the reign of liberty. The essence of what I said [in *The Constitution of Liberty*] was really the fact that the laws under which government can use coercion are equal for all responsible adult members of that society. Any kind of discrimination—be it on grounds of religion, political opinion, race, or whatever it is—seems to be incompatible with the idea of freedom under the law. Experience has shown that separate never is equal and cannot be equal."[23] He believed, however, that on a private basis, people should be allowed to discriminate.

He acknowledged the existence of racism in the United States when, after discussing the possibility of sending his children to the United States during

World War II, he remarked that "I should perhaps add that this was based on the tacit assumption that my children would there be placed with a white and not with a coloured family."[24] He opposed direct government provision of education in part on the grounds that it is "the provision of education by government which creates such problems as that of the segregation of Negroes in the United States."[25] He said of university admissions in his South African interview that in "so far as the universities are in a strict sense public [that is, government funded] institutions, according to my philosophy they ought by definition to be equally open to all. If they are strictly private institutions, I would say that private institutions would have the right to discriminate."[26]

Hayek was intellectually defined by his youth in Austria, young and middle adulthood in England, dozen years in Chicago, and later great renown in Great Britain after Margaret Thatcher became prime minister. What Schumpeter said of Keynes—that his "advice was in the first instance always English advice"[27]—could in many ways also be said of Hayek. He was naturally at home in Britain, and it was only as a result of personal circumstances that he did not live out his days there.

On March 26, 1980, he gave an address to the Monday Club in London, a Conservative Party caucus, on "the muddle of the middle." He ended this talk on the thought that the battle for Britain to survive as a wealthy and important nation was being fought in the Conservative Party, and that Britain's continued survival would depend on the elimination of trades union privileges, control of inflation, and rejection of the concept of social justice. In 1984, Hayek happily participated in a Mont Pelerin Society conference in Cambridge. In a write-up of the conference for the *National Review*, John Chamberlain wrote that "the most encouraging thing about the Mont Pelerin Cambridge meeting was that it took place in an academic environment that is no longer fashionably leftist. . . . This is a far cry from the Cambridge of the Thirties, which the Communists found to be a great harvesting ground for Party members and even outright traitors. The Cambridge of 1984 was ready to accept the homecoming of Hayek as a popular figure."[28]

Margaret Thatcher wrote Hayek shortly after she became prime minister that "I am very proud to have learnt so much from you over the past few years. I hope that some of those ideas will be put into practice by my Government. As one of your keenest supporters, I am determined that we should succeed. If we do so, your contribution to our ultimate victory will have been immense."[29]

She wrote him again in 1982 in response to a letter of his apparently regarding the success of the Chilean government in reducing government expenditures as a proportion of the gross domestic product. "The progression from Allende's socialism to the free enterprise capitalist economy of the 1980s is a striking example of economic reform from which we can learn many lessons," she wrote. "However, I am sure you will agree that, in Britain with our democratic institutions and the need for a high degree of consent, some of the measures adopted in Chile are quite unacceptable. Our reform must be in line with our traditions and our Constitution. At times the process may seem painfully slow. But I am certain we shall achieve our reforms in our own way and in our own time. Then they will endure."[30]

On the occasion of his ninetieth birthday in 1989, Thatcher sent him a letter saying, "It is ten years this week since I was privileged to become Prime Minister. Many people have been most kind in their comments on what the Government has been able to achieve in that time. There is of course still so much to do. But none of it would have been possible without the values and beliefs to set us on the right road and provide the right sense of direction. The leadership and inspiration that your work and thinking gave us were absolutely crucial; and we owe you a great debt."[31]

CHAPTER THIRTY-EIGHT

Opa

ALTHOUGH HAYEK DID NOT SPEND MUCH TIME WITH HIS CHILDREN while they were growing up and particularly during their young adulthood, he became closer to them, especially his son, during his long old age. Once, answering a 1978 interview question about his family, he replied, "A boy and a girl. The boy is married; he's a doctor, or rather has become now a bacteriologist. He lives in Devon, in ideal conditions. He has three children—an English girl is his wife. My daughter is an entomologist in the British Museum of Natural History in London."[1]

Hayek's son, Larry; daughter-in-law, Esca; and their three children (two girls and a boy) lived in southern England. During the 1970s and early '80s, Hayek visited them regularly, once or twice a year or so. Finances were easier now following the Nobel Prize. He made these trips to England alone. A typical trip was for about a week. He would spend a couple of days in London, talking to his publisher, visiting the IEA, dropping in at the Reform Club, and perhaps whispering in the ear of a politician or two. Then he would go to Devon for several days where his son's family had a lovely home on the edge of the countryside. Esca Hayek remembers her father-in-law as a "family man—he loved his family and adored his grandchildren."[2] He was called "*Opa*," the Austrian familiar form of grandfather. He read his grandchildren stories and enjoyed taking the family out to dinner. Esca Hayek recalls that "he adored coming down here, walking on the High Street. He would say, 'If my friends could only see me now!' We were his secret."[3]

His children remember that Hayek's "life was his work."[4] His family once gave him a self-winding watch as a present, but he could not use it because he was not active enough to keep it wound. He wore a signet ring on which was engraved the family coat-of-arms—a naval design—which now serves as the crest on the title pages and covers of *The Collected Works of F. A. Hayek*. He would sit in the easy chair in his son's home, facing the fire, with a cat in his lap. His family visited him in Germany as he moved into his later eighties and became unable to travel. His grandchildren were fond of their grandfather, as he was of them.

On one occasion, Lionel (by now, Lord) Robbins came to Devon to spend time with Hayek. Hayek remarked in 1978 that when he first came to England in 1931, Robbins became his "closest friend, and still is, although we see each other very rarely now."[5] Robbins enjoyed regaling the Hayek family with inside stories on the latest doings in and gossip from the House of Lords. In a 1983 interview, Hayek recounted a final interaction with his old friend, whom he had just seen. When asked how Robbins was, he responded, "Not very good, it was depressing. In some ways he was rather worse than the first time I saw him after the stroke. Mentally, what he does say, with great effort, is perfectly clear, but it is evidently an enormous effort for him to concentrate, to speak. He makes the impression of a dead tired man, and what shocked me the most is the change in the expression of his face. For me it was frightfully sad."[6]

A happy late interaction with Robbins occurred on January 27, 1981 (before Robbins' strokes), when Hayek gave his final lecture at LSE, "The Flow of Goods and Services," fifty years to the day after his first lecture at the school. As a half-century before, Robbins was in the chair. The room was packed and members of Hayek's family attended. His former student Bill Letwin recalls that it was a "pleasure just to hear Hayek lecture one more time."[7] More wanted to attend than the room could hold. Hayek said in the preface of his talk that his 1931 LSE lectures were the first time he made use of what became the leading idea in much of his later work—the signaling function of prices.

He also visited Helene's son's family in Vienna during later years, accompanying her. These were generally annual trips in the summer for about a week. Here, too, he found familial contentment, as "Onkel Fritz"—"Uncle Fritz." His wife's son, a professor in physics at the University of Vienna, recalls him as "fascinating," "the most factual man" he has ever met, and a good listener who talked about what he was currently writing.[8] Each year, his thought developed, and it was interesting to track progress in his work. To both sides of the family he conveyed the impression of a scientist, one who considered himself merely an instrument for the truth. He himself was unimportant. What was important was the truth.

During the late 1970s and early '80s, Hayek participated in conferences and symposia around the world in such exotic locales as Iceland, Portugal, South America (including Argentina, Venezuela, Peru, and Brazil), South Korea, and Hong Kong, as well as his more regular haunts in West Germany, Austria, England, and the United States. He visited South Africa in 1978. This was the first time he had been in the country since 1963. His trip there gives an idea of the itinerary he followed at this time. He stayed for twenty-eight days, gave eleven lectures, participated in two seminars, and gave short talks at a number of other functions. In a report by the South African Free Market Foundation on his visit, its executive director, Leon Louw, said Hayek was "guest of honour at twenty-one luncheons, dinners, banquets or receptions which were attended by some 480 prominent South Africans, including the majority of South Africa's most prominent business leaders, government officials, academics and financial editors and journalists."[9] There were two television and two radio interviews, two press conferences, and several published interviews. In his letter to the seventy-nine-year-old Hayek after the visit, Louw wrote, "Many, many thanks for coming to South Africa in spite of your very heavy schedule," and "Finally, might I repeat how very impressed everyone was with you both [Hayek and his wife], with your energy—mental and physical—and your insight into and intimate knowledge of so many disciplines. No doubt you find that reaction wherever you go." Summing up Hayek's opinions concerning the South African political situation, Louw wrote that "although he personally disagrees with many of South Africa's policies he considers the double standards, hostility and interference of the international community to be 'scandalous.' It is not surprising that in response many South Africans rally behind the government when they might not otherwise do so."[10] Immediately before he went to South Africa, Hayek had been in Japan for talks with the Japanese prime minister and minister of economic affairs. He had also recently been consulted by the West German and Chilean governments.

Some of Hayek's lectures were remunerative. He gave an address in 1981 to the Annual Conference of Visa International on "The Future Unit of Value." Visa contacted him regarding the creation of money by private institutions. He received a fee of $15,000, plus travel and accommodation expenses for himself and Helene.

While participating in a 1981 Venezuelan forum on "Economy, Politics and Society," he made the following observations. He saw a "revival of liberalism with the young. Not what most people call liberalism; that's socialism. But libertarianism."[11] He became genuinely more optimistic about the prospects for the type of society in which he believed. In the introduction to a 1985 work, he wrote that "as late as the early 1970s it seemed to me that hardly anyone was listening to the argument for liberalism. But in the last five or ten years I have seen a change I never thought would come."[12] Asked by a Venezuelan interviewer about "totalitarian" regimes in Latin America, he replied, "Don't confuse totalitarianism with authoritarianism. I don't know of any totalitarian governments in Latin America. The only one was Chile under [former Marxist president Salvador] Allende. Chile is now a great success. The world shall come to regard the recovery of Chile as one of the great economic miracles of our time."[13]

In a January 1980 letter to the London *Times*, published under the title "Freeing the Hostages in Tehran," he expressed foreign policy views. He wrote that he was "genuinely puzzled by the restraint shown by the United States in the recent emergency. It seems to me that the future of peaceful international relations and the safety of persons in foreign countries would have been much better served if the United States Government had at once sent an ultimatum saying that, unless every single member of the embassy staff were within forty-eight hours handed over unharmed to representatives of the United States Government, bombs would be falling at an increasing rate at the seat of the Iranian Government."[14]

In 1983, he experienced criticism in Argentina for the following letter to the *Times* during the Falklands War, "Argentina ought perhaps to be reminded that no rule of international law would forbid to retort to another attack on what for 150 years had been under the jurisdiction of Britain by some counter-attack on the geographical sources of such bellicose action. That might well be a more effective protection than turning the Falklands into a fortress."[15] He hoped that this letter would lead to public discussion, but was disappointed by the response.

He stated his views on Reaganomics and defense policy in early 1983:

Q: The world economy is in the grip of the most protracted recession since the end of World War II. We have market-economy models for overcoming that recession, and we have socialist models. What do you think of President Reagan's market-economy model?

A: The American President is moving in entirely the right direction. So why are things happening so slowly in America? I have serious doubts about the famous theory that you can increase tax revenue by cutting taxes. To a certain extent you undoubtedly can; but the quantitative factor is very much open to question. I wonder whether the expectations based on Reagan's announcement that he was going to balance his budget by means of tax cuts were not over-optimistic from the start.

Q: Isn't high arms expenditure also a factor here?

A: I am convinced Reagan is right not to reduce arms expenditure. World peace depends upon America staying strong. The real problem is whether we have got ourselves into a situation in which the Soviets can intimidate us to such an extent that we knuckle under completely. The West must stay at least as strong as the Soviet Union. I don't believe any Russian is daft enough to start a nuclear war. But if ever the Soviets are in a position to intimidate us with military superiority, they won't hesitate to do whatever they want.[16]

He was greatly concerned about United States federal government budget deficits. In a letter to the *Times,* he wrote "Sir, you would do a public service if you displayed in capital letters the elementary truth that IF THE UNITED STATES GOVERNMENT BORROWS A LARGE PART OF THE WORLD'S SAVINGS TO FINANCE CURRENT EXPENDITURE, THE CAPITAL AVAILABLE ANYWHERE FOR INVESTMENT MUST BECOME SCARCE AND EXPENSIVE."[17] This was not the first time he wrote to a newspaper recommending the use of capital letters. In 1978, he wrote a letter-to-the-editor to the *Wall Street Journal*, "Could you print in front of every issue in headline letters the simple truth that INFLATION IS MADE BY GOVERNMENT AND ITS AGENTS: NOBODY ELSE CAN DO ANYTHING ABOUT IT. It might do some good!" though he noted in his scrapbook that the letter was published only once and in small print.[18]

In 1983, Hayek was asked by the newsmagazine the *Economist* to participate in a centenary critique on Keynes. His final word on his old Cambridge friend was contained in the June 11 edition. There he wrote that he was "claiming that perhaps the most impressive intellectual figure I have ever encountered and whose general intellectual superiority I have readily acknowledged was wholly wrong in the scientific work for which he is chiefly known."[19] He was a bit kinder in an earlier newspaper interview, when he responded to the question, "Are there any similarities between your economic theory and that of Keynes?" "No. I think basically Keynes was also a free trader and an economic liberal. But with many qualifications and restrictions. He was never quite consistent. We were personal friends but we rarely agreed on economics."[20]

In December 1980, Hayek was one of twelve Catholic Nobel laureates to meet with new Pope John Paul II to dialogue, discuss views in their fields, communicate regarding the relationship between Catholicism and science, and "bring to the Pontiff's attention the problems which the Nobel Prize Winners, in their respective fields of study, consider to be the most urgent for contemporary man."[21] Hayek issued a statement in connection with this meeting that he believed the "greatest contribution" Nobel laureates could make to mankind would be to warn against the "progressive destruction of human values by scientific error. To tell our fellows that science and technology are not omnipotent, that we owe what we have achieved to submitting to those moral restraints on our desires which were never designed as a means to serve the satisfaction of our known pleasures, but which made possible the formation of an order of human actions more extended than any human mind can fully comprehend, seems to me the most urgent moral duty now placed upon scientists on whom mankind has placed special distinction."[22]

~

During the mid-1980s glory years of Thatcher and Reagan, the sun could hardly have been in a better place as far as Hayek was concerned. Newspaper writer Henry Allen wrote in a 1982 profile that Hayek was "everything you want an eight-three-year-old Viennese conservative economist to be. Tall and rumpled. A pearl stickpin in his tie. A watch chain across his vest, even though he wears a digital wristwatch. An accent which melds German Z's and British O's."[23]

Gitta Sereny, Mises' stepdaughter, depicted him in a 1985 London *Times* story on his eighty-sixth birthday:

On the wall of the study in Friedrich August von Hayek's beautiful old flat in Freiburg in the Black Forest, hang two affectionate caricatures he received, fifty years apart, from the London School of Economics. The first shows him upright and buoyant, with the caption: "Why man he doth bestride the narrow world like a Colossus and we petty men . . ." In the second he staggers, fragile, with the weight of the Conservative cabinet on his shoulders. He chuckled when he pointed out the drawings, but typically for him, added at once: "It is, of course, not true that I advise Mrs. Thatcher." . . .

A tall, elegant man, now rather thin, he is deaf in one ear. "It has its advantages," he quipped, pointing at his hearing aid. "I can now turn people on and off." . . .

[Regarding the Nobel Prize] "A complete surprise to me. I didn't approve of Nobel Prizes for economists—until they gave it to *me*, of course!" He laughs. "Of course there is a very big advantage to fame: People suddenly listen to you." He rattles off, with relish, anecdote after anecdote, quite often making fun of himself, but never of others.[24]

Hayek enjoyed joking in later years that while Marx was deaf in his right ear, he was deaf in his left.

He inhaled snuff during his later years. He had this exchange:

Q: I can't resist talking some more about snuff. You said you have this shop in London.

A: Yes, it's a very special snuff. It's a very old shop, Fribourg and Treyer, which like an English shop, still uses the same label which they used in the 18th century. And I've now discovered and tried his thirty-six different snuffs. The one I decided was much the best has the beautiful name of Dr. James Robertson Justice's Mixture.

Q: That sounds good.

A: And it is very good.

Q: Why do you use snuff?

A: Well, I was stopped from smoking by the doctor and was miserable for a long time. I was a heavy pipe smoker. I took some snuff and found the longing at once stopped. So I started taking it up and I've become completely hooked. It is as much a habit-forming thing, and you get all the nicotine you want; but the worst thing about smoking, of course, is the tar, which you don't get. So I get my pleasure without the real danger.[25]

He had this to say about other worldly pleasures:

Q: Where did you learn about wines?

A: Beyond Burgundies, I have never been very expert. Burgundies I just liked very early and took every opportunity to drink them.

Q: Did your parents have wine every night at dinner?

A: No. So far as they drank anything, it was beer rather than wine. I am not particularly fond of the Viennese wines. In general, 'til fairly recently, my preference was red wines. It's only now that in this fortunate position at Freiburg, where all around they produce first-class, very small vintages of white wines, that I'm getting very interested in wines.[26]

He remarked of his later work habits that, while most of his life he could work from morning through evening, now, he no longer worked on original material in the evening—he could merely read in the evening. In the morning, his energy lasted two hours or so. "I usually, if I am not disturbed, as soon as I have read my newspaper, sit down to work." Sometimes a cup of coffee helped him work a little bit longer, "but not very much longer."

Q: When you're working, are you at your desk writing, or do you pace and think, or what works?

A: In an easy chair, leaning back and writing on my knees. I should say I have my reading periods and my writing periods. When I really want to read extensively, I cannot write at the same time. Sometimes it's a question of two or three months that I do only reading, practically. Well I'm making notes all the time, but I don't attempt to pursue systematically a train of thought. While once I settle down to writing, I consult books, but I no longer read systematically, at least on that subject. In the evening I will be reading something else.[27]

His characteristic method of composition was to begin with notecards on which he wrote ideas, and then to "write and write and write." He began with cards; he always carried note cards with him so that he could write his ideas down. "All my ideas I first put down in this form. Then I still write it out longhand from these cards, and this is the longest process. Then I go on myself typing it out in what I suppose is clean manuscript. And then starts the problem of correcting, giving it to a typist, correcting it again; so I suppose that everything of substance which I have written has been in written-out form three or four times."[28]

He said of his health that on the whole he had been healthy throughout life, notwithstanding his later health episodes. For most of his life, he was healthy.

When asked in a 1978 interview about how his career might have been different, what he would have changed, he replied, "I don't know. I never thought about this. In spite of my age, I'm still thinking much more about the future than about the past. It's so difficult to know what the consequences of particular actions have actually been, and since all evolution is largely the product of accidents, I'll be very hard put to say what particular decisions of my own have had particular consequences. It is my general view of life that we are playing a game of luck, and on the whole I have been lucky in this game."[29]

He was made a member of the Order of the Companions of Honour in 1984 by Queen Elizabeth II on recommendation of Prime Minister Thatcher for his "services to the study of economics." His secretary Charlotte Cubitt remembers him as at times hoping he might receive a baronetcy. Previous members of the Order of the Companions of Honour included Churchill, Attlee, and Robbins. After receiving this honor, he sent a letter to friends asking to be called the English version of Friedrich, "Frederick," but few ever complied with this request.[30]

Of his awards, he was especially moved by being made a Companion of Honour, which included a twenty-minute audience with the queen. His family recalls him as, going into the audience, not expecting it to be particularly significant. He had met many heads of state. After he came out, it was a different matter. According to Esca Hayek, he was "absolutely besotted"[31] by the queen. He considered her one of the most gracious, informed, and knowledgeable people he had ever met. He remarked the next year, "I was amazed by her. That ease and skill, as if she'd known me all my life."[32]

The audience was followed by dinner with family and friends at the Institute of Economic Affairs. As his daughter-in-law dropped him off at the Reform Club later in the evening, she remembers him in top hat, leaning on his umbrella, with a big smile on his face, saying, "I've just had the happiest day of my life."[33]

CHAPTER THIRTY-NINE

The Fatal Conceit

THE GREAT PROJECT OF THE LAST YEARS OF HAYEK'S CAREER was *The Fatal Conceit,* subtitled *The Errors of Socialism.* One should not think that most of Hayek's time during his last years was spent in travel or incidental activities. Rather, from about 1978 to 1985, he was passionately involved in the preparation of *The Fatal Conceit,* which he thought, as he wrote in a letter early during its composition, might become his most important work.[1]

Hayek intended that *The Fatal Conceit* would be the culmination of his life's career in societal philosophy. As a young man, he noticed the vital importance of the signaling function of prices to guide economic production. In "Economics and Knowledge," he extended this concept to explain that prices help to overcome the division of human knowledge. In The Abuse and Decline of Reason, he intended to present the historical development of socialist ideas, but when this took too long, he decided to write an advance popular sketch, *The Road to Serfdom,* of the consequences of socialist ideas. This, in turn, led him to recognize that classical liberalism was not properly understood, and he wrote *The Constitution of Liberty* to remedy this deficiency. Then, in *Law, Legislation and Liberty,* he attempted to go beyond traditional classical liberalism and formulate some of his own ideas. Finally, in *The Fatal Conceit* he was going to present the upshot of his entire work—an evolutionary interpretation of the growth of human civilization.

Hayek was passionately committed to western civilization. He thought that mankind has better hope for attaining peace and prosperity through the ideas of the western heritage than through those of any other tradition. He thought that western civilization has evolved over centuries, not infrequently in unknown and unforeseen directions. The crucial issue, in his mind, was to create rules for societies that allow continued material progress.

His outlook was nonetheless largely spiritual. Although he adopted a material measure for the success of human societies, he thought that the rules men and women adopt are largely internal. The order of society is an abstract order. It is an internal vision held by the members of a society as to how a society should physically look, what patterns of relationships should exist in a society and what the material outcomes of these patterns will be. Capitalism, Hayek thought, is the physical manifestation of the historical western moral code.

There is, moreover, the tie between what people empirically believe and their normative, ethical, actions. If individuals believe that society may be structured so as to allow efficient central government control of all of the details of economic activity, they may favor different rules and laws than those who do not believe such control can be efficient. The holding of empirical beliefs affects people's actions. Thus Hayek's philosophy was deeply committed to truth. Only in truth—as accurate an appraisal as possible of the way that things are and can be—could humanity reach the stars.

The Fatal Conceit was derived from the originally uncontemplated epilogue of *Law, Legislation and Liberty*, "The Three Sources of Human Values," given by Hayek as the L. T. Hobhouse Lecture at LSE on May 17, 1978. As Hayek completed *Law, Legislation and Liberty* after several years of rest, he returned to the issue of socialism's intellectual origins—the empirical propositions on which its normative prescriptions are based. He thought that these empirical propositions prevailed in the society of his time, and he sought to thwart them through his writings to the greatest extent he could.

He frankly stated that, at this time, the greatest challenge to the western traditions of liberty through law, property, exchange, contract, and traditional family and sexual morés came from the left. He had nothing but disgust for the purveyors of ideas that are inconsistent with traditional western values that have evolved and who would substitute in their place conceptions for optimal societies founded on the empirical proposition that discretionary control by government is preferable to known general laws applicable to all. He sought order through laws.

It is, in turn, through order that the greatest material progress will occur. Only as mankind are as relatively sure as they can be about the consequences of their actions will they interact with each other as effectively—as materially productive as possible—as they can. Rules are necessary in every society. The golden question is what rules should be.

As Hayek completed *Law, Legislation and Liberty* during the later 1970s, he was reluctant to publish what he thought would be his last major work without "at least indicating in what direction" his ideas were heading. He added an epilogue, the Hobhouse Lecture, to the work, which expressed "more directly the general view of moral and political evolution which has guided me in the whole enterprise."[2] He originally thought that *Law, Legislation and Liberty* would be his final work, on which he endeavored longer than any other project during his career.

Sixteen years elapsed between when Hayek commenced work on *Law, Legislation and Liberty* in 1962 and when he completed it in 1978. He became more of a libertarian in the concluding chapter of *Law, Legislation and Liberty*. In the third to last section, "The devolution of internal policy to local government," he spoke in favor of "most service activities rendered by central government" being "devolved to regional or local authorities." He thought the "result would be the transformation of local and even regional governments into quasi-commercial corporations competing for citizens."[3]

Hayek foresaw a communitarian future through the implementation of libertarian practices. Communitarianism is the supremacy of local values and local institutions, and of diversity among communities. Communitarianism is not similar values and institutions throughout a geographical area. Communitarianism is diversity of communities, not necessarily diversity in communities. Communitarian diversity is diversity of communities. Diversity is differentiation. Singularity of communities is uniformity, not diversity.

At the same time, true communitarianism is not the preservation of past modes of human society and organization for their own sake. Writing eloquently that it is desirable, both for individuals and for society as a whole, to allow the disappearance of past, premodern ways of life, Hayek stated that "We should be showing more respect for the dignity of man if we allowed certain ways of life to disappear altogether instead of preserving them as specimens of a past age."[4] The communities that emerge in a libertarian order are those that are chosen by their adult members as long as they do not physically harm others.

In the penultimate section of *Law, Legislation and Liberty,* "The abolition of the government monopoly of services," Hayek wrote the most libertarian sentiments of his career. He stated that there is "of course no need for central government to decide who should be entitled to render different services, and it is highly undesirable that it should possess mandatory powers to do so. This means that any governmental agency allowed to use its taxing power to finance such services ought to be required to refund any taxes raised for these purposes to all those who prefer to get the services in some other way."[5] These words were even more significant because of the government services to which he applied them—"without exception to all those services of which government possesses a legal monopoly, with the only exception of maintaining and enforcing the law and maintaining for this purpose an armed force, i.e. all those from education to transport and communications, including post, telegraph, telephone and broadcasting services, all the so-called 'public utilities,' the various 'social' insurances and, above all, the issue of money." In the last pages of *Law, Legislation and Liberty,* published in 1979, Hayek the classical liberal became Hayek the libertarian.[6]

Hayek described the early evolution of *The Fatal Conceit* in a February 1979 talk:

> About a year ago, it occurred to me that the moment had arrived in which it would be worthwhile to organize a great public discussion on the question "Was socialism a mistake?" I gained the support of twelve fellow members of the Mont Pelerin Society to act as a team in the affirmative, and our plan was to challenge a similar team to a public discussion.
>
> This proved to be impractical for two reasons. One is that an affair like this, on the scale on which I had contemplated, is very expensive. Evidently, the capitalists did not have an interest in the intellectual defense of capitalism. But that was not the main point.
>
> A much more serious consideration arose when we assembled at the Mont Pelerin meeting in Hong Kong. It was then suggested that if we selected the opposite team, it would have no credibility. The upshot of this discussion was that I was asked to write out the challenge in book form, submit it to the twelve members on our side, elaborate it, with help of their criticism, into a small book, and make the book the challenge, by inviting the other side to organize its own team for the public discussion.[7]

This idea for a debate occurred to Hayek right as he was finishing *Law, Legislation and Liberty,* conterminous with writing "The Three Sources of Human Values." He identified the key insight in "The Three Sources of Human Values" that led him to a new formulation of his views as a line he added in the final stages of the epilogue's publication, "Man has been civilized very much against his wishes"[8]—"That, I think, is the upshot of the whole argument—it's not our intelligence which has created civilization, but really the taming of many of our innate instincts which resisted civilization."[9] Human nature wars with capitalism. Morals required for an open society do not necessarily cohere with the savage instincts inherited from humanity's primordial past.

He expended a considerable amount of time and energy on the proposed debate. The Mont Pelerin team was originally to be comprised of, in his plan, P. T. Bauer, James Buchanan, Ronald Coase, Milton Friedman, Armin Gutowski, Ralph Harris, Emil Küng, Gaston Leduc, Warren Nutter, Joaquin Reig, Ben Rogge, Arthur Shenfield, and Christian Watrin. The socialist team could, he thought, include such luminaries as James Meade, Noam Chomsky, Leszek Kolakowski, Arthur Lewis, and Gunnar Myrdal, with Michael Harrington and Jean-Paul Sartre as possible substitutes. Raymond Aron agreed to serve as moderator.

When Hayek formulated his debate plan in 1978 and invited a number of classical liberal and libertarian-oriented scholars to participate, he wrote Friedman, who could not participate because of other commitments in filming the television version of *Free to Choose.* Hayek then wrote Friedman a second time, saying Friedman was the man he needed most, and exclaiming that Friedman should help him.

Friedman displayed deference, modesty, and far-sightedness in his second letter to Hayek explaining why he could not participate:

> I certainly approve heartily of your plan for the confrontation in Paris. My situation is, however, very simple. My first commitment at the moment is to work on completing the TV series in which I am involved. As I wrote you, that has proved extremely time-consuming. Much more important, from the point of view of your project, is that it has involved me in open-ended commitments. The problem is that it depends not simply on me but on . . . [a] fair number--a half dozen or more--of other people. The timing schedule turns out to be very rigid and to leave little leeway if we are in fact going to have the series on TV by our target date, which is the fall of 1979.
>
> I go to such length in explaining my situation to make it clear that my inability to give a commitment is not out of lack of enthusiasm for your project but rather solely out of a prior commitment to a project that may not be equally important but that hinges to a much greater extent on my own personal participation.[10]

Hayek's debate did not come off. He added as final sentences to "The Three Sources of Human Values" as published in *Law, Legislation and Liberty* in 1979 that in "concluding this epilogue I am becoming increasingly aware that it ought not to be that but rather a new beginning. But I hardly dare hope that for me it can be so."[11] He added further, however, in the preface to the 1982, one-volume consolidated edition of *Law, Legislation and Liberty,* "I said in the concluding words that what I said in that Epilogue should not be an Epilogue but a new beginning. I am glad to be able to say now that it has turned out to be such and that that Epilogue has become the outline of a new book of which I have now completed a first draft."[12]

He spent much of the late 1970s and early '80s working on *The Fatal Conceit,* never completing it to his liking. The work grew from a relatively brief debate challenge to a treatise in three parts, similar to *The Constitution of Liberty* and *Law, Legislation and Liberty.* There were a number of draft versions of *The Fatal Conceit,* a title he took from a phrase of Adam Smith, "the overweening conceit," which he thought Smith applied to falsely proud intellectuals who believe that they can design society in a superior manner to a competitive market.[13]

There are two basic versions of drafts that Hayek wrote of *The Fatal Conceit.* Describing the first, Buchanan writes that "By the early 1980s, Professor Hayek seemed to be well along with his project. Steve Pejovich organized, and Liberty Fund financed, a small conference in Obergurgl, Austria, the site of Hayek's summer retreat for some thirty years, for the express purpose of assisting Hayek in the final stages of preparation. There were some fifteen of us assembled in August 1982, a group that included Peter Bauer, Ronald Coase and George Stigler. We were, I must say, not very happy with the draft we received, and, as critics who, at the same time, maintained the highest respect for Professor Hayek, we felt that we should not recommend publication."[14] The second version of *The Fatal Conceit* that Hayek worked on were drafts and redrafts he wrote during the latter part of 1982, 1983, 1984, and the first months of 1985 before illness forced him to discontinue work permanently.

The role of William Warren Bartley, III in editing the published *The Fatal Conceit* was unique for any of Hayek's works. Bartley was to be Hayek's official biographer and general editor of his *Collected Works.* As Hayek became ill in 1985, Bartley assumed a much more significant role with *The Fatal Conceit* than was originally planned. Bartley died on February 5, 1990. He was succeeded as general editor of Hayek's *Collected Works* by Stephen Kresge, Bartley's close friend. In addition, Walter Morris, a retired businessman, played a key role in initiating *The Collected Works of F. A. Hayek.*

The Fatal Conceit was not entirely well received when it was published in 1988. While there was respectful reference to flashes of wisdom and Hayek's genius, *The Fatal Conceit* was not perceived as having met his earlier high-stated hopes for it. Hayek was, by the time *The Fatal Conceit* was published, incapacitated. His professional career was over.

He worked on *The Fatal Conceit* for about seven years, from when he wrote the speech "The Three Sources of Human Values" during the first half of 1978, until the first half of 1985. He had a little over a decade of Indian summer between when he received the Nobel Prize in December 1974 until he became permanently ill and unable to work. Particularly as he labored over the second version of *The Fatal Conceit* during the early and mid 1980s, he began to suffer from health difficulties. During the late 1970s and first half of the '80s, he suffered from extended illnesses several times.

He was initially enthusiastic about *The Fatal Conceit,* but his secretary Cubitt recalls him coming to wonder whether he had not written much, if not most, of what was in it elsewhere and better before and whether the work was not too repetitive. He was also disappointed that he did not complete the work himself.

Hayek's ultimate moral message in *The Fatal Conceit* was that "life has no purpose but itself."[15] The purpose of life is to be flourishing, abundant, diverse, joyous. The basic idea of *The Fatal Conceit,* which comes through most clearly in the introduction and first chapters, is that the development of human life is conterminous with the development of knowledge, technology, and material creation, and that the society in which these are most developed is the best society. Moreover, that the growth of trade and civilization are one.

He described the work in progress a number of times during the late 1970s and first half of the '80s. He said in a 1978 interview:

What I am writing at the moment is called "The Reactionary Character of the Socialist Conception." My argument is essentially that our instincts were formed in the small face-to-face society where we serve the visible needs of other people. Now, the [open] society was built up by our obeying signals which enabled us to serve unknown persons, and to use unknown resources for that purpose. Now our instinct still is that we want to see to whom we do good, and we want to join with our immediate fellows in serving common purposes. Now, both of these things are incompatible with the [open] society. The society becomes possible when, instead of aiming at known needs of known people, one is guided by the abstract signals of prices. . . .

You have real evolution only under freedom. Wherever you have a community completely commanded by an authoritarian system, there is no evolution. Evolution is made possible by freedom, and what you get in unfree systems is due to the fact that the emergence of the better has been prevented.

. . . morals which existed in the small face-to-face band that determined our biologically inherited instincts, which are still very strong in us. And I think all civilization has grown up by these natural instincts being restrained. We can even use the phrase that man was civilized very much against his wishes. He hated it. The individual profited from it, but the general abandoning of these natural instincts, and adapting himself to obeying formal rules which he did not understand, was an extremely painful process. And man still doesn't like them. . . .

The function of government very frequently is to prevent further evolution.[16]

He said in the summer of 1985 of the emerging work that the "whole idea, which is basic, [is] that part of our order of cooperation is based not on deliberate designs which we understand but on traditions which have prevailed because [they] enabled more people to live than other traditions. A sort of quasi-Darwinian solution, which however differs from biological Darwinism by not being based on selection of individuals. . . . [The traditions] only show themselves in the aggregate success of the group. I am using for this purpose now the conception of an extended order of human cooperation. By extended I mean an order which transcends our vision. Just the simple fact that we all are working for people whom we do not know, and being supplied by people whom we do not know, we live in an order which is, in this sense, not perceivable."[17]

He held in 1984 that "socialism assumes that all the available knowledge can be used by a single, central authority. It overlooks that the modern society is based on the utilisation of widely dispersed knowledge. And once you are aware that we can achieve that great utilisation of available resources only because we utilise the knowledge of millions of men, it becomes clear that the assumption of socialism that a central authority is in command of this knowledge is just not correct. I think the nicest form to put it in is to say that socialism, protesting against production for profit and not for use, objects to what makes the extended society possible. Profit is the signal which tells us what we must do in order to serve people whom we do not know. By pursuing profit, we are as altruistic as we can possibly be, because we extend our concern to people who are beyond our range of personal conception."[18]

The question of who should be trusted with material, physical resources is ideally resolved in capitalism by who makes the most profits. Hayek wrote in the published *The Fatal Conceit* that "profits are all that most producers need to be able to serve more effectively the needs of men they do not know. They are a tool for searching—just as, for the soldier or hunter, the seaman or air pilot, the telescope extends the range of vision." Expanding the same thought, he also said that in the "evolution of the structure of human activities, profitability works as a signal that guides selection towards what makes man more fruitful; only what is profitable will, as a rule, nourish more people, for it sacrifices less than it adds."[19] Profits and prices are the invisible hands.

CHAPTER FORTY

Neustift am Wald

HAYEK WORKED VERY LITTLE AFTER 1985. Cubitt recalls that he would not purchase the word processor that would have facilitated completion of *The Fatal Conceit* by himself. He came to consider the market as the prototype for society as a whole. Just as, in the market, the more productive and effective practices survive, so it should be for institutions and societies.

He gave his conception of the morality underlying his thoughts on optimal societal order in response to the question, "Would you comment on the command to love thy neighbor as thyself?"

> I think the comment has to be that we have to restrict the concept of neighbor much more than was possible in the past. In fact, the phrase in the Bible is "neighbor" and it has to be taken very literally—those people for whom we work in concrete knowledge of their persons. It is no longer applicable once we have to work for people of whose very existences we do [not] know. . . .
>
> These [religious] rules were developed as guides for action toward a small group of personally known people. Once we have left the primitive group, we must leave these inborn morals behind, and except for our relations with our immediate circle—what is now called the "nuclear family"—observe what I have called the "commercial morals."[1]

It is not enough to know that one should love others. One must also know *how* to love others. Hayek's point was that by following the impersonal rules of the

market—which sometimes preclude doing immediate, visible good, and sometimes appear to require the opposite—people are most likely to love one another
to the greatest extent possible and be happiest.

He appeared at a Freiburg conference in 1987 where, after a sharp and
alert morning, he dozed in the afternoon. Greeting a Mont Pelerin regional
meeting later in 1987, Hayek wrote that "after forty years of the existence of
the Mont Pelerin Society it is bitter to resign oneself to the fact that it will have
to continue without me. But though I am no longer actually ill, two years of
sickness have made me an old man. This summer vacation in the Tyrolean
mountains is the first time that I have again been able to leave home, and at
eighty-eight years of age I can hardly hope that I shall again be able to travel
for longer distances. So I must confine myself to send all the participants of the
meeting all my best wishes for its success and for an effective continuation of
the efforts of the Society."[2]

A magazine article depicted him in 1989, in perhaps his last meeting with
a reporter:

> *Forbes* called on Hayek at his apartment in a large stucco house on
> Urachstrasse in Freiburg, West Germany. His health is not good; he has
> never fully recovered from a recent bout with pneumonia, during which he
> lay critically ill for six weeks in hospital. But he cheerfully agreed to an
> interview. A tall, thin man whose bearing even now recalls his days as an
> officer in the Austrian army in World War I, Hayek welcomed *Forbes* at the
> door of his book-strewn and elegantly furnished third-floor apartment.
> Leaning on a cane, he ushered his visitor into a small sunroom whose
> windows look out on pine-covered Schauinsland Mountain.
>
> Hayek told *Forbes* that he is more optimistic about the future of
> capitalism than he was ten years ago. He believes that the public has come
> to understand some of the problems posed by central planning. Around the
> world—from Algeria to Burma to China to Yugoslavia—promises of the
> better life through socialist planning have soured. In particular, Hayek sees
> a greater appreciation for the market among the younger generation. Today
> unemployed youth in Algiers and Rangoon riot not for a centrally planned
> welfare state but for opportunity: the freedom to buy and sell—jeans, cars,
> whatever—at whatever prices the market will bear.
>
> Hayek now believes that the West will probably win the battle with
> collectivism—even though the fight is by no means over. Pulling a blanket
> further up his lap, he remarks: "Communism has ended." What of Ronald
> Reagan and Margaret Thatcher and their battles against government control
> of the economy? Here Hayek surprises. He does not disapprove of Reagan

and Thatcher, but he has no high opinion of modern politicians in general. He does, however, say that Reagan's and Thatcher's policies "are as reasonable as we can expect at this time. They are modest in their ambitions."[3]

Listed over the doorbell on the front door to his apartment building was "Prof. Dr. Friedrich A. von Hayek." It was not an exceptionally posh apartment by American upper-income standards. His library contained perhaps 4,000 volumes that ranged across a number of disciplines, including economics, psychology, anthropology, and political philosophy. The furniture was not new nor the interior recently painted. The ceilings were high, and the kitchen—in which, according to his daughter, Christine, who helped to care for him during his last years, he was proud to boast he "never stepped foot"[4]—was slightly run down. A picture of Winston Churchill hung over his office desk for many years. On his desk, he had a photograph of his second wife as a beautiful young woman in Vienna, many years before.

Hayek lived long enough to see the momentous collapse of Communism in eastern Europe during the fall of 1989 and in the Soviet Union itself during 1991. In October 1989, Ed Crane, president of the Cato Institute, presented a bust of Hayek in Moscow to Yevgeny Primakov, a future foreign minister. Hayek wrote Crane that "I am of course deeply pleased by the news. . . . I could not imagine a more impressive symbol of the ultimate victory of our side. . . . I hardly expected to live to experience this."[5]

Hayek perhaps best summarized the signaling function of prices— perhaps his greatest intellectual contribution—in one of his last publications (if not the last) that he himself saw through to print, "The Moral Imperative of the Market" (1986):

> In 1936, I suddenly saw that my previous work in different branches of economics had a common root. This insight was that the price system was really an instrument which enabled millions of people to adjust their efforts to events, demands and conditions, of which they had no concrete, direct knowledge. The problem I had first identified in studying industrial fluctuations—that false price signals misdirected human efforts—I then followed up in various other branches of the discipline.
>
> Here my thinking was inspired largely by Ludwig von Mises' conception of the problem of ordering a planned economy.
>
> It took me a long time to develop what is basically a simple idea. I gradually found that the whole economic order rested on the fact that by using prices as a guide, or as signals, we were led to serve the demands and

> enlist the powers and capacities of people of whom we knew nothing. Basically, the insight that prices were signals bringing about the co-ordination of efforts became the leading idea behind my work.

To convince the "leaders of public opinion" of this idea became his "chief task, and it has taken me something like fifty years to be able to put it as briefly and in as few words as I have just attempted."[6]

On December 13, 1991, Hayek dictated his final remarks on political, economic, philosophical, and moral questions in response to a reporter's written questions read to him by his son. Hayek stated that "questions about the influence of socialism are increasingly more difficult to answer as the word socialism has so many meanings. The idea that the inequalities of incomes can be greatly reduced has come to be recognized as largely impractical. Practically all endeavours at just distribution express more or less arbitrary conceptions of what is just and the central idea of Marxian socialism of a rationalisation of the means of production has been largely abandoned as technically impracticable. I believe that in general the idea of justice is more closely met by a freely competitive market than by any deliberate allocation of income to some imagined ideal of the kind."[7] The great voice became still.

Following several very bad years, Hayek died on March 23, 1992, in Freiburg, a month and a half shy of his ninety-third birthday. There were calls, letters, and obituaries from around the world. Larry Hayek remembers that during his last years, his father would characterize his days as "tolerable" or "misera-ble."[8] His remains are buried in Neustift am Wald cemetery on the northern outskirts of Vienna.

His funeral service was held Saturday, April 4. About 100 family members and invited guests attended. The day was windy and overcast, but the sun broke through the clouds. There were flowers and wreaths from around the world. Neustift am Wald is located on a hillside overlooking vineyards and the Vienna woods in which he played as a young boy. The start of the service was delayed to allow Vaclav Klaus, then finance minister and later prime minister of the Czech Republic, to attend.

Father Johannes Schasching officiated and conducted the burial rites of the Roman Catholic Church. He spoke in German in his homily along these lines:

It is impressive how in the time of economic and political crisis of Austria, great men left the country and contributed outside, especially in the United States, in an important way to the solution of political, economic, and social problems. Among them was Friedrich von Hayek.

Today we celebrate Friedrich von Hayek. At the end of the Second World War, he tried to help Europe rebuild in year zero, formulating tasks for reconstruction. One of these was that Europe needs institutions and forces to encourage people to contribute freely—not collectively—to the common good.

He was also always somebody looking for an answer to the problem of religion and he had a continuous internal battle with the concept we call God. He always resisted an anthropomorphic God. He didn't want a God just a little bit more than man.

He was one looking for solutions to the great problems of mankind. He tried to find an answer. He was himself convinced that his answers were merely a piece within a larger mosaic.

I am sure Friedrich von Hayek after a passionate life of continuous research and personal battles entered the light and the peace we call eternity and God.[9]

At the end of the service, Father Schasching led the coffin to the gravesite, preceded by the cross and followed by the assemblage. The dark earth of the grave was covered from top to bottom with small green tree branches. Father Schasching blessed the grave. The casket was lowered. Father Schasching placed a small shovel of dirt in the grave, and this was repeated by Hayek's widow, then children, then the other members of the community of family and friends. The only sound was the dirt as it hit the top of the coffin.

The stone for his headstone came from the area of the Tyrolean Alps in which he vacationed so happily each summer. Engraved on the rough-hewn stone, beneath the cross, reads:

F. A. Hayek
1899–1992

CHAPTER FORTY-ONE

"Universal Order of Peace"

THE LIBERTARIAN AGE IS AT HAND. Friedrich Hayek's great contributions included the enunciation of a world order in which humanity could live at peace. His exposition of spontaneous order, though he traced the concept to Adam Smith and Carl Menger, was his own. He attempted to demonstrate that, absent an orderer, human society can achieve great orderliness. Government need not be omniscient, omnipotent, omnipresent, and omnibenevolent in order to attain an optimal society, which, in any event, government is not and cannot be—and it is counterproductive for it to attempt to be, as the twentieth century appears manifestly to have shown.

Hayek best stated his ideal of one world living at peace in *Law, Legislation and Liberty:*

> The ideal underlying the Open Society [is] that the same rules should be applied to all human beings. It is an ideal which I, for one, hope we shall continue gradually to approach because it seems to me the indispensable condition of a universal order of peace. . . .
>
> The extension of the obligation to obey certain rules of just conduct to wider circles and ultimately to all men must lead to an attenuation of the obligation towards fellow members of the same small group. . . .

Only slowly and gradually do those general rules of conduct towards all fellow men come to prevail over the special rules which allowed the individual to harm the stranger if it served the interest of his group. Only this process has made possible the rise of the Open Society, and offers the distant hope of a universal order of peace.[1]

Hayek's focus on law was revealed through his ideal of a universal order of peace. Ultimately there should be not world government but world law.[2] The ideal underlying this conception is that all men and women are moral equals.

One of the most significant messages that can be derived from Hayek's work is that the laws of societies should come to reflect no more than laws among individuals. Ultimately, the only laws there should be are laws that one individual can apply to all others without requirement of government. He wrote in *Law, Legislation and Liberty,* though intending a different meaning, that it is "only by extending the rules of just conduct to the relations with all other men, and at the same time depriving of their obligatory character those rules which cannot be universally applied, that we can approach a universal order of peace which might integrate all mankind into a single society."[3] His writings will serve as a beacon to enlighten centuries.

Appendix

THE QUESTION OF THE RELATIONSHIP BETWEEN WORDS AND PHYSICAL REALITY can be derived both from the thought of Hayek and his contemporaries, including Ludwig Wittgenstein and the Vienna circle of logical positivists. Hayek's view of the nature of reality was not really bifurcated between sociological and natural facts. While he thought that we consider sociological facts from the inside and natural facts from the outside, still, it was the case that for both types of facts we construct a theory of the facts, and we then utilize this theory. Knowledge, for Hayek, whether in the social or physical fields, always is theoretical.

In the epilogue of *Law, Legislation and Liberty,* he wrote (referring in part to *The Sensory Order*) that "a tradition of rules of conduct, existing apart from any one individual who had learnt them, began to govern human life. It was when these learnt rules, involving classifications of different kinds of objects, began to include a sort of model of the environment that enabled man to predict and anticipate in action external events, that what we call reason appeared."[1] What Hayek appears to have meant here is that human understanding of the world precedes reason. Rules incorporate knowledge. As a result of the existence of rules, individuals are able to predict the consequences of their actions. This prediction is reason. While this passage is of interest for the light it sheds on Hayek's conception of the importance of rules for material productivity, it is also interesting because it does not differentiate between facts of nature and of the social sciences. In his view, a theory of the fact is constructed by the individual mind. There is, thus, no meaningful difference, Hayek thought, between the facts of the natural and social sciences.

On November 19, 1942, Hayek presented to the Cambridge University Moral Science Club a lecture titled "The Facts of the Social Sciences," which was later reprinted in *Individualism and Economic Order.* Here, while Hayek held that there are different kinds of facts ontologically between the realms of

society and the natural sciences, he did not ascribe much weight to these differences. Social, like natural, phenomena are constructed in the mind from theory.

The primary error of intellectuals that Hayek identified in "The Facts of
the Social Sciences" was "the belief that, when we turn from the action of the
individual to the observation of social collectivities, we move from the realm of
vague and subjective speculation to the realm of objective fact."[2] Here Hayek
particularly had in mind such thinkers as Marx, Hegel, and Comte, about whom
he was comtemporaneously studying and writing. Comte, Hegel, and Marx believed it is possible to predict the stages of development through which humanity will pass and made such predictions. Hayek did not believe this sort of
prediction is possible.

However, Hayek's essential point was not the ontological differences between the facts of the natural sciences and those of society. Rather, it was that
intellectual leaders had claimed too often to know more about social collectives
than about the individual elements of social collectives—that is, individual human beings. He characterized his perspective in this area as methodological individualism.

Hayek did not consider in as great depth the ontological divide between
facts in the realms of senses and of society, and it is important to consider this
difference. Hayek considered "social" facts to be essentially compositive, composed of many elements. A historical event is "created" by the historian in "an
act of construction or interpretation."[3] As Goethe said, and as Hayek quoted
him, "all that is factual is already theory."[4]

There is, however, another sense in which facts in the realm of society
often differ from facts in the natural world—not merely in compositive complexity, but in actual ontological essence. While this is a difficult point to get
across, there is all the difference in the world between mainly sociological facts
(for example, the "President of the United States") and purely and truly natural
facts of the physical world. While in the physical world, material facts exist,
in the world of society, conceptual facts hold an entirely different ontological
status.

There is a metaphysical chasm between the president of the United States
and a stone. While the stone absolutely exists, it is not so in the same sense for
the president. The "President of the United States" is merely a shared way of
looking at the world, a mind-set, a paradigm, a Weltanschauung. Excepting the
person, of course, if people cease to believe in the concept of a president of
the United States (and take the necessary political steps to abolish the office),
the "entity" ceases to exist. This is not so with the stone. It always exists,

regardless of what people think. Facts in the world of society do not exist in the same way as facts in the physical world.

This distinction is related in part to Hayek's frequent criticism of John Stuart Mill for a passage in *Principles of Political Economy* where Mill stated that the "laws and conditions of the production of wealth partake of the character of physical truths. . . . It is not so with the distribution of wealth. . . . The things once there, mankind, individually or collectively, can do with them as they like."[5] Hayek thought that this was a ridiculous statement because it implied that Mill thought any societal organization is possible.

Mill's point, though, was not so dissimilar to one that Hayek made. Mill immediately went on in *Principles of Political Economy* that "society can subject the distribution of wealth to whatever rules it thinks best; but what practical results will flow from the operation of those rules, must be discovered, like any other physical or mental truths, by observation and reasoning."[6] In other words, Mill did not say that any type of social organization is possible, the position Hayek criticized as "constructivism." Mill simply said that societies have considerable choice in the rules they adopt, and that the practical results of these rules should be discovered—like anything else—by observation and reasoning.

The importance of the ontological divide between facts in the world of society and facts in the natural sciences is that this distinction reaffirms the crucial role of free will. While we may not be able to make of the future whatever we wish, the future is what we make of it.

Hayek wrote in the closing paragraph of the text proper of *Law, Legislation and Liberty* that "we ought to have learnt enough to avoid destroying our civilization by smothering the spontaneous process of the interaction of individuals by placing its direction in the hands of any authority."[7] This was his great message—individuals should have great freedom. He concluded *The Road to Serfdom:* "A policy of freedom for the individual is the only truly progressive policy."[8]

Chronology of Hayek's Major Works

Monetary Theory and the Trade Cycle	1929/33
Prices and Production	1931/35
Collectivist Economic Planning (ed.)	1935
Monetary Nationalism and International Stability	1937
Profits, Interest and Investment: and Other Essays on the Theory of Industrial Fluctuations	1939
The Pure Theory of Capital	1941
The Road to Serfdom	1944
Individualism and Economic Order	1948
John Stuart Mill and Harriet Taylor: Their Friendship and Subsequent Marriage	1951
The Counter-Revolution of Science: Studies on the Abuse of Reason	1952
The Sensory Order: An Inquiry into the Foundations of Theoretical Psychology	1952
Capitalism and the Historians (ed.)	1954
The Constitution of Liberty	1960
Studies in Philosophy, Politics and Economics	1967
Law, Legislation and Liberty: A New Statement of the Liberal Principles of Justice and Political Economy	
Vol. 1 Rules and Order	1973
Vol. 2 The Mirage of Social Justice	1976
Vol. 3 The Political Order of a Free People	1979

Bibliographical Essay

WORKS BY HAYEK

In addition to the preceding chronology of Hayek's major works, the emerging *Collected Works of F. A. Hayek* will provide new material and republication of Hayek's major works. Volumes already published are below.

Vol. 1   *The Fatal Conceit: The Errors of Socialism* (1988) (William Bartley, ed.)

Vol. 3   *The Trend of Economic Thinking: Essays on Political Economists and Economic History* (1991) (William Bartley and Stephen Kresge, eds.)

Vol. 4   *The Fortunes of Liberalism and the Austrian School: Essays on Austrian Economics and the Ideal of Freedom* (1992) (Peter Klein, ed.)

Vol. 5   *Good Money, Part 1: The New World* (1999) (Stephen Kresge, ed.)

Vol. 6   *Good Money, Part 2: The Standard* (1999) (Stephen Kresge, ed.)

Vol. 9   *Contra Keynes and Cambridge: Essays, Correspondence* (1995) (Bruce Caldwell, ed.)

Vol. 10 *Socialism and War: Essays, Documents, Reviews* (1997) (Bruce Caldwell, ed.)

About twenty volumes will ultimately be published in all.

Roy McCloughry (ed.), *Money, Capital, and Fluctuations: Early Essays* (University of Chicago Press, 1984) is a collection of Hayek's early economic essays that had previously appeared only in German. Chiaki Nishiyama and Kurt R. Leube, *The Essence of Hayek* (Stanford: Hoover Institution Press, 1984), contains selections across Hayek's career, including "Two Pages of Fiction: The Impossibility of Socialist Calculation"—Hayek's final shot in the socialist calculation debate in 1982—and his 1983 lecture at the Hoover Institution, "The Origins and Effects of Our Morals: A Problem for Science." Nishiyama notes in his introduction that when he was a student at the University of Chicago, Hayek "used to tell me that he was writing for the next century" (lx). *Knowledge, Evolution, and Society* (London: Adam Smith Institute, 1983) is a collection of four late lectures on themes in *The Fatal Conceit.*

In the preface to his 1978 *New Studies,* Hayek remarked that "much the greater part of what I published during the last ten years were preliminary studies for that work [*Law, Legislation and Liberty*] which had little importance once the chief conclusions had found their final form in that systematic exposition" (*NS,* vii). A number of his articles can be seen as off-shoots from larger projects on which he endeavored.

Stephen Kresge and Leif Wenar (eds.), *Hayek on Hayek* (University of Chicago Press, 1994) is the published collection of Hayek's autobiographical notes, and mainly covers Hayek's life and career before he went to Chicago. John Raybould (comp.), *Hayek: A Commemorative Album* (London: Adam Smith Institute, 1998) contains excellent pictures from Hayek's life.

Hayek gave a number of interviews. Some of the best and most readily accessible include "Friedrich Hayek on the Crisis," *Encounter* (May 1983); "Economics, Politics and Freedom," *Reason* (February 1975); "The Road from Serfdom," *Reason* (July 1992); and "An Interview with Friedrich Hayek," *Libertarian Review* (September 1977).

The fiftieth anniversary edition of *The Road to Serfdom* (University of Chicago Press, 1994) contains an introduction by Milton Friedman, and Hayek's 1956 and 1976 prefaces. Other works of Hayek worthy of particular notice include *A Tiger by the Tail: The Keynesian Legacy of Inflation* (Sudha Shenoy, compiler and introducer; London: Institute of Economic Affairs, 1972, 1978) and *The Political Ideal of the Rule of Law* (Cairo: National Bank of Egypt, 1955).

The essential archival collection of Hayek's work is at the Hoover Institution on War, Revolution and Peace at Stanford. A most valuable collection of interviews with Hayek is available through the UCLA Oral History Program, Department of Special Collections, Charles E. Young, Research Library. There is also material at the London School of Economics, including Nadim Shehadi's valuable interviews of Hayek and other 1930s LSE economists. Another valuable interview with Hayek, perhaps his last, was with Gary North and Mark Skousen, a considerable portion of which is incorporated in *Hayek on Hayek.* Charlotte Cubitt's private collection of Hayek material across his career, but particularly regarding *The Fatal Conceit,* is noteworthy, as is material in the possession of Stephen Kresge. An Institute of Economic Affairs video, "Hayek: His Life and Thought" (1984), is worthwhile.

WORKS PERTAINING TO HAYEK'S LIFE

Richard Cockett, *Thinking the Unthinkable: Think-Tanks and the Economic Counter-Revolution, 1931-1983* (Great Britain: HarperCollins, 1994) is the vital intellectual history of economic liberalism's revival in British political and academic life from the 1930s to 1980s, emphasizing Hayek's role.

Many books have been written on the Austro-Germanic background and Viennese milieu in which Hayek was raised, including William M. Johnston, *The Austrian Mind* (Berkeley: University of California Press, 1972), which Hayek did not like; Allan Janik and Stephen Toulmin, *Wittgenstein's Vienna* (New York: Touchstone, 1973); Hilde Spiel, *Vienna's Golden Autumn, 1866-1938* (London: Weidenfeld and Nicolson, 1987); Carl E. Schorske, *Fin de Siècle Vienna: Politics and Culture* (New York: Vintage Books, 1981); Robert A. Kann, *A History of the Habsburg Empire 1526-1918* (University of California Press, 1974); A. J. P. Taylor, *The Habsburg Monarchy 1809-1918* (London: Penguin, 1948); and Robert Musil's novel *The Man Without Qualities* (New York: Capricorn Books, 1965).

Earlene Craver, "The Emigration of the Austrian Economists," *History of Political Economy* (Spring 1986) is an exceptional article based on interviews with a number of economists who emigrated from Austria during the 1930s, including Hayek. Also see Arthur M. Diamond, Jr., "The Austrian Economists and the Late Hapsburg Viennese Milieu," *Review of Austrian Economics* (1988). The fourth volume of Hayek's *Collected Works* contains much biographical and historical information on Austrian economists. Ludwig von Mises, *The Historical Setting of the Austrian School of Economics* (New Rochelle, N.Y., 1969; also contained in Bettina Bien Greaves, *Austrian Economics: An Anthology* [Irvington-on-Hudson, N.Y.: Foundation for Economic Education, 1993], including other relevant works) provides background on the Austrian school. Ludwig von Mises, *Notes and Recollections* (South Holland, Ill.: Libertarian Press, 1978), is autobiographical. Margit von Mises, *My Years with Ludwig von Mises* (Cedar Falls, Iowa: Center for Futures Education, 1984) is a unique and revealing look at Mises' life.

Friedrich Engel-Janosi, . . . *aber ein stolzer Bettler: Erinnerungen aus einer verlorenen Generation* (. . . *but a proud beggar: Memories of a lost generation*) (Graz, Austria: Styria, 1974) is a German-language memoir of a Hayek Viennese associate and fellow-participant in the *Geistkreis* and Mises' seminar. Paul Silverman, *Law and Economics in Interwar Vienna: Kelsen, Mises, and the Regeneration of Austrian Liberalism,* Ph.D. thesis (University of Chicago, 1984), includes valuable historical and theoretical background on societal thought in Austria during the first decades of the twentieth century as well as insightful analysis of Mises' views. Barry Smith, "On the Austrianness of Austrian Economics," *Critical Review* (Winter-Spring 1990) argues for distinct Austrian and German philosophical traditions.

Many histories have been written on the London School of Economics. The most recent and comprehensive is Ralf Dahrendorf, *LSE: A History of the London School of Economics and Political Science 1895-1995* (Oxford University Press, 1995). Other works on the history of LSE include Hayek's own, excellent "The London School of Economics 1895-1945," *Economica* (February 1946) and Joan Abse (ed.), *My LSE* (London: Robson Books, 1977). The March 1982 issue of the *Atlantic Economic Journal* was devoted to "LSE and Its Contributions to Economics," and features contributions by Gerard M. Koot, A. W. Coats, and Ronald Coase. Coase's "Economics at LSE in the 1930's: A Personal View" is also included in his *Essays on Economics and Economists* (University of Chicago Press, 1994).

Lionel Robbins, *Autobiography of an Economist* (London: Macmillan, 1971) is an invaluable memoir for history of LSE, Robbins' career and life, and his relationship with Hayek. For more information on Robbins' life, see Henry Phelps Brown, "Lionel Charles Robbins 1898-1984," *Proceedings of the British Academy 1987* (Oxford University Press, 1988), and for consideration of his thought, D. P. O'Brien, *Lionel Robbins* (London: Macmillan, 1988). John Hicks, "The Hayek Story," in *Critical Essays in Monetary Theory* (Oxford: Clarendon Press, 1967) is frequently noted for a statement Hicks made about Hayek's influence at LSE during the early 1930s. Hicks also said, though, in this 1967 essay, that "Hayek's economic writings . . . are almost unknown to the modern student" (203)—indicating the black hole in which Hayek's economic work fell.

Elizabeth Durbin, *New Jerusalems: The Labour Party and the Economics of Democratic Socialism* (London: Routledge & Kegan Paul, 1985) is an exceptional history of the development of democratic socialist thought in Great Britain during the first half of the twentieth century, emphasizing the 1930s and including discussion of Hayek and LSE. Alan Ebenstein, *Edwin Cannan: Liberal Doyen* (London: Routledge/Thoemmes Press, 1997) is the only biography on Cannan. Colin Clark, "The 'Golden' Age of the Great Economists," *Encounter* (June 1977) is an interesting memoir of early 1930s British economic policy and thought. *Hayek's 'Serfdom' Revisited* (London: Institute of Economic Affairs, 1984) includes "Recollections" by Arthur Seldon. Walter Grinder's introduction to Ludwig Lachmann, *Capital, Expectations, and the Market Process* (Kansas City: Sheed Andrews and McMeel, 1977) paints a picture of the changing world of British academic economics during the 1930s.

Don Lavoie, *Rivalry and Central Planning: The Socialist Calculation Debate Reconsidered* (Cambridge University Press, 1985) is an erudite study of the meaning and significance of the socialist calculation debate, arguing especially Mises' position but considering Hayek's and Robbins' contributions. Lavoie perspicaciously observes that, contrary to what Hayek maintained, the socialists believed at the time and for some decades after that they had won the debate.

Robert Skidelsky, *John Maynard Keynes: The Economist as Savior 1920-1937* (New York: Penguin Books, 1994) is the second volume of his exceptional biography. *The Economist as Savior* provides much historical detail on the times as well as an approachable presentation of Keynes' comprehensive thought. Skidelsky also discusses Hayek in a work published in Britain under the title *The World After Communism: A Polemic for Our Times* (London: Macmillan, 1995), which appeared a year later in the United States under the Hayekian title *The Road from Serfdom: The Political and Economic Consequences of the End of Communism.* In a London *Times Literary Supplement* (September 20, 1996) review of Andrew Gamble's *Hayek: The Iron Cage of Liberty,* Skidelsky writes that Hayek was "the dominant intellectual influence of the last quarter of the twentieth century" (4), and that "the theory of spontaneous order is Hayek's finest achievement" (5).

There is, as yet, no comprehensive history of the University of Chicago. Works from which information about the University of Chicago and Hayek's time there may be obtained include Edward Shils, *Remembering the University of Chicago: Teachers, Scientists, and Scholars* (University of Chicago Press, 1991); William H. McNeill, *Hutchins' University: A Memoir of the University of Chicago 1919-1950* (University of Chicago Press, 1991); and *One in Spirit: A Retrospective View of the University of Chicago on the Occasion of Its Centennial* (University of Chicago Press, 1991). There is also information in a number of biographies and autobiographies about the era of Hayek's time at the University of Chicago, including George Stigler, *Memoirs of an Unregulated Economist* (New York: Basic Books, 1985)—Stigler wrote of Hayek that his "orderly mind could not comprehend the survivability of our disorderly world" (147). Milton and Rose Friedman's memoirs, *Two Lucky People* (University of Chicago Press, 1998), is the essential work on their life. James M. Buchanan, "I Did Not Call Him 'Fritz': Personal Recollections of Professor F. A. v. Hayek," *Constitutional Political Economy* (vol. 3, no. 2, 1992) is a fond reminiscence. Buchanan says of Hayek's later work that Hayek changed his focus from economic theory to the "philosophical foundations of a liberal order" (131).

Karen I. Vaughn, *Austrian Economics in America* (Cambridge University Press, 1994) is a history of the Austrian movement in economics during the recent decade emphasizing Mises, though also considering Menger, Hayek, and to a lesser extent Ludwig Lachmann and Israel Kirzner.

The Mont Pelerin Society is the subject of a history, Max Hartwell, *A History of the Mont Pelerin Society* (Indianapolis: Liberty Fund, 1995). George H. Nash, *The Conservative Intellectual Movement in America Since 1945* (Wilmington, Delaware: Intercollegiate Studies Institute, 1976, 2nd ed. 1996) is the definitive and authoritative work in its field. In describing the "roots of postwar American conservatism" (3), Nash gives pride of place to Hayek. Nash's essential work discusses in detail virtually all significant writers in a broad stream of postwar American conservatism and, to a lesser extent, libertarianism through 1975, and provides a postscript in the second edition on later developments.

John L. Kelley, *Bringing the Market Back In: The Political Revitalization of Market Liberalism* (New York University Press, 1997) is a mixture of practical political developments and economic and political theory and theorists, including Hayek. He says that Hayek and Mises "exaggerated the danger that the American mixed economy might fall prey to totalitarian temptations. Perhaps this is explained by the fact that both of them were central Europeans who had little experience with the strengths of a pluralistic democracy" (34). Caniel Yergin and Joseph Stanislaw, *The Commanding Heights: The Battle Between Government and the Marketplace that is Remaking the Modern World* (New York: Simon and Schuster, 1998) is a history of the transformation from government-driven to market-driven economies throughout the world during the last decades of the twentieth century. Dennis Kavanagh, *The Reordering of British Politics: Politics After Thatcher* (Oxford University Press, 1997) discusses influences on Thatcher's government, including Hayek, Friedman, and the Institute of Economic Affairs.

WORKS ON HAYEK'S THOUGHT

Many works have been written on Hayek's thought. Some of the better ones include Norman P. Barry, *Hayek's Social and Economic Philosophy* (London: Macmillan, 1979); Eamonn Butler, *Hayek: His Contribution to the Political and Economic Thought of Our Time* (New York: Universe Books, 1983); Jeremy Shearmur, *Hayek and After: Hayekian Liberalism as a Research Programme* (London: Routledge, 1996); G. R. Steele, *The Economics of Friedrich Hayek* (London: Macmillan, 1993); and Graham Walker, *The Ethics of F. A. Hayek* (Lanham, Md.: University Press of America, 1986).

Barry's work is a solid contribution on Hayek's comprehensive thought. *Hayek's Social and Economic Philosophy* is filled with insightful observations and deep scholarship. Barry is profound when he observes that it is not "the selfish aspect of the 'economic man' . . . that is significant, it is the fact of his ignorance. . . . Morality may well change, but what cannot change is ignorance. If a man were supremely altruistic or completely egoistic he would still only be able to comprehend the facts of a narrowly circumscribed area" (9). Barry's "The Tradition of Spontaneous Order," *Literature of Liberty* (Summer 1982) is a historical presentation of this idea and discussion of Hayek's perspective.

Butler's *Hayek* was conceived as an "introduction to Hayek's thought which covered his main arguments but which could be understood by the general reader" (v). Hayek wrote to Butler of *Hayek* that he very accurately conveyed his views (HA, 9-3). Also see Butler's *Milton Friedman: A Guide to His Economic Thought* (New York: Universe Books, 1985) and *Ludwig von Mises: Fountainhead of the Modern Microeconomic Revolution* (1988).

Shearmur's work is a study of Hayek's political thought. Shearmur says that it is "simply mistaken to try to make of him [Hayek] a conservative" (41), also noting that there are unresolved tensions and inconsistencies in Hayek's thought. Also see Shearmur, *The Political Thought of Karl Popper* (London: Routledge, 1996) and an interview of Shearmur on Popper and Hayek in *The Laissez Faire City Times,* vol. 4, no. 8 (February 21, 2000).

G. R. Steele provides a comprehensive account of Hayek's thought, focusing on his early economic thought. Steele greatly supports Hayek, saying that there is "no doubt that Hayek's work will secure its rightful place at the apex of twentieth century philosophy" (xii), and, "I unashamedly confess to be among those for whom 'the roll call of Hayek's works on the fundamental problems of society arouses . . . a peak of admiration'" (xiii).

Graham Walker's *The Ethics of F. A. Hayek* (Lanham, Md.: University Press of American, 1986) is a slim but valuable volume. Walker writes from the perspective of a conservative Catholic. As such, he is both attracted to and repelled by aspects of Hayek's thought. The best part of Walker's work is his discussion of the naturalistic and evolutionary character of Hayek's ethical and societal thought. He accurately observes that Hayek was often far closer in ultimate philosophical perspective to the collectivists he derided than to the liberals he exalted. Regarding Hayek's intellectual orientation, Walker writes that Hayek was a "thoroughgoing naturalist. He firmly rejects any notion of transcendence, both for the nature of reality in general and for ethics in particular. Ethics are fully immanent, fully of this world, fully the result of the process of cultural evolution. They have no transcendent, immutable or eternal referent" (35). Unlike most "naturalist-materialists" (as Walker terms them) (33), however, Hayek did not believe in the power of an individual's reason to replace the role of God. Thus his thought has not been susceptible to political excesses to which the thought of many other naturalist-materialists has led. For Hayek, the self-generating order replaced both God and a divine-like individual reason.

John Gray, *Hayek on Liberty,* 3d edition (London: Routledge, 1998) includes the most complete and readily accessible bibliography of Hayek's works and also contains an excellent bibliography of works on and about Hayek. Gray has moved away from Hayek's thought since the middle 1980s.

British socialist writer Andrew Gamble, *Hayek: The Iron Cage of Liberty* (Cambridge, England: Polity Press, 1996), finds much of value in Hayek's work, though disagreeing with his practical conclusions. According to Gamble, Hayek has "much to contribute to the renewal of the socialist project. . . . The implications of his theories are towards decentralized, local forms of governance" (192, 190).

Hannes Gissurarson, *Hayek's Conservative Liberalism* (New York: Garland, 1987) is an analysis of tensions in Hayek's thought between conservatism and liberalism, noting Hayek's similarities with and debts to various conservative and liberal thinkers. Gissurarson's work is informed by excellent scholarship in political philosophy. He cites Roy Harrod that, "responding to Hayek's paper from 1946 on 'Individualism: True and False,' . . . Harrod argued that by transferring the concept of the invisible hand from economic to social life, Hayek was 'roughing in a philosophical defence not of individualism, but of the best type of conservatism'" (126). Gissurarson affirms that, despite tensions and inconsistencies in Hayek's thought, his ultimate commitment was to liberalism.

Calvin M. Hoy, *A Philosophy of Individual Freedom: The Political Thought of F. A. Hayek* (Westport, Conn.: Greenwood Press, 1984) is a short but stimulating presentation. Hoy well covers the main points. The works discussed most are *The Constitution of Liberty* and *Law, Legislation and Liberty,* though Hoy is well grounded in the whole range of Hayek's work. Hoy's discussion is provocative for the pithy summaries he makes of Hayek's thought: "Without understanding the importance of prices in Hayek's political philosophy, one cannot understand Hayek's argument" (62); "Rules are necessary because of human ignorance" (81); "Freedom is possible only within a market order. . . . [T]his order can persist only if individuals are governed by law, that is, abstract rules of conduct" (119); "Problems involving civil liberties receive too little attention from Hayek. . . . Hayek somewhat surprisingly does not much discuss the related ideas of resistance, rebellion, or revolution" (122-3).

Barbara M. Rowland, *Ordered Liberty and the Constitutional Framework: The Political Thought of Friedrich A. Hayek* (Westport, Conn.: Greenwood Press, 1987) is a brief, critical examination of Hayek's thought. Rowland's analysis is valuable in calling attention to conservative elements in especially his later, evolutionary thought. She says of his later work that the "role of reason appears to dwindle away at an alarming rate" (35). She states that, for Hayek, "liberty is not an absolute or natural right" (97), and there is "no attention to individual rights as such in Hayek" (ibid.).

Chandran Kukathas, *Hayek and Modern Liberalism* (Oxford: Clarendon Press, 1990) is an examination both of Hayek's moral and political theories and their place in modern societal thought, emphasizing Hume and Kant. It is true, as Eugene Miller holds, that Hayek is "deeply influenced by the Kantian view that sense data are never accessible to consciousness in their original or pure state, but only as they are transformed by the mind's own apparatus of classification" (in Robert L. Cunningham [ed.], *Liberty and the Rule of Law* [Texas A & M University Press, 1979], 258). It is also the case, as Tibor Machan remarks, that Hayek's "conception of how we are aware of reality manifests his basically Kantian framework (something he shares with . . . Mises)" (Ibid., 271). Hayek's primary debt to Kant was in ontology, not societal philosophy. On the crucial issue of liberty, Hayek and Kant had different views. Hayek stated in *The Constitution of Liberty,* in obvious reference to Kant, that "philosophers have sometimes defined freedom as action in conformity with moral rules. But this definition of freedom is a denial of the freedom with which we are here concerned" (*CL,* 79). Hayek noted in "Kinds of Rationalism" that "constructivist rationalism . . . tinged the views" (*Studies,* 94) of Kant. Kant's influence on Hayek was in ontology not societal philosophy, nor was it as extensive as Kukathas contends.

Other book length considerations of Hayek include Brian Lee Crowley, *The Self, the Individual, and the Community: Liberalism in the Political Thought of F. A. Hayek and Sidney and Beatrice Webb* (Oxford: Clarendon Press, 1987); Joao Carlos Espada, *Social Citizenship Rights: A Critique of F. A. Hayek and Raymond Plant* (London: Macmillan, 1996); Roland Kley, *Hayek's Social and Political Thought* (Oxford: Clarendon Press, 1994); Brian McCormick, *Hayek and the Keynesian Avalanche* (New York: St. Martin's Press, 1992); Gerald P. O'Driscoll, Jr., *Economics as a Coordination Problem: The Contributions of Friedrich A. Hayek* (Kansas City: Sheed Andrews and McMeel, 1977); Chris Matthew Sciabarra, *Marx, Hayek and Utopia* (Albany: State University of New York, 1995); and Jim Tomlinson, *Hayek and the Market* (London: Pluto Press, 1990).

Crowley's work is a comparison of Hayek and the Webbs. Crowley concludes regarding Hayek that at "many levels Hayek offers us a much richer theory than the Webbs were able to do, just as his work is more stimulating and exciting" (287). Crowley sees both the Webbs and Hayek in the liberal tradition.

He has, in addition, narrated an excellent two-part radio series for the Canadian Broadcasting System, "The Ideas of F. A. Hayek," available through Laissez-Faire Books, San Francisco.

McCormick's *Hayek and the Keynesian Avalanche* is a work in intellectual recovery. McCormick recreates the pre-Keynesian world at LSE and suggests the continuing potential relevance of this line of economic thought.

O'Driscoll's *Economics as a Coordination Problem* is an interpretation of Hayek's early economic work from a Misesian perspective. Hayek wrote in a foreword to this book that it is a "curious fact that a student of complex phenomena may long himself remain unaware of how his views of different problems hang together and perhaps never fully succeed in clearly stating the guiding ideas which led him in the treatment of particulars. I must confess that I was occasionally myself surprised when I found in Professor O'Driscoll's account side by side statements which I made at the interval of many years and on quite different problems, which still implied the same general approach" (xx).

Tomlinson's *Hayek and the Market* is a perceptive and sympathetic, yet critical, account of Hayek by a British social democrat. "The basic paradox of . . . [Hayek's] evolutionism, that history has allegedly 'gone wrong' with the rise of collectivism over the last 100 years, and yet this has been accompanied by the most rapid population growth ever, supposedly the measure of evolutionary progress, is not resolved" (122).

There are a number of good edited collections on Hayek's thought. Some include Jack Birner and Rudy van Zifp (eds.), *Hayek, Co-Ordination and Evolution* (London: Routledge, 1994), an excellent collection of essays on Hayek's thought in economics, political and legal theory, philosophy, and the history of ideas; Robert L. Cunningham (ed.), *Liberty and the Rule of Law* (Texas A & M University Press, 1979); Stephen Frowen (ed.), *Hayek: Economist and Social Philosopher A Critical Retrospect* (Great Britain: Macmillan, 1997); and Arthur Seldon (ed.), *Agenda for a Free Society: Essays on Hayek's* The Constitution of Liberty (London: Institute of Economic Affairs, 1961), an exceptional collection.

Cunningham (ed.) is a superior collection of papers delivered by distinguished participants at a 1976 conference in honor of Hayek. The paper by Joseph Raz, "The Rule of Law and Its Virtue," is particularly noteworthy: "A legal system that in general observes the rule of law . . . presupposes that . . . [people] are rational, autonomous creatures. . . . The rule of law provides the foundation for the legal respect for human dignity" (15). A paper by Eugene F. Miller, "The Cognitive Basis of Hayek's Political Thought," discusses *The Sensory Order* and Hayek's other epistemological work. According to J. R. Lucas, "Professor Hayek is jealous for liberty. Not only does he argue, trenchantly and convincingly, that liberty is a great good, but he often argues also that no other good is to be compared with it, and that in any case of conflict other goods must always be compromised in order that the overriding claims of liberty may not be in any way abated" (146).

Frowen (ed.) is an excellent collection of essays. Contributors include Lord Desai, Barry Smith, Manfred Streit, Karl Milford, Tony Lawson, and G. R. Steele. This volume includes Popper's memorial tribute to Hayek.

Fritz Machlup (ed.), *Essays on Hayek* (New York University Press, 1976) is a collection of essays originally delivered at a Mont Pelerin Society conference in 1975. William F. Buckley writes that Hayek always took "scrupulous care to give credit, if it is faintly plausible . . . , to others who articulated ideas before he did, and indeed sometimes, on reading the footnotes to *The Constitution of Liberty,* one almost has the feeling that the book is a collection of after-dinner toasts by Hayek to great philosophers, political thinkers, and economists, from Thales to Ludwig von Mises. But he cannot shrug off the credit for having brought much of it all together" (95). Gottfried Dietze, "Hayek on the Rule of Law" is excellent.

M. Colonna et al. (eds.), *Money and Business Cycles,* vol. 1 *The Economics of F. A. Hayek,* and *Capitalism, Socialism and Knowledge,* vol. 2 *The Economics of F. A. Hayek* (England and the United States: Edward Elgar, 1994) are two good collections of essays from a conference held on Hayek in 1992. The first volume is primarily devoted to Hayek's early, technical economic work, and the second to capital, socialist calculation, and methodology.

Christopher Frei and Robert Nef (eds.), *Contending with Hayek* (Bern, Switzerland: Peter Lang, 1994) is a collection of essays presented at a 1992 colloquium on Hayek. One of the best aspects of this collection, which includes essays by a number of prominent Hayek scholars, is that they are not all "for" Hayek; several of the pieces are quite critical of him.

Erich Streissler (ed.), *Roads to Freedom: Essays in Honour of Friedrich A. von Hayek* (New York: Augustus M. Kelley, 1969) is a *Festschrift* presented at the meeting of the Mont Pelerin Society following Hayek's seventieth birthday. Streissler is the leading contemporary historian of the historical Austrian school of economics and has written many articles in this area.

Hayek is the subject of a number of chapters in books, including in Richard Bellamy, *Liberalism and Pluralism* (London: Routledge, 1999), the first chapter of which is "Trading Values: Hayek and the Dethronement of Politics by Markets"; Anthony de Crespigny and Kenneth Minogue (eds.), *Contemporary Political Philosophers* (London: Methuen & Co., 1975); William Ebenstein and Alan Ebenstein, *Great Political Thinkers,* 6th ed. (Fort Worth, Tex.: Harcourt Brace, 2000) and Alan Ebenstein, William Ebenstein, and Edwin Fogelman, *Today's Isms: Socialism, Capitalism, Fascism, Communism, Libertarianism,*

11th ed. (Englewood Cliffs, N.J.: Prentice-Hall, 2000); Richard P. F. Holt and Steven Pressman (eds.), *Economics and its Discontents: Twentieth Century Dissenting Economists* (Cheltenham, U.K.: Edward Elgar, 1998), one chapter of which is by Laurence Moss, "Friedrich A. Hayek: Super-Dissenter"; Murray Rothbard, *The Ethics of Liberty* (Atlantic Highlands, N.J.: Humanities Press, 1988), of which chapter 28 is "F. A. Hayek and the Concept of Coercion," a critical view; William E. Scheuerman, *Carl Schmitt: The End of Law* (Lanham, Md.: Rowman and Littlefield, 1999), which includes a chapter discussing the legal theories of Schmitt and Hayek; and Walter B. Weimer and David S. Palermo (eds.), *Cognition and the Symbolic Processes,* vol. 2 (Hillsdale, N.J.: Lawrence Erlbaum Associates, 1982).

Crespigny's "F. A. Hayek, Freedom for Progress" is an excellent brief introduction to Hayek's thought based mostly on *The Constitution of Liberty.* Crespigny remarks that, for Hayek, "freedom is to be valued not so much from the standpoint of the individual as from that of society" (57). According to Moss, Hayek "adopted an enlightenment view of a world in which all people, united by trade and mutual understanding, may increase their living standards indefinitely and without limit" (85). Weimer and Palermo's work contains a chapter by Hayek, "*The Sensory Order* After 25 Years"; a chapter by Weimer, "Hayek's Approach to the Problems of Complex Phenomena: An Introduction to the Theoretical Psychology of *The Sensory Order,*" in which Weimer states that "[t]he major theme in Hayek's work·is that there are constraints upon the nature of knowledge" (241); and a discussion between Hayek and Weimer. Hayek remarked in the discussion, "I should tell you that in a way, I was a Popperian before he published *The Logic of Scientific Discovery*" (323).

Lawrence H. White, "Monetary Nationalism Reconsidered," in Kevin Dowd and Richard H. Timberlake, Jr. (eds.), *Money and the Nation State* (New Brunswick, N.J.: Transaction Publishers, 1998) is a discussion largely of Hayek's 1937 *Monetary Nationalism and International Stability.*

Two general histories of economic thought including discussion of Hayek are Ben Seligman, *Main Currents in Modern Economics* (New Brunswick, NJ: Transaction Publishers, 1990) and Henry W. Spiegel, *The Growth of Economic Thought* (Englewood Cliffs, NJ: Prentice-Hall, 1971). J. R. Hicks and W. Weber (eds.), *Carl Menger and the Austrian School of Economics* (Oxford University Press, 1973) is a fine collection of papers given at a 1971 Vienna symposium celebrating the 100th anniversary of Menger's *Principles of Economics,* including a paper by Hayek. Hicks said in his essay that "though the origins of the Austrian theory of capital are in Menger . . . I shall take the theory . . . in the form I learned it myself from Professor Hayek. There were four years, 1931-5, when I was myself a member of his seminar in London; it has left a deep mark upon my thinking. In much of my work it has been overladen by other influences, but it has survived" (190). Hayek said in his contribution that, "though there is no longer a distinct Austrian School, I believe there is still a distinct Austrian tradition" (13).

T. W. Hutchison, *The Politics and Philosophy of Economics: Marxians, Keynesians and Austrians* (New York University Press, 1981) contains two particularly relevant chapters, "Carl Menger on Philosophy and Method" and "Austrians on Philosophy and Method (since Menger)." Hutchison's work brought a response from Bruce Caldwell which, together with a rejoinder from Hutchison, is included in the 1992 edition of Warren Samuels (ed.), *Research in the History of Economic Thought and Methodology* (JAI Press).

Willem Keizer, et al. (eds.), *Austrian Economics in Debate* (London: Routledge, 1997) contains a number of papers on the development of the Austrian movement in economics during recent decades. Ebeling says that "Hayek was the most prominent proponent and refiner of the Wicksell-Mises business-cycle theory. Indeed it is no exaggeration to say that the theory gained world renown among economists through him. Yet Hayek's use of the Wicksell-Mises theory has a uniquely distinct twist to it" (59). Steve Fleetwood puts forward in his contribution:

> It appears that Hayek sets out *the* crucial question for economics in 1937 but cannot answer it satisfactorily until 1960. The question is this: How can the socio-economic activity of millions of unconnected individuals be coordinated when this requires the prior coordination of their plans, which in turn requires the discovery, communication and storage of an enormous quantity . . . of knowledge that exists only as a decentralized and fragmented totality?
>
> The answer comes in two temporally divided parts. In a 1945 paper, Hayek argues that coordination occurs due to the discovery, communication and storage of knowledge being facilitated by the telecom system—. . . the price mechanism. . . . In his work after 1960 Hayek argues that the discovery, communication and storage of knowledge is facilitated not by the telecom system *alone,* but by the telecom system articulating with, and embedded within, a dense web of social rules of conduct. (134)

Also see Fleetwood's *Hayek's Political Economy: The Socio-Economics of Order* (London: Routledge, 1995).

Israel Kirzner, *Competition and Entrepreneurship* (University of Chicago Press, 1973) notes similarities between Hayek and Mises in the ignorance implied by subjectivism, but at the same time says that there "can be no doubt that, on key elements in the Misesian system, Hayek is no Misesist at all" (119). Kirzner, *The Meaning of Market Process: Essays in the Development of Modern Austrian Economics* (Routledge: London, 1992) includes his *New Palgrave* article, "The Austrian School of Economics." Kirzner's "Divergent Approaches in Libertarian Thought," *Intercollegiate Review* (January-February, 1967) highlights differences between Chicago and Austrian perspectives.

Ludwig Lachmann, *Capital, Expectations, and the Market Process: Essays on the Theory of the Market Economy* (Kansas City: Sheed Andrews and McMeel, 1977) is a collection of articles that include consideration of Hayek. Hayek remarked in 1978 of his own work in capital that "I think the most useful conclusions drawn from what I did are . . . in Lachmann's book on capital (UCLA, 243)," *Capital and Its Structure* (1956). Also see Lachmann's "The Salvage of Ideas: Problems of the Revival of Austrian Economic Thought," *Journal of Institutional and Theoretical Economics* (1982), which includes considerable discussion of Hayek's capital theory juxtaposed to Knight's criticisms of it.

George L. S. Shackle (Stephen F. Frowen, ed.), *Business, Time and Thought* (New York University Press, 1988) contains an essay, "Hayek as Economist," discussing Hayek's early economic and epistemological work. Shackle said of Hayek, "On any reckoning he must be accorded by friend or foe his unquestioned place amongst the giants" (191). Hayek recalled in a 1978 interview: "I discovered Shackle. . . . Shackle sent to me . . . an essay he'd written; nobody knew him. But I encouraged him to elaborate it for *Economica*. . . . I was very impressed and got him a scholarship at the London School of Economics" (UCLA, 191).

Viktor Vanberg, *Rules and Choice in Economics* (London: Routledge, 1994) is an outstanding collection of essays. "Hayek's inquiry into the interrelation between the *order of rules* and the *order of actions* . . . his message that changes in the order of rules are the principal means by which we can hope to improve the socio-economic-political order under which we live" (5); "What we call a market is always a system of social interaction characterized by a specific *institutional framework*, . . . a *set of rules*. . . . Hayek has to be credited for having addressed this . . . more explicitly and more systematically than most 'free market economists'" (77, 93). Hayek thought well of Vanberg's work.

Hundreds of articles have been written on Hayek over the decades. A few of these include Bruce Caldwell, "Hayek and Socialism," *Journal of Economic Literature* (December 1997), an excellent scholarly presentation of the intellectual context in which Hayek developed ideas in *The Road to Serfdom,* and Caldwell, "Hayek's Transformation," *History of Political Economy* (Winter

1988), which traces development of Hayek's economic thought during the 1930s and '40s. For a view similar to Caldwell's, see William Butos, "Hayek and General Equilibrium Analysis," *Southern Economic Journal* (October 1985).

Critical Review has devoted two issues to Hayek, the Spring 1989 issue, including David Miller's and Leland Yeager's reviews of *The Fatal Conceit,* and the Winter 1997 issue.

Murray Forsyth, "Hayek's Bizarre Liberalism: A Critique," *Political Studies* (June 1988) provides this view: "The heart of the criticism that must be levelled at the version of liberalism that Hayek seeks to vindicate . . . [is that] it has no qualitative, substantive content. . . . [I]t is liberalism purged of all its classical truths" (250).

Scott Gordon, "The Political Economy of F. A. Hayek," *Canadian Journal of Economics* (August 1981) is a critical review of *Law, Legislation and Liberty.* Gordon writes that Hayek's "dedication to liberty is profound and sincere, but one wonders whether his defence does not have the effect of making it rather unattractive. There is a heaviness of spirit which pervades his writings, not merely because his style is devoid of grace or wit or because of his pessimism concerning western civilization, but because his own ideal society wears a grim-God aspect. Hayek's liberty is a starch-collared, tight-lipped, no-compromise liberty; constrained not by coercive authorities but by hard, self-imposed, moral imperatives, scrupulously dutiful in obedience to principle, but solemn, suspicious, and cramped" (486-7).

Ronald Hamowy, "Law and the Liberal Society: F. A. Hayek's *Constitution of Liberty,*" *Journal of Libertarian Studies* (Winter 1978) is critical of Hayek on laws' generality. Also see Hamowy, "The Hayekian Model of Government in an Open Society," *Journal of Libertarian Studies* (Spring 1982), critical of Hayek's proposed form of representative government.

Marlo Lewis, "The Achilles Heel of F. A. Hayek," *National Review* (May 17, 1985) is an insightful criticism of Hayek's views on societal evolution from the perspective of natural law theory. "The American intellectual conservative movement may be said to have been born in 1944, with the publication of Friedrich A. Hayek's *The Road to Serfdom,*" Lewis writes; and, "To Hayek, apparently, the only justification for traditional morality is its utility in promoting interests that are in themselves non-moral" (32).

Theodore Rosenof, "Freedom, Planning, and Totalitarianism: The Reception of F. A. Hayek's *Road to Serfdom,*" *Canadian Review of American Studies* (Fall 1974) is a good account of philosophical issues current at the time of publication of *The Road to Serfdom.* Rosenof observes that the "Hayekian tendency to stress the impact of ideas . . . and to deemphasize or even ignore the role of concrete conditions was sharply questioned" (155). He notes as well that "one of the most interesting things about Hayek's critics—most of whom were New Deal liberals and democratic socialists—was the extent to which they shared Hayek's fear of the totalitarian specter and warned against 'too much' government economic intervention" (156). Rosenof also says that Hayek was "accused by critics of subsuming all concrete phenomena under the aegis of inclusive 'systems,' traditions, and cultural patterns. . . . [T]his was in a sense a variant of a Marxist and socialist mode of thought. . . . For socialists, too, sometimes tended to subsume all social, economic, and political phenomena under the aegis of an all-inclusive 'system'" (160).

Arthur M. Diamond, Jr., "F. A. Hayek on Constructivism and Ethics," *Journal of Libertarian Studies* (Fall 1980) argues that Hayek "endorses four ethical positions that cannot all be reconciled: relativism, Institutional Social Darwinism, utilitarianism, and contractarianism. Apart from their mutual inconsistency, at least one, and perhaps . . . three, of the positions are also inconsistent with Hayek's condemnation of the broad philosophical approach he identifies as 'constructivism'" (353).

Among older articles, Frank H. Knight, "Professor Hayek and the Theory of Investment," *Economic Journal* (March 1935) was a stinging criticism of Hayek's emerging theory of capital, all the more so because Hayek had previously cited Knight in support of his position. Knight did not concur with Hayek that an increase in the amount of capital necessarily results in a lengthening of a structure of production. Also see Knight, "Laissez Faire: Pro and Con," *Journal of Political Economy* (October 1967) for a harsh criticism of Hayek's political philosophy and *The Constitution of Liberty* in particular.

Jacob Viner, "Hayek on Freedom and Coercion," *Southern Economic Journal* (January 1961) is a review of *The Constitution of Liberty.* Viner noted that Hayek's "positive proposals for government action in the 'welfare' field . . . [are] a substantial enough program to destroy any claims Hayek may have to the laissez faire label" (236). Lionel Robbins' review of *The Constitution of Liberty* in part making the same point is included in the February 1961 edition of *Economica.*

John Cunningham Wood and Ronald N. Woods (eds.), *Friedrich A. Hayek: Critical Assessments,* 4 volumes (London: Routledge, 1991) is an excellent collection of 96 articles on Hayek's thought throughout his career. Part of the "Critical Assessments of Contemporary Economists" series, these volumes naturally concentrate on his economic work but also include other aspects of his thought. Volume 1 largely includes articles on and reviews of his early economic work; volume 2, *The Road to Serfdom, The Counter-Revolution of Science,* and *The Constitution of Liberty;* and volumes 3 and 4, his later economic thought.

Virginia Postrel, *The Future and Its Enemies: The Growing Conflict Over Creativity, Enterprise, and Progress* (New York: Free Press, 1998) is a work in the Hayekian tradition. Postrel well describes the possibility of continued material progress through technological advance, the ideas necessary to fortify a society to realize this future, and the threats to progress from government efforts to stifle freedom, creativity, and competition. She distinguishes between "dynamism" and "stasis"—change and keeping things the way they are. She concludes her work in defence of Hayek against the charge that he has a strictly material vision of progress with no emphasis on spirit: "'It is in the process of learning,' Hayek reminds us, 'in the effects of having learned something new, that man enjoys the gift of his intelligence'" (218).

Jim Powell, *The Triumph of Liberty* (New York: Free Press, 2000) is an excellent history of liberty told through its leading protagonists in diverse fields, including chapters on Hayek, Friedman, Mises, Rand, and many others.

Mark Skousen, *The Structure of Production* (New York University Press, 1990) is the most Hayekian presentation of the economic process by a contemporary economist. Skousen links Hayek's work in capital, money, industrial fluctuations, and gold.

Thomas Sowell, *A Conflict of Visions: Ideological Origins of Political Struggles* (New York: William Morrow and Company, 1987) considers Hayek and Hayekian themes extensively, particularly in his discussion of justice. Sowell observes that, for Hayek, it is "especially unwarranted for the individual to place himself outside or above the society which makes his understanding possible" (82). Hayek greatly praised Sowell's *Knowledge and Decisions* (1980).

Aaron L. Friedberg, *In the Shadow of the Garrison State: America's Anti-Statism and Its Cold War Grand Strategy* (Princeton University Press, 2000) states that "[m]uch postwar rhetoric regarding the dangers of excessive state control of the economy can be traced to a single source . . . *The Road to Serfdom*" (51). According to Caniel Yergin and Joseph Stanislaw in *The Commanding Heights* (1998), "In the postwar years, Keynes' theories of government management of the economy appeared unassailable. But a half century later, it is Keynes who has been toppled and Hayek, the fierce advocate of free markets, who is preeminent. The Keynesian 'new economics' . . . may have dominated the . . . 1960s, but it is the University of Chicago's free-market school that is globally influential in the 1990s" (14-5). According to Friedman in Brian Lamb, *Booknotes: Life Stories* (New York: Times Books, 1999), "Hayek was not a conservative. . . . We are radicals" (250-1).

Works published while the present book was itself in the proof pages stage of publication or which were published or became known to this writer after they could be fully incorporated here include Malachi Haim Hacohen, *Karl Popper–*

The Formative Years, 1902-1945: Politics and Philosophy in Interwar Vienna (Cambridge University Press, 2000), the first extensive intellectual biography of Popper, particularly of the first half of his life. Hacohen's work is informed by deep scholarship—he apparently worked about fifteen years on this book. He has done a superb job of bringing to light much information on Popper's life and intellectual development. The work is also a substantial, balanced presentation of the development of Austro-Germanic intellectual thought.

Hacohen emphasizes Hayek's practical assistance to Popper. More lines are devoted to Hayek than to any other contemporary in the index, which, because they did not meet until 1935, is particularly significant. Hacohen summarizes that "Popper's encounter with Hayek turned out to be one of the most important in his life" (316), and stresses Popper's debt to Hayek in the development of his political philosophy.

Another major intellectual biography to be published only as the present book was in the proof pages stage is Robert Skidelsky, *John Maynard Keynes: Fighting for Britain 1937-1946* (London: Macmillan, 2000), the third volume of his monumental biography. The infrequency of Hayek's appearance in this work indicates that his relationship with Keynes was more important to Hayek than it was to Keynes (which is not to say Keynes did not consider Hayek one of his many friendly acquaintances and intellectual interlocutors). Hayek wrote Lydia Lopokova, Keynes' widow, on Keynes' death that Keynes was "the one really great man I ever knew, and for whom I had unbounded admiration. The world will be a very much poorer place without him" (472). Skidelsky calls attention to Hayek's relative deprecation of fiscal policy compared to monetary policy in *The Road to Serfdom* to make the point that activist fiscal policies are a step closer to state socialism than activist monetary policies (which Hayek, at this time, was more inclined to favor). However, he probably overemphasizes the extent to which Hayek was concerned about fiscal policy this way. Hayek immediately went on to say, following the passage Skidelsky cites (284) to make this case, that "the very necessary efforts to secure protection against . . . [business] fluctuations do not lead to the kind of planning which constitutes such a threat to our freedom" (*RS*, 91).

Skidelsky describes Hayek as a "philosopher of liberalism," and notes that the discussion between Hayek and Keynes of "how much government intervention is compatible with a free society was never properly joined" (550). He expresses a similar thought in the second volume of his biography, *The Economist as Saviour* (supra), when he speculates that had Keynes lived longer, he might have written a work in societal and political philosophy. "Capitalism," Skidelsky there writes, "may have vanquished socialism, but the debate between *laissez-faire* and Keynes's philosophy of the Middle Way is still fiercely joined" (228-9).

Israel Kirzner, *The Driving Force of the Market* (London: Routledge, 2000) is a collection of essays in the Austrian movement in postKeynesian economics. Part III is "Studies in the Mises-Hayek Legacy," also included is Kirzner's obituary of Hayek. In "Hedgehog or Fox? Hayek and the Idea of Plan-Coordination," Kirzner notes Hayek's "reinterpretation of equilbrium as expressing the mutual compatibility of independently-made plans" and the "extension by Hayek of his economic insights of 1937 to his political philosophy insights of the 1960s" (193, 196). He notes that Mises "never did focus explicitly on plan-coordination . . . ; he never did focus on the dispersed character of knowledge, and on the consequent coordination problem. (This does not mean that Mises's seminal insights in each of the above two areas cannot be faithfully articulated in plan-coordination terms; it merely means that Mises himself never explicitly recognized this possible articulation.)" (198).

Kirzner emphasizes that "Perhaps the single most important and original insight which Hayek contributed to economic understanding is contained in his 1937 detailed interpretation of the state of equilibrium as being simply the state in which 'the different plans which the individuals . . . have made for action in time are mutually compatible" (191). Kirzner quotes from Hayek's 1981, final LSE lecture that his original 1931 LSE lectures, which were published as *Prices and Production*, "'made use' of what became the leading theme of most of my later work, an analysis of the signal function of prices'" (in ibid., 183).

Gottfried von Haberler had this exchange in 1979 with Richard Ebeling, in an interview recently published in *The Austrian Economics Newsletter*, vol. 20, no. 1 (Spring 2000):

Q: What led you to question the relevance of the Hayekian business cycle theory?

A: I realized that you can't explain a deep depression by real maladjustments emphasized by Mises and Hayek. It was the so-called "secondary deflation" which made the Great Depression so bad, and not any enormous real maladjustments. . . .

Q: Do you think, though, that the Mises-Hayek analysis has relevance at least in explaining the primary distortions?

A: Well, that may be so, but the particular type of maladjustment that Hayek has in mind, I believe, is not really a very important factor—what he calls the "vertical" maladjustments in the structure of production. What impresses me is that on other occasions our economy handles very large maladjustments, as, for example, during a transition from war to peace and from peace to war, without much trouble. But in Hayek's theory those so-called vertical maladjustments are supposed to bring about the enormous disaster of the Great Depression. To my mind, that makes no sense.

Kenneth Hoover, "Ideologizing Institutions: Laski, Hayek, Keynes and the Creation of Contemporary Politics," *Journal of Political Ideologies* (February 1999) contains biographical information. According to John Cassidy, "The Price Prophet," *New Yorker* (February 7, 2000), "Hayek got some things wrong (he was tardy about acknowledging the need for government action to reduce unemployment during the thirties, for example) and he neglected others (such as inequality and pollution); but on the biggest issue of all, the vitality of capitalism, he was vindicated to such an extent that it is hardly an exaggeration to refer to the twentieth century as the Hayek century" (45). Bruce Caldwell, "The Emergence of Hayek's Ideas on Cultural Evolution," *The Review of Austrian Economics* (February 2000) discusses Hayek's work in *The Sensory Order* and the application of his ideas there to societal evolution. Finally, "The Friedrich Hayek Scholars' Page," maintained on the internet by Gregory Ransom (www.hayekcenter.org), is an excellent resource for information on, and to research and discuss, Hayek.

Abbreviations

HAYEK'S WORKS

CEP   *Collectivist Economic Planning* (London: Routledge & Kegan Paul, 1950)

CL   *The Constitution of Liberty* (University of Chicago Press, 1960)

CRS   *The Counter-Revolution of Science* (New York: Free Press, 1955)

CW   *Collected Works of F. A. Hayek* (University of Chicago Press, 1988) (volume number follows *CW*)

DM   *Denationalisation of Money* (London: Institute of Economic Affairs, 1990)

HH   *Hayek on Hayek: An Autobiographical Dialogue* (Stephen Kresge and Leif Wenar, eds.) (University of Chicago Press, 1994)

KES   *Knowledge, Evolution, and Society* (London: Adam Smith Institute, 1983)

IEO   *Individualism and Economic Order* (University of Chicago Press, 1948)

LLL   *Law, Legislation and Liberty* (University of Chicago Press, 1973-79) (volume number follows *LLL*)

"LSE"   "The London School of Economics 1895-1945," *Economica* (February, 1946)

MCF   *Money, Capital, and Fluctuations: Early Essays* (Roy McCloughry, ed.) (University of Chicago Press, 1984)

MNIS   *Monetary Nationalism and International Stability* (New York: Augustus M. Kelley, 1964)

MTTC   *Monetary Theory and the Trade Cycle* (New York: Augustus M. Kelley, 1966)

NS   *New Studies in Philosophy, Politics, Economics and the History of Ideas* (London: Routledge, 1978)

PII   *Profits, Interest and Investment* (Clifton, N.J.: Augustus M. Kelley, 1975)

PP   *Prices and Production* (New York: Augustus M. Kelley, 1967)

PTC   *The Pure Theory of Capital* (University of Chicago Press, 1975)

RS   *The Road to Serfdom* (London: Routledge, 1944)

SO   *The Sensory Order* (London: Routledge, 1952)

Studies   *Studies in Philosophy, Politics and Economics* (University of Chicago Press, 1967)

TT   *A Tiger by the Tail: The Keynesian Legacy of Inflation* (Sudha Shenoy, compiler and introducer) (London: Institute of Economic Affairs, 1978)

OTHER SOURCES

Cockett   Richard Cockett, *Thinking the Unthinkable: Think-Tanks and the Economic Counter-Revolution, 1931-1983* (Great Britain: HarperCollins, 1994)

HA   Hayek Archive, Hoover Institution, Stanford University (box and file number given)

Hartwell   R. M. Hartwell, *A History of the Mont Pelerin Society* (Indianapolis: Liberty Fund, 1995)

IEA   Transcript of "Hayek: His Life and Thought" video (London: Institute of Economic Affairs, 1984)

Keynes *CW* *The Collected Works of John Maynard Keynes* (Cambridge, Engl.: 1971-1989) (volume number follows "Keynes *CW*")

Robbins   Lionel Robbins, *Autobiography of an Economist* (London: Macmillan, 1971)

UCLA   "Nobel Prize-Winning Economist Friedrich A. von Hayek," Oral History Program, University of California at Los Angeles (1983)

Notes

INTRODUCTION

1. John Stuart Mill, *On Liberty* (introduction by Gertrude Himmelfarb, London: Penguin, 1974), 78.
2. Paul A. Samuelson and W. D. Nordhaus, *Economics,* 13th ed. (New York: McGraw Hill, 1989), 837.
3. I am indebted to Art Rupe for the comparison of Hayek to Darwin, Marx, and Freud in their emphases on evolutionary processes.
4. Palgrave, R. H. Inglis (ed.), *Dictionary of Political Economy,* vol. II (London: Macmillan, 1896), 704.
5. *Time* (April 6, 1992), 19.
6. *LLL* II, 144.

CHAPTER 1

1. UCLA, 474-5.
2. UCLA, 23.
3. Allan Janik and Stephen Toulmin, *Wittgenstein's Vienna* (New York: Touchstone, 1973), 13.
4. In ibid., 36-7 (original Musil paragraph cited here—Robert Musil, *The Man Without Qualities* [New York: Capricorn Books, 1965], 32-3).
5. Hilde Spiel, *Vienna's Golden Autumn, 1866-1938* (London: Weidenfeld and Nicolson, 1987), 7.
6. *NS,* 50-4. Hayek's favorite philosopher, Hume, remarked—perhaps along the lines of Hayek's distinction between puzzlers and masters of their subject: "The greater part of mankind may be divided into two classes; that of *shallow* thinkers, who fall short of the truth; and that of *abstruse* thinkers, who go beyond it. The latter class are by far the most rare: and I may add, by far the most useful and valuable. They suggest hints, at least, and start difficulties, which they want, perhaps, skill to pursue; but which may produce fine discoveries, when handled by men who have a more just way of thinking. At worst, what they say is uncommon; and if it should cost some pains to comprehend it, one has, however, the pleasure of hearing something new. An author is little to be valued, who tells us nothing but what we can learn from coffee-house conversation" (David Hume, *Essays Moral, Political, and Literary* [Indianapolis: Liberty Classics, 1985], 253).
7. Joseph Schumpeter, in *NS,* 51.
8. *RS,* 110.

9. *CW* IV, 177.
10. *IEO*, 25-6.
11. *HH*, 39.
12. F. A. von Hayek, *Die Irrtümer des Konstruktivismus* (Walter Eucken Institute, 1975), 3.
13. *HH*, 37-8.
14. *CW* IV, 176.
15. August Hayek's massive, three-volume, 2,500 page *Prodromus Florae peninsulae Balcanicae* (*Introducing Flora of the Balkan Penisula*), in part published posthumously, remains a standard botanical work and was republished in 1970. It was characterized in the 1970 republication as "monumental" ([Germany: Otto Koeltz Verlag], i).
16. UCLA, 397-8.
17. Ibid., 23.
18. Frank Johnson, "The Facts of Hayek," *Daily Telegraph Magazine* (September 26, 1975), 33.
19. *HH*, 40.
20. Johnson, *Daily Telegraph*, 32.
21. UCLA, 20.
22. *HH*, 41.
23. *NS*, 52.
24. UCLA, 22.
25. *HH*, 39.
26. "Obituary: Hayek's Life and Times," *Economic Affairs* (June 1992), 20.

CHAPTER 2

1. Karl Popper, *Unended Quest* (Great Britain: Fontana, 1982), 13-5.
2. UCLA, 21-2.
3. 3. *HH*, 46.
4. Streissler, Erich (ed.), *Roads to Freedom: Essays in Honour of Friedrich A. von Hayek* (New York: Augustus M. Kelley, 1969), xi.
5. Hayek, by choice, did not make friends readily. Outside of family, the only individuals with whom he had a "du" relationship in German (the familiar form of "you") were childhood friend Magg, fellow officers during World War I, fellow University of Vienna student Fürth, and Popper.
6. Charlotte Cubitt diary, June 13, 1983.
7. UCLA, 175.
8. *HH*, 153.
9. Unpublished autobiographical notes in the possession of Charlotte Cubitt.
10. CLA, 71.
11. Ibid., 11.

CHAPTER 3

1. UCLA, 2.
2. Ibid., 1-2.
3. Hayek-North/Skousen interview.
4. *CW* IV, 20-1.
5. UCLA, 12.

6. Ibid.
7. *CW* IV, 20.
8. *HH,* 48.
9. Johnson, *Daily Telegraph,* 33.
10. UCLA, 248, 174.
11. *CW* IV, 62.
12. In Bettina Bien Greaves, *Austrian Economics: An Anthology* (Irvington-on-Hudson, N.Y.: Foundation for Economic Education, 1996), 47.
13. *CW* IV, 62.
14. Carl Menger, *Principles of Economics* (Grove City, Penn.: Libertarian Press, 1994), 55-7.
15. *CW* IV, 79.
16. *CRS,* 83.
17. Carl Menger, *Investigations into the Method of the Social Sciences with Special Reference to Economics* (New York University Press, 1985), 149; 151; 130.
18. Hayek-North/Skousen interview.
19. UCLA, 49-50.
20. *KES,* 18.
21. Joseph Schumpeter, *Ten Great Economists* (London: George Allen & Unwin), 80, 83-4.
22. Ibid., 84.
23. Menger, *Principles of Economics,* 49.
24. UCLA, 13-4.
25. Ibid., 25.
26. *CW* IV, 173.
27. UCLA, 24-5.
28. Ibid., 27-8.
29. Ibid., 25, 28.
30. Ibid., 29.
31. Ibid., 27-30.
32. IEA, 13.
33. Hayek-North/Skousen interview.
34. *NS,* 52.
35. Hayek-Shehadi interview.

CHAPTER 4

1. UCLA, 26.
2. Ibid., 373.
3. Ibid., 374.
4. *CW* IV, 35.
5. Letwin-Ebenstein interview.
6. *HH,* 22
7. *CW* V, 8.
8. Ibid.
9. *MCF,* 1.
10. F. A. Hayek, "Germany's Finance," *New York Times* (August 19, 1923).
11. UCLA, 373.
12. Ibid., 25-6.

CHAPTER 5

1. UCLA, 409.
2. Ibid., 273.
3. *KES,* 17.
4. UCLA, 273.
5. Hayek-Greaves interview.
6. Earlene Craver, "The Emigration of Austrian Economists," *History of Political Economy* (Spring 1986), 16.
7. Stephan Boehm, "The Private Seminar of Ludwig von Mises" (paper presented at History of Economics Society, May 1984 meeting), 2.
8. Hayek-Greaves interview.
9. UCLA, 37; 17. According to Smith, who was in personal communication with Hayek, Hayek "seriously considered joining the Vienna circle" (Barry Smith, *Austrian Philosophy: The Legacy of Franz Brentano* [Chicago: Open Court, 1994], 304).
10. *MCF,* 1.
11. UCLA, 176. According to Ebeling: "It is not meant to detract from Hayek's own contributions to suggest that many areas in which he later made his profoundly important mark were initially stimulated by . . . Mises. This is most certainly true of Hayek's work in monetary and business-cycle theory, his criticisms of socialism and the interventionist state, and in some of his writings on the methodology of the social sciences" ("Friedrich A. Hayek: A Centenary Appreciation," *Freeman* [May 1999], 29).
12. In T. W. Hutchison, *The Politics and Philosophy of Economics: Marxians, Keynesians and Austrians* (New York University Press, 1981), 206.
13. Ludwig von Mises, *The Ultimate Foundations of Economic Science* (Princeton, N.J.: Van Nostrand, 1962), 71. Cf. Ebeling: "Hayek followed Wieser and Mises in distinguishing between the natural and social sciences on the basis of their sources of knowledge" (*Austrian Economics: A Reader* [Hillsdale, Mich.: Hillsdale College Press, 1991], 48); Hutchison: "Wieser was the predecessor whom Mises most closely followed with regard to the 'necessity' and certainty of the results of introspection" ("Hayek and 'Modern Austrian' Methodology," *History of Economic Thought and Methodology* [1992], 20); Eamonn Butler: "Although Mises wrote disparagingly of Wieser, he did absorb Wieser's 'psychological method,' the point that the economist has a 'huge advantage' over the natural scientist because he or she can draw on 'inner observation' to understand directly the values and purposes that motivate individuals" (*Ludwig von Mises: Fountainhead of the Modern Microeconomic Revolution* [Hants, England: Gower, 1988], 331); and Lawrence White: "Mises not only claims that praxeology provides aprioristic truth, but also that it 'conveys exact and precise knowledge of real things.' As Wieser attempted to do, Mises must forge a bridge from his deductions to the real world" (*Methodology of the Austrian School* [New York: Center for Libertarian Studies, 1977], 9).
14. Ludwig von Mises, *Socialism* (Indianapolis: Liberty*Classics,* 1981), 12.
15. Ibid., 13.
16. Ibid., 461.
17. Ibid., 13-14.
18. Ibid., 460-1.
19. Ludwig von Mises, *Human Action,* 3rd ed. (Chicago: Contemporary Books, 1966 ed.), 880.
20. UCLA, 136.

21. In Mises, *Socialism*, xix-xx.
22. *KES*, 18.
23. *MCF*, 2.
24. UCLA, 377.
25. *MCF*, 2-3.
26. Ibid., 27-8. Greaves maintains of Austrian trade cycle theory that there "can be no doubt that it must be attributed to Mises, not Hayek" (February 18, 1999 letter to author). She emphasizes in addition to Mises' *The Theory of Money and Credit* his *Monetary Stabilization and Cyclical Policy* (1928); and Mises' presentation in these books resembles some (though not all) of Hayek's presentation.

    The conventional approach in the Austrian movement in post-Keynesian economics is to ascribe Austrian trade cycle theory jointly to Mises and Hayek. Murray Rothbard wrote that Hayek "develop[ed] Mises' insights into a systemic business cycle theory" and referred to "Mises-Hayek cycle theory" (in Ludwig von Mises, *The Theory of Money and Credit* [Indianapolis: Liberty Fund, 1980], 15-16). Alexander Shand wrote in his 1984 *The Capitalist Alternative: An Introduction to Neo-Austrian Economics:* "The importance of Mises' theory is that it was upon it that Hayek developed his theory of the trade cycle which has become almost synonymous with the neo-Austrian approach" ([New York University Press], 149). According to Kirzner: "Hayek's vigorous exposition and extensive development of the theory . . . unmistakably left [his] imprint on the fully developed theory" (Israel Kirzner, *The Meaning of Market Process: Essays in the Development of Modern Austrian Economics* [London: Routledge, 1992], 63).
27. Hayek-Greaves interview.
28. Ludwig von Mises, *Notes and Recollections* (South Holland, Ill.: Libertarian Press, 1978), 97-8.
29. In Margit von Mises, *My Years with Ludwig von Mises* (Cedar Falls, Iowa: Center for Futures Education, 1984), 205-7.
30. Ibid., 203.
31. Friedrich Engel-Janosi, . . . *aber ein stolzer Bettler: Erinnerungen aus einer verlorenen Generation* (Graz, Austria: Styria, 1974), 112 (trans. by Andrew Ebenstein).
32. *CW IV*, 154-5.
33. UCLA, 180. Friedman has written in response to a query from Mark Skousen: "I believe Ludwig von Mises was certainly of a quality that would have made him an entirely appropriate recipient of a Nobel Prize" in Economics (Friedman letter to Mark Skousen, March 5, 1996). Mises comes off well in his correspondence with Hayek, which extended over decades (in extant, accessible form), and was typically in English though occasionally in German. Mises was a particularly frequent correspondent to Hayek during the early 1940s just after he came to the United States. Hayek helped Mises to resolve his affairs in Europe. Mises typically wrote Hayek in letters of beautiful, old-fashioned handwriting, and would begin with such salutations as "My dear friend" or "My dear Professor Hayek." Hayek always wrote, "Dear Professor Mises."

    On July 27, 1944, Mises wrote Hayek that *The Road to Serfdom* was "really excellent." He noted that "even before the publication of the American edition your success in this country is remarkable." Several references had been published in the *New York Times*.

    On December 1, 1944, Mises wrote Hayek that *The Road to Serfdom*, which by this time had been published by the University of Chicago Press, "has had a tremendous success in this country. . . . But don't be mistaken. The Veblen-Hansen ideology dominates public opinion in this country no less than does the Laski-Keynes ideology in Great Britain." Mises remarked in a December 22, 1940 letter that he was "sorry to learn" that Keynes and Marx were "the idols of youth in this hemisphere too," the "other favourites" being "your colleague L[aski] and Bertrand R[ussell]. . . . Is it not dreadful?"

Mises wrote Hayek in February 1945 that the "news of your impending lecture tour is very gratifying. It is almost a public sensation. You probably do not realize how great the success of your book is and how popular you are in this county. The newspaper-men will watch all your steps and publicize all your dicta" (HA, 38-24).

Hugh Gaitskell, a future leader of the British Labour Party, had an unfavorable recollection of Mises when he visited Vienna (apparently in part on Hayek's advice) and attended Mises' seminar during the early 1930s: "There is no discussion. He is just incapable of it. There's one exception—the *English* are allowed to speak . . . but if any Austrian or German student raises his voice Mises shuts him up at once" (in P. M. Williams, *Hugh Gaitskell: A Political Biography* [London: Jonathan Cape, 1979], 53).

34. Paul Silverman, *Law and Economics in Interwar Vienna: Kelsen, Mises, and the Regeneration of Austrian Liberalism,* Ph.D. thesis (University of Chicago, 1984), 834.
35. Hayek-Greaves interview.
36. Hayek could be indignant in later years when it was suggested that he left Austria as a refugee.
37. Margit von Mises, 41.
38. Ibid., 17.
39. *MCF,* 2.
40. Ibid., 3.
41. In Cockett, 24.
42. Obituary of August von Hayek by K. Fritsch, *Mitt. Nat. Ver. Steirermark* (Graz, 64-5).
43. Robbins, 91.
44. *CW* IV, 129.
45. In Margit von Mises, 205.
46. William Johnston, *The Austrian Mind* (Berkeley: University of California Press, 1972), 402.
47. In *London Times* (May 9, 1985).
48. *CW* IV, 145-6. Hayek praised Mises greatly on a number of occasions. He concluded his introduction to Mises' *Notes and Recollections:* "That they had one of the great thinkers of our time in their midst, the Viennese have never understood" (*CW* IV, 159). He remarked of Mises in a 1978 lecture: "There is no single man to whom I owe more intellectually" (*KES,* 17).

CHAPTER 6

1. Robert Skidelsky, *The World After Communism: A Polemic for Our Times* (London: Macmillan, 1995), 70-1.
2. *CW* IX, 85.
3. *CW* IV, 29.
4. *Studies,* 195-6.
5. In Alan Ebenstein, *Edwin Cannan: Liberal Doyen* (London: Routledge/Thoemmes, 1997), 392.
6. *LSE,* 6.
7. Edwin Cannan, *The Economic Outlook* (London: Routledge/Thoemmes, 1997), 11, 13.
8. Edwin Cannan, *Elementary Political Economy* (London: Routledge/Thoemmes, 1997), 119.

9. Ibid., 133.

10. Hayek-Shehadi interview.

11. Ibid. Cannan had enough exposure to Hayek's views to express a joking opinion of them in an early 1930s letter to his friend C. R. Fay, commenting on the LSE economics department: "I'm still busy over the 'nature of saving.' That fellow Hayek has corrupted them all, and ought to be deported" (in Alan Ebenstein, *Edwin Cannan,* 359).

12. In Ebenstein, *Edwin Cannan,* 332.

13. Joseph Schumpeter, *History of Economic Analysis* (Great Britain: Allen & Unwin, 1954), 1120-21.

14. John Strachey, *The Nature of Capitalist Crisis* (London: Victor Gollancz, 1935), 58.

15. John Hicks, *Critical Essays in Monetary Theory* (Oxford University Press, 1967), 204.

16. Richard F. Kahn, *The Making of Keynes' General Theory* (Cambridge University Press, 1984) 181-2.

17. Hayek-Shehadi interview.

18. *CW* IX, 119-20.

19. Robert Skidelsky, *John Maynard Keynes: The Economist as Saviour* (London: Penguin, 1992), 456.

20. Hayek-North/Skousen interview.

21. Robbins, 127.

22. Hayek-North/Skousen interview.

23. William Ebenstein, *Political Thought in Perspective* (New York: McGraw Hill, 1957), 335.

24. Isaac Kramnick and Barry Sheerman, *Harold Laski: A Life on the Left* (London: Allen Lane, 1993), 320.

25. Ibid., 589.

26. Milton and Rose D. Friedman, *Two Lucky People: Memoirs* (University of Chicago Press, 1998), 257.

27. *Fatal Conceit* draft version in the possession of Charlotte Cubitt.

28. F. A. Hayek, "Hayek on Laski," *Encounter* (June 1984), 80.

29. UCLA, 113; *HH,* 85; UCLA, 113.

30. Kramnick, 501.

31. Ibid., 2.

32. In Michael Newman, *Harold Laski: A Political Biography* (London: Macmillan, 1993), 355. A standing joke at LSE was that Hayek's seminar produced socialists, and Laski's, liberals.

33. Robbins, 87.

34. "LSE," 6.

35. UCLA, 113.

36. In Ralf Dahrendorf, *LSE* (Oxford University Press, 1995), 42.

37. Lord Beveridge, *Power and Influence* (New York: Beechhurst Press, 1955), 170.

38. Robbins, 137.

CHAPTER 7

1. Robbins, 119.

2. Hayek-North/Skousen interview.

3. Robbins, 132-3.

4. Ibid., 133-4.

5. Gerard Koot, "An Alternative to Marshall: Economic History and Applied Economics at the Early LSE," *Atlantic Economic Journal* (March 1982), 3.

6. Skidelsky, *Keynes: Saviour,* 368.

7. *CW* IX, 122.

8. Ibid., 121; 122; 128.

9. Ibid., 128.

10. Ibid., 154. Keynes editor Donald Moggridge observes that Hayek to some extent invited Keynes' critique of *Prices and Production,* for Hayek referred readers to it in his review of *A Treatise on Money:* "If at any point my own analysis seems to English readers to take too much for granted, perhaps I may be permitted to refer to my *Prices and Production* in which I have attempted to provide a broad outline of the general theoretical considerations which seem to me indispensable" (*CW* IX, 122-3; Moggridge, *Maynard Keynes: An Economist's Biography* [London: Routledge, 1992], 534). Keynes remarked in his review article, "Reading Dr. Hayek's *Economica* article in the light of his book *Prices and Production,* I fancy that I see at last where the stumbling block really is" (*CW* IX, 151).

11. *CW* IX, 159.

12. Kahn, 181.

13. John Maynard Keynes, *The General Theory of Employment, Interest, and Money* (New York: Harcourt Brace Jovanovich, 1953), 20.

14. In Fritz Machlup (ed.), *Essays on Hayek* (New York University Press, 1975), 61.

15. John Hicks, *Value and Capital,* 2nd ed. (Oxford University Press, 1946), vi.

16. John Hicks, *Money, Interest and Wages, Collected Essays on Economic Theory,* vol. II (Harvard University Press, 1982), 3.

17. Ronald Coase, *Essays on Economics and Economists* (University of Chicago Press, 1994), 211.

18. Correspondence between Arthur Seldon and author, October 17, 1997. Seldon continues: "By 1946 Hayek had become the most formidable champion of classical liberalism at the LSE (and the world?)" (ibid.).

19. *Studies,* 196. Hayek commented in an interview, in the context of his distinction between "two types of mind": "That describes very much the relation between me and Robbins. He was the absolute master of his subject, and what he had read he remembered. . . . I never remembered; I always had to think it out anew, which led me sometimes to original ideas. While Robbins . . . had really few original ideas. He was much the better teacher, he was a brilliant lecturer, strong and clear, but not what I call a puzzler" (Hayek-Shehadi interview).

20. Arthur Lewis, in William Breit and Roger W. Spencer (eds.), *Lives of the Laureates,* 2nd ed. (Cambridge, Mass.: MIT Press, 1990), 3.

21. Kaldor-Shehadi interview.

22. *New Palgrave,* vol. III, 167.

23. Arthur Seldon, "Professor F. A. Hayek-Obituary," *Independent* (March 25, 1992), 33.

24. Coase, *Essays,* op. cit., 213.

25. Ronald Coase, in Breit and Spencer, *Lives of the Laureates,* 3rd ed. (Cambridge, Mass.: MIT Press, 1995), 231.

26. Seldon-Ebenstein interview.

27. Robbins, 126-7.

28. Arnold Plant, "A Tribute to Hayek—The Rational Persuader," *Economic Age* (Jan.-Feb., 1970), 5.

29. *CL,* 455.

30. *Studies,* 196; 195.

31. Robbins, 131.

32. UCLA, 364-5. Transcript corrected from audiovisual tape.

33. Plant, "A Tribute to Hayek," 5-6.

34. Robbins, 131-2; fragment of poem, William Wordsworth, *The Prelude, Book xi.*

35. *HH,* 81.

CHAPTER 8

1. Colin Clark, "The 'Golden' Age of the Great Economists," *Encounter* (June 1977), 81.
2. John Maynard Keynes, *The Economic Consequences of the Peace* (New York: Penguin Books, 1988), 10-2.
3. In Skidelsky, *Keynes: Savior,* 235.
4. Ibid., 521.
5. Keynes, *Economic Consequences,* 254.
6. *HH,* 89; *CW* IX, 240.
7. Robert Skidelsky, *John Maynard Keynes: Hopes Betrayed* (London: Macmillan, 1983), 1.
8. In *CW* IX, 29.
9. Keynes *CW* V, 178.
10. Ibid.
11. Keynes *CW* XIII, 243.
12. Bert Tieben and Willem Keizer write that it is "argued that Hayek deliberately sought this conflict [with Keynes] to establish himself as a leading theorist" (Willem Keizer, et al., *Austrian Economics in Debate* [London: Routledge, 1997], 11). According to G. Mongiovi: "Hayek saw his review of the *Treatise* as an opportunity to draw attention to his own ideas about the trade cycle," also noting Hayek's "profoundly unfavorable review of Keynes' *Treatise*" (G. Mongiovi, "Keynes, Hayek and Sraffa: On the Origins of Chapter 17 of *The General Theory,*" *Economie Appliquée* [1990, no. 2], 135, 133).
13. Keynes *CW* XIII, 265. Friedman has characterized Hayek and Keynes' correspondence, originally published in the Keynes *Collected Works:* "Hayek comes out very badly in those letters, in my opinion. Keynes comes out like the kindly, generous uncle, while Hayek comes out like a very arrogant, self-centered young man, which he was" (Friedman-Ebenstein interview).
14. Keynes *CW* XIII, 265.
15. *CW* IX, 173.
16. Skidelsky, *Keynes: Saviour,* 459.
17. Ibid.
18. Keynes *CW* XIII, 90.
19. Skidelsky, *Keynes: Saviour,* 459.
20. Keynes *CW* XXVII, 385. Keynes took a camouflaged shot at Hayek in *The General Theory:*

> It has been usual to suppose that an increase in the quantity of money has a tendency to reduce the rate of interest . . . [The neo-classical school has] inferred that there must be *two* sources of supply to meet the investment demand-schedule; namely, savings proper . . . *plus* the sum made available by any increase in the quantity of money . . . This leads on to the idea that there is a "natural" or "neutral" or "equilibrium" rate of interest, namely, that rate of interest which equates investment to classical savings proper without any addition from "forced savings"; and finally to what, assuming they are on the right track at the start, is the most obvious solution of all, namely, that, if the quantity of money could only be kept *constant* in all circumstances, none of these complications would arise, since the evils supposed to result from the supposed excess of investment over savings proper would cease to be possible. But at this point we are in deep water. "The wild duck has dived down to the bottom—as deep as she can get—

and bitten fast hold of the weed and tangle and all the rubbish that is down there, and it would need an extraordinarily clever dog to dive after and fish her up again." [*General Theory*, 182-3]

Chicago economist Harry Johnson, who was a student and lecturer at Cambridge, wrote in a reminiscence titled "Cambridge as an Academic Environment in the Early 1930s" that the "older, pre-*General Theory* Cambridge style was much gentler and more sophisticated, though it had the same basic ingredients: concentration on criticism of the work of a few eminent British economists, often not identified directly by name and reference (a scathing attack on Hayek in the *General Theory,* for example, is indexed under 'wild duck')" (in Don Patinkin and J. Clark Leith, *Keynes, Cambridge and* The General Theory (University of Toronto Press, 1978), 112.

21. *CW* IX, 221-2.
22. In Willem Keizer, et al., 96.
23. Kurt Leube and Albert Zlabinger, *The Political Economy of Freedom: Essays in Honor of F. A. Hayek* (Munich: Philosophia Verlag, 1984), 9.
24. Stephan Boehm, "L. M. Lachmann (1906-1990): A Personal Tribute," *Review of Political Theory* (July 1991), 366. In an interview with William Bartley, Lachmann said that there never was a debate between Keynes and Hayek (Bartley-Lachmann interview, in LSE archives with Nadim Shehadi interviews).
25. Hicks, *Critical Essays,* 205.
26. *Studies,* 345.
27. *CW* IX, 228.
28. Coase-Ebenstein interview.

CHAPTER 9

1. LSE history archive file.
2. Theodore Draimin correspondence to author, August 2, 1995.
3. In Joan Abse (ed.), *My LSE* (London: Robson Books, 1977).
4. In Don Patinkin and J. Clark Leith (eds.), *Keynes, Cambridge and* The General Theory (University ofToronto Press, 1978), 74.
5. P. M. Toms correspondence to author, August 4, 1995.
6. Vera Hewitt correspondence to author, August 4, 1995.
7. In Patinkin and Leith, 40.
8. John Hicks, *Money Interest and Wages; Collected Essays on Economic Theory,* vol. 2 (Harvard University Press, 1982), 3.
9. *PP,* 94.
10. Ibid., 114.
11. Ibid., 118-9.
12. *MTTC,* 19.
13. Ibid., 20.
14. *PP,* 162.

CHAPTER 10

1. Hayek mistakenly recalled that Keynes told him, after he wrote *A Treatise on Money,* that he no longer believed in the ideas in it. Rather, as Keynes wrote Hayek in a March 29, 1932 letter responding to a question from Hayek about whether Keynes would reply

to the second half of Hayek's review of *A Treatise on Money* in *Economica:* "I doubt if I shall return to the charge. . . . I am trying to re-shape and improve my central position, and that is probably a better way to spend one's time than in controversy" (*CW* IX, 173). Cf. Skidelsky: "There is no support in this exchange for Hayek's later claim that 'after the appearance of the second part of my article, Keynes told me that in the meantime he had changed his mind and no longer believed what he said [in the *Treatise*]'" (*Keynes: Savior,* 458-9).

After World War II, Robbins recanted his earlier Misesianism and Hayekianism in technical economics, though he retained a strong market emphasis. Robbins later explained what he thought was wrong with his and Hayek's early 1930s approach:

> Now I still think that there is much in this theory as an explanation of a *possible* generation of boom and crisis. But, as an explanation of what was going on in the early '30s, I now think it was misleading. Whatever the genetic factors of the pre - 1929 boom, their *sequelae,* in the sense of inappropriate investments fostered by wrong expectations, were completely swamped by vast deflationary forces sweeping away all those elements of constancy in the situation which otherwise might have provided a framework for an explanation in . . . [our] terms. The theory was inadequate to the facts.
>
> Nor was this approach any more adequate as a guide to policy. Confronted with the freezing deflation of those days, the idea that the prime essential was the writing down of mistaken investments and the easing of capital markets by fostering the disposition to save and reducing the pressure on consumption was completely inappropriate. To treat what developed subsequently in the way which I then thought valid was as unsuitable as denying blankets and stimulants to a drunk who has fallen into an icy pond, on the ground that his original trouble was overheating. [Robbins, 154]

Hayek's critics at the time said that his theory amounted to a contention that there existed in Britain during the Great Depression what they pejoratively referred to as "Hayeks"—half completed capital projects littering the countryside.

2. Patrick Deutscher, *R. G. Hawtrey and the Development of Macroeconomics* (London: Macmillan, 1990), 190-1, 194.
3. Keynes, *General Theory,* 379-80.
4. In William and Alan Ebenstein, *Great Political Thinkers,* 6th ed. (Fort Worth, Tex.: Harcourt, 2000), 805. *The Middle Way* was the title of a popular 1938 book by future British Conservative prime minister Harold Macmillan. Another popular work of about this time was Marquis Childs' *Sweden: The Middle Way* (1936).
5. Friedman-Ebenstein interview.
6. *PTC,* v.
7. Ibid., 4.
8. *HH,* 78.
9. Ibid.
10. Ibid.
11. Ibid.
12. Hayek-Shehadi interview.
13. *HH,* 80.
14. Brian McCormick, *Hayek and the Keynesian Avalanche* (New York: St. Martin's Press, 1992), 45-7, 136.

15. Hayek-Shehadi interview.
16. Sudha Shenoy provides a thumbnail sketch of Austrian capital theory:

> Austrian capital theory views capital not as a homogeneous stock but as a network of interrelated goods: a diversified structure of complementary elements, rather than a uniform lump. The process of production is seen as occurring in a series of "stages", extending from final consumption to stages successively further removed. . . .
>
> . . . [A] miscellaneous jumble of non-consumption goods will *not necessarily* raise final output. Individual capital investments . . . must fit into an integrated capital structure, completed to the final consumption stage, if they are to add to final consumption output. Investments that do not form such an integrated structure are (or become) *mal*-investments yielding capital and operating losses. . . .
>
> The essential role of prices . . . only if there exist markets in which prices reflect (changing) relative scarcities of the different sorts of capital goods involved can the capital structure as a whole be integrated, and mal-investments be revealed. [in F. A. Hayek, *Full Employment at Any Price?* (London: IEA, 1975), 51-2]

17. G. L. S. Shackle, *Business, Time and Thought* (New York University Press, 1988), 179, 173, 181, 180. John Hicks later remarked of Hayek's technical economic thought: "Something, one has long realized, had gone wrong with it; but just what?" (Hicks, *Critical Essays,* ix). Trade cycle historian Robert Aaron Gordon commented that the "monetary overinvestment theory in the particular form developed by the Austrian School is a highly sophisticated explanation which impresses the reader both by its theoretical subtlety and also by its lack of touch with reality" (*Business Fluctuations,* 2nd ed. [New York: Harper & Brothers, 1961], 358).
18. Christine Hayek-Ebenstein interview.

CHAPTER 11

1. *London Observer* (March 29, 1992). Galbraith also recalls in his autobiography of his sojourn at LSE: "I attended the seminars of Friedrich von Hayek and Lionel Robbins— seminar in each case being a conventional term that described a convocation of some seventy-five or hundred contentiously articulate and deeply dissenting participants from all over the globe. Most notably present were the recent migrants from the repressive regimes in Germany, Austria, Hungary and Poland" (J. K. Galbraith, *A Life in Our Times* [Boston: Houghton Mifflin, 1981], 78).
2. Hayek-Shehadi interview.
3. Beatrice Webb, *The Diary of Beatrice Webb,* vol. 4 (ed. Norman and Jeanne MacKenzie) (London: Virago Press, 1985), 372.
4. Robbins, 143-4.
5. Breit and Spencer, *Lives of the Laureates,* 4.
6. Fowler-Ebenstein interview.
7. Coase-Ebenstein interview.
8. Elizabeth Durbin, *New Jerusalems: The Labour Party and the Economics of Democratic Socialism* (London: Routledge & Kegan Paul, 1985), 108.

9. *MNIS,* xiii.

10. Ibid., 73.

11. Mark Skousen, *The Structure of Production* (New York University Press, 1990), 266.

12. *MNIS* xi, xii, xiii, 94.

CHAPTER 12

1. Henry W. Spiegel, *The Growth of Economic Thought* (Englewood Cliffs, N.J.: Prentice-Hall, 1971), 539.

2. In *CEP,* 87-8.

3. February 18, 1999 correspondence from Bettina Bien Greaves to author.

4. Mises, *Human Action,* 698.

5. In *CEP,* 110.

6. In Karen Vaughn, *Austrian Economics in America* (Cambridge University Press, 1994), 50.

7. Richard Ebeling, "An Interview with Friedrich Hayek," *Libertarian Review* (September 1977), 11.

8. UCLA, 225-6.

9. UCLA, 415.

10. *CW* III, 19, 26, 32.

11. *IEO,* 121.

12. *CRS,* 122. Kirzner remarks concerning "the possibility of economic calculation under socialism" that the "writers who affirmed this possibility . . . apparently did so on the assumption that the central planning authorities would already possess all necessary information. But of course it is precisely the mobilization of information which is under debate" (*Competition and Market Entrepreneurship* [University of Chicago Press, 1973], 230-1).

13. *IEO,* 174.

14. In *CEP,* 118.

15. *CEP,* 219.

16. *IEO,* 175.

17. *RS,* 30.

18. *CEP,* 202.

19. Decades later, Hayek returned to the socialist calculation debate. In 1982, he sent Seldon a letter saying that he was "particularly indignant about the steadily repeated silly talk of Lange having refuted Mises" (in *Hayek's 'Serfdom' Revisited* [London: IEA, 1984], xxvi), and enclosing a piece he suggested for publication by the Institute of Economic Affairs. Hayek commenced this article: "There is endless repetition of the claim that Professor Oskar Lange . . . refuted the contention advanced . . . by Ludwig von Mises that 'economic calculation is impossible in a socialist society.' The claim rests wholly on theoretical argument by . . . Lange in little more than two pages. . . . It will be timely to analyse this argument:

> Professor Mises' contention that a socialist economy cannot solve the problems of rational allocation of its resources is based on a confusion concerning the nature of prices. As Wicksteed has pointed out, the term "price" has two meanings. It may mean either price in the ordinary sense, i.e. the exchange ratio of two commodities on a market, or it may have the generalized meaning of "terms on which alternatives are offered." Wicksteed says, "'Price,' then, in the narrower sense of "the money for

which a material thing, a service, or a privilege can be obtained," is simply a special case of "price" in the wider sense of "the terms on which alternatives are offered to us." It is only prices in the generalized sense which are indispensable to solving the problem of the allocation of resources.

"Wicksteed's honest warning that for the purposes of analysis he would use the term 'price' in a wider sense in no way indicates that those quasi-prices can generally operate as substitutes for the money prices where they are known. . . . That the 'alternatives which are offered to us' become known to us in most instances only as *money* prices is Mises' chief argument" (in Chiaki Nishiyama and Kurt R. Leube [eds.], *The Essence of Hayek* [Stanford, Cal.: Hoover Institution Press, 1984], 53-4.). Seldon noted that in this late contribution, Hayek was "fairly aggressive, certainly more so than in his younger or middle years" (*Hayek's 'Serfdom' Revisited,* xxvii).

CHAPTER 13

1. *IEO,* 50, 54.
2. Hayek held in "The Facts of the Social Sciences," employing a Wieserian and Misesian methodology: "While at the world of nature we look from the outside, we look at the world of society from the inside" (*IEO,* 76). The idea of a priori knowledge is prominent in Germanic idealist philosophy, tracing its path through Immanuel Kant, whose central problem in *Critique of Pure Reason* was to establish how "synthetic a priori" judgments can exist. Barry Smith writes: "German philosophy is determined primarily by its orientation around epistemology: attention is directed not to the world, but to our knowledge of the world" (*Austrian Philosophy: The Legacy of Franz Brentano* [Chicago: Open Court, 1994], 4). Kant, Hegel, Mises, Wittgenstein, Hayek, and thinkers generally in the Germanic philosophical tradition emphasize mind.
3. *IEO,* 41.
4. Ibid., 42.
5. *PTC,* 14.
6. John Stuart Mill, *Principles of Political Economy,* vol. II (New York: Colonial Press, 1899), 259-61.
7. *IEO,* 44-5.
8. Ibid., 51, 42.
9. Kirzner, *Competition and Market Entrepreneurship,* 218-9.
10. *CW* IV, 55-6.
11. UCLA, 57-8.
12. In T. W. Hutchinson, "Hayek and 'Modern Austrian' Methodology," *Research in the History of Economic Thought and Methodology,* vol. 10 (JAI Press, 1992), 23.
13. *CW* IX, 62.
14. *HH,* 79.
15. Milton Friedman, *The Essence of Friedman* (Stanford: Hoover Institution Press, 1987), 22.
16. *IEO,* 77-8.
17. Ibid., 134-5.
18. *LLL* I, 45-6.
19. Ibid., 91.
20. *HH,* 80-1.
21. Hayek-North/Skousen interview.

22. UCLA, 425-6. Hayek remarked in "Economics and Knowledge" that "quite a number of . . . recent attempts . . . to push theoretical investigations beyond the limits of traditional equilibrium analysis" involved questions of "foresight," and that "[t]he stimulus which was exercised in this connection by the work of Frank H. Knight may yet prove to have a profound influence far beyond its special field" (*IEO*, 33-4).
23. *Studies*, 91-2.

CHAPTER 14

1. *CW* X, 36.
2. *HH*, 137.
3. Robbins, 168.
4. Winston Churchill, *Their Finest Hour* (Boston: Houghton Mifflin, 1949), 25.
5. Larry Hayek-Ebenstein interview.
6. In Joan Abse (ed.), *My LSE* (London: Robson Books, 1977), 47.
7. "LSE," 28.
8. *CW* IX, 244-5.
9. Hayek-North/Skousen interview. War or no war, even in the truncated fourth part of *The Pure Theory of Capital*, Hayek criticized Keynes: "I cannot help regarding the increasing concentration on short-run effects . . . not only as a serious and dangerous intellectual error, but as a betrayal of the main duty of the economist and a grave menace to our civilisation. . . . It is not surprising that Mr. Keynes finds his views anticipated by the mercantilist writers and gifted amateurs. . . . Are we not even told that, 'since in the long run we are all dead,' policy should be guided entirely by short-run considerations? I fear that these believers in the principle of *apres nous le déluge* may get what they have bargained for sooner than they wish" (409-10).

   Hayek ultimately came to favor incremental interest rate adjustments to guide national economic production. He wrote in *Profits, Interest and Investment* (1939) that "what amount of changes in the rate of interest would be necessary to prevent the recurrence of cumulative processes in either direction [toward overinvestment or underinvestment] we do not know because such a policy has never been tried. And it is, of course, true that in the absence of an automatic mechanism making rates of interest move with rates of profits it would require superhuman wisdom to adjust them perfectly by deliberate policy. But this by no means proves that we might not get much nearer to the ideal than we have done. If we have to steer a car along a narrow road between two walls, we can either keep it in the middle of the road by fairly frequent but small movements of the steering wheel; or we can wait longer when the car deviates to one side and then bring it back by more or less violent jerks, probably overshooting the mark and risking collision with the other wall; or we can try to keep the steering wheel stiff and let the car bang alternately into either wall with a good chance of leading the car and ourselves to ultimate destruction" (*PII*, 69-71). When most of his fellow economists had come to emphasize fiscal policy, Hayek continued to emphasize monetary policy.

   The answer to the question of why Hayek did not write a review of or response to Keynes' *General Theory* is apparently mostly that he was writing his own treatise, what became *The Pure Theory of Capital*. Hayek said that he worked on *The Pure Theory of Capital* for seven years; the preface is dated June 1940, so this means he could have been working on it as early as mid-1933, over two years before *The General Theory* was published in February 1936. Hayek's own major project was well underway before *The General Theory* appeared. According to Bruce Caldwell: "Rather than interrupt his effort in order to spar with Keynes, he [Hayek] decided to continue working on his own model. . . . This, in my opinion, . . . is the principal reason why he decided not to review *The General Theory*" ("Why Didn't Hayek Review Keynes's *General Theory?*," *History of Political Economy* [Winter 1998], 564). Cf. Mark Blaug: "What Hayek was really doing in the late 1930s was writing *The Pure Theory of Capital*" (in Bruce Caldwell [ed.], *Carl Menger and His Economic Legacy* [Durham, N.C.: Duke University Press, 1990], 187).

10. *HH,* 99.
11. UCLA, 228.
12. F. A. Hayek, *The Counter-Revolution of Science* (Indianapolis: Liberty*Press,* 1979), 9.
13. Ancient Greeks believed that *hubris,* arrogance, was punished by *Nemesis,* the goddess of retribution, particularly of human presumption.
14. *IEO,* 6-7.
15. F. A. Hayek, "The Counter-Revolution of Science," Part I, *Economica* (February, 1941), 9.
16. *IEO,* 9.
17. *CRS,* 121.
18. Ibid.
19. *RS,* 18.
20. *CRS,* 136.
21. Ibid., 194.

CHAPTER 15

1. *HH,* 98.
2. "LSE," 29.
3. Kingsley Martin, *Harold Laski* (London: Victor Gollancz Ltd., 1953), 128-9.
4. Joan Abse, *My LSE.*
5. Ian Gilbert, "LSE at Cambridge," *LSE Magazine* (Winter 1999), 28.
6. Geoffrey Stern, "Anne Bohm," *LSE Magazine* (n.d.), 26.
7. July 10, 1995 letter from Eric Rose to author.
8. *CRS,* 31.
9. Ibid., 70.
10. Ibid., 39.
11. *Studies,* 34.

CHAPTER 16

1. *RS,* 1.
2. *CW* X, 135-6.
3. *RS,* 1.
4. Ibid., viii.
5. Ibid., 3.
6. UCLA, 106.
7. Ibid., 76.
8. *HH,* 101.
9. Karl Mannheim, *Man and Society in an Age of Reconstruction* (London: Kegan Paul, 1940), 4, 193, 350.

10. In *RS*, 144.

11. Herman Finer, *Road to Reaction* (Boston: Little, Brown and Co., 1946), 5.

12. Friedrich Hayek, "Freedom and the Economic System," *Contemporary Review*, 438; *RS*, 10.

13. *RS*, vi.

14. Ibid., v.

15. In William Ebenstein, *Today's Isms: Communism, Fascism, Capitalism, Socialism* (Englewood Cliffs, N.J.: Prentice-Hall, 1973), 214.

16. *RS*, 53.

17. Ibid., 52-3.

18. *The Federalist*, no. 51.

19. In his presentation of the limited inherent value of democracy—and of the manner in which demand for democracy came to replace concern for individual liberty—Hayek followed John Stuart Mill, who held in *On Liberty:* "A time . . . came, in the progress of human affairs, when men ceased to think it a necessity of nature that their governors should be an independent power, opposed in interest to themselves. It appeared to them much better that the various magistrates of the State should be their tenants or delegates, revocable at their pleasure. In that way alone, it seemed, could they have complete security that the powers of government would never be abused to their disadvantage. By degrees this new demand for elective and temporary rulers became the prominent object of the exertions of the popular party, wherever any such party existed; and superseded, to a considerable extent, the previous efforts to limit the power of the rulers. As the struggle proceeded for making the ruling power emanate from the periodical choice of the ruled, some persons began to think that too much importance had been attached to the limitation of the power itself. *That* (it might seem) was a resource against rulers whose interests were habitually opposed to those of the people. What was now wanted was, that the rulers should be identified with the people; that their interest and will should be the interest and will of the nation. The nation did not need to be protected against its own will. There was no fear of its tyrannising over itself" (in William Ebenstein, *Great Political Thinkers*, 587). Like Mill, Hayek feared that a nation could tyrannize over itself. See chapter 24 here on Mill for more discussion of this passage and Hayek's later misinterpretation of it.

20. Hayek, "Freedom and the Economic System," 440.

21. In Jim Powell, *The Triumph of Liberty* (New York: Free Press, 2000), 364.

22. Ibid., 66.

23. Ibid., 68.

24. Ibid., 177.

25. Ibid., 15, 11.

26. Jeremy Bentham, *An Introduction to the Principles of Morals and Legislation* (London: Methuen, 1982), 12.

27. *RS*, 11.

28. Ibid.

29. Ibid.

30. Ibid., 54.

31. Ibid., 13.

32. Ibid., 60, 29.

33. *CW* X, 194-5.

34. *RS*, 27.

35. Ibid., 13.

36. University of Chicago Roundtable, "The Road to Serfdom," a radio discussion by Friedrich Hayek, Maynard Krueger, and Charles E. Merriam, 581st broadcast in cooperation with the National Broadcasting Company, No. 370 (April 22, 1945).
37. In Cockett, 101.
38. University of Chicago Roundtable.
39. *RS*, 161-2.
40. Ibid., vii.

CHAPTER 17

1. *Studies*, 217.
2. Cockett, 85.
3. In ibid.
4. Ibid., 78.
5. Ibid.
6. HA, 106-8.
7. Cockett, 80.
8. Cockett, 81.
9. UCLA, 229. Wootton testified to Hayek's academic collegiality in her *Freedom under Planning* (1945), a contemporary response to themes in *The Road to Serfdom:* "I have also to thank Professor F. A. Hayek for his kindness in letting me have an early view of his *Road to Serfdom.* Much of what I have written is devoted to criticism of the views put forward by Professor Hayek in this and other books. Intellectual controversy on serious practical and political issues is not always conducted in an atmosphere of personal goodwill. It is on that account the greater pleasure to express here my appreciation and reciprocation of the unchanging friendliness of Professor Hayek's attitude" ([Chapel Hill: University of North Carolina Press], v). Not all of his academic interactions were so friendly. Herman Finer wrote in a footnote in *Road to Reaction* concerning Hayek's discussion of the rule of law: "I had hoped to avoid personal reminiscence, but it is impossible in view of Hayek's evasiveness. When he first breached his peculiar personal idea of the Rule of Law and Planning to the author and a few friends . . . all who heard him, being scholars of world repute, immediately denounced his history of the Rule of Law as false" (48-9).
10. UCLA, 228-9.
11. April 4, 1944 letter from Keynes to Hayek, LSE archive.
12. Keynes *CW* XXVII, 385-7.
13. George Orwell, *As I Please, 1943-1945* (New York, 1968), 117-9.
14. Arthur Cecil Pigou, back cover of *IEO*.
15. R. H. Tawney, *The Attack and Other Papers* (New York: Harcourt Brace, 1953), 93.
16. *Studies*, 217.
17. Ibid., 217-8.
18. William Miller, *The Book Industry,* 12.
19. W. T. Couch, "The Sainted Book Burners," *Freeman* (April 1955), 423.
20. Friedman-Ebenstein interview.
21. Miller, *The Book Industry,* 11.
22. In Hartwell, 23.
23. In C. Hartley Grattan, "Hayek's Hayride: Or, Have You Read a Good Book Lately?," *Harper's* (July 1945), 48
24. Jim Powell, "*The Road to Serfdom*—Inside Story of a 50-Year Phenomenon," *Laissez Faire Books* (October 1994), 9.

25. Grattan, "Hayek's Hayride," 48.
26. In Friedrich Hayek, *The Road to Serfdom* (University of Chicago Press, 1994), xviii.
27. John Chamberlain, *A Life with the Printed Word* (Chicago: Regnery Gateway, 1982), 125.
28. In Hayek, *The Road to Serfdom* (University of Chicago Press, 1944), v-vi.
29. Henry Hazlitt, *New York Times Book Review* (September 24, 1944).
30. In Hayek, *The Road to Serfdom* (University of Chicago Press, 1994), xviii-xix.
31. UCLA, 464-6 (cf. *HH,* 105).
32. Lawrence Frank, "The Rising Stock of Dr. Hayek," *Saturday Review* (May 12, 1945), 5.
33. "Poor Mr. Hayek," *New Republic* (April 23, 1945), 543.
34. Stuart Chase, "Back to Grandfather," *Nation* (May 19, 1945), 565.
35. Finer, *Road to Reaction,* xii, citations on back cover of *IEO.*
36. William Ebenstein, *Man and the State: Modern Political Ideas* (New York: Rinehart, 1947), 471. In a later work, Ebenstein described *The Constitution of Liberty* as "[t]he most scholarly and best argued case for the free-enterprise system based on constitutional government and the rule of law available in English" (*Modern Political Thought: The Great Issues,* 2nd ed. [New York: Holt, Rinehart and Winston, 1960], 854). Hayek referred to the latter work in *Law, Legislation and Liberty* (*LLL* III, 193).
37. In Kramnick, 481.
38. Harold Macmillan, *Tides of Fortune, 1945-1955* (New York: Harper & Row, 1969), 32.
39. In Kramnick, 483. Hayek later said that as if to "provide an illustration for my remarks on the nationalist tendencies of socialism, [Labour leaders] attacked the book [*The Road to Serfdom*] on the ground that it was written by a foreigner" (*Studies,* 217). Churchill began his speech preceding Attlee's, though, by saying that he wanted to inform his listeners about "this continental conception of human society called socialism" (in Kramnick, 481). Attlee received a copy of *The Road to Serfdom* in spring 1944 (Cockett, 92).
40. *HH,* 106-7.
41. *Manchester Guardian* (June 6, 1945).
42. *Evening News* (June 6, 1945).
43. *Sunday Graphic* (June 17, 1945).
44. In Kramnick, 484.
45. Ibid., 484-5.
46. Kramnick, 482.
47. Cockett, 95-6.

CHAPTER 18

1. *CW* III, 46, 48.
2. HA, 105-10.
3. HA, 106-4. Interestingly, given his later efforts to revive the intellectual tradition of the University of Vienna, Hayek suggested that the English-speaking college of social studies to re-educate German leaders should be located in Vienna.
4. HA, 106-10. Hayek remarked decades later when asked about *The Road to Serfdom*'s origins that, "basically, there was no difference between socialism and fascism" (IEA, 26).
5. *CW* IV, 203.
6. Ibid., 208.
7. Ibid., 215.

8. *CW* IV, 191.

9. Cockett, 9. Lippmann's work suggested to Hayek the title of the second part of his intended The Abuse and Decline of Reason. He quoted Lippmann in *The Road to Serfdom:* "'The generation to which we belong is now learning from experience what happens when men retreat from freedom to a coercive organization of their affairs. Though they promise themselves a more abundant life, they must in practice renounce it; as the organized direction increases, the variety of ends must give way to uniformity. That is *the nemesis of the planned society* and the authoritarian principle in human affairs [emphasis added]'" (in *RS,* 21).

10. *CW* IV, 192.

11. Cockett, 102-3.

12. In ibid., 104.

13. *IEO,* 194.

14. Later members of the Mont Pelerin Society to receive the Nobel Prize in Economic Sciences are James Buchanan, Ronald Coase, and Gary Becker.

15. Greg Kaza, "The Mont Pelerin Society's 50th Anniversary," *The Freeman* (June 1997), 347-8.

16. *CW* IV, 237-8.

17. Hartwell, 38.

18. E. R. Noderer, "7 Nations Map Freedom Fight in Secret Talk," *Chicago Tribune* (April 3, 1947).

19. Cockett, 116.

20. Friedman-Ebenstein interview.

21. In Fritz Machlup (ed.), *Essays on Hayek* (Hillsdale, Mich.: Hillsdale College Press, 1976), xii-xiii. A preliminary version of what became a Mont Pelerin Society Statement of Aims that was drafted with Hayek's participation was more influenced by him:

> 1. Individual freedom can be preserved only in a society in which an effective competitive market is the main agency for the direction of economic activity. Only the decentralization of control through private property . . . can prevent those concentrations of power which threaten individual freedom.
>
> 2. The freedom of the consumer in choosing what he shall buy, the freedom of the worker in choosing his occupation and his place of employment, are essential. . . .
>
> 5. The preservation of an effective competitive order depends upon a proper legal and institutional framework. The existing framework must be considerably modified to make the operation of competition more efficient and beneficial. . . .
>
> 10. . . . Complete intellectual freedom is so essential to the fulfillment of all our aims that no consideration of social expediency must ever be allowed to impair it. [in Hartwell, 49-50]

Hayek emphasized the importance of freedom of speech and other forms of expression. Kaldor once remarked that he remembered Hayek telling him that "academic freedom was so important a principle that they [LSE] must tolerate Laski, whatever nuisance he is" (Kaldor-Shehadi interview). Given Hayek's views of Laski, and Kaldor's of Hayek, this statement is of particular relevance.

22. *HH,* 133.

23. UCLA, 126-7.

24. Cockett, 115.

25. Jewkes wrote in prefacing his British best-selling *Ordeal by Planning* (Macmillan, 1948) criticizing the postwar Labour government: "Everything that I have to say here, and indeed much more, is to be found in Professor Hayek's masterly *Road to Serfdom*" (ix).

26. *CW* IV, 192. Friedman emphasizes the significance of Hayek's founding of the Mont Pelerin Society. He writes in his memoirs that "[i]n the early decades, the society played an important role in enabling individuals who were intellectually isolated in their own countries to spend a week or so with a group of like-minded intellectuals. . . . The collegial atmosphere was not so important for those of us from the U.S., because there were more partisans of free markets and free enterprise here than in most other countries. But it was extremely important for Europeans, and later, for Japanese and Latin Americans"(*Two Lucky People,* 333). Joseph Schumpeter provided the following early appraisal of the Mont Pelerin Society's effectiveness, when, after listing various socialist policies, he wrote in 1949 that "I believe . . . there is a mountain in Switzerland on which congresses of economists have been held which express disapproval of all or most of these things. But these anathemata have not even provoked attack" (in Antonio Martino, "Ideas and the Future of Liberty," in Hardy Bouillon [ed.], *Libertarians and Liberalism* [Adershot, Engl: Ashgate Publishing, 1996], 288).

CHAPTER 19

1. *HH,* 126.

2. Ibid., 125.

3. UCLA, 138-9.

4. Ibid., 152.

5. In D. J. O'Connor, *A Critical History of Western Philosophy* (New York: Free Press, 1964), 497.

6. *CL,* 64.

7. *HH,* 62.

8. F. A. Hayek, in Walter Weimer and David Palermo (eds.), *Cognition and Symbolic Processes,* vol. 2 (Hillsdale, N.J.: Lawrence Erlbaum Associates, 1982), 287-8.

9. *SO,* 165.

10. *CRS,* 208.

11. Ibid., 272.

12. *SO,* v.

13. *HH,* 153.

14. UCLA, 153.

15. In Weimer and Palermo, 325.

16. *SO,* xviii.

17. In Bruce Caldwell, "Hayek and Socialism," *Journal of Economic Literature* (December 1997), 1856.

18. London *Times,* (May 9, 1983).

19. UCLA, 229.

20. UCLA, 182.

21. Coase-Ebenstein interview.

22. Friedman-Ebenstein interview.
23. *HH,* 125.
24. Synopsis of November 2, 1947 letter from Hayek to L. B. Miller provided by Charlotte Cubitt.
25. *CL,* 395.
26. *CW* IX, 46.
27. *Studies,* 217.
28. *HH,* 105.

CHAPTER 20

1. In Cockett, 28.
2. Ibid., 120.
3. Karl Popper, in Stephen F. Frowen (ed.), *Hayek: Economist and Social Philosopher* (Great Britain: Macmillan, 1997), 311.
4. Ian Jarvie and Sandra Pralong (eds.), *Popper's* Open Society *After Fifty Years* (London: Routledge, 1999), 21.
5. Ibid., 22.
6. Popper, *Unended Quest,* 120.
7. The only other books Hayek dedicated at all were *The Road to Serfdom* and *The Constitution of Liberty.*
8. UCLA, 16-20.
9. Terence Hutchison, *The Politics and Philosophy of Economics: Marxians, Keynesians and Austrians* (New York University Press, 1981), 213-4; *CEP,* 11.
10. Terence Hutchison, "Hayek and 'Modern Austrian' Methodology," *Research in the History of Economic Thought and Methodology* (JAI Press, 1992), 21.
11. Ibid., 30.
12. Popper, in Frowen, 311. Hayek provided the following interesting summary of his conception of the development of the idea of spontaneous order from Smith and Menger in a footnote to "The Results of Human Action but not of Human Design":

> The more recent revival of this conception seems to date from my own article on "Scientism and the Study of Society" where I argued that the aim of social studies is "to explain the unintended or undesigned results of many men." From this it appears to have been adopted by Karl Popper, "The Poverty of Historicism," where he speaks of "the undesigned results of human action" and adds in a note that "undesigned social institutions may emerge as *unintended consequences of rational actions* . . . (I cannot agree, however, with . . . [Popper's] statement . . . based on a suggestion of Karl Polanyi, that "it was Marx who first conceived social theory as the study of the *unwanted social repercussions of nearly all our actions."* The idea was clearly expressed by Adam Ferguson and Adam Smith, to mention only the authors to whom Marx was unquestionably indebted.) [*Studies,* 100]

13. Marjorie Grice-Hutchinson, "Luncheon Address–Reflections on F. A. Hayek, R. S. Sayers and Spain" (n.d.), LSE archive, 3-4.
14. Ibid.
15. July 8, 1995 correspondence from Henry Toch to author. According to Joan Abse, another former student: "Professor Hayek's lecture on economics often defeated me

(do I dream or did he really stand on chairs or pile them on top of each other to illustrate his points?)" (Joan Abse [ed.], *My LSE* [London: Robson Books, 1977], 11). Kari Leavitt, a socialist student and later academic, remembers that as "we knew him then, he was very central European, had a very large mustache, and at that time spoke in very heavily accented English, and he had a habit of lecturing with his back to the students and his face to the blackboard, which he covered with enormous amounts of diagrams with chalk flying all over everything including his suit. So as a lecturer he was not very successful at that time. I would say that he was simply totally irrelevant, and that he was considered generally as something from the past, just a museum piece" (in Brian Crowley [author and compiler], transcript of "The Ideas of F. A. Hayek," Canadian Broadcasting System [n.d.], 12).

16. Cockett, 82.
17. Ibid., 82
18. Jeremy Shearmur, *Hayek and After* (London: Routledge, 1996), 64, 229.
19. Ibid., 64.
20. In Jarvie and Pralong, *Popper's* Open Society *After Fifty Years,* 26.
21. Malachi Haim Hacohen, *Karl Popper—The Formative Years, 1902-1945* (Cambridge University Press, 2000), 462, 486.
22. In Ibid., 486.
23. Ibid., 502
24. Ibid., 502, 501.
25. Jeremy Shearmur, *The Political Thought of Karl Popper* (London: Routledge, 1996), 22, 27.
26. Michael H. Lessnoff, *Political Philosophers of the Twentieth Century* (Oxford: Blackwell, 1999), 148.
27. *SPPE,* viii.
28. In Cockett, 84.
29. University of Chicago Roundtable.
30. UCLA, 422-3.
31. *RS,* 156-7.
32. *CL,* 79.
33. *RS,* 52.

CHAPTER 21

1. *HH,* 137.
2. HA, 58-116; Popper Archive, Hoover Institute, Stanford University, 305-14.
3. HA, 37-39.
4. Kane-Ebenstein interview.
5. UCLA, 394-5.
6. Ibid., 395 (VHS tape version). Hayek broke down crying when he heard of his first wife's death.

CHAPTER 22

1. Hayek-Shehadi interview.
2. *New Palgrave,* vol. III, 139. Friedman writes in a letter that "[w]ith respect to the Chicago school, I believe there is a sense in which it dates back to James Laurence Laughlin's appointment as head of the Department of Economics. Throughout the

whole period from then to now, there has been a real distinction between the
Department of Economics on the one hand and the Chicago school of economics on the
other" (October 20, 2000 letter from Friedman to author, in the possession of author).

3. *New Palgrave,* vol. III, 55.

4. Edward Shils (ed.), *Remembering the University of Chicago* (University of Chicago
   Press, 1991), 244.

5. In Breit and Spencer, 83.

6. Spiegel, 642.

7. Breit and Spencer, 83.

8. George J. Stigler, *Memoirs of an Unregulated Economist* (New York: Basic Books,
   1988), 148.

9. John Nef, *The Search for Meaning* (Washington, D.C., 1973), 37. Chicago University
   historian William McNeill calls *The Search for Meaning* a "confused and confusing
   autobiographical essay written in old age" (*Hutchins' University* [University of
   Chicago Press, 1991], 179).

10. Friedman-Ebenstein interview.

11. Ibid.

12. Johnson-Ebenstein interview.

13. Hayek-North/Skousen interview.

14. Hayek-Shehadi interview.

15. UCLA, 182.

16. George Nash, *The Conservative Intellectual Movement in America* (New York: Basic
    Books, 1976), 20, 353.

17. UCLA, 124-5. Knight, Friedman, Stigler, and Director were charter members of the
    Mont Pelerin Society. In a 1981 discussion including Milton and Rose Friedman,
    George Stigler, Ronald Coase, and Aaron Director, the participants mention Hayek's
    appointment on the Committee on Social Thought and other circumstances that might
    have influenced this appointment. They note that the economics department or
    administration at Chicago turned down Franklin D. Roosevelt "brain trust" member
    and adviser Rexford Tugwell and George Stigler about the time Hayek was suggested
    for the economics department, and Henry Simons did not receive a position in the
    department but instead was given a post in the law school. Friedman himself would not
    have come to Chicago in 1946 if it had been up to the economics department, who
    preferred Stigler. As well, Director came to the law school at Chicago in 1946, not the
    economics department (and like Hayek, through the Volcker Fund). Hayek stayed with
    Director, who is Rose Friedman's brother, when he came to the United States in January
    1950. Director originally suggested to Nef that Hayek come to the University of
    Chicago through the Committee on Social Thought, and, Director recalled, Nef
    "carried it through" (in Edmund W. Kitch [ed.], "The Fire of Truth: A Remembrance
    of Law and Economics at Chicago, 1932-1970," *Journal of Law and Economics* [April
    1983], 188).

18. *HH,* 128, 126.

19. *CL,* 3.

20. *Studies,* 253.

21. In a 1981 review greatly praising Thomas Sowell's *Knowledge and Decisions,* Hayek
    wrote that "I now hope I have not done more harm than good by expressing my
    considered view . . . so frankly. But I trust the time is past when it was possible, as
    happened 32 years ago at a meeting of the American Economic Association, for an
    unknown young author whom I congratulated on the achievement of a book of his I had
    just read to afterwards be teased by his friends for having been seen receiving the kiss

of death" ("The Best Book on General Economics in Many a Year," *Reason* [December 1981], 49).

22. UCLA, 130-1. The question of the development of the explicit "Chicago school of economics" is uncertain. While some, in retrospect, tie this development to Knight, this was not necessarily the case at the time. Stigler wrote in his autobiography that

> Professor Viner and his students . . . have testified that they had not encountered the name or the belief that there was a distinctive Chicago School during this early period [the 1930s and 1940s], and I have found no hints of such a belief in the economics profession before about 1950, and no widespread recognition of the school for another five years. . . . By the 1960s, however, the profession had widely agreed that there was a Chicago School of Economics. Edward H. Chamberlin had written a chapter on the Chicago School . . . in 1957, the earliest such explicit essay I have found. . . . H. Lawrence Miller wrote perhaps the first comprehensive article on the school and its central views in 1962" (*Memoirs*, 149-50).

> Viner wrote in a 1969 letter that it was

> not until after I left Chicago in 1946 that I began to hear rumors about a "Chicago School" which was engaged in *organized* battle for laissez faire and "quantity theory of money" and against "imperfect competition" theorizing and "Keynesianism." I remained sceptical about this until I attended a conference sponsored by University of Chicago professors in 1951. . . . From then on, I was willing to consider the existence of a "Chicago School" (but not one confined to the economics department and not embracing all of the department) and that this "School" had been in operation, and had won many able disciples, for years before I left Chicago. But at no time was I consciously a member of it (in Don Patinkin, *Essays On and In the Chicago Tradition* [Durham, N.C.: Duke University Press, 1981], 266).

In the general public mind (as distinct from the economics profession), the emergence of the explicit "Chicago school of economics" is tied to the rise of Friedman's fame during the 1960s.

CHAPTER 23

1. *HH*, 126.
2. McNeill, 120-1.
3. HA, 3-14
4. Grene-Ebenstein interview.
5. Mary Ann Dzuback, *Robert M. Hutchins: Portrait of an Educator* (University of Chicago Press, 1991), 215.
6. In Machlup, 147. Gary Becker also participated in Hayek's Chicago seminar.
7. In Leo Szilard, 94-5.
8. In Machlup, 148.
9. Hayek-Shehadi interview.
10. Friedman-Ebenstein interview.

11. Grene-Ebenstein interview.
12. Eugene Miller, in Robert Cunningham (ed.), *Liberty and the Rule of Law* (Texas A & M Press, 1979), 242-3.
13. June 26, 1995 correspondence from James Vice to author.
14. August 29, 1995 correspondence from Stanley Heywood to author.
15. In John Raybould (comp.), *Hayek: A Commemorative Album* (London: Adam Smith Institute, 1998), 70.
16. Ronald Hamowy, "F. A. Hayek, on the Occasion of the Centenary of His Birth," *Cato Journal* (Fall 1999), 285.
17. August 24, 1995 correspondence from Richard Stern to author.
18. May 1, 1996 correspondence from Todd Breyfogle to author.
19. Hayek-Shehadi interview.

CHAPTER 24

1. *HH,* 140.
2. In John Stuart Mill, *The Spirit of the Age* (Chicago, 1942), xxxiii.
3. *JSMHT,* 15; 33; 83; 16.
4. *RS,* 5.
5. *CL,* 8; 30; 222, 492; 220.
6. Ibid., 113.
7. Ibid., 402.
8. Ibid., 223, 492.
9. Ibid., 376, 526.
10. Ibid., 394.
11. *HH,* 129.
12. John Robson, *The Improvement of Mankind* (University of Toronto Press, 1968), 51, 53.
13. Ruth Borchard, *John Stuart Mill the Man* (London: Watts, 1957), ix.
14. Michael St. John Packe, *The Life of John Stuart Mill* (London: Secker and Warburg, 1954), xii.
15. Ibid., xiv.
16. *Collected Works of John Stuart Mill,* vol. 12, vii.
17. Ibid., xxiv.
18. Robert L. Cunningham (ed.), *Liberty and the Rule of Law* (Texas A&M University Press, 1979), ix.
19. Norman Barry, *Hayek's Social and Economic Philosophy* (London: Macmillan, 1979), 70.
20. John Gray, *Hayek on Liberty* (Oxford: Basil Blackwell, 1984), 149.
21. *LLL* II, 63-4.
22. Ibid., 111, 186.
23. *LLL* III, 3.
24. Ibid.
25. Ibid., 178.
26. See chapter 16, note 19.
27. In William Ebenstein, *Great Political Thinkers,* 587.
28. *CL,* 107.
29. Ibid., 444.
30. *FC,* 149.
31. In *CL,* 502-3.

32. Mill, *Principles of Political Economy*, 443-4.
33. In William Ebenstein, *Great Political Thinkers*, 614.
34. In Andrew Gamble, *Hayek: The Iron Cage of Liberty* (Cambridge, England: Polity Press, 1996), 133-4.
35. Hartwell, 95-6.
36. John Davenport, Mont Pelerin Society newsletter (n.d.), 7.
37. In Nash, 182.
38. In Hartwell, 219.
39. James Buchanan, "I Did Not Call Him 'Fritz': Personal Recollections of Professor F. A. v. Hayek," *Constitutional Political Economy* (vol. 3, no. 2, 1992), 130.
40. Gandil-Ebenstein interview.
41. Friedman-Ebenstein interview.
42. UCLA, 412.
43. *SO*, ix. Hella Hayek translated Hayek's 1931 edition of Richard Cantillon's *Essai sur la nature du commerce en général* into German.
44. HA, 56-116.
45. *RS*, 160.
46. UCLA, 253.

CHAPTER 25

1. *HH*, 129.
2. HA, 28-29.
3. *HH*, 129-30.
4. Friedrich Hayek, *The Counter-Revolution of Science* (Indianapolis: Liberty Press, 1979), 12.
5. *CL*, 11.
6. Ibid., 416.
7. In ibid., 162.
8. In *RS*, 62.
9. *CL*, 208. Hayek approvingly quoted F. W. Maitland in *The Constitution of Liberty*: "Known general laws, however bad, interfere less with freedom than decisions based on no previously known rule" (449).
10. Ibid., 13.
11. Ibid., 52-3.
12. Ibid., 46-7.
13. Ibid., 42, 44.
14. Thomas Hobbes, *Leviathan* (Oxford: Basil Blackwell, 1946), 80. Hobbes is not typically considered a liberal thinker, but his emphasis on philosophical realism helped prepare the way for later British empiricists in the liberal tradition.
15. John Locke, *An Essay Concerning Human Understanding*, vol. 1 (New York: Dover, 1959), 121-2; *Second Treatise of Civil Government* (Oxford: Basil Blackwell, 1946), 4-5.
16. In Steven Fraser (ed.), *The Bell Curve Wars* (New York: Basic Books, 1995), 98.
17. *CL*, 31.
18. Ibid., 86-7.
19. *CL*, 87.
20. IEA, 30.
21. Ronald Hamowy, "Hayek's Concept of Freedom: A Critique," *New Individualist Review* (April, 1961), 32-4.

22. Friedrich Hayek, "Freedom and Coercion: A Reply to Mr. Hamowy," *New Individualist Review* (Summer 1961), 70-2.
23. Hamowy, 32.
24. Hayek, "Freedom and Coercion," op. cit., 70.
25. Ibid.
26. *CL,* 22.
27. Ibid., 24, 39.
28. *CL,* 23.
29. Ibid., 69.
30. Ludwig von Mises, "Liberty and Its Antithesis," *Christian Economics* (August 1, 1960), 1, 3.
31. UCLA, 230.
32. Raymond Moley, "Book Offers Clue to Nixon's Creed, *Chicago Daily News* (August 10, 1960).
33. HA, 62-67.
34. Sydney Hook, *New York Times Book Review* (February 21, 1960), 28.
35. John Davenport, "An Unrepentant Old Whig," *Fortune* (March 1960), 134.
36. George Morgenstern, *Chicago Sunday Tribune Magazine of Books* (February 14, 1960).
37. Arthur Kemp, *Journal of the American Medical Association* (February 20, 1960), 125.
38. "The Busy Nibblers at Individualism," *Wall Street Journal* (June 8, 1960).
39. Lionel Robbins, *Economica* (February 1961); 67, 69-70.
40. *Studies,* 222.
41. *CL,* 404-5.
42. Ibid., 410-1.
43. Ibid., 411.

CHAPTER 26

1. In *CL,* 112-3.
2. *MN,* xii.
3. *CRS,* 206.
4. *CL,* 411.
5. In *LLL* I, 161.
6. *DM,* 17.
7. John Maynard Keynes, *The General Theory,* 383-4; cf. *IEO,* 108.
8. *CL,* 112.
9. Ibid.
10. Lee Edwards, *Goldwater* (Washington, D.C.: Regnery, 1995), 274, 281.
11. Barry Goldwater, *Goldwater* (New York: Doubleday, 1988), 110.
12. Barry Goldwater, *The Conscience of a Conservative* (Washington, D.C.: Regnery, 1990), 7. Buckley and Bozell write: "Not only is it *characteristic* to create institutions and to defend them with sanctions. Societies *must* do so—or else they cease to exist. The members of a society must share certain values if that society is to cohere" (in Nash, 107).
13. Ronald Reagan, *An American Life* (Norwalk, Conn.: Eaton Press, 1990); 142. Reagan described himself as a "libertarian" in a 1975 appearance on CBS's "60 Minutes" (in John L. Kelly, *Bringing the Market Back In* [New York University Press, 1997], 134). When challenged by then–Libertarian Party chairman Ed Crane on his use of the term, Reagan replied: "I have used the expression on some occasions that libertarianism is at

the very heart of conservatism. That's libertarianism with a small 'l' and makes no reference to your party. I don't believe that anything I have said can be confusing to Libertarian Party members, but certainly the conservative approach to individual freedom, in contrast to the liberal's big government philosophy, gives validity to my use of the word" (ibid., 134-5).

14. Roland Evans and Robert Novak, *The Reagan Revolution* (New York: E. P. Dutton, 1981), 229. According to Reagan advisor Martin Anderson: "For over twenty years he [Reagan] observed the American economy, [and] read and studied the writings of some of the best economists in the world, including the giants of the free market economy— Ludwig von Mises, Friedrich Hayek and Milton Friedman" (Martin Anderson, *Revolution* [Orlando, Fl.: Harcourt Brace Jovanovich, 1988], 164). Reagan reporter Lou Cannon writes of this statement, though: "This is an exaggeration" (*President Reagan: The Role of a Lifetime* [New York: Simon & Schuster, 1991], 238).

15. Kelley, 226.

16. Meese-Ebenstein interview.

17. HA, 3-11.

18. David Stockman, *The Triumph of Politics* (New York: Avon, 1987), 33.

19. Elizabeth Durbin writes of historical interest in Hayek from the left in Britain: "Many socialists, including [Evan] Durbin, Kaldor and Lerner, were strongly influenced by Hayek's theories" (*New Jerusalems,* 108).

20. Cannon, 282.

21. *HH,* 131.

22. Frank Johnson, "The Facts of Hayek," *Daily Telegraph Magazine* (September 26, 1975), 32.

23. Horowitz-Ebenstein interview.

24. *HH,* 131.

25. Hayek-Shehadi interview.

26. Friedman-Ebenstein interview.

27. Milton Friedman, in *New Individualist Review* (Indianapolis, Liberty Press, 1981), ix-x.

28. Both the Heritage Foundation and the Cato Institute funded secretarial assistance for Hayek during the 1980s. There is an auditorium named after Hayek at the Cato Institute.

29. HA, 9-21.

30. Ayau-Ebenstein interview.

31. Larry Hayek-Ebenstein interview.

32. Hartwell, 82.

33. Ibid., 97.

34. In ibid., 102.

35. Ibid., 108.

36. Ibid.

37. Ibid., 109.

38. Ibid., 116.

39. James Buchanan, "I Did Not Call Him 'Fritz,'" 131.

40. *CW* IX, 255.

41. HA, 114.3.

42. HA, 116.10.

43. In Margit von Mises, 215-6.

44. IEA, 28.

CHAPTER 27

1. Esca Hayek–Ebenstein interview.
2. *HH,* 131.
3. Ibid.
4. *LLL* I, 2.
5. *LLL* III, xiii.
6. In Jeremy Shearmur, *Hayek and After,* 89.
7. *HH,* 28.
8. *CL,* 493.
9. A. P. d'Entreves, *Natural Law* (London: Hutchinson University Library, 1951), 85-6.
10. *Sunday Telegraph* (September 30, 1962).
11. *Studies,* 251.
12. Ibid., 251-2.
13. *HH,* 131.
14. *Studies,* 251.

CHAPTER 28

1. In William Ebenstein, *Great Political Thinkers,* 391.
2. UCLA, 457-8.
3. In William Ebenstein, *Great Political Thinkers,* 364.
4. *DM,* 84.
5. Ibid., 132.
6. *LLL* III, 152.
7. *DM,* 132-3.
8. *LLL* III, 43.
9. *LLL* III, 62.
10. *CL,* 22.
11. Ibid., 451.
12. *LLL* II, 57.

CHAPTER 29

1. Skidelsky, *Keynes: Saviour,* 457.
2. In Stephen Frowen (ed.), *Hayek: Economist and Social Philosopher A Critical Retrospect* (Great Britain: Macmillan, 1997), 1-6.
3. Hayek's early 1930s lecture file "The Marxian Theory of Crises" has twenty pages of notes and a bibliography including works by Marx, Hilferding, Tougan-Baranovsky, and Spiethoff. Regarding Tougan-Baranovsky (who based his work on Marx), Hayek wrote in his lecture notes that his "work was first published in 1894. . . . It has probably had a more profound influence on modern trade cycle theory than any other single book." Hayek wrote as lecture points on book II of Marx's *Capital*: "magnificent wealth of material," "almost in the position of Adam Smith in general economics," "no exposition without interpretation possible," "but also no interpretation where I have not the authority of some Marxian writer on my side" (file in the possession of Charlotte Cubitt).

4. In Ben Seligman, *Main Currents in Modern Economics* (New Brunswick, N.J.: Transaction Publishers, 1990), 63.

5. Karl Kühne, *Economics and Marxism* (New York: St. Martin's Press, 1979); vol. I, 44; vol. II, 222-3.

6. *MTTC,* 41.

7. Ibid.

8. In addition to those identified in the main text, others who observe similarities between Hayek's (or Austrian) and Marx's economic thought include:

> Chris Sciabarra: "Business Cycle Theory: Marxian-Hayekian Parallels . . . Marx's description of capitalist crisis . . . [i]n many significant ways . . . resembles the Hayekian-Austrian theory of the business cycle" (*Marx, Hayek, and Utopia* [Albany: State University of New York Press, 1995], 76).

> Frank Vorhies: "For those familiar with the Austrian-school analysis of the business cycle, Marx's theory will appear strikingly similar. . . . Marx argued that central banking brought about the very instability it was supposed to correct. . . . Both Marx and the Austrians focus on the monetary factors behind capitalist economic crises, pinpointing the destabilizing effects of artificial credit expansion made possible by central banking" ("Marx on Money and Crises," *Critical Review* [Summer/Fall, 1989], 533, 538-9).

> Alexander Shand: "Hayek's analysis of the origin of trade depression . . . resembles that of Marx" (*The Capitalist Alternative,* 157).

> Peter Rosner: "Hilferding, . . . a follower of Marx, and Hayek . . . rely on similar theories of capital while constructing a theory of business cycles. . . . Hayek wanted to demonstrate that any policy to interfere with the business fluctuations is at best useless. . . . [H]e considered business cycles to be inevitable, due to money creation through the banking system . . . Hilferding's *Finance Capital* served a similar purpose. . . . There is no way for the working class to influence events" ("A Note on the Theories of Business Cycle of Hilferding and by Hayek," *History of Political Economy* [Summer, 1988], 316-7).

> Joseph Schumpeter: "The Böhm-Bawerkian theory of interest and . . . period of production are only two elements in a comprehensive model of the economic process, the roots of which may be discerned in Ricardo and which parallels that of Marx" (*A History of Economic Analysis* [originally 1954], 846).

9. *PTC,* 425-6.

10. File in possession of Charlotte Cubitt.

11. *PP,* 101, 103.

12. Michael Perelman, *Marx's Crises Theory: Scarcity, Labor and Finance* (New York: Praeger, 1987), 183.

13. Ibid., 216-7.

14. *PP,* 101.

15. Karl Marx, *Communist Manifesto,* first chapter.

16. Ibid.
17. Ibid.
18. *CW* III, 121.
19. *NS*, 269.
20. *FC*, 124.
21. *LLL* III, 54.
22. *LLL* I, 23.
23. *LLL* III, 132.
24. *FC*, 24.
25. *LLL* I, 153; ibid., 23.
26. *DN*, 132-3.
27. *LLL* III, 63-4.
28. *Studies*, 194.
29. *LLL* III, 146.
30. *CL*, 352.
31. UCLA, 319. In *The Constitution of Liberty*, Hayek remarked on "competition between municipalities" (*CL*, 352). From the *polis* to the *polis?*
32. *LLL* I, 65.
33. Ibid., 64-5.
34. Ibid., 62.

CHAPTER 30

1. Hans Kelsen, *The Pure Theory of Law* (Berkeley: University of California Press, 1970), 4. .
2. *LLL* I, 99.
3. Ibid., 44.
4. *CL*, 160-1.
5. *LLL* I, 1.
6. Hayek remarked in *Law, Legislation and Liberty* that the "insight into the significance of our . . . ignorance in the economic sphere, and into the methods by which we have learnt to overcome this obstacle, was . . . the starting point for those ideas which in the present book are systematically applied to a much wider field" (*LLL* I, 13).
7. Ibid., 9.
8. *CW* X, 134.
9. UCLA, 274-5, 148, 81.
10. *LLL* I, 14.
11. Ibid., 49; "Moral Imperative of the Market," 147.
12. Mill, *On Liberty,* 68.
13. *CL*, 146.
14. Ibid., 62-3; *HH,* 24.
15. *CL*, 146-7.
16. Cockett, 110.
17. *CW* IV, 13-4.
18. *New Palgrave,* vol. II, 188.
19. UCLA, 341.
20. *CW* IV, 193-4.
21. Ibid., 189, 191.
22. *Studies,* 253, 252.
23. *CW* IV, 190.

24. *Studies,* 200.
25. Henry Hazlitt, back cover of Wilhelm Röpke, *A Humane Economy* (Indianapolis: Liberty Fund, 1971).
26. Ibid.
27. *CW* IV, 192.
28. *Encounter,* 55.
29. *LLL* II, 180.
30. London *Times* (December 31, 1976).
31. *RS,* viii.
32. Hayek's position on an acceptable extent of government has often been noted, and criticized:

> The key distinction for Hayek was not big government versus small government, but between a government of laws in which all coercive action is constrained by general and impartial rules, and a government of men in which coercion may be arbitrarily exercised to achieve whatever ends the government, or even the majority on whose behalf it acts, wishes to accomplish. Though Hayek contemplated with little enthusiasm the absorption by the state of a third or more of national income, the amount and character of government spending were to him very much a secondary issue that directly involved no fundamental principle. [David Glasner, *Commentary* (October 1992), 50]
>
> Taxation as a proportion of national income is a rough measure of the domains of collective versus individual sovereignty over material resources. It sounds almost like deadpan black humor to state that "except for raising the means," government need not rely on coercion to render services. . . . There is an infinity of services to be rendered; they all satisfy some need. How much should be provided? We are in an ideological void in which minimal state, maximal state and anything in between are equally admissible. [Anthony de Jasay, *Critical Review* (Spring, 1989), 296]
>
> He allows as a proper exercise in government the grant of national minimum support to those who for any reason cannot support themselves; but he does not indicate what rule, if any, would regulate the level of this grant. He even gives the impression that in this, as in other matters, so long as the provision applies equally to the whole class the level is a matter for government discretion. [Geoffrey Vickers, "Controls for Freedom," *Futures* (August 1979), 347]
>
> Hayek's view regarding the role of market and state cannot systematically be distinguished from that of a modern Socialdemocrat . . . . [T]he difference between Hayek and a modern Socialdemocrat boils down to the question whether or not the postal service should be privatized (Hayek says "yes"). [Hans-Hermann Hoppe, in *Contending with Hayek,* 127, 130].

CHAPTER 31

1. HA, 93-11.
2. *SO,* 185.
3. Ibid., 191, 192.

4. *CW* IV, 178.
5. John Gray, *Hayek on Liberty* (Oxford: Basil Blackwell, 1984), 13.
6. Ludwig Wittgenstein, *Tractatus Logico-Philosophicus* (London: Routledge, 1995), 3.
7. *SO*, 192. In *The Counter-Revolution of Science*, Hayek wrote that "[t]o assert that we can explain our own knowledge is to assert that we know more than we do know, a statement which is non-sense in the strict meaning of that term" (*CRS*, 89).

In a summer, 1974 interview, Hayek had this exchange:

A: . . . there is an irreducible basis of facts which must be facts for all the people with whom we can communicate at all. This seems certain.

Q: There are a number of philosophical inquiries in the twentieth century for which this topic is central. . . . One of the major influences in America has been Ludwig Wittgenstein. . . . Have you had any thoughts on Wittgenstein . . .?

A: . . . My earliest recollection of him was in 1917 and I had since seen him off and on on various occasions and have read his two main works very closely. All the other material which has been published from his manuscripts I haven't. I don't think, frankly, that Wittgentstein's work is very relevant to the social sciences. I'm not even sure whether the work produced during a certain phase of his life is anything as important as his present disciples make out. They're very suggestive, deal with interesting problems, but I at least didn't derive much benefit from studying them ["Economics, Politics and Freedom: An Interview with F. A. Hayek," *Reason* (February, 1975), 8].

This was a somewhat different sentiment than Hayek expressed in his 1977 *Encounter* article (cited in the main text), where he indicated that the *Tractatus Logico-Philosophicus* made a "great impression" on him. (The 1974 interview may have been when Hayek still suffered from significant depression.) Hayek apparently only referred once to Wittgenstein in his published work, in "Rules, Perception and Intelligibility," where he cited Wittgenstein as a reference for his own statement that "there is no reason why . . . the sense of justice . . . should not . . . consist in . . . a capacity to follow rules which we do not know in the sense that we can state them" (*Studies*, 45). His reference to Wittgenstein was: "'Knowing' it only means: being able to describe it" (in ibid.). The extent to which Hayek was influenced by Wittgenstein in his psychological ideas is called into question by the fact that Hayek apparently wrote his student paper that later became *The Sensory Order* before the *Tractatus Logico-Philosophicus* was published in late 1921.
8. F. A. Hayek, "The Sensory Order After 25 Years," in Walter B. Weimer and David S. Palermo (eds.), *Cognition and the Symbolic Processes* (Hillsdale, N.J.: Lawrence Erlbaum Associates, 1982), 288.
9. *CRS*, 40.
10. Hayek, "The Sensory Order After 25 Years," 325.
11. Ibid., 329. Heinrich Klüver wrote in introducing *The Sensory Order* that Hayek's theory was that "[e]very sensation, even the 'purest,' must . . . be regarded as an interpretation of an event in the light of the past experience of the individual or the species" (*SO*, xix).
12. Hayek, "The Sensory Order After 25 Years," 290.
13. *Studies*, 18.

14. *HH*, 28.
15. *Studies*, 67.
16. Spiegel, 545.
17. Schumpeter, *History of Economic Analysis*, 689.
18. Ben Seligman, *Main Currents in Modern Economics* (New Brunswick, N.J.: Transaction Publishers, 1990), 342.
19. *CW* III, viii.
20. Vera Smith, *The Rationale of Central Banking and the Free Banking Alternative* (Indianapolis: Liberty Press, 1990), 167.
21. *HH*, 128.
22. *Studies*, 109.
23. *CL*, 420.
24. *Studies*, 110.
25. In Susan Mendus and David Edwards, *On Toleration* (Oxford: Clarendon Press, 1987), 35.
26. *Studies*, 111-2.
27. Cf. John Gray: "There is in Hayek as in Hume . . . a fundamental utilitarian commitment in their theories of morality. It is a very indirect utilitarism that they espouse, however" (*Hayek on Liberty*, 59); Graham Walker: "Hayek must be considered an ethical utilitarian" (Walker, 37-8); and Leland Yeager: "Hayek employs the utilitarian criterion of appraisal" (*Critical Review*, 333); other writers have also noticed Hayek's utilitarian approach and sentiments. Hayek expressed utilitarian views in a number of places in *Law, Legislation and Liberty* ("*The Good Society is one in which the chances of anyone selected at random are likely to be as great as possible*" (v. II, 132; see also v. I, 103; v. II, 106, 115), as well as throughout his work.
28. In *The Constitution of Liberty*, Hayek referenced Mill's discussion of rule, as opposed to act, utilitarianism: "It is true enough that the justification of any particular rule of law must be its usefulness . . . But, generally speaking, only the rule as a whole must be justified, not its every application" (159, 425). Mill wrote that "in the conduct of human beings towards one another, it is necessary that general rules should for the most part be observed, in order that people may know what they have to expect" (J. S. Mill, *On Liberty* [Oxford University Press, 1981], 94). The leading article in the area of rule utilitarianism remains J. O. Urmson's brilliant, often reprinted "The Interpretation of the Moral Philosophy of J. S. Mill," *Philosophical Quarterly* (1953) (cf. *CL*, 158-59, 455, where Hayek terms "act" utilitarianism "extreme" utilitarianism): "A particular action is justified as being right by showing that it is in accord with some moral rule."
29. In *Studies*, 111.
30. Ibid., 112.
31. Ibid., 121. Hayek said later that "Hume has come closer to a critique of rationalism than any other author I kn[o]w. Again and again I've found in Hume statements of ideas which I had already independently arrived at. I am impressed especially with Hume's account of the formation of social institutions of all kinds" ("Economics, Politics & Freedom: An Interview with F. A. Hayek," *Reason* [February 1975], 8).
32. *NS*, 250, 264.
33. In *Studies*, 99.
34. *NS*, 269.
35. A thinker on whom Hayek did not individually write, but whose thought was congruent with his own, particularly in the area of the gradual, organic development of society, was Burke. Hayek concluded *The Constitution of Liberty* that the more he learned "about the evolution of ideas, the more I have become aware that I am simply an

unrepentant Old Whig" (*CL,* 409); here also commenting that "Burke remained an Old Whig to the end" (401).

In a preliminary introduction of *The Fatal Conceit,* Hayek mentioned that authors whom he thought followed similar approaches to his own but whose work he had only glanced at or read so long before that he no longer remembered what he learned from them included Herbert Spencer, Henry Sidgwick, Alfred North Whitehead, Ernst Cassirer, and José Ortega y Gasset. In a preliminary bibliography of *The Fatal Conceit,* others whom he listed as from whom he could have learned more included Johann Gottfried von Herder, Wilhelm von Humboldt, Charles Babbage, Frederic Bastiat and Sewall Wright. He here, too, emphasized his indebtedness to Menger, Böhm-Bawerk, Wieser, and Mises. It was also here that he mentioned he had in the first version of *The Fatal Conceit* headed each section with a quotation by Mises. He here as well distinguished between continental and British liberalism, and said British liberalism was best represented by Smith and Burke.

Another thinker who influenced Hayek but on whom he did not individually write was Adam Ferguson, who was, with Smith and Hume, a part of the Scottish Enlightenment that greatly influenced Hayek. Ferguson emphasized the importance of property to civilization and, in Hayek's works, "defined the savage as one who was not yet acquainted with property" (in Mendus and Edwards, 38).

36. *CH,* 10, 3. It would be inaccurate to leave discussion of Hayek's contributions in the history of ideas without mentioning that much of his presentation in his great works in societal philosophy—*The Road to Serfdom, The Constitution of Liberty, Law, Legislation and Liberty,* and *The Fatal Conceit*—was historical. His discussion in *The Constitution of Liberty* of the *Rechtsstaat* was largely historical, and his presentation of the development of law in *Law, Legislation and Liberty* followed the same approach. *The Fatal Conceit* was in significant part a work in historical interpretation.

CHAPTER 32

1. *LLL* III, xi.
2. Hayek-Shehadi interview.
3. Hayek-North/Skousen interview.
4. *HH,* 130.
5. *HH,* 135.
6. *LLL* II, xiii.
7. In John Cassidy, "The Price Prophet," *New Yorker* (February 7, 2000), 50.
8. *HH,* 130.
9. *CL,* 125.
10. Ibid., 447.
11. In *The Essence of Hayek,* xxvii.
12. Ibid.
13. "Economics, Politics and Freedom: An Interview with F. A. Hayek," *Reason* (February 1975), 12.
14. *LLL* II, xii.
15. Translation of letter to *Die Presse* (February 1977).
16. Patrick Cosgrave.
17. UCLA, 380.
18. Hayek-North/Skousen interview.
19. In J. R. Hicks and W. Weber (eds.), *Carl Menger and the Austrian School of Economics* (Oxford University Press, 1973), 13.

20. Hayek-North/Skousen interview.
21. James Buchanan, "I Did Not Call Him 'Fritz': Personal Recollections of Professor F. A. v. Hayek," *Constitutional Political Economy* (vol. 3, no. 2, 1992), 132. Buchanan also recalls that Hayek told him "he simply could not survive, intellectually, without the *Times (London) Literary Supplement*" (ibid.).
22. *HH,* 131.
23. Shenoy intended at one time to write a biography of Hayek.
24. *TT,* 112.
25. Ibid., 41-2.
26. Ibid., 136.
27. *HH,* 137.
28. "Economics, Politics, and Freedom," 12.
29. Hayek-North/Skousen interview.

CHAPTER 33

1. UCLA, 204.
2. "Myrdal and von Hayek Share a Nobel," *New York Times* (October 10, 1974), 1.
3. Ibid.
4. *Wall Street Journal* (October 24, 1974), 18.
5. HA, 3-7.
6. Friedman-Ebenstein interview. Friedman also remarked in response to the comment, "he [Hayek] was to some extent brought back from obscurity during the early '70s . . .": "It was because of the Nobel Prize entirely."
7. IEA, 34.
8. "Economics, Politics and Freedom," *Reason* (January 1975), 33.
9. *CL,* 255; *Studies,* 220
10. IEA, 41.
11. Hayek-North/Skousen interview.
12. IEA, 41.
13. Grinder-Ebenstein interview.
14. UCLA, 478

CHAPTER 34

1. Milton Friedman, *Capitalism and Freedom* (University of Chicago Press, 1982), xi, 2.
2. *RS,* 53.
3. Friedman, *Capitalism and Freedom,* 2.
4. *RS,* 100.
5. In Machlup, xxi.
6. Friedman-Ebenstein interview, October 1995.
7. Friedman has mentioned in an interview that he was closer personally to Lionel Robbins than to Hayek, giving an idea of Hayek and Friedman's personal relationship (Friedman-Ebenstein interview).
8. In Shils, 138, 141, 146 (order of paragraphs rearranged).
9. Daniel Yergin and Joseph Stanislaw, *The Commanding Heights* (New York: Simon & Schuster, 1998), 144.
10. Friedman-Ebenstein interview, October 1995.
11. Friedman-Ebenstein interview, October 1995.

12. Milton and Rose Friedman, *Two Lucky People* (University of Chicago Press, 1998), 333.
13. Milton Friedman, *The Essence of Friedman* (Stanford, Cal.: Hoover Institution Press, 1987), 363.
14. Brian McCormick, *Hayek and the Keynesian Avalanche* (New York: St. Martin's, 1992), 260.
15. Cubitt-Ebenstein interview.
16. "Obituary: Hayek's Life & Times," *Economic Affairs* (June 1992), 21.
17. Friedman-Ebenstein interview, October 1995.
18. UCLA, 182.
19. Hayek-North/Skousen interview (cf. *HH*, 144-5; Hayek spoke in a soft as well as highly accented voice, and his taped words are not always intelligible. Different transcribers, therefore, sometimes present slightly different versions of what he said).
20. *CW* IV, 40.
21. Friedrich Hayek, "The Road from Serfdom," *Reason* (7/92), 32.
22. UCLA, 144. Friedman agreed with the following interview exchange:

> Q: Hayek would say that: Friedman is a macroeconomist. He doesn't take a microeconomic perspective, and aggregates and averages don't explain anything. All he's really saying is that—he's not saying that you don't take a microeconomic approach; he's saying that you don't agree with his Austrian conception of trade cycle theory with the lengthening, the deepening of the capital structure. It's really not even a micro versus macro distinction.
>
> A: No it's not. (Friedman-Ebenstein interview, November 2000)

23. In Susan Mendus and David Edwards (eds.), *On Toleration* (Oxford: Clarendon Press, 1987), 31.
24. Milton Friedman, *Essays in Positive Economics* (University of Chicago Press, 1953), 4, 7, 9, 12, 40, 42.
25. Friedman-Ebenstein interview (November 2000). In a nutshell, Popper's methodological beliefs are (1) the test of a scientific theory is its capability to be falsified (2) scientific theories cannot be verified; they can merely be falsified, and (3) theories that claim to be unfalsifiable are unscientific.
26. Friedman-Ebenstein interview (October 1995).
27. *IEO*, 51.
28. "The Road to Serfdom," 32.
29. *MTTC*, 32.
30. Ibid., 28.
31. Friedman, *Essays*, 4.
32. Cubitt-Ebenstein interview.
33. Michael S. Berliner (ed.), *Letters of Ayn Rand* (New York: Dutton, 1995), 299.
34. Ibid., 308.
35. In Annelise Anderson and Dennis L. Bark (eds.), *Thinking About America: The United States in the 1990s* (Stanford University: Hoover Institution Press, 1988), 455, 463-4.
36. Kelley, 85.
37. "The Liberty Poll," *Liberty* (February 1999), 17. In the area of academic influence, Peter Boettke has compiled information showing about 250 social science citations for Hayek per year since 1989, about the same as James Buchanan and Ronald Coase, but fewer than Milton Friedman and George Stigler. Hayek broke 200 citations only in 1985; he had only

49 citations in 1973. By way of comparision, Friedman had 328 citations in 1973 (Peter Boettke [ed.], "Which Enlightenment, Whose Liberalism? Hayek's Research Program for Understanding the Liberal Society" [HayekList@aol.com]).

38. *National Review* (April 27, 1992), 35. Just a few of many others influenced by Hayek include Robert Lucas, 1995 Nobel laureate in Economics, who is influenced by Hayek's approach to a business cycle (Robert E. Lucas, Jr., *Studies in Business-Cycle Theory* [Cambridge, Mass.: MIT Press, 1981], 215-6). Political scientist Theodore Lowi wrote in the preface to the second edition of *The End of Liberalism*: "And, although he is very probably unaware of this book and of my work in general, I want to express a very belated thanks to Friedrich A. Hayek. His work had much more of an influence on me than I realized during the writing of the First Edition" (*The End of Liberalism*, 2nd ed. [New York: W. W. Norton & Co., 1979], xiv). Philosopher Robert Nozick said in a 1977 interview: ". . . how I became a libertarian. I came as a graduate student in philosophy to Princeton in 1959. It must have been around 1960 that there was another graduate student in the department who was already an articulate libertarian. . . . And this graduate student put me onto some of Hayek's writings" ("An Interview with Robert Nozick," *Libertarian Review* [December 1977], 11).

Chinese Prime Minister Zhu Rongji has Hayek on his bookshelf (*Newsweek* [June 29, 1998], 31). Yegor Gaidar, who was one of former Russian President Boris Yeltsin's key advisers on privatization and liberalization of the Russian economy, and who was deputy prime minister and finance and economy minister from 1991 to 1994, responded to a question about who the most influential western writers were for his generation of economists in the Soviet Union who questioned the effectiveness of communism: "Of course, Hayek. He gave a very clear and impressive picture of the world, as impressive as Marx in his way" (in Yergin and Stanislaw, 277). Hayek stood in very high standing among the dissidents in Eastern Europe and the Soviet Union.

CHAPTER 35

1. *NS,* 23.
2. Ibid., 192.
3. Friedrich Hayek, "Monetarism and hyper-inflation," *Times* (March 5, 2000).
4. *DN,* 80.
5. Hayek, "Monetarism and hyper-inflation"; *DN,* 81.
6. Ian Bradly, London *Times* (November 21, 1980).
7. Hayek, "Monetarism and hyper-inflation."
8. *CL* 297; 216, 490.
9. Friedrich Hayek, *A Conversation with Friedrich A. von Hayek: Science and Socialism* (Washington, D. C.: American Enterprise Institute, 1978), 16.
10. *NS,* 197.
11. *Encounter,* 57.
12. UCLA, 183-4
13. *Listener,* 331.
14. *Now!* (January 31, 1981), 41.
15. Frank Johnson, "The Facts of Hayek," *Daily Telegraph Magazine* (September 26, 1975), 32.
16. *NS,* 224.
17. *DM,* 23.
18. Ibid., 26.

19. Ibid., 12. In addition to his advocacy of competitive currencies to combat inflation, Hayek favored this radical reform to eliminate a business cycle. He ultimately came around to the Chicago view that a primary source of monetary and economic instability is less-than-full currency reserve requirements. He held: "What the original issue of a [private] currency could do and would have to do is not to repeat the mistakes governments have made, as a result of which control of . . . secondary or parasitic issues has slipped from their hands. It must make clear that it would not be prepared to bail out secondary issuers by supplying the 'cash' (i.e. the original notes) they will need to redeem their obligations. By adhering strictly to this principle they would force the secondary issuer to practise something very close to '100 per cent banking'" (ibid., 65). "The abolition of the government monopoly of money was conceived to prevent the bouts of acute inflation and deflation which have plagued the world for the past 60 years. It proves on examination to be also the much needed cure for a more deep-seated disease: the recurrent waves of depression and unemployment that have been represented as an inherent and deadly defect of capitalism" (ibid., 130).

20. Nigel Lawson, *The View from No. 11* (New York: Doubleday, 1993), 939.

21. Margaret Thatcher, *The Downing Street Years* (London: Harper Collins, 1995), 715-6.

CHAPTER 36

1. UCLA, xii. Alchian also characterizes Hayek as "a man for all generations, who believes mightily in the freedom of the individual, convinced that the open, competitive survival of diffused, decentralized ideas and spontaneous organizations, customs, and procedures in a capitalist, private-property system is preferable to consciously rational-directed systems of organizing the human cosmos" (ibid., xiii).

2. Eamonn Butler, *Hayek: His Contribution to the Political and Economic Thought of Our Time* (New York: Universe Books, 1983), 13.

3. George L. S. Shackle, *Business, Time and Thought* (New York University Press, 1988), 165. Robbins wrote in his 1971 autobiography that what Maria Edgeworth said of David Ricardo could equally be said of Hayek: "I never argued or discussed a question with a person who argues more fairly, or less for victory and more for truth. He gives full weight to every argument brought against him, and seems not to be on any side of the question for one instant longer than the conviction of his mind on that side. It seems quite indifferent to him whether you find the truth, or whether he finds it, provided it be found" (in Robbins, 128).

4. HA, 114-16.

5. UCLA, 241.

6. Ibid., 56-7.

7. *DM*, 10. Vaughn observes of the 1974 Institute for Humane Studies meeting that "Hayek's work took a distinct back seat to Mises' at South Royalton. Although his work on business cycle and inflation was discussed and treated with respect, there was no sense that he might in any way be Ludwig von Mises' professional equal in Austrian economics" (*Austrian Economics in America* [Cambridge University Press, 1994], 108). She also perceptively states that "although Hayek emigrated to America in the late 1940s, it was his older colleague Mises who was responsible for bringing Austrian economics to America. While I believe Hayek's ideas ultimately proved more important in shaping the Austrian revival, it was because of Mises that there was a revival at all" (in Bruce Caldwell [ed.], *Carl Menger and His Economic Legacy* [Durham, N.C.: Duke University Press, 1996], 396).

8. Milton Friedman, in Yergin and Stanislaw, 98.

9. *CW* IV, 192-3.

10. ICL, 6.

11. In *Hayek's "Serfdom" Revisited.*

12. Dennis Kavanagh, *The Reordering of British Politics: Politics After Thatcher* (Oxford University Press, 1997), 96-7. Friedman was perhaps a more important source of inspiration to the IEA from the late 1960s through the 1970s than Hayek. Cockett remarks: "Friedman became the Institute's most celebrated exponent of monetary stability, or what came to be called 'monetarism'"; "Friedman became the most famous exponent of the free-market economy during the 1970s. . . . His TV programme *Free to Choose* had an enormous impact on British public opinion"; "during the 1970s Friedman was to be central to the IEA's campaign for monetarism" (Cockett, 149, 152, 154). Seldon refers to the "Friedmanite counter-revolution against Keynes 'sponsored' at the IEA" (*Hayek's 'Serfdom' Revisited,* xxii).

13. Hayek-North/Skousen interview.

14. Butler, *Hayek,* 7.

15. Ibid.

16. Ibid.

17. UCLA, 442.

18. Cf. William Ebenstein, *Great Political Thinkers,* 16.

19. *Hayek's "Serfdom" Revisited,* xxiii-xxiv.

20. Cockett, 141-2, 156.

21. Arthur Seldon (memorial talk given at LSE in Hayek's honor).

22. Ibid. An important document, *Letters on a Birthday: The Unfinished Agenda of Arthur Seldon* (Marjorie Seldon, ed. [Economic and Literary Books, 1996]), contains 119 letters from scholars and others around the world that testify to Seldon's contribution to modern classical liberalism. The comments of Vernon Bogdanor are typical: "On your eightieth birthday you can feel proud of having been responsible for a real revolution in ideas and in government. Of how few can that be said!" Digby Anderson, director of the Social Affairs Unit, wrote: "It's sixteen years since we first met at the IEA. And the direct and rapid result was the founding of the SAU. . . . We have now published over 200 authors and although few of them or their readers know it, not one would have been published without the original help of Arthur Seldon." Lord Harris expressed: "You were always the senior by virtue of the leadership you patiently gave me and hundreds of others to advance your transformation, first of the intellectual climate, then of the Party debate, and finally, let's hope, of the political landscape. . . . [T]he credit belongs to you more than to any other individual—not excluding FAH [Hayek], MF [Friedman], JEP [Enoch Powell], KJ [Keith Joseph] or (even) MT [Thatcher]." Lady Thatcher wrote: "You have made an invaluable contribution to the political and economic map of Britain. . . . At a time when free enterprise and the free market were unfashionable you championed their cause, laying the foundations for their revival in the 1970s. . . . When I became leader of the Party, I greatly valued the advice of the IEA as we moved forward with new policies. . . . [Y]ou inspired much of our success during the '80s."

CHAPTER 37

1. Margaret Thatcher, *The Path to Power* (London: Harper Collins, 1995), 50.

2. Thatcher, *The Path to Power,* 85.

3. Cockett, 175-6.

4. Ibid., 174.

5. UCLA, 482.

6. August 28, 1979 letter from Friedrich Hayek to Margaret Thatcher, in the possession of Larry Hayek.

7. *Daily Mirror* (May 23, 1976).

8. *Daily Mirror* (January 12, 1980).

9. *Daily Mirror* (June 20, 1980).

10. Cosgrove, 141.

11. *Daily Telegraph* (April 14, 1978).

12. *Economic Affairs* (June 1992), 21. Larry Hayek remembers his father as not having thought much of Reagan intellectually after meeting him (Larry Hayek-Ebenstein interview).

13. In McCormick, 235.

14. London *Times* (February 11, 1978), 15.

15. Ibid. (February 14, 1978).

16. Ibid.

17. Ibid. (February 15, 1978).

18. Ibid.

19. Ibid. (February 16, 1978).

20. Ibid. (March 9, 1978).

21. Hayek once responded to an interview question "about people you dislike or can't deal with": "I don't have many strong dislikes. I admit that as a teacher—I have no racial prejudices in general—but there were certain types, and conspicuous among them the Near Eastern populations, which I still dislike because they are fundamentally dishonest. . . . It was a type which, in my childhood in Austria, was described as Levantine, typical of people of the eastern Mediterranean. But I encountered it later, and I have a profound dislike for the typical Indian students at the London School of Economics, which I admit are all one type—Bengali moneylender sons. They are to me a detestable type, I admit, but not with any racial feeling. I have found a little of the same amongst the Egyptians" (UCLA, 490).

    Hayek could be obtuse and insensitive of anti-Semitism. He wrote in a piece after World War II: "It is scarcely easier to justify the prevention of a person from fiddling [playing in the Vienna Symphony] because he was a Nazi than the prevention because he is a Jew" ("Re-Nazification at Work," *Spectator* [January 31, 1947], 134).

22. *RS,* 166.

23. "Conversation with Systematic Liberalism," *Forum* (September 1961), 6.

24. *LLL* II, 189.

25. *CL,* 379.

26. "Conversation with Systematic Liberalism," 7.

27. Joseph A. Schumpeter, *Ten Great Economists* (London: George Allen & Unwin, 1956), 274.

28. John Chamberlain, "Hayek Returns to Cambridge," *National Review* (January 11, 1985), 61.

29. May 18, 1979 telegram from Margaret Thatcher to Friedrich Hayek, in the possession of Larry Hayek.

30. HA, 101-26.

31. In Cockett, 175.

CHAPTER 38

1. UCLA, 396.

2. Esca Hayek-Ebenstein interview.
3. Ibid.
4. Ibid.
5. UCLA, 109. That Hayek remarked in 1978 that Robbins was his "closest friend," notwithstanding that they saw each other most infrequently (quite apart from their decade of non-communication), indicates how few close friends Hayek had.
6. Hayek-Shehadi interview.
7. Letwin-Ebenstein interview.
8. Hans Warhanek-Ebenstein interview.
9. HA, 4-25.
10. Ibid.
11. *Daily Journal* (Venezuela) (May 15, 1981), 4.
12. In Arthur Seldon (ed.), *The 'New Right' Enlightenment* (Kent, England: E & L Books, 1985), vii.
13. *Daily Journal* (Venezuela) (May 15, 1981), 4.
14. London *Times* (January 12, 1980)
15. London *Times* (February 17, 1983).
16. *Encounter* (May 1983), 54. In a 1968 Japanese newspaper exchange of essays, Hayek wrote of the larger world conflict between the United States and Soviet Union that he had "little doubt that out of the ideological conflict the ideal of personal freedom and free enterprise will emerge victorious. What I am not so sure is who will in the end represent that idea. If things go on as at present, I don't think that it is at all impossible that . . . the Russians with a newly discovered capitalism will conquer the world. . . . I can well conceive a development which will produce a situation in which the Russians will call old-fashioned capitalism 'communism' and the West under the name 'capitalism' produce something much nearer old-fashioned communism" ("Exchange of Letters," *Yomiuri* [8/12/68]). In a 1950 speech to the Economic Club of Chicago, he proposed the admission of West Germany to the United States, to be followed by other western European nations. A contemporary news article reported: "Admission to statehood in the American union of the eight states of western Germany was proposed yesterday by Friedrich A. Hayek. . . . This step was advocated as a preliminary to the entry of other countries of western Europe into the United States. . . . Hayek said the states of western Germany would eagerly embrace the plan. Later France and England would find it desirable to enter the American union. . . . Other smaller European nations, including the Scandinavian countries, would soon clamor to get in" (Thomas Furlong, "Admit German States to U.S., Hayek Urges," *Chicago Daily Tribune* [November 4, 1950]).
17. London *Times* (February 27, 1985).
18. *Wall Street Journal* (December 4, 1978).
19. *CW* IX, 252.
20. Chang Tsan-Kuo, "Economic Aid to Socialist Third World a Waste, Says Economist Hayek," *China News* (Taipei, November 14, 1975).
21. HA, 63-1.
22. HA, 63-2.
23. *International Herald Tribune* (December 18, 1982).
24. Gitta Sereny, London *Times* (May 9, 1985)
25. UCLA, 461-2.
26. Ibid., 392-3.
27. Ibid., 417-8.
28. Ibid., 378-9.
29. Ibid., 204-5.

30. Cubitt-Ebenstein interview.
31. Esca Hayek-Ebenstein interview.
32. Sereny, *Times*. Hayek enjoyed telling the story about how, when the queen's usher asked how his name should be pronounced, he startled him by replying, "Hi-yek, as in high explosive" (*Economic Affairs,* June 1992, 21).
33. Esca Hayek-Ebenstein interview.

CHAPTER 39

1. Hayek's assistant Kurt Leube wrote in a 1984 biographical sketch of Hayek of *The Fatal Conceit* that "[w]hen not lecturing throughout the world, Hayek devotes himself entirely to the completion of this great work, which will contain some of the most significant developments in his intellectual thought" (*Essence of Hayek,* xxix).
2. *LLL* III, xi.
3. *LLL* III, 146.
4. *CL,* 364.
5. *LLL* III, 147.
6. Ibid.
7. Ibid., 5-6.
8. *LLL* III, 168.
9. UCLA, 68-9.
10. July 12, 1978 letter from Milton Friedman to Hayek, in the possession of Charlotte Cubitt.
11. *LLL* III, 176.
12. Consolidated version of *LLL,* xxi.
13. "The Overweening Conceit" was a preliminary title of what became *The Fatal Conceit.* Hayek's family recalls him as having thought *"The Fatal Conceit"* a very good title, expressing both the great magnitude of the error and the vanity of socialism.
14. Buchanan, 133.
15. *FC,* 133.
16. UCLA, 79-81, 286, 290.
17. Hayek-North/Skousen interview.
18. IEA, 14-5, 17.
19. *FC,* 104, 46.

CHAPTER 40

1. Friedrich Hayek, *A Conversation with Friedrich A. von Hayek: Science and Socialism* (Washington, D. C.: American Enterprise Institute, 1979), 17-8.
2. MPS newsletter, 11.
3. *Forbes* (May 15, 1989), 43-4.
4. Ebenstein-Christine Hayek interview.
5. October 1989 letter from Hayek to Ed Crane (HayekList@aol.com)
6. Seldon, *Festschrift,* 143-4.
7. Larry Hayek-Ebenstein interview.
8. Larry Hayek-Ebenstein interview.
9. The homily presented here is not a verbatim transcription of Father Schasching's remarks, but an after-the-fact condensation made by the author with Schasching's participation in 1996.

CHAPTER 41

1. *LLL* II, 57-8; 89-91; 148.
2. Hayek expressed world federational ideas throughout his career. He held in a 1968 newspaper letter that "what we need is international law not international government: a system of rules which bind the individual states both in their relations to each other and in their relations to the[ir] citizens. . . . But you cannot have an international authority so long as the individual states are free to do what they please. International order will therefore be achieved only by reducing the powers of government all around . . ." ("Exchange of Letters," *Yomiuri* [August 12, 1968]) He was quoted in a 1945 talk that a "practicable postwar world organization for peace would have to rest on international rules of law and create the machinery rather than the authorities for direction. It would have to be something like a federal system where federal authority is a restraining power which yet allows individuals and individual states freedom of direction" ("Hayek Asks 'Federal' World Machinery to Keep Peace," *Minneapolis Morning Tribune* [April, 1945]). He wrote in 1939 that "the abrogation of national sovereignties and the creation of an effective international order of law is a necessary complement and the logical consummation of the liberal program." That nineteenth-century liberalism did not develop in the direction of interstate liberalism was, he held, one of its chief failings. "Real liberalism . . . [is] true to its ideal of freedom and internationalism" (*IEO,* 269-71).
3. *LLL* II, 144.

APPENDIX

1. *LLL*, III, 157.
2. *IEO*, 69.
3. Ibid, 72.
4. In *SO*, xviii.
5. John Stuart Mill, *Principles of Political Economy*, vol. I (New York: Colonial Press, 1900, 196–7).
6. Ibid.
7. *LLL*, III, 152.
8. *RS*, 178. I am indebted to Rob Ebenstein for his suggestion of how to conclude the appendix.

Index

of Names and Hayek's Works in the Main Text and Bibliographical Essay